KATHERINE MANSFIELD
A Biography

KATHERINE MANSFIELD

A Biography

JEFFREY MEYERS

HAMISH HAMILTON
LONDON

First published in Great Britain 1978
by Hamish Hamilton Ltd
Garden House 57-59 Long Acre London WC2E 9JZ
Second impression October 1979

Copyright © 1978 by Jeffrey Meyers

British Library Cataloguing in Publication Data

Meyers, Jeffrey
    Katherine Mansfield.
    1. Mansfield, Katherine 2. Novelists,
    New Zealand – Biography
    823   PR6025.A57Z/
    ISBN 0-241-89888-9

Printed and bound in Great Britain by
REDWOOD BURN LIMITED
Trowbridge & Esher

For Val, again

CONTENTS

ILLUSTRATIONS

Between pages 82 *and* 83

1*

8(a) S. S. Koteliansky, portrait by Mark Gertler, 1917
      (Courtesy of The Hon. M. M. Michael Campbell)
  (b) Katherine, 1913
      (Alexander Turnbull Library, Wellington, New Zealand)

Between pages 178 *and* 179

9(a) Leslie Beauchamp, 1915
      (Alexander Turnbull Library, Wellington, New Zealand)
  (b) Francis Carco as a student aviator, 1917
10(a) Virginia and Leonard Woolf, Sussex, 1914
      (The Hogarth Press)
  (b) Lady Ottoline Morrell at Garsington, *c.* 1922
      (Courtesy of Mrs Julian Vinogradoff)
11   Katherine Mansfield, portrait by Anne Estelle Rice, 1918
      (National Art Gallery, Wellington, New Zealand)
12   Katherine and Murry, 1918
      (Alexander Turnbull Library, Wellington, New Zealand)
13   Elizabeth Bibesco, portrait by Augustus John, 1919
      (Laing Art Gallery, Newcastle, and Tyne and Wear County
      Council Museums)
14(a) Katherine with Connie Beauchamp, Mrs Dunare and
      Jinnie Fullerton at the Villa Flora, Menton, 1920
      (Alexander Turnbull Library, Wellington, New Zealand)
  (b) Katherine with Dorothy Brett and Ida Baker at Sierre,
      1921
      (Alexander Turnbull Library, Wellington, New Zealand)
15(a) Violet Schiff, portrait by Wyndham Lewis, 1924
      (Courtesy of Mrs Wyndham Lewis and the Tate Gallery)
  (b) Sydney Schiff, caricature by Max Beerbohm, 1925
      (Courtesy of Mrs I. Collis)
16(a) Katherine at the Isola Bella, Menton, 1920
      (Ida Baker Collection, Alexander Turnbull Library,
      Wellington, New Zealand)
  (b) George Gurdjieff

Every effort has been made to trace the copyright holders of the
illustrations used. Should there be any omissions in this respect,
we apologise and shall be pleased to make the appropriate
acknowledgments in future editions.

ACKNOWLEDGMENTS

It is a pleasure to acknowledge the generous assistance I received while writing this book. The University of Colorado provided two grants for research in New Zealand and in England. Margaret Scott, who is editing Katherine Mansfield's letters, allowed me to read copies of all the correspondence she had collected. My friends helped me in important ways. I am grateful to Dr Sheldon Cooperman for expert advice in medical matters; to Werner and Elisabeth Alferink for valuable information about Wörishofen; to Ron Billingsley for photographs; to Felipe Orlando for addresses in Spain; and to Freddie and Naomi Earlle for splendid hospitality while I was working in London.

For personal interviews and letters I would like to thank William Craddock Barclay, Edith Bendall, Gerald Brenan, Dorothy Brett, David Drey, A. S. Frere, David Garnett, Ruth Herrick, Enid Hilton, Lady Juliette Huxley, Christopher Isherwood, Patrick Lawlor, Frank Lea, John Manchester, Colin Murry, who spoke to me for twelve hours, Mary Murry, Richard Murry, Dorothy Richards, Frank Swinnerton, Oliver Trowell, Julian Vinogradoff, Montague Weekly, and Dame Rebecca West.

For letters about Katherine I am grateful to Enid Bagnold, Ida Baker, Barbara Barr, Anne Bennett, Sylvia Berkman, Jean Bickler, Sharon Clark, Adam Curle, Georgina D'Angelo, Robert G. Davis, William Gerhardie, Ian Gordon, Anne Hardham, Tara Heinemann, Alfred Knopf, Gerald Lacy, Dan Laurence, Wallace Martin, Lucy O'Brien, Jeanne Renshaw, Elinor Short, Catherine Stoye, William Targ, E. W. Tedlock, Douglas Trowell, Craig Wallace, Sylvia Townsend Warner, John Waterlow, Seymour Weiner, Celeste Wright and George Zytaruk.

Mary Dalton of the University of Windsor, Ontario, kindly sent me copies of Katherine's letters to Garnet Trowell; and I also received useful information from Donald Eddy of Cornell University, Joseph McCarthy of Fordham University, P. J. Croft of King's College, Cambridge, Mary Trott of Smith College, David Farmer of the University of Texas, Helen Slotkin of the University of Cincinnati, Thomas Whitehead of Temple University, P. B. Freshwater of Birmingham University, John Isard of the Guildhall School of Music, Francis Puslowski of the Polish Institute of Arts and Sciences, and Stefan Traugott of the Instytut Badan Literakich in Warsaw. Florence Schwartz did research for me in the New York Public Library. My wife provided rigorous scrutiny and critical insight. Aladeen Smith was a superb editor and typist.

For arranging my lectures on Katherine Mansfield I would like to thank Carl Stead of the University of Auckland, James Traue of the Alexander Turnbull Library in Wellington, who gave me full access to the Katherine Mansfield papers, Roger Robinson of Victoria University of Wellington, Stephanie Fierz of Queen's College, London and Charles Rossman of the University of Texas.

Every effort has been made to communicate with all copyright holders.

The author and publishers are also grateful to the following for permission to quote: © 1978 the Estate of Katherine Mansfield; The Society of Authors as the literary representative of the Estate of Katherine Mansfield for extracts from letters of Katherine Mansfield; The Society of Authors as the literary representative of the Estate of John Middleton Murry for extracts from his published works and those of Katherine Mansfield; Laurence Pollinger Ltd and the Estate of the late Mrs Frieda Lawrence for extracts from D. H. Lawrence, *Collected Letters*, ed. H. Moore, and other published works; Faber and Faber Ltd and R. Gathorne-Hardy for extracts from *Ottoline at Garsington*; Jonathan Cape for extracts from A. Alpers' *Katherine Mansfield*; Weidenfeld and Nicolson for extracts from Ronald Clark's *The Life of Bertrand Russell*; the Literary Estate of Leonard Woolf and the Hogarth Press for extracts from Leonard Woolf's *Beginning Again*; the Literary Estate of Virginia Woolf and the Hogarth Press for extracts from *The Question of Things Happening—Letters of Virginia Woolf*, edited by Nigel Nicolson; Ida Baker and Michael Joseph Ltd for extracts from *The Memoirs of LM*; Miss C. Oliver for an extract from her letter to Mrs M. Amoore of 5 July 1968; Methuen and Co Ltd and F. A. Lea for extracts from *The Life of John Middleton Murry*; Frank Swinnerton for extracts

from *Georgian Literary Scene* and *An Autobiography*; Gordon
Fraser Gallery Ltd and H. S. Ede for extracts from *The Savage
Messiah*; Secker and Warburg Ltd and the late D. Brett for extracts
from *Lawrence and Brett: A Friendship*; to the editor of *Adam* for
extracts from: Katherine Mansfield's 'Letters to Sydney and
Violet Schiff', *Adam* (1965), 'Fifteen Letters to Virginia Woolf',
Adam (1972–3), and D. Brett and J. Manchester, 'Reminiscences
of Katherine Mansfield', *Adam* (1972–3), to Anne Hardham for an
extract from *Elizabeth of the German Garden* by Leslie de Charms.

CHAPTER ONE

Childhood, 1888–1902

THE ANCESTORS of Kathleen Mansfield Beauchamp (who used the pen-name of Katherine Mansfield) can be traced to prosperous goldsmiths in the reign of Charles II. On November 14, 1660, the diarist Samuel Pepys recorded: 'I went into Cheapside to Mr. Beauchamp's, the goldsmith, to look out a piece of plate . . . and did choose a gilt tankard.'[1] The family business continued well into the nineteenth century, when it was inherited by Katherine's great-grandfather, John Beauchamp, who loved fox-hunting and the works of Byron and Coleridge, and was known to his High-gate neighbours as 'the Poet of Hornsey Lane'. His brother-in-law was the friend and biographer of the painter, John Constable, who visited Beauchamp's works in 1833.[2] But when John Beauchamp abandoned his traditional craft and began to manu-facture imitation 'British Plate', the business failed, and in 1848 his four sons emigrated to the antipodes. The eldest son, Henry Herron Beauchamp, was the father of the best-selling novelist, Elizabeth von Arnim, who wrote *Elizabeth and Her German Garden*; his brother, Arthur Beauchamp, was the grandfather of Katherine Mansfield.

Arthur Beauchamp made the three-month voyage to Welling-ton to claim a thousand acres of land left to him by his wealthy sister. But legal complications between the British government and the New Zealand Company prevented him from taking possession. Arthur moved to the penal colony of Australia when gold was discovered there in 1850 and married Mary Elizabeth Stanley, the daughter of a Lancashire silversmith, a few years later. In 1858 Katherine's father, Harold Beauchamp, was born in the gold fields of Ararat, a hundred miles north-west of Mel-bourne. Three years later the restless Arthur, who had no luck as a gold miner, returned to New Zealand and established him-self as a general merchant and auctioneer in Picton, which was situated on a sheltered harbour at the top of South Island and was then the seat of the government. Arthur was elected to the New Zealand parliament in 1866, a year after Wellington became the capital, and died in 1910 at the age of eighty-three.

Samuel Butler, who had been a sheep farmer near Christchurch from 1860 to 1864 (and portrayed the beauty of the New Zealand landscape in the opening chapters of *Erewhon*), describes the dominance of materialism over culture which would later disturb Katherine Mansfield: 'New Zealand seems far better adapted to develop and maintain in health the physical than the intellectual nature. The fact is, people here are busy making money; that is the inducement which led them to come in the first instance, and they show their sense by devoting their energies to the work. . . . It does not do to speak about John Sebastian Bach's Fugues or pre-Raphaelite pictures.'[3] Though Butler 'only saved his soul by escaping to New Zealand',[4] Katherine felt she had saved her soul by escaping *from* that raw pioneering country which either rejected culture entirely or pursued it with 'gauche eagerness'.[5]

Travellers to New Zealand towards the end of the nineteenth century recorded the dominant characteristics of the people, who were (and still are) conservative, conformist, respectable, decorous and diligent. At the turn of the century they lacked style and elegance, had simple tastes and unsophisticated habits, and were 'solid and reliable, narrow and egotistical'. Visitors described 'the drabness of the towns and the bleakness of the landscape, the crude empiricism of the politicians, and the intellectual apathy of the people' in that 'comfortable and colourless' country. The political style, popularized by Richard Seddon, who was Prime Minister from 1893 until 1906, combined 'energy, good fellowship, the common touch, [and] a crude intelligence unhampered by reflection'.[6]

Katherine's father, who was proud of being a settler type, a self-made tycoon and a friend of politicians, had many of Seddon's qualities. He left school at fourteen, entered his father's firm in 1872, and joined the importing house of W. M. Bannatyne in 1877. The following year he met the fourteen-year-old Annie Burnell Dyer, the daughter of a Sydney pioneer and sister of his fellow clerk. Six years later, in 1884, Harold married the exceptionally beautiful and aristocratic-looking Annie.

Their daughter, Katherine Mansfield Beauchamp, was born at

eight o'clock on a spring morning, October 14, 1888, at 11 Tinakori Road. It was a white, wooden, red-roofed house over-looking the splendid natural harbour, within sound of the foghorns and close to the shops and quays of the wet and windy city.

Katherine's father soon made his fortune. He became a partner of Bannatyne's in 1889, a member of the Wellington Harbour Board in 1895, a director of the Bank of New Zealand in 1898 and Chairman in 1907. Marion Ruddick, a young Canadian girl whose father worked in Wellington, described Harold Beauchamp in 1898 as 'a big man with sandy hair greying at the temples . . . and a ruddy complexion'.[7] The architect William Craddock Barclay spoke of his second cousin as a shrewd but straight trader with a keen financial brain, and thought the strong-willed and pompous Harold was a colourful and impressive figure, a polished rather than a rough diamond. Barclay illustrated Harold's love of money with the perhaps apocryphal but never-theless revealing story of how he lent a sovereign to a cousin who was leaving for the Great War and then asked for it back when he returned several years later.[8] Another story relates how Harold chartered an exclusive railway car and would not allow the people who were clinging to the outside of the train to enter his car. Though his family pleaded with him, Harold insisted: 'I paid for it and it's mine!'

Katherine portrayed her domineering father, who believed in 'Duty' and often reminded his daughter 'one cannot live on mulberry leaves like a silkworm',[9] in many letters and stories including 'A Birthday' and 'The Stranger'. Though she imagina-tively transformed reality, her intensely autobiographical stories create a composite portrait of her family and illuminate the experiences and emotions of her childhood. In 'Juliet' (1906), a fragmentary and unfinished novel, she incisively describes her father as 'a tall grey bearded man, with prominent blue eyes, large ungainly hands, and inclining to stoutness. He was a general merchant, thoroughly commonplace and commercial.'[10] In 1919 she diminished his stature and confirmed his limitations in a letter to Lady Ottoline Morrell: 'He is not tall, very healthy looking with white hair and a small clipped beard, large blue eyes, and expansive voice. In fact he looks a typical Colonial banker!!'[11]

Harold Beauchamp also appears in 'Prelude' (1918) as the energetic and authoritative, blustering and egotistical, brutish and pathetic Stanley Burnell. The delicate Linda Burnell (Katherine's mother's second name) resents her husband's rather predatory demands and thinks: 'If only he wouldn't jump at her so, and bark so loudly, and watch her with such eager, loving eyes. He was too strong for her.' And she warns her aggressive husband: ' "You know I'm very delicate. You know as well as I do that my heart is affected, and the doctor told you I may die at any moment".'[12] His daughter was also frightened of him, and wrote in 'The Little Girl' (1912) that 'he was a figure to be feared and avoided'.[13]

Harold was the classic Beauchamp 'Pa man': overbearing, independent, commonsensical and benevolent; Katherine was torn between her hatred of his philistine domination and her desire for his love and protection. In 1913, when she was twenty-five, she still felt childishly insecure about him, and wrote: 'I feel towards my Pa man like a little girl. I want to jump and stamp on his chest and cry "You've *got* to love me".'[14] She spent a great deal of her adult life trying to win the affection and respect of her prosaic father, who built an ugly bus shelter in Wellington as a memorial to his imaginative child.

Katherine's mother, Annie, had a severe attack of rheumatic fever in her teens, suffered from chronic heart trouble, and resented the physical and emotional burdens of motherhood. Though Annie was something of an invalid, she gave Katherine an intense response to life and a courageous spirit. As Katherine wrote to Dorothy Brett after her mother's death in 1918, when she had painfully acquired her own understanding of illness: 'She *lived* every moment of life more fully and completely than anyone I've ever known—and her gaiety wasn't any less real for being *high courage*—courage to meet anything with. . . . [Her death] has made me realize more fully than ever before that I love *courage*—spirit—poise (do you know what I mean? all these words are too little) more than anything.'[15] Though Katherine praised her mother's brave response to life, despite her illness, she portrayed Annie in 'At the Bay' (1922) as an ethereal, languid and remote invalid who dreads and resents having children: 'She was broken, made weak, her courage was gone, through child-bearing. And what made it doubly hard to bear was, she did not love the children. It was useless pretending. Even if she had had the strength she would never have nursed and played with the little girls.'[16]

In 1890, when the newest baby was born, Katherine was brought in to see it:

'Her name is Gwen,' said the grandmother. 'Kiss her.'
I bent down and kissed the little goldy tuft. But she took no notice.
She lay quite still with her eyes shut.
'Now go and kiss mother,' said the grandmother.
But mother did not want to kiss me. Very languid, leaning against some pillows, she was eating some sago.[17]

In this crucial moment of emotional rejection, when Katherine is supplanted as the baby of the family (significantly, the grandmother holds Gwen while Annie attends to her own needs), her self-absorbed mother refuses to kiss her and makes the child doubt her love. The search for and disappointment in love was a dominant pattern of Katherine's life.

A few weeks after she was born her parents took a long holiday in England and left Katherine, who had jaundice when she was three months old, in the care of her grandmother. Margaret Mansfield Dyer lived with the family and looked after the six children: Vera, who was born in 1885, Charlotte in 1887, 'Kass' in 1888, Gwendoline (who died in infancy) in 1890, Jeanne in 1892, and a brother, Leslie, in 1894. In 'Prelude' Katherine's beloved grandmother appears as Mrs. Fairfield (a literal translation of Beauchamp), gladly assumes the maternal role abandoned by her daughter, and gives the children the warmth and affection they failed to receive from their self-absorbed parents. Linda's child-like but precise physical description of her mother subtly suggests the old lady's moral qualities: 'There was something comforting in the sight of her that Linda felt she could never do without. She needed the sweet smell of her flesh, and the soft feel of her cheeks and her arms and shoulders still softer. She loved the way her hair curled, silver at her forehead, lighter at her neck, and bright brown still in the big coil under the muslin cap. Exquisite were her mother's hands, and the two rings she wore seemed to melt into her creamy skin. And she was always so fresh, so delicious. The old woman could bear nothing but linen next to her body and she bathed in cold water winter and summer'.[18] When Katherine was lonely and ill in Bavaria in 1909, she comforted herself with the memory of her grandmother's tender care: 'The only adorable thing I can imagine is for my Grandmother to put me to bed and bring me a bowl of hot bread and milk, and standing, her hands folded, the left thumb over the right, say in her adorable voice: "There, darling, isn't that nice?" Oh, what a miracle of happiness that would be! To wake later to find her turning down the bedclothes in a little pink singlet, softer than a cat's fur.'[19] As Katherine's sister, Jeanne Renshaw, writes: 'Grandmother Dyer, a widow who lived with us, played a *very* big part in our life. Looking back on my parents —that strong dynamic Father who fell in love with Mother when she was 14. They married when she was 19. Mother I could not have loved more. Small and fragile—my parents so sensitive and tender hearted.'[20] But their tenderness was directed more towards each other than towards their children; and in 1919 Katherine characterized her own selfish withdrawal by stating: 'I am become—Mother. I don't care a rap for people.'[21]

At Easter 1893 the Beauchamps moved from Tinakori Road to Karori, a rural retreat in an upland valley about four miles from the town. In 'Prelude' Katherine describes the first of a great number of moves in her short life. The village, which had about 1200 people, included a general store, wooden church, hall, library and blacksmith. Chesney Wold, 'a great old rambling house' with large bay windows and ornamented porch, was 'planted lonesomely in the midst of huge gardens, orchards and paddocks'[22] and had a solitary aloe and a quick stream. It was built in the mid-1860s and had been the residence of a former Prime Minister. The house was looked after by the likeable Irish handyman, Pat Sheehan, who wore a dignified brown bowler hat and drove Harold to and from work every day. Harold, who bought a bigger house to mark each stage of his financial success, enjoyed playing the role of traditional land owner, country squire and Justice of the Peace in Karori.

Annie's brother-in-law, Valentine Waters, a musician, clerk in the post office and model for Jonathan Trout in 'At the Bay', soon followed the Beauchamps to Karori. His two boys joined their cousins in the small school, which 'had been on its present site since 1875 and in 1893 had three classrooms, one for the infants and two for standards 1 to 7'.[23] In 'The Doll's House' (1922), Katherine portrays her parents' rather snobbish attitude towards the unfortunately democratic school, which she attended from 1895 until 1898: 'The school the Burnell children went to was not at all the kind of place their parents would have chosen if there had been any choice. But there was none. It was the only school for miles. And the consequence was all the children of the neighbourhood, the Judge's little girls, the doctor's daughters, the store-keeper's children, the milkman's, were forced to mix together. Not to speak of there being an equal number of rude, rough little boys as well.'[24] A friend has described an incident that reveals Katherine's youthful sympathy and courage: 'When the teacher of the school rebuked a lad for sleeping at his desk, Katherine spoke up to explain that he was forced to rise at three o'clock each morning to help with the family milk delivery, and the boy escaped a caning.'[25]

In 1893, the year of the move to Karori, the family began to spend their summers swimming, boating and fishing in Anakiwa, near Picton. In 'The Voyage' (1921), Katherine describes Fenella's journey across the Strait to visit her paternal grandfather, with his white tuft of hair, rosy face and long silver beard, and her arrival at the old family home: 'Up a little path of round white pebbles they went, with drenched sleeping flowers on either side. . . . The blinds were down in the little house; they mounted the steps on to the verandah.'[26]

In 1898 the Beauchamps moved back to 75 Tinakori Road—a large house with a spacious garden, tennis court, and magnificent view of the harbour and distant mountains—which looked down Saunders Lane at the cottages of the poor and was the setting of 'The Garden Party'. In her *Journal* of 1916 Katherine describes the house which 'stood far back from the road. It was a big, white-painted square house with a slender pillared verandah and balcony running all the way round it. In the front of the verandah edge the garden sloped away in the terraces and flights of concrete steps—down—until you reached the stone wall covered with nasturtiums that had three gates let into it—the visitors' gate, the tradesmen's gate, and a huge pair of old iron gates that were never used.'[27] In 1898 Harold also bought a modest holiday bungalow at 3 Main Road, Day's Bay. There was no highway around the wide harbour in those days, and the park, pavilion, pier and beach could only be reached by the ferry described in 'At the Bay'.

In modern Wellington the hideous motorway that slashes through old Thorndon and the centre of the city has destroyed Katherine's homes at 75 Tinakori Road (now a severed street) and 47 Fitzherbert Terrace, where she lived during 1907–1908. Though Chesney Wold still stands in the suburbs at 372 Karori Road, the lovely façade was torn off and the house ruined when it was converted into four flats. Only her birthplace at 11 Tinakori Road and the small summer cottage in Day's Bay still survive intact. Katherine is very modestly commemorated in her birthplace by a small park, by Katherine Street off Fitzherbert Terrace and by Beauchamp Street off Karori Road.

Katherine's family had wealth, influence and social prestige, but her childhood—despite its rich teas and grown-up dinners, charades and theatricals, boat trips and birthdays—was far from idyllic. The affectionate Vera was the favourite child; and Katherine's sisters, like her mother, were extremely attractive and perfectly obedient. By contrast, the fat and homely Katherine, who wore steel-rimmed spectacles and had a disabling stutter, was anxious, highly strung and rebellious. She appears in childhood photographs with a pinched mouth, pudgy face, and a severe and solemn look. In 'The Little Girl' Katherine writes that 'She never stuttered with other people—had quite given it up—but only with father, because then she was trying so hard to say the words properly'.[28] And in 'New Dresses' (1912), when the mother blames the child and refuses to accept the reality and psychological significance of the stutter, the father rather casually dismisses the problem:

'I really shall have to see Dr. Malcolm about her stuttering, if only to give her a good fright. I believe it's merely an affectation she's picked up at school—that she can help it.'
    'Anne, you know she's always stuttered. You did just the same when you were her age, she's highly strung.'[29]

Katherine expressed her anxiety, resentment and loneliness in fits of temper that drew attention to herself and provoked her father's hostility. As she wrote to her sister Jeanne in 1921: 'I remember one birthday when you bit me! It was the same one when I got a doll's pram and in a rage let it go hurling by itself down the grassy slope outside the conservatory. Father was *awfully* angry and said no one was to speak to me.'[30]

Katherine attended Wellington Girls' High School during 1898 and 1899, where she formed her first real friendship with the Canadian girl, Marion Ruddick; published her first story, 'Enna Blake', which the Headmistress felt 'showed promise of great merit'; and received prizes in arithmetic, French and English. Though she was eager to transfer to the élite Miss Swainson's School on Fitzherbert Terrace and to wear its distinctive red and blue ribbon on her straw hat, she was unpopular and 'utterly idle' there during her years of adolescence from 1900 to 1903. Her compositions were 'poorly written, poorly spelled, and careless',[31] one teacher called her 'dumpy and unattractive—not even cleverly naughty',[32] and the Headmistress classified her as 'a surly sort of a girl' who was 'imaginative to the point of untruth'.[33] In 'Juliet', the most revealing description of her childhood, she characterizes herself, with considerable insight, as an ugly, moody, angry, critical girl, who withdrew from her family and friends into her own imaginative existence:

Juliet was the odd man out of the family—the ugly duckling. She had lived in a world of her own, created her own people, read anything and everything which came to hand, was possessed with a violent temper, and completely lacked placidity. She was dominated by her moods which swept through her and in number were legion. She had been as yet, utterly idle at school, drifted through her classes, picked up a quantity of heterogeneous knowledge—and all the pleading and protestations of her teachers could not induce her to learn that which did not appeal to her. She criticised everybody and everything with which she came into contact, and wrapped herself in a fierce white reserve.[34]

It was not until many years later that her Headmistress retrospectively realized, 'The family was very conventional; Kass was the outlaw. No one here saw that the unconventionality and rebellion had something behind it. Nobody, I think, understood that or her. They just tried to make her conform'[35]—and she refused to do so.

Though Katherine's parents and teachers did not understand her, she made two intimate friends during this period who encouraged her unconventional behaviour and profoundly influenced her life. At Miss Swainson's School she met and fell passionately in love with a half-caste Maori princess and heiress, a year or two older than herself, who had been educated in English schools. Maata Mahupuka (or Martha Grace) had a soft, gentle and sensuous face, and her golden skin and flashing dark eyes reflected the exotic beauty of her race. In the fragment of an unfinished novel written in the winter of 1913, Katherine portrayed Maata as a sensitive and responsive girl who enchanted everyone in her family. Though she sensed Maata's emotional uneasiness, she attributed her own feelings to her friend: 'Maata felt half suffocated by the strain of the child's little eager body, her smothering kisses, her fumbling hands, and yet it comforted her. . . . It was something real and human and safe.'[36] And in a recently discovered confessional passage, suppressed in her *Journal* of 1907, the rather naive but honest Katherine gives full expression to her powerful lesbian feelings: 'Do other people of my age feel as I do I wonder so absolutely powerful *licentious* so almost physically ill—I alone in this silent clock filled room have become powerfully—I want Maata I want her—and I have had her—terribly—this is unclean I know but true. What an extraordinary thing—I feel savagely crude—and almost powerfully enamoured of the child.'[37] Though Katherine felt guilty about her 'unclean' feelings, Maata allowed her, for the first time in her life, to express her deepest emotions and taught her that she could love a woman as well as a man.

Katherine had loved Maata for two years when in 1900 she met the 'cellist Arnold Trowell, who was also born in 1888, at a musical evening in her home. Arnold, who was the child prodigy of Wellington, practised for eight hours a day and was planning to study in Europe. In 'Juliet', which was written four years later and concerns her tragic love for the sensitive and inspired musician, she idealizes the 'thin stripling, with red hair, [prominent teeth], and no pretensions to good looks'[38] as David, 'A boy of very much her own age. . . . He stood beside a great lamp and the light fell full on his face and his profusion of red-brown hair. Very pale he was, with a dreamy exquisite face, and a striking suggestion of confidence and Power in every feature.'[39] Later on in the story David confesses that their very similarities prevent him from loving her: ' "I feel as though I ought to love her—to me she is an angel, she has always been an angel—but I do not. She is too like me. I understand her too well. We are both too moody, we both feel too much the same about everything. That is what I feel, and so she does not attract me".'[40] When Juliet is later reminded of her 'past *affaire de coeur*' with David, she regrets her submission and adoration, and cries: ' "To think of it makes me feel overwhelmingly sick. When I think how he filled, swayed my whole life, how I worshipped him—only I did. How jealous I was of him! I kept the very envelopes of his letters, for years".'[41]

Arnold, the first real artist she had ever known, inspired Katherine's musical as well as sexual passion, for 'when he drew his bow across the strings her whole soul woke and lived for the first time in her life'.[42] Katherine felt that ' "he was the first person with whom she could really be herself". Arnold felt that "she really understood him". They "told each other everything" '[43] and carried on an intimate correspondence for six years, until he lost interest in Katherine and she transferred her love to his fraternal-twin brother, Garnet.

After hearing Arnold perform in Wellington Katherine began to take 'cello lessons from his father, Thomas Trowell. Thomas had been born in Birmingham and had come to New Zealand in 1880 to marry Kate Wheeler, whom he had first courted in England. Their eldest son, Lyndley, had died of pneumonia at the age of ten; and Thomas, who was a violinist and music master at St. Patrick's, a Catholic college for boys, then devoted himself to the musical education of the prodigious twins. He was a Unitarian, with a free and independent mind, a good sense of humour and a bad temper; and had a large forehead, bright eyes, high straight nose, long drooping moustache and rather pudgy hands. Thomas, a great music teacher, was a father-figure to Katherine, who dressed in brown so that her clothes would 'tone' with her instrument.[44]

Arnold initiated Katherine into the world of art, turned her thoughts beyond the limited confines and conventional values of Wellington, and confirmed her desire to go to Europe. Though it was not a common practice, a few wealthy families sent their daughters to complete their education in the superior English schools, which gave them a refined accent and considerable prestige among those who had never been 'Home'. The

Beauchamps chose Queen's College in London because their
three Payne cousins were attending the school and had recommended it. They arranged for Annie's younger sister, Belle Dyer
(the restless, dreamy and vain Beryl of 'Prelude'), to remain in
England with the three eldest girls and act as assistant to Miss
Wood, the head of the college hostel.

In January 1903 the entire family accompanied the girls to
England on the *Niwaru*, and Vera recalls: 'We were a party of
nine and had the entire accommodation of a cargo passenger ship.
It took us 42 days—with one day at Las Palmas on the way. . . .
We had a clavichord to practise on, a canary in a cage, a sewing
machine, and all the amenities that a ship of that kind could
provide.'[45] The ship stopped briefly in the Canary Islands,
Uruguay and Mexico, where Katherine sent love letters to
Arnold.

When she sailed for England at the age of fourteen, Katherine
had already absorbed the experiences she would later portray in
her stories of New Zealand. On this voyage she made a strong
impression on an elderly gentleman, who noticed her distinctive
powers of observation, her seriousness and her maturity: 'She
struck him as intensely alert, with a deep curiosity altogether
different from the flighty, excited curiosity usual in children. She
turned things over in her head and asked him questions which
surprised him. She was sometimes with her grandmother and the
other children, but oftener alone, going about the boat, looking
the world over with quiet satisfaction.'[46]

In New Zealand Katherine was an unconventional and rebellious outsider who opposed her parents' values but inherited their
unusual mixture of toughness and sensitivity, experienced her
emotional awakening and linked sexual with imaginative freedom, and saw herself as an artist who lived in a world of her own.
In the more congenial though idealized milieu of England, she
would gain confidence in her own beliefs and desires, and would
gradually learn to transform experience into art.

CHAPTER TWO

Queen's College, 1903–1906

QUEEN'S COLLEGE was founded in 1848 by Frederick Denison Maurice, clergyman, author and leader of the Christian Socialism movement, who was a close friend of Tennyson and a charter member of the brilliant Apostles Club at Cambridge. At Queen's, which was originally created to educate governesses but soon developed into a college of further education for women, there were no regulations or grades and the atmosphere was more like a university than a school. Maurice recruited the faculty from King's College, London, where he held the Chair of Divinity, and his colleagues were men of considerable intellect.

The two outstanding teachers during 1903–06, when Katherine was a student, were John Adam Cramb and Walter Rippmann. Cramb, balding and short-sighted with a huge drooping moustache, was born in Scotland in 1862 and became professor of modern history at Queen's College in 1893. He was a friend of Ottoline Morrell, whose biographer writes that 'he taught what he called "the whole life": painting, music, philosophy, as well as history. He was a strong imperialist and later became Lord Roberts's speech-writer.'[1] Cramb predicted the Great War in his influential *Germany and England*, which was based on his lectures at Queen's in February–March 1913. Katherine was extremely impressed by him and said: 'He was "history" to me. . . . Cramb striding up and down, filled me up to the brim. I couldn't write down Cramb's thunder, I simply wanted to sit and hear him.'[2]

Walter Rippmann, who was born in London of a German father and English mother, was professor of German at Queen's from 1896 to 1912. Ruth Herrick, a lively New Zealander who was at the College with Katherine, says that the popular Rippmann, who was younger than most of his colleagues and an exciting lecturer as well as a polished flatterer, was the only teacher entirely acceptable to the students.[3] He took a personal interest in the intellectual life of exceptional and advanced girls like Katherine; invited them to his rooms in Notting Hill, which were decorated with modernistic colours, contemporary posters and Japanese prints; and introduced them to the works of Pater, Wilde, Symons, Dowson and other Decadents of the 1890s. Katherine was rather in love with Rippmann, and in 1904 wrote to her cousin Sylvia Payne: 'I am *ashamed* at the way in which I long for German. I simply can't help it. It is dreadful. And when I go into the class I feel I must just stare at him the whole time. I never liked anyone so much. Every day I like him more.'[4]

Katherine and her two sisters, Vera and Charlotte, dressed in black velour hats and sailor coats with brass buttons, and chaperoned by their somewhat officious Aunt Belle, entered Queen's College in April 1903. The College, a handsome Georgian building at 45 Harley Street, had a spacious Waiting Room with a beautiful ceiling; a decorous Library with a rich carpet and portrait of the Founder over the fireplace; and a rather grand main staircase. Katherine lived next door at number 41 with about forty boarders, had a cubicle of her own, and looked out of the Library and across Harley Street to Mansfield Mews. A passage in 'Juliet' describes her anxious yet expectant first impressions of her surroundings and establishes her superiority to the philistine English girls:

> Juliet looked round her room curiously. So this is where she was to spend the next three years—three years. It did not look inviting. She noticed two texts, ornamented with foxgloves and robins . . . and decided that they must come down. The three large windows looked out upon the Mews below—the houses built all round in a square. She wondered who would share this sanctum. Some English girl, stiff and sporting, who would torture the walls with pictures of dogs, and keep a hockey stick in the corner. Heaven forbid, she thought. She sat down by the side of the bed and pulled off her long gloves. How strange and dim the light was. She was alone in London —glorious thought. Three years of study before her, and then all Life to plunge into.[5]

Katherine played tennis in Regent's Park; attended concerts at Queen's Hall; and took additional 'cello lessons at the London

Academy of Music where De Monk Beauchamp, her second cousin and official guardian in England, was a teacher. Her musical ability was not very great, but she studied the 'cello because it was Arnold Trowell's instrument.

Katherine appears in photographs of this period with a rather puffy face, frizzy hair parted in the middle and springing outward, and dowdy high-necked blouses and long dark skirts. Ruth Herrick observes that she was far from the fair and fluffy Edwardian ideal, exemplified by her sisters, whom she liked though she did not share their looks or their values. Katherine, who had an undistinguished academic career, admired Rippmann and little else. She was not interested in college, did very little work, and was at loggerheads with the professors: 'Most of them, I'm afraid, thought her troublesome. She was certainly very lazy.' Ruth Herrick also says, 'She was a strange girl, and she had an intensity beyond the understanding of most of her schoolfellows'. She did not get on well with the other pupils, and was fond of saying, 'Don't bother me, girls: I'm going to have a mood!'[6] Ruth Herrick never knew what to believe, for Katherine once claimed she had been 'raped', thought she was pregnant and wanted to see a woman doctor. Though she asked her friend to come with her, they never actually went: 'Mimicry was her strong suit and her sense of drama was faultless—she could think herself into any part.'[7]

Katherine's *Journal*, which records the physical rather than the intellectual aspects of the school, confirms her lack of interest in academic life: 'I was thinking yesterday of my *wasted, wasted* early girlhood. My college life, which is such a vivid and detailed memory in one way, might never have contained a book or a lecture. I lived in the girls, the professor [Rippmann], the big, lovely building, the leaping fires in winter and the abundant flowers in summer.'[8] Katherine's story, 'Carnation' (1917), describes a terribly boring French class on a 'wasted' hot afternoon when 'all of them lolled and gaped, staring at the round clock, which seemed to have grown paler, too; the hands scarcely crawled. . . . The great difficulty was, of course, if you felt at all feeble, not to get the most awful fit of the giggles.'[9] When the lecturer on Bible History asked if any of the young ladies had ever been chased by a wild bull and Katherine falsely claimed that she had (since no one else volunteered), he condescendingly replied: 'I am afraid you do not count. You are a little savage from New Zealand.'[10]

Yet a recent letter from the Registrar of Queen's College reveals that Katherine's work, especially in modern languages, was certainly above average and considerably better than she had remembered: 'French and German were clearly her "best" subjects, her reports for these ranging from "good" to "excellent", but she seems to have done well in most of her classes, except for one term when her English language was "unsatisfactory" and literature "disappointing" (Christmas 1905). Past students who were her contemporaries have said that she was not generally popular because she was very shy and reserved.'[11] Though reserved, Katherine was active in music, in debating the question of whether teachers spoil Shakespeare by making him a duty instead of a pleasure, and in the college magazine. Between December 1903 and December 1905 she published five stories about children and her own childhood, including 'About Pat' (which was reprinted in her *Scrapbook*), and 'Die Einsame' (The Lonely One) about an alien and solitary spirit, drawn into the agony of exile, which may well have been influenced by her reading Moore's *Life and Letters of Byron* and the exotic romances of Anthony Hope.

Katherine's friendships at Queen's were undoubtedly more important to her than her teachers, her school work, her writing and even her music. Her older cousins, Sylvia and Evelyn Payne, whose father was a successful doctor, lived in nearby Wimpole Street. In 1903 Katherine spent the Christmas holidays in Bexley, Kent, at the house of her great uncle, Henry Herron Beauchamp, the father of Elizabeth of the German Garden. From there she sent Sylvia, a strange child who wore spectacles and had long red hair, a charming invitation to friendship: 'I like you much more than any other girl I have met in England, and I seem to see less of you. We just stand upon the threshold of each other's heart and never get right in. What I mean by "heart" is just this: My heart is a place where everything I love (whether it be in imagination or in truth) has a free entrance. . . . I wish we could know each other, so that I might be able to say, "Sylvia is one of my *best* friends".'[12]

Katherine's friendship with another girl, the small, dark and slender 'Mimi' Bartrick-Baker (who later married Murry's friend J. W. N. Sullivan), was both emotional and intellectual, and their 'advanced' reading was highly suspect in the eyes of the Headmistress. Mimi relates that Katherine was 'definitely most enthusiastic in temperament, even to the extent of stammering very slightly from sheer excitement when much aroused.'[13] 'Of course Katherine Mansfield and I had long discussions over Tolstoy, Maeterlinck and Ibsen, in the lower corridor. We came an hour earlier for this, and were suspected of immorality. Miss Croudace was *stupefied* when she asked what we talked about and I told her.'[14]

Ida Baker, Katherine's most intimate friend at Queen's and throughout her life, somewhat jealously records that Katherine and Ruth Herrick swaggered around London in 'aesthetic' clothes: 'They went to concerts together in large, floppy, black ties, and wide, soft felt hats and assumed a rather slouching walk, imagining themselves to be young bohemian musicians. Ruth became devoted to Katherine, perhaps too devoted.'[15] Ruth Herrick recalls that Katherine insisted on conversing in French though they knew only ten words between them.

Ida Constance Baker was born in Suffolk in January 1888, was taken when she was two months old to Burma, where her father was an army doctor, and brought back to England in 1895, when the family settled in Welbeck Street. Her sister, May, was crippled by polio, her mother, who was named Katherine, died of typhoid fever in the spring of 1903, and her moody and irascible father, Colonel Oswald Baker, who was 'a dried up old stick'[16] and a model for Constantia's father in 'The Daughters of the Late Colonel', shot himself after World War I. Ida, who was used to nursing her sister, attended Queen's College school in 1897, entered the College itself in 1901, and met Katherine just after her mother's death, when she was asked to show the three Beauchamp sisters to their room on the top floor. It was Katherine 'who suggested that they *choose* each other. "Let's be friends," she said, and for a moment startled the dreaming Ida out of her void. "*Be* friends!" thought Ida. "But you can't just *be* friends. A friend is something you become".'[17]

Katherine called her friend 'Lesley Moore' (a composite of the first name of her brother and the maiden name of Ida's mother) because she felt that Ida Baker was 'the ugliest name on earth';[18] Ottoline Morrell later labelled her 'The Mountain' because of her

overshadowing height. Katherine, who was extremely fond of
pet names and pseudonyms, and liked to enhance reality with
fantasy, also called her prosaic friend 'Adela*ida*', 'Betsy', 'Jones'
and (ironically) 'The Godmother', 'The Faithful One' (F.O.),
'The Dwarf' and 'The Rhodesian Mountain' (for Ida spent 1914–
1916 in southern Africa).

The graceless and awkward Ida, who was lonely and desperately in need of affection after the death of her mother, soon
became attracted to the clever, strong-willed Katherine. Ruth
Herrick, who answered Ida's jealousy with hostility, was 'not
impressed by Ida's intellect' and was sickened by the adoration of
the 'lymphatic lump of humanity', whom Katherine treated like
a slave.[19] The girls heard Katherine cry: ' "Ida! Get my handkerchief from the left-hand bureau drawer!" And they heard
Ida's quiet reply: "Yes, Katie, darling".'[20] Katherine was
genuinely fond of the gentle and devoted Ida, but she enjoyed
dominating her.

While at Queen's Katherine continued to write love letters to
Arnold Trowell, whose photograph stood on her dressing-table.
In the summer of 1903 Arnold and Garnet won a grant from the
New Zealand government (subscribed to by Harold Beauchamp)
to study music in Europe. They had played in all the principal
towns of New Zealand, and toured Australia and South America
before completing their formal training in the conservatories of
Frankfurt and Brussels. When the two boys came to London for
their holidays, Katherine would go to concerts with them. In
the spring of 1906 Katherine and her two sisters, escorted by
Aunt Belle Dyer, spent two weeks in Belgium; and Katherine
told Ida they had bathed naked on a sheltered part of the coast.
They visited the Trowells in Brussels; met their bohemian friend
Rudolf, who appears in 'Juliet', and heard Arnold's 'cello
performance.

On March 31, 1906, the music critic of the *European Express* in
Brussels praised Arnold's virtuosity and enthusiastically wrote:
'M. Arnold Trowell's recital on the violoncello at the Grande
Harmonie on Tuesday evening was attended by an overflowing
audience, many persons in the side Galleries having to stand
throughout the evening. The efforts of this artist were rewarded
with immense applause. . . . M. Trowell displayed great sentiment
and delicacy in his delivery of Schumann's "Abendlied" and

Bach's "Aria in D".' After a number of concerts on the Continent, a Wellington newspaper proudly announced that after two years of study in Brussels, 'Arnold Trowell, a clever young New Zealand 'cellist, who has won fame all over Europe, is to make his debut before a London audience in April.'[21] Arnold's recitals at the Bechstein Hall in London were received with enthusiasm, and he had a distinguished career as a 'cello soloist.[22]

Katherine was enormously proud of Arnold's artistic success, fell more in love than ever before and began to write the autobiographical 'Juliet' in May 1906. One girl at Queen's, who saw her with the Trowells, was clearly impressed, and thought them 'the most extraordinary beings I had ever met. Red-haired, pale, wearing huge black hats . . . [they were] smoking the longest cigarettes I had ever seen.'[23] But Katherine's meetings with Arnold were sometimes unhappy, and the highly strung girl would return to the College, throw herself on the bed and weep violently.

In 1906 Katherine also had an emotional reunion with Maata, who had finished her education in Paris and become sophisticated in dress and behaviour. The two girls rode blissfully down Regent Street in a hansom cab and exchanged intimate sections of their diaries.

Katherine's parents came to England in April 1906 and remained there until October when the girls, who had finished college, returned to New Zealand with them. In a letter to Sylvia Payne, Katherine announced her departure, and reversed her aesthetic priorities, at the insistence of her father, who discouraged her unhealthy imitation of Arnold: 'Father is greatly opposed to my wish to be a professional 'cellist or to take up the 'cello to any great extent—so my hope for a musical career is absolutely gone—It was a fearful disappointment. . . . In the future I shall give *all* my time to writing.'[24]

Katherine, who loved London and Arnold Trowell, and anticipated a dreary exile in remote New Zealand, tried to persuade her parents to allow her to remain in England. As she despairingly wrote in 'Juliet': 'If I do once go back all will be over. It is stagnation, desolation that stares me in the face. I shall be lonely, I shall be thousands of miles from all that I care for and once I get there I can't come back.' And in the story her father impatiently replies: 'What have I got for my money? . . . You are behaving badly. You must learn to realize that the silken cords of parental authority are very tight ropes indeed. I want no erratic spasmodic daughter. I demand a sane healthy-minded girl.'[25] Harold, who was not pleased by the 'unhealthy' changes he had observed in Katherine after three years at Queen's, under Rippmann's influence, vowed 'I'll never send the two younger children "home" to be educated',[26] and rejected his daughter's pleas. Only Aunt Belle, who had become engaged to a wealthy shipowner, remained in England. The Beauchamps sailed back on the *Corinthic*, and the battle between the authoritative parent and the erratic daughter broke out almost immediately.

CHAPTER THREE

Return to New Zealand, 1907–1908

KATHERINE'S RETURN voyage to the bottom of the world on the *Corinthic* was a paradigm of her eighteen months in New Zealand. It reflects her opposition to her family's conventions and values, her condemnation of their 'vulgar' materialism, her desire to return to London, her struggle against restraints, her quest for sexual freedom, and her passionate determination to be an artist despite the 'tyranny' and 'inferiority' of her intolerable parents. Though her elder sister Charlotte (like other members of the family) fostered the myth of a happy and well-adjusted Katherine and claimed 'We had a M.C.C. team on board and they were a very gay lot and Katherine thoroughly enjoyed herself',[1] Katherine's rather savage diary entry about her parents, written aboard ship in November 1906, reveals that she felt bitterly trapped from the moment she left London:

> They are worse than I had even expected. They are prying and curious, they are watchful and they discuss only the food. They quarrel between themselves in a hopelessly vulgar fashion. My Father spoke of my returning as damned rot, said look here, he wouldn't have me fooling around in dark corners with fellows. His hands, covered with long sandy hair, are absolutely cruel hands. A physically revolted feeling seizes me. He wants me to sit near. He watches me at meals, eats in the most abjectly, blatantly vulgar manner that is describable. . . . *She* is constantly suspicious, constantly overbearingly tyrannous. . . . I shall never be able to live at home. I can plainly see that. There would be constant friction. For more than a quarter of an hour they are quite unbearable, and so absolutely my mental inferiors.[2]

Ruth Herrick felt that Katherine was a 'foreigner' to Harold Beauchamp, whom she described as a fine-looking man but 'soapy, humbuggy and a thorough hypocrite'. She thought that

Annie Beauchamp was a pleasant and kindly woman who had a difficult time with Harold, especially about money.[3] In Katherine's autobiographical story, 'New Dresses' (1910), the mother says: 'They're a hell upon earth, every month, these bills'; and Katherine told Ida Baker 'of the family trials each time the weekly accounts had to be submitted to him. Her mother, who called her husband "Mr. Businessman", had a weekly allowance which made a torture of each reckoning day.'[4] Harold had rapidly made his fortune and was a director of shipping, insurance, gas and chemical companies; and though Katherine enjoyed her father's wealth in girlhood, she would (like her mother) suffer from his stinginess throughout her adult life.

When Katherine returned to Wellington in December 1906 she found the household changed. Aunt Belle Dyer had stayed in England and her twelve-year-old brother, Leslie, was away at school. Her grandmother Dyer, who had moved to the house of her eldest daughter, died on December 31, before Katherine had visited her; and Katherine's self-absorption and failure to see her grandmother must have intensified both her grief and her guilt about the kindly old lady. In April 1907, when Harold became Chairman of the Bank of New Zealand, the family moved to 47 Fitzherbert Terrace. The two-storey white wooden house was even larger than Chesney Wold and 75 Tinakori Road, and had a music room, front bay windows, an arched carriage porch, a croquet lawn and a picket fence around the splendid garden.

Edith Bendall, a close friend of Katherine during this period of her life, dismissed the Beauchamps as 'bridge and golf people', and felt that Vera and Charlotte shared their parents' values and liked their social life while Katherine frequently withdrew into surly solitude.[5] Katherine, who had the temperament but had not yet developed the power of the artist, was intensely irritated when the banalities of everyday existence impinged upon her imaginative reveries and wrote in October 1907: 'Damn my family! O Heavens, what bores they are! I detest them all heartily. . . . Even when I am alone in my room they come outside and call to each other, discuss the butcher's orders or the soiled linen and—I feel—wreck my life.'[6] Her cosmopolitan experience merely emphasized the philistine vulgarity of her native land, and the angry and moody girl, who was considered 'posey and affected', decided to be as rude and 'difficult' as possible in order to force her parents to allow her to return to England.

Rupert Brooke, who later met Katherine at Garsington, passed through Wellington in January 1914 and wrote to his mother: 'New Zealand isn't a frightfully interesting country, I fancy',[7] and even today it is rather provincial, philistine and smug. Katherine wrote ironically that 'colonial men are not the brightest specimens', and the writer who had once whispered about Maeterlinck and Ibsen echoed Samuel Butler when she said that Wellington 'is still trying to swallow Rossetti, and *Hope* by Watts is looked upon as very advanced'.[8] The expatriate New Zealand painter, Frances Hodgkins, entirely agreed with Katherine. Miss Hodgkins, who was also disillusioned by her experiences in Wellington in 1905 and disliked the complacency of her countrymen, later wrote: 'Wellington is *not* an artistic centre. Neither I nor my work was ever popular there.'[9]

Katherine expressed the conflict between her artistic individuality and the dull conformity of her country in letters to her sister and her friends; and advocated a rather hopeless programme of cultural regeneration: 'I am ashamed of young New Zealand, but what is to be done. All the firm fat framework of their brains must be demolished before they can begin to learn. They want a purifying influence—a mad wave of pre-Raphaelitism, of super-aestheticism, should intoxicate the country. They must go to excess in the direction of culture, become almost decadent in their tendencies for a year or two and then find balance and proportion. We want two or three persons gathered together to discuss line and form and atmosphere.'[10]

A month later, in a letter to Sylvia Payne filled with self-pity and irony, she emphasizes her isolation and longs for the misty, *fin-de-siècle* London of Wilde and of Whistler: 'I feel absolutely ill with grief and sadness here—it is a nightmare. . . . I can't see how it can drag on—I have not one friend—and no prospect of one— My dear—I know nobody—and nobody cares to know me— There is nothing on earth to do—nothing to see—and my heart keeps flying off to Oxford Circus—Westminster Bridge at the Whistler hour—London by hansom—my old room—and a corner in the Library—it haunts me all so much—and I feel [I] must come back soon—How people ever wish to live here I cannot think.'[11]

And a letter to her father, written at the end of her life, contrasts his cosmopolitan independence with the colony's narrow-minded mentality, its envy of European experience and its accommodation to conventional mediocrity: '[It is] all part of that Colonial "New Zealand's good enough for me" attitude which is so disconcerting. It is a refusal to regard anything except from a purely local standpoint: they grudge you your wider vision and range of experience. In fact, what it comes to is they are frightened of anything approaching power in any shape or form. Like all little people, they are uneasy at knowing there is some one among them who is their superior. It must be intensely disheartening at times.'[12]

Though Katherine told Edie Bendall, 'If I had to live here, I'd go and die under a *manuka* tree', Ruth Herrick observed that Katherine liked New Zealand as long as she did not have to live there and 'raved about it' while she was in England. Though she wrote to Garnet Trowell, soon after she returned to London: 'This evening I had my New Zealand letters; they always strangely depress me. I think the shadow of the old life creeps over me, and I feel so out of touch with them—they hurt me bitterly',[13] her New Zealand experience was not all shadows and bitterness. Besides stimulating Katherine's responsiveness to natural beauty, New Zealand gave her something tangible to rebel against and led to that 'internal emigration' which was important to her artistic development. Katherine was an outsider in New Zealand as well as in English society.

Despite Katherine's diatribes against New Zealand and her lamentation to Vera: 'Here there is really no scope for development, no intellectual society, no hope of finding any',[14] she made significant intellectual progress during her reluctant exile from England, which was a profitable and relatively happy period of her life. She spent most of her time reading modern authors, writing short stories behind locked doors while burning incense, playing the 'cello, and pursuing the interests that had been encouraged by Walter Rippmann at Queen's. While in Wellington she attended the Technical School, published her first professional works, made a passionate new friendship, travelled in the wild Maori country, and led a full social life. She felt the protection and security, as well as the irritations, of her family, and enjoyed good health for the last time in her life.

The numerous quotations from *Dorian Gray* in Katherine's *Journal* of 1906–08 reflect the overwhelming influence of Oscar Wilde, the defiant dandy 'who was so absolutely the essence of *savoir faire*'. Katherine attempted to put Wilde's ideas into practice while in Wellington (despite Harold's insistence that he 'wouldn't have her fooling around in dark corners with fellows'), and Oscar kept a 'firm stronghold' in her soul.[15] Wilde also provided aesthetic justification for the rebellious and rarefied spirit whose clothes 'toned' with her 'cello and whose life was 'wrecked' by soiled linen. Like Wilde, she claimed the sexual and intellectual freedom of the artist and felt intensity was the touchstone of experience:

The only way to get rid of temptation is to yield to it.
Be always reaching for new sensations. . . . Be afraid of nothing.
Push everything as far as it will go.
To love madly perhaps is not wise, yet should you love madly,
   it is far wiser than not to love at all.[16]

Katherine got a ticket to the General Assembly Library, a grey-green Victorian gingerbread building next to Parliament, and devoured her favourite authors—Morris and Meredith, Ruskin and Shaw, Whitman and Carpenter, D'Annunzio and the Brontës—not only to learn how to write, but to learn how to live. She was also seriously reading the Russians: Tolstoy, Dostoyevsky, the young painter and diarist Marie Bashkirtseff, and quite probably Chekhov, for R. E. C. Long's translation of *The Black Monk and Other Stories* (1903) had been in the Library since August 1904. Marie Bashkirtseff, whose tragic fate foreshadowed Katherine's, was most important to her at this time, and she felt intense sympathy for the artist who wrote, in the last year of her life: 'My weakness and the preoccupation of my thoughts keep me apart from the real world which, however, I have never seen so clearly as I do now. All its baseness, all its meanness, stand out before my mind with a saddening distinctness.'[17]

Katherine resumed her music lessons with Thomas Trowell, who was then resident conductor for visiting companies at the opera house; her friendship with the Trowells, one of the few artistic families in Wellington, was a vital link with Arnold as well as with music. She describes a successful lesson as if it were a lovers' tryst, and shows how dependent she was on his sympathy and how proud of his praise: 'A happy day. I have spent a perfect day. Never have I loved Mr. Trowell so much or felt so in accord with him; and my 'cello expressing everything. . . . He came, and in one instant we understood each other, and I think he was happy. O joyous time! It was almost inhuman. And to hear that "Bravely done! You've a real grip of it all. Very good!" I would not have exchanged those words for all the laurel wreaths in existence.'[18] She was intensely unhappy when the Trowells left Wellington in September 1907 to join the twins in London; her farewell letter to Mr. Trowell expressed her profound gratitude for his inspiring teaching: 'I cannot let you leave without telling you how grateful I am and must be all my life for what you have done for me and given me. You have shown me that there is something so immensely higher and greater than I had ever realized before in music, and therefore too, in life.'[19]

Millie Parker, a musical friend, noticed that Katherine was different from the other girls and unusually self-possessed, perhaps because of her London finishing school and her 'ultra-modern' behaviour. Katherine seemed 'almost a little foreign by way of strange temperament. . . . She was at that time only about eighteen, but very mature and experienced for her age and often delighted and amused when people mistook her age for twenty-eight.'[20] Katherine still had a plump figure, fat face and pinched mouth, wore her hair rolled high on her head and dressed in unflattering clothes, but her lively sophistication (and perhaps her father's money) led to the novel experience of being popular with men.

In May 1908 Katherine entered Wellington Technical School to learn typing and bookkeeping. She described her orderly existence and unusual social success in a letter to the beautiful Vera: 'You know I go to the Technical School every day. Library until five in the afternoon, then a walk, and in the evenings I read *and* write. . . . Here is a little news—don't call me conceited. I think I am more popular than almost any girl here at dances— isn't it funny—it makes me glad in a way but it's a little trying.'[21] Katherine also confided to an English friend: 'Do you know *five* men have asked me to marry them. It is the stupid truth.'[22] She dismissed one promising suitor with the casual notation: 'I used him merely for copy';[23] and after another flirtation with a 'bloated lover of a thousand actresses, [and] roamer of every city under the sun', she wrote: 'I'm glad about the whole affair. I shall pervert it . . . make it fascinating.'[24] But this popularity also had its dangers. In December 1907 her vigilant parents were alarmed when they discovered her highly-coloured description of an incident that occurred when she sat out a dance with an ardent admirer.

Her pretty friend Edie Bendall, who was nine years older than Katherine and had returned to Wellington after studying art in Sydney, usually accompanied her on the five o'clock walks. The two girls planned a book about children in which Edie would illustrate Katherine's poems and stories; Katherine wrote to her friend that 'The child with the fringe is fascinating me—in fact, all of the [drawings] are wonderfully beautiful.'[25] Though the book was never published, Katherine later used Edie's surname for characters in a story of 1909[26] and in 'Sixpence' (1921). The girls became intimate friends and often went to the small family cottage near the sea in Day's Bay, which Katherine (who was used to grand houses) described in her *Journal* of June 1907: 'I sit in the small poverty-stricken sitting-room, the *one* and only room which the cottage contains, with the exception of a cabin-like bedroom fitted with bunks, and an outhouse with a bath and wood-cellar, coal-cellar complete. On one hand is the sea, stretching right up to the yard; on the other the bush growing close down almost to my front door.'[27]

But Katherine's dominant interest was writing and she declared: 'My plans, they are work and struggle and learn and try and lead a full life—and get this great heap of MSS off my hands—and write some more'.[28] With the help of her father, who took paternal pride in her work, Katherine succeeded in publishing her first professional sketches of London and Wellington: 'Vignette', 'Silhouette' and 'In A Café' in *The Native Companion* of Melbourne during October, November and December of 1907, and she placed a fourth piece, 'Study: The Death of a Rose', in the *Triad* of Dunedin in July 1908. The quality of the prose and the heady influence of Wilde can be seen in this characteristic sentence from 'Silhouette': 'I want the night to come, and kiss me with her hot mouth, and lead me through an amethyst twilight to the place of the white gardenia.'[29]

During a cricket match Harold Beauchamp told Tom Mills, a Wellington journalist, about his daughter's work, and asked him

to read the sketches and suggest a place of publication. Mills was
impressed by the six precocious stories 'of the sex problem type'
and 'discovered in this literary Beauchamp a girl bright, well read
and informed on general topics, obviously a thinker, and not the
least bit diffident about her writings. She was quite convinced in
herself that she could write—that she had the gift to write.'[30]
Mills advised her to send her work to E. J. Brady, the editor of
The Native Companion.

The sketches were typed by Harold's secretary and sent to
Melbourne; when they were accepted Katherine confidently
replied to Brady in September 1907: 'You ask me for some
details as to myself. I am poor—obscure—just eighteen years of
age—with a rapacious appetite for everything, and principles as
light as my purse. If this pleases you—this Mss.—please know
that there is a great deal more where this comes from.'[31]
Katherine's statement that she was only eighteen made Brady
suspect the originality of her 'mature' work, so he sought, and
received, reassurance from Harold: 'you need never have any
hesitation in accepting anything from her upon the assumption
that it may not be original matter. She herself is, I think, a very
original character, and writing—whether it is good or bad—
comes to her quite naturally. In fact, since she was eight years of
age, she has been producing poetry and prose. . . . I may add that
she has always been an omnivorous reader, and possesses a most
retentive memory.'[32] Katherine, who signed these sketches with
her pen-name, 'Katherine Mansfield', was extremely excited when
she received her first cheque and the October issue of the magazine. Fifteen years later she wrote to her father: 'It is strange to
remember buying a copy of *The Native Companion* on Lambton
Quay and standing under a lamppost with darling Leslie to see if
my story had been printed.'[33]

Though Edie Bendall remembers that Katherine was 'always in
love with someone', she remained passionately in love with
Arnold (whom she called 'Caesar') throughout her stay in New
Zealand and recorded her extremes of emotion in her *Journal* of
June 1907: 'I hate everybody, loathe myself, loathe my life, and
love Caesar'.[34] And on August 11 she expressed her complete
adoration of her distant lover and her longing for sexual surrender: 'Beloved, though I do not see you, know that I am yours
—every thought, every feeling in me belongs to you. I wake in

the morning and have been dreaming of you—and all through the day, while my outer life is going on steadily, monotonously, even drearily, my inner life I live with you, in leaps and bounds. I go through every phase of emotion that is possible, loving you. To me you are man, lover, artist, husband, friend—giving me all—and I surrendering you all—everything.'[35]

But even Katherine realized that she could not sustain nor Arnold reciprocate this intensity of emotion, and the printed passage ends with the fearful plea: 'Do not suddenly crush out this one beautiful flower—I am afraid—even while I am rejoicing'.[36] In a revealing passage, which was omitted from the published *Journal*, Katherine continues her rhetorical but prophetic apprehensions, reaffirms her barely repressed physical desires and (like the fictional Juliet) preserves the envelopes of Arnold's letters as fetishes of love: 'But whatever happens—tho' you marry another—tho' we never meet again—I belong to you—we belong to each other. And whenever you want me, with both my hands [I'll] say—unashamed, fiercely proud—exultant—triumphant—satisfied at last—"take me". Each night I go to sleep with your letters under my pillow & in the darkness I stretch out my hand & clasp the thin envelope close to my body so that it lies there warmly & I smile in the darkness and sometimes—my body aches as though with fatigue—but I understand.'[37]

Katherine's plan to marry Arnold when she returned to England was apparently encouraged by Mr. Trowell, for on August 27 she wrote: 'If I marry Caesar—and I thought of him all the time—I think I could prove a great many things. Mr. Trowell said: "She must share his glories and always keep him in the heights".'[38] Yet the very next day she received a letter from Ida Baker, whom she had written to for insight about Arnold's feelings, which confirmed her fears of abandonment and plunged her into numb despair: 'I had a letter from Aida today about Arnold Trowell, and at present I have no idea how I felt. First, so sorrowful, so hurt, so pained, that I contemplated the most outrageous things; but now only *old*, and angry and lonely.'[39] That crisis eventually subsided, perhaps because the Trowells left for England in September, steadied Arnold's life and turned his thoughts back to Katherine. Ida continued to send clippings about Arnold's performances, and in January 1908 Katherine

proudly told Vera of Arnold's musical triumphs: Arnold 'has
had the most magically successful concert—you know, a packed
hall, and glowing notices even from *The Times*. I am so glad.
He played this Reverie then, and also at Queen's Hall where the
Duke of Connaught was present.'[40] In 1908 Arnold published
his *Six Morceaux* for violin, which were 'Dedicated to my dear
Friend Kathleen M. Beauchamp'.

Though Katherine loved Arnold, he remained an idealized
figure in far-off London, and though she dismissed the Wellington
beaux as literary fodder (for they paled in comparison to
'Caesar'), she needed an outlet for her passions and found it—
once again—in a girlfriend who could return her love. 'Caesar is
losing hold of me,' she wrote early in 1907. 'Edie is waiting for
me. I shall slip into her arms. They are safest. Do you love me?'[41]
When Katherine extinguished the lights and played the 'cello for
Edie, Harold knocked at the door and asked: 'What are you in
the dark for?'

The 1927 edition of the *Journal* omitted all the lesbian passages,
the 1954 edition gives a glimpse of her brief but intense love
affair with Edie (who is not identified in the crucial entries), and
the unpublished passages from her Notebook of June 1907 reveal
the depths of her emotions and her shrewd self-analysis. In the
published entry of June 1, 1907, when the girls were together at
Day's Bay, Katherine expresses her ambivalent feelings of love
and guilt, takes the male role, and recognizes that her passion for
Edie is more intense, realistic and genuine than anything she had
ever felt for Arnold:

Last night I spent in her arms—and to-night I hate her—which,
being interpreted, means that I adore her: that I cannot lie in
my bed and not feel the magic of her body: which means that
sex means as nothing to me. I feel more powerfully all those
so-termed sexual impulses with her than I have with any man.
She enthrals, enslaves me—and her personal self—her body
absolute—is my worship. I feel that to lie with my head on her
breast is to feel what life can hold. . . .

In my life—so much Love in imagination; in reality 18 barren
years—never pure spontaneous affectionate impulse. Adonis
was—dare I seek into the heart of me—nothing but a pose.
And now she comes—and pillowed against her, clinging to her

hands, her face against mine, I am a child, a woman, and more than half man.[42]

At this point in the *Journal* there is the editorial excuse: 'After an indecipherable page the journal becomes legible again'. But it is possible to decipher the somewhat masochistic deleted passage in which Katherine describes the anguish of her love as a 'combat' and a 'crucifixion', expresses her fear of uncontrollable urges, and prophesies the suffering she will experience in the 'hard course of loving': 'I cannot sleep I shall not sleep again. This is madness I know—but it is too real for sanity it is too simply incredible to be doubted—Once again I must bear this changing of the tide—my life is a Rosary of Fierce combats for Two—each bound together with the powerful magnetic chain of sex—and at the end—does the emblem of the crucified—hang—surely—I do not know I do not wish to look—but I am so shocked with grief that I feel I cannot continue my hard course of loving—and being unloved— of giving loves only to find them flung back at me—faded worm eaten.'[43] Though a nightmare of 'hideous forms of Chinamen' follows this deleted passage, the published version concludes with an hysterical catharsis, a tender reconciliation and a longing for sexual oblivion: '[I] sat on the edge of the bed, trembling, half crying, hysterical with grief. Somehow silently she woke, and came over to me—took me again into the shelter of her arms. We lay down together, still silently, she every now and then pressing me to her, kissing me, my head on her breasts, her hands round my body, stroking me, lovingly—warming me to give me more life again. Then her voice, whispering "Better now, darling?" . . . I drew close to her warm sweet body . . . the past once more buried, clinging to her, and wishing that this darkness might last for ever.'[44]

By the end of June Katherine's love affair had peaked and expired, and both girls seemed weary of each other and embarrassed by what had happened. Katherine notes her tedium in the published *Journal*: 'But this afternoon has been horrible. E.K.B. bored me, I bored her. I felt unhappy, and I think so did she. But she never took the initiative.'[45] In the deleted passage she criticizes their relationship and Edie's character, and returns to the question of her susceptibility to sexual impulses: 'And now E.K.B. is a thing of the Past—absolutely irrevocably—thank

Heaven! It was, I consider, retrospectively, a frantically maudlin relationship & one better ended—also she will not achieve a great deal of greatness [?] she has not the necessary impetus of character. Do other people of my own age feel as I do I wonder—so absolutely powerful *licentious*.'[46] It is rather extraordinary that this passage about concluding her affair with Edie runs directly into her confession (quoted in Chapter 1) that she had been Maata's lover when they were pupils at Miss Swainson's School in 1903: 'I want Maata I want her—and I have had her—terribly—this is unclean I know but true.'[47] It seems that Edie revived Katherine's feelings for Maata, and that she used her memory of Maata to compensate for the loss of Edie.

The full story of Katherine's relationship with Edie Bendall suggests that she exulted in her powerful sexual impulses but was afraid of her inability to control them. At the early age of fourteen (with Maata) and again at eighteen (with Edie), she defied social conventions and moral restraints in her quest for love and for the kind of 'experience' she could use in her art. In Queen's College and in Wellington her behaviour was usually regulated by her teachers and parents, but when she returned to London her destructive surrender to the 'hard course of loving' would have tragic results. Katherine's ability to sustain simultaneous love for both Edie and Arnold foreshadowed her relationship with her friend, Ida Baker, and her husband, John Middleton Murry. And Katherine's need (like Wilde's) to love men and women at the same time helped her to form friendships with the bisexual Dora Carrington and Virginia Woolf.

In November 1907, at the beginning of the New Zealand summer, after the Trowells had left for England and Katherine had her first stories published, she intensified her bitter campaign to return to London and her father provisionally agreed to her departure. He then arranged for her to travel for a month through the Maori-speaking Urewera country, to cool her passions, to distract her, to get rid of her for a while and to teach her something about her own country.

Cannibalism and the wars against the Maoris on North Island had lasted until the early 1870s; a historian writes that though 'the completion of the main trunk railway from Auckland to Wellington in 1908 may be taken to symbolize the opening of the island, there was still a great amount of backblocks land to be brought into cultivation, and a good deal of arduous and isolated pioneering to be survived before this was complete.'[48] When I travelled to Te Whaiti in the Ureweras in June 1976 I found that very little had changed since Katherine had been there at the turn of the century. As I rode from the plains into the mountains the tidy sheep farms gave way to thick bush with semi-tropical vegetation, vast forests, deep gorges, high waterfalls and rushing streams 'like fierce wolves'. The bus went there only three times a week, the road was unpaved after Murupara, there were very few settlements and Maori was still spoken by most of the people. A 1907 photograph of Te Whaiti shows Katherine with her hand on her hip and a gloomy expression on her face, standing between her guide and companion and behind a rather miserable-looking group of Maoris, some wrapped in blankets and others wearing vests.

Katherine took the train to Hastings on the east coast, and the party then travelled in two horse-drawn covered caravans to the centre of the island, from Bay View to Rotorua. She then went south to Taupo and took the train home. There were eight people in the party, four men and four women, plus the driver, and all but one were strangers to Katherine. One of the women, Elsie Webber, later said: 'Our sleeping quarters consisted of one large tent with a division between. On one side the women slept, and on the other the men.'[49] Katherine wrote to her mother of her companions: 'I'm quite fond of all the people—they are ultra-colonial but . . . kind & goodhearted & generous—and always more than good to me.'[50] But she privately expressed displeasure with her countrymen after meeting an English family: 'It is splendid to see once again real English people. I am so tired and sick of the third-rate article. Give me the Maori *and* the tourist, but nothing between.'[51]

Katherine's moods varied enormously on the trip—from admiration of the spectacular scenery and interest in the Maori way of life, to disgust with the crude conditions of travel and revulsion for the ugly mud volcanoes which reminded her of hell. In a vivid letter to her mother she conveys the excitement of new discoveries, the grubbiness of the camp site and the sensual pleasures of the velvety mineral baths, while alluding to Lewis Carroll's parody of Wordsworth's 'aged man' and the awful food at the Queen's College hostel:

The greatest sight I have seen was the view from the top of
Turungakuma. You draw rein at the top of the mountains &
round you everywhere are other mountains—bush covered—
& far below you in the valley little Tarawera & a silver ribbon
of river—I could do nothing but laugh—it must have been the
air—& the danger. . . .

We reached the Tarawera Hotel in the evening, & camped
in a little bush hollow. *Grubby*, my dear. I felt dreadful—my
clothes were white with dust—we had accomplished 8 miles of
hill climbing—so after dinner (broad beans cooked over a
camp fire and tongue & cake and tea) we prowled round and
found an 'aged aged man' who had the key of the mineral
baths. . . . He guides us through the bush track by the river. . . .
I don't think he ever had possessed a tooth & he never ceased
talking—you have the effect?

The Bath House is a shed—three of us bathed in a great pool
—waist high. . . . The water was very hot & like oil—most
delicious . . . & when we came out drank a great mug of
mineral water—luke warm & tasting like Miss Wood's eggs
at their worst stage—But you feel inwardly & outwardly like
velvet.[52]

Katherine particularly disliked the steaming stench of Rotorua,
where the Maoris had built their village amid the explosive
geysers and pockets of volcanic mud. She complained about the
'*fearful* rain—up to the ankles—the wet camp—the fear of having
to move',[53] and concluded: 'I must say I hated that town. It did
not suit me at all. I never felt so ill and depressed.'[54] But at the
end of the journey, when she reached Lake Taupo, she expressed
her blissful contentment:

All is harmonious and peaceful and delicious. We camp in a
pine forest—beautiful. There are chickens cheeping; the
people are so utterly benevolent. We are like children here with
happiness. We drive through the sunset—then supper at the
hotel. And the night is utterly perfect. We go to the mineral
baths. The walk there down the hill is divine. The suggestion
of water and cypresses; it is very steep. Not a fire bath, though
very hot—so pleasant. Then we go home—tired—hot—happy
—blissfully happy. We sleep in the tent—wake early and wash
and dress and go down to the hotel again. The birds are

magical. I feel I cannot leave, but pluck honeysuckle. The splashes of light lie in the pine woods.[55]

The trip to the Ureweras introduced Katherine to the gentle ways of the primitive Maori (so different from the sophisticated Maata), to the wild natural beauty of North Island, and to the conditions her grandfather and father had found when they came to New Zealand in the 1860s. She captured some of this in 'The Woman at the Store' (1911), a story of murder in the bush country, as she described the curious twilight 'when everything appears grotesque—it frightens—as though the savage spirit of the country walked abroad and sneered at what it saw'.[56]

Though Katherine had enjoyed her trip, she was still eager to return to London and to Arnold, and told her sister Jeanne: 'England draws me. I have to go back. I'll never gain the experience I have to go through, here in New Zealand.'[57] In her *Journal* of September 1907 she urged herself to overcome her father's opposition to her destiny: 'Prove yourself. Be strong, be kind, be wise, and it is yours. Do not at the last moment lose courage. Argue wisely and quietly. . . . Convince your Father that it is *la seule chose*.'[58] Her strategies eventually succeeded, and in 1908 her father agreed to give her an allowance of £100 a year. Harold was more kind and intelligent than Stanley Burnell in 'Prelude', and though he had well-founded reservations about his daughter's emotional stability, he understood her better than her mother did, for Katherine was more a Beauchamp than a Dyer. In his *Reminiscences and Recollections* of 1937 Harold conceded: 'After living in New Zealand for eighteen months, she begged to be allowed to go to London, confident that she could make good in the real world of letters. Work she had done showed undoubted promise. There could be no question of standing in her light.'[59] In July 1908 Katherine left New Zealand forever to encounter the 'reality of experience'. But when Harold discovered what this reality was, he declared: 'We'll keep Jeanne at home.'[60]

CHAPTER FOUR

Disorder and Early Sorrow, 1908–1909

KATHERINE'S FIRST adult year in Europe was a disastrous period of her life and confirmed all her father's fears. Her violent rebellion against Harold's values was an acknowledgment of his power and influence over her, the reluctant homage of disobedience to authority. Within ten months of her arrival she had had an unhappy love affair with one man, conceived his illegitimate child, married a second man and left him the next day, endured a period of drug addiction and suffered a miscarriage. Though Katherine was afraid of her uncontrollable feelings, she believed she had to 'experience' life before she could write about it. But her raw emotion was only thinly veiled by a pose of sophistication, and she abandoned herself to a destructive sexual extremism that expressed both her craving for and her repudiation of men. She clearly revealed the masochistic side of her personality when she wrote of an attractive young man she had met on the *Corinthic* when sailing back to New Zealand in November 1906: 'When I am with him a preposterous desire seizes me. I want to be badly hurt by him. I should like to be strangled by his firm hands.'[1]

Katherine arrived in Plymouth on August 24, 1908; was met at the boat-train by Ida Baker, who took her home for a few days; and under the aegis of De Monk Beauchamp was installed in a hostel with twenty women who were studying music. Beauchamp Lodge, as it was fortuitously called, was a large white five-storey building located at 2 Warwick Crescent in Paddington and run by two liberal-minded women who were also musicians. A contemporary of Katherine's later reported that 'Rules were reduced to a minimum, the bed-sitting rooms were bright and cheerful, meals were on a generous scale and the tariff was low'.[2] Katherine's room had a French window and a small balcony that overlooked the canals of Little Venice.

Yet Katherine had abandoned the security and authority of

the rich, and was always short of money. Her first husband, George Bowden, later wrote to Murry that 'her allowance was almost worse for her than nothing',[3] and spoke of 'her period of obscurity and her pinched existence on what was barely pin money'.[4] Dorothy Brett, who met Katherine in 1915 and shared a house with her in Gower Street, said that Katherine was very poor, had inadequate shoes and clothing, could not afford cabs, and that poverty affected her delicate health.[5] And Katherine, who called her father 'the richest man in New Zealand, and the meanest', exclaimed 'I must say I hate money, but it's the lack of it I hate most'.[6] Katherine had just enough to live on, but could not buy the luxuries or even the comforts to which she was accustomed. She found it difficult to adjust downward to relative poverty, especially when she was with wealthy friends.

Ida says that in the autumn of 1908 Katherine was able to earn some extra money and 'to use her great gift for recitation, mimicry and music, as in those days hostesses often provided entertainment for their guests. . . . She was soon offered professional invitations, at a guinea an evening.'[7] Katherine had a pure, dramatic voice, and Ruth Herrick and many other friends praised her 'faultless sense of drama' and talent as an actress. In a letter to Garnet Trowell she revealed her naive and grandiose plans to perform her own works in public: '[I want] to write—and recite what I write—in a very fine way—you know what I mean. Revolutionize and revive the art of elocution—take it to its proper plane . . . and express in the voice and face and atmosphere all that you say. Tone should be my secret—each word a variety of tone. . . . I should like to do this—and this is in my power because I know I possess the power of holding people. . . . I could then write just what I feel would suit me—and would popularize my work—and also I feel there's a big opening for something sensational and new in this direction.'[8]

Rebecca West recalls that in 1913 she saw Katherine in Freda Strindberg's ultra-modern Cave of the Golden Calf, which had been decorated by Wyndham Lewis and Jacob Epstein: 'I saw K.M. only once, when she was *commère* at a cabaret show in a nightclub in Regent St., run by one of Strindberg's wives. She did not do it very well, but looked very pretty in a Chinese costume. She was very attractive, with her beautiful dark hair.'[9] Rebecca West's vivid memory, after more than sixty years, suggests that Katherine, whose porcelain mask of a face must have accentuated her oriental costume, was a confident and self-possessed young woman. From 1913 to 1916 Katherine occasionally acted as an extra in the cinema. In December 1916 she wrote to Bertrand Russell: 'Tomorrow I am acting for the movies—in "exterior scene in walking dress" '; the following month she wearily added: 'My last day with the "movies"—walking about a big bare studio in what the American producer calls "slap up evening dress" has laid me low ever since.'[10] Katherine's story 'Pictures' (1919), which ends as a desperate penniless actress is picked up by a lecherous and threatening man, is based on her experience in films.

Katherine's poverty, obscurity and solitude intensified her feeling of being an outsider in London. Even after she had lived in the city for many years, she characterized herself as an alien and asked: 'Why should they make me feel like a stranger? Why should they ask me every time I go near: "And what are *you* doing in a London garden?" They burn with arrogance and pride. And I am the little Colonial walking in the London garden patch—allowed to look, perhaps, but not to linger.'[11] In her review of Jane Mander's *The Story of a New Zealand River* (1920), she emphasized this feeling of estrangement and identified herself with the New Zealand heroine: 'How is this timidity to be explained, then? One would imagine that round the corner there was a little bank of jeering, sneering, superior persons ready to leap up and laugh if the cut of the new-comer's jacket is not of the strangeness they consider admissible.'[12]

Katherine, who naturally turned to the familiar and 'colonial' Trowell family for comfort, security and love, spent a good deal of time at their large grey house at 52 Carlton Hill, St. John's Wood, and even lived with them for several weeks as a paying guest. Many years later, in a letter to Dorothy Brett, she recalled her pleasant memories of those days among the artists and musicians who then lived in Carlton Hill: 'What a pity it is you can't get a house in St. John's Wood. I think it is the *one* darling part of London. . . . But perhaps that is because I lived there in Carlton Hill for a long time when I was young and very very happy. I used to walk about there at night—late—walking and talking on nights in Spring with two brothers. Our house had a real garden, too, with trees and all the rooms were good—the top rooms lovely. But it's all the musical people who make St. John's Wood so delightful.'[13]

But Katherine's carefully nurtured idealization of Arnold inevitably clashed with reality after eighteen months of passionate correspondence and grim forebodings, for he was totally committed to his musical career, and probably found her emotional expectations and demands far too exacting. In 'Juliet', she expresses his worldly and rather patronizing *congé* in a series of romantic clichés: ' "How we change, Juliet. When we first knew each other [five years ago], both so young, so full of quaint, romantic impossibilities—but those two children are dead now, and we are man and woman. All is different. You have made a mistake".'[14] Katherine's love for Arnold, who was accustomed to adulation, was rather one-sided, and in the autumn of 1908 (the year Arnold met his future wife) Katherine symbolized her break with him by selling her expensive 'cello for only three pounds.

When Katherine was rejected by Arnold, she quickly transferred her love to his twin brother Garnet, who was less attractive and more withdrawn than his brother. Ida describes him as tall, pale, gentle, sweet-tempered and quiet. Garnet was not, like Arnold, an intense and highly strung virtuoso soloist, but a violinist in the orchestra of a travelling opera company. He was forced to spend many dreary and boring hours in boarding-houses while touring the provinces, and must have been flattered to receive the love—and the love letters—that had formerly been reserved for his idolized brother. Garnet was much more receptive and responsive to Katherine's love than Arnold had been, though his amorous triumph over Arnold may have been tempered by the knowledge that he was her second choice. Katherine's twenty letters to Garnet, written between September and November 1908, just before and after her twentieth birthday, are highly emotional and filled with gushes, dashes, italics, exclamations, effusions, foreign phrases and poems for Garnet to set to music. They are very like her *Journal* entries about Arnold: lamenting the agony of separation and counting the days until his return.

All the extremely passionate letters are written in Katherine's sophisticated schoolgirl manner, and reveal that her love for Garnet, whom she called 'Husband', was immediate, sincere and ardent:

You are my life, now. I feel as though your kisses had absorbed my very soul into yours. (September 1908)

When I think for one moment of what the future holds for us together, what days, and oh, my husband, *what nights*—I feel really that I do not belong to this earth—it's too small to hold so much. (September 23, 1908)

I shall go to bed—come soon. I feel lonely tonight, and yet almost savagely passionate. Let us go up the stairs together and look in at little [sister] Doll's room—she is sleeping. And, lying in your arms, I fancy the world is beating to the beating of our hearts. I love you—I love you passionately with my whole soul and body. (*c.* October 4, 1908)

You see, my beloved, you have taught me so much of the joy of life—that the world is a glorious thing—and to be alive in it a tremendous delight—that I feel I must communicate it wherever I go. (September 17, 1908)

I feel as tho' Nature said to me—'Now that you have found your true self—now that you are at peace with the world, accepting instead of doubting—now that you love, you can see.' (October 17, 1908)

Do you know, Garnet, I feel so immensely that you are the complement of me—That ours will be the Perfect Union. (October 3, 1908)

Katherine's unpublished letters to Garnet, the only ones extant from these years, present an unusually detailed account of this obscure period of her life and build up to a tragic conclusion. Though their mood is constantly ecstatic, there is considerable variation, from sexual innuendo, aesthetic bliss and wifely concern to social observation, lyric description and dream visions.

Katherine enjoys exciting Garnet and herself by a euphemistic anticipation of their sexual reunion: 'People always persist in confiding in me the most intimate facts of their domestic relations— in the first breath—so when we are together, j'ai peur that we will never get the landladies out of the room' (October 7, 1908). She shared with Garnet, as with Arnold, a devotion to music and to 'the splendid artist calling', and often described their love in a high-flown and overwrought musical metaphor: 'Oh, you and I, we stand on the shore of an ocean—boundless—untried—over the horizons how many magic isles—lie hidden in clouds of rose colour? But we stand, hearing only that marvellous symphonic rush of sound . . .' (November 4, 1908). Katherine also expressed tender solicitude about Garnet's delicate health and anxiety about the treacherous northern winters: 'Please take care of yourself for this poor little girl who cannot take care of you. I think—yes, I'm rather afraid, Beloved—you'll have a very tyrannical wife! . . . I feel as though I've been married to you for years—As though I ought to be looking after you' (October 17 and 29, 1908).

Coming home from the theatre one night Katherine passed a group of men who were carrying a revolutionary flag and protesting against their poverty, and she expressed her fearful sympathy with the oppressed as she had done for the poor children at Karori School: 'In the Edgware Road we passed a great procession of the unemployed. They carried a scarlet banner. You cannot think how horrible and sinister they looked—tramping along—hundreds of them—monotonously, insistently—like a grey procession of dead hours' (October 13, 1908).

The launching of a ship in the west of England by Asquith was an exciting event for the girl who had grown up within sight and sound of a busy harbour; and Katherine personifies the ship to make its birth more vivid: 'And all the time, we heard inside the ship, a terrible knocking—they were breaking down the supports—but it seemed to me almost symbolical as tho' the great heart of the creature pulsated—And suddenly a silence so tremendous that the very winds seemed to cease—then a sharp wrenching sound and all the great bulk of her swept down the inclined plank into the sun' (November 5, 1908).

At the end of October Katherine visited Paris and attended a naval wedding with the family of Margaret Wishart, a violin student and daughter of an admiral (who had probably arranged for Katherine to see the launching), whom she had met at Beauchamp Lodge. Katherine sent Garnet a euphoric description of the luxurious art of Versailles, the pleasures of a popular fair and the grand sights of the capital:

Yesterday we spent the day at Versailles—starting by train quite early in the morning—through Paris—by the riverside—through the gates—past St. Cloud, and into the beautiful French country and then to the Palace & Gardens. Looking

back from it all, I feel I must have dreamed so much beauty—
The pictures, the rooms which Louis the XV gilded with the
very blood of the people—the chapel built by Madame de
Maintenon to 'purify the Palace'—the theatre where Madame
de Pompadour sat with Louis XV—the statuary—the ball-
rooms—and above everything the marvellous gardens and
fountains—Avenues of chestnut trees, darling, burning a red
bronze with the fires of Autumn—and among them these
marvellous marble figures—Apollo—Venus—the Four Seasons
—Cupid—etc. etc. Then the fountain of Apollo—the fountain
of Neptune—the fountain where Latona is seen beautiful as a
flower turning the inhabitants of a village into frogs & lizards
and turtles—the grotto of Apollo set above with trees—and the
lake where yellow leaves flooded like sunlight—the green lawns
—and always the marvellous distance effect—One feels it is an
eternal magic world—that Versailles is indeed the hunting
grounds of gods & goddesses—It was full of ghosts in the day,
what would *they* be at night!! We left the gardens in the
evening—outside there was a great Fair—long—brilliantly
lighted booths which made me feel like a child—especially the
toys and gingerbread—and kites and cakes and books and
sweets. I bought you a little packet of most fascinating things
which I will send you from London—Felt we two were bringing them together—and the queer little Frenchman seemed to
be so pleased with my delight that he made me a present tied
with ribbon of confiserie fearful and wonderful. We got back
here, dined and went to a Reception where I sat on a sofa &
talked to an English Naval Lieutenant until after 11, and this
poor child was so tired & ennuyée that I almost saw 'double'.
You know that degree of fatigue? I came home, my darling,
and went to bed, thinking of you—dreaming of you all the
night through. Today I have been to the Arc de Triomphe and
the very top of Notre Dame—and the Tomb of Napoleon and
the Luxembourg—I feel very tired with so much beauty and
fascinating new thoughts & conceptions.

On November 5, 1908, shortly before the conclusion of the
series of letters, Katherine relates two rather transparent dreams,
which signify her symbolic defloration and (in the metaphor of
Garnet's musical instrument) the death of their love:

I have been wandering through a castle with barred windows, locked doors—helplessly. At last I come to the gates—and you have unlocked them and you are there. I give you the keys—and you say it is so simple, 'it is like this,' unlocking the door of my castle. . . .

I dreamed last night that we were at a Tschaikovsky concert together last night—And in a violin passage, swift and terrible—I saw to my horror, a great flock of black wide winged birds—fly screaming over the orchestra.[14a]

Toward the end of November, when Katherine could no longer bear their separation, Garnet got her a small part in the opera chorus. In order to save money and avoid the (anticipated) difficulties with inquisitive boarding-house landladies, Katherine pretended to be Garnet's wife when she joined him in Hull, shared his bed and—probably at this time—became pregnant.

The next few months are extremely obscure, but it is most likely that Katherine remained with Garnet and that the lovers spent the Christmas holidays with the Trowells at Carlton Hill. Thomas Trowell continued to exercise his parental role while she lived in his London house and apparently did not discourage her obvious infatuation with Garnet. Yet Garnet's sister Dolly (who used to sip chocolate with Katherine at the Blenheim Café in Bond Street, a gathering place for artists) recalls that early in 1909, when she was fifteen years old, Thomas (who had a bad temper) was shocked to discover the love affair of Katherine and Garnet, and was extremely angry with the pregnant Katherine rather than with his son. Katherine left their house and never returned; and Dolly, who loved her dearly, felt wretched and heartbroken.[15]

Though Katherine, whose 'emotional instability was well known'[16] to the Trowells, probably had seduced Garnet (as she later seduced Murry), Thomas protected Garnet from what he considered a disastrous marriage and placed all the guilt and responsibility on Katherine. Garnet, who may have been ashamed of his moral cowardice, never spoke about Katherine either to his sister or to his sons. Katherine's complete emotional and physical commitment to her first lover at the most vulnerable moment of her life, when her parents were 12,000 miles away and she could not confide in any adult, suggests that Garnet's betrayal and

Thomas's condemnation had a profound effect. She was horribly shocked and permanently wounded by the rejection of her love, and this experience helps to explain why she became hard, tough, defensive and embittered.

Katherine had seen Ida Baker as soon as she returned to England, and naturally turned in this moment of crisis to the selfless friend who had been a passive observer of the love affair with Garnet, just as she would later turn to Ida when she felt rejected by Murry. On October 4, 1908, Katherine, who called Ida their 'Godmother', told Garnet: 'She never by any chance takes the initiative—Must be shown everything—never thinks for herself and is content, yes, radiantly content, to have a little spare room in our life, and presumably, sew on buttons.'

Though sexual life at Queen's College had been severely repressed, it was obvious to all the girls that Ida loved Katherine. Katherine's brother-in-law, Richard Murry, confirms that Ida's love continued into adult life and writes that Ida, like Katherine's friend Koteliansky, was jealous of John Murry.[17] Even Harold in distant Wellington heard of the girls' friendship and asked Alexander Kay, the London director of the Bank of New Zealand in Queen Victoria Street and manager of Katherine's financial affairs, to find out about their relationship. According to Ida, Kay (who had flirted with Katherine) invited Ida to lunch to question her, but failed to discover anything.[18]

Ida was 'afraid of life' and frightened of men, and she admits 'I was always . . . demanding a fuller expression of [Katherine's] feeling'.[19] It is clear that their friendship was determined by Katherine (Ida 'never took the initiative'); that Ida, who craved affection, would have done whatever Katherine wanted; and that their emotional and psychological relationship was intimate. In March 1914 Katherine wrote about Ida: 'Her body was obedient [to the touch], but how slowly and gravely it obeyed, as though protesting against the urge of her brave spirit.'[20] Ida worshipped Katherine, quite literally devoted her life to her, became a buffer between Katherine and the harsh world of men, and was at once friend, nurse, slave and scapegoat.

At the beginning of 1909, after she had left Garnet and returned to Beauchamp Lodge, Katherine quite characteristically turned to Ida as she had turned to Edie Bendall, and fled from the agonizing rejection of a man to the healing love of a woman. But since Ida could not help her solve the problem of the child she was bravely determined to have, she adopted another stratagem in the 'fierce combats' with her musical lovers.

Katherine met the singer George Bowden, who was eleven years her senior, through the Trowells's musical circle in St. John's Wood. Bowden writes: 'Our first meeting occurred in the winter of '08-09 at a dinner party followed by music at the house in Hamilton Terrace, London, of Dr. C. W. Saleeby, whose wife was the daughter of the poetess Alice Meynell.'[21] Murry wrote condescendingly of Bowden, who was a contemporary of E. M. Forster at King's College from 1899 to 1902: 'He had advanced into the profession by the flowery path of a choral scholarship at Cambridge. He had education and refinement; he was the gentleman artist with the bedside manner of the type afterwards depicted with subtle understanding in "Mr. Reginald Peacock's Day [1917]".'[22] But Bowden, in a letter to Murry of December 1933, just after this description had been published in the Mantz-Murry biography of Katherine, insisted that he respected Katherine's art and that 'she found in me a congenial and sympathetic response to her literary enthusiasms and ambitions'.[23]

Bowden immediately began to send long letters to Katherine at Beauchamp Lodge and spoke of 'laying himself at the feet of her genius'. Ida Baker writes, more objectively than Murry, that Bowden 'was a kindly person, and, I believe, very much in love with Katherine. His letters were full of humble devotion and understanding. . . . I don't think marrying Bowden seemed very important [to Katherine] and he was extremely persistent.'[24] Katherine spent a great deal of time at Bowden's bachelor flat, and his considerable vanity and lofty idealism about women led him to misinterpret Katherine's true feelings and motives. He stated: 'It was at another of these [Saleeby] parties that the engagement of K.M., as she was known to her friends, and myself was announced';[25] but also said, as late as 1950: 'The reasons which induced K.M. to take this step of marriage remain an insoluble mystery to me.'[26]

Katherine, who obviously wanted security and a father for her child, and was torn between the bohemian and the bourgeois way of life, wrote three fictional accounts of her marriage to Bowden. In 'Mr. Reginald Peacock's Day' she emphasizes the weakest and most vulnerable side of her character and portrays herself as 'a pathetic, youthful creature, half child, half wild untamed bird, totally incompetent to cope with bills and creditors and all the sordid details of experience'.[27] In 'The Swing of the Pendulum' (1911), the heroine also stresses her desperate need for protection and says: 'I was not in love. I wanted somebody to look after me —and keep me until my work began to sell—and he kept bothers with other men away. And what would have happened if he hadn't come along? I would have spent my wretched little pittance, and then—. Yes, that was what decided me, thinking about that "then".'[28]

She also explained her 'cowardly' and impulsive marriage in a *Scrapbook* sketch of 1915: ' "Then I got ill, and my voice went— and a hard time came," she said. "And then you know, out of pure cowardice—yes, really—I couldn't fight any more and I hadn't the courage to—I married." Louise turned her grave glance to her. "I didn't love him a bit," said Nina, shaking her head,—"just because I was afraid." . . . "And then—oh, well, it served me right—he was a brute and my——" she hesitated a second, "my baby died and I left him." '[29]

But Bowden was, in fact, tolerant rather than brutish, and she left him *before* rather than after Garnet's baby died. Ottoline Morrell, one of the few friends who realized Katherine 'has had a very hard life, and that puts her on the defensive', reports that Katherine spoke 'of her marriage to a man called Bowden, who married her "to protect her". I didn't understand what the real position was, but she said that he took advantage of her and wanted to live with her which she had not bargained for. . . . Obviously she disliked him and refused to live with him.'[30] Bowden, quite reasonably, failed to see that Katherine wanted a marriage without a husband.

Bowden writes that 'K's uncle [i.e., her second cousin, De Monk Beauchamp], possibly relieved at the prospect of seeing her "settle down", had written to New Zealand, but the idea of delay for family consent, perhaps of having to wait their convenience for coming to London, was repugnant to her.'[31] Though

Bowden was older than Katherine and extremely respectable, he was overwhelmed by her personality, submitted to her wishes and also acted in an impulsive way. On March 2, 1909, when she was about three months pregnant, Katherine put on a black dress and a shiny black straw hat, falsely claimed she was twenty-two so she could wed without parental consent and, accompanied only by Ida Baker, married George Bowden in the dirty and depressing Paddington Registry Office. Though Katherine's mourning dress was grotesque and she was playing a tragi-comic role, Bowden did not seem to notice. Ida, who had helped Katherine pack, left a note in the dressing-case urging her to 'bear up'; Katherine promised to meet her friend at a concert the next afternoon.

The newlyweds spent a pleasant day at dinner and the theatre, but the marriage was not consummated. Bowden reports that Katherine exhibited a 'sudden and complete frigidity after we had reached the hotel suite where we were to spend the night. . . . The anti-climactic dénouement came as a complete surprise—not to say shock—to me.'[32] Though he naively believed 'Her mind would be somewhere above her body', Bowden loved Katherine and naturally expected to sleep with his wife on their wedding night. His reference to 'the realization of an incompatibility which made married life between us impossible', euphemistically disguises the fact that Katherine never told the 'kindly' Bowden that 'she disliked him' and would not allow him to 'take advantage of her' and to live with her. Katherine's 'sudden frigidity' was her cruel method of revenging herself on Bowden for the rejections of Arnold and Garnet, and of conveying the bitter truth about their 'marriage'—which he failed to understand as late as 1950. Katherine left Bowden the very next morning, and while longing for Garnet and suffering from insomnia, she had recourse to veronal. Bowden took an entire week to find Katherine, and when he finally discovered her in a wretched bedroom in Baker Street (she could not return to Beauchamp Lodge which was a hostel for single women) she was 'dry-eyed and firm in her determination to go her own way alone'.[33] All she would say in response to his questions was: 'I can't come.'[34]

Katherine went her own way but was not entirely alone, for she returned to bohemian life with Garnet, who was then touring in Liverpool, and to her minor role in the opera company. Murry writes that 'She used to tell of cooking kippers over a fish-tail gas-flame in her bedroom; and she sometimes sang, with all the absurd gestures required of an opera chorus, snatches of her former parts'.[35]

After a squalid and ultimately unhappy month with Garnet, in which she failed to recapture his love and persuade him to marry her, Katherine felt England had become dead, barren and sterile. She went to Belgium for a brief holiday at Easter 1909, travelling in the name of Mrs. K. Bendall, and wrote to her lover: 'The carriage is full but Garnie I feel that I am going *home*. To escape England—it is my great desire. I loathe England.'[36] Two stories, 'The Journey to Bruges' and 'A Truthful Adventure' (both 1910), describe this trip. The former is merely a realistic account of the boat-train and channel ferry, but in the latter the heroine meets in Bruges a New Zealand school friend who has recently married and had a baby, and is unable to respond to her friend's overtures. The story concludes on a quietly bitter note when the happy friend remarks: 'You know, after the strenuous life in London, one does seem to see things in such a different light in this old world city', and the apathetic heroine ironically responds: 'Oh, a very different light indeed.'[37] Katherine did not see Garnet again, but continued to write to him from Germany in 1909. Though Arnold fulfilled his early promise with a distinguished musical career, Garnet passed into obscurity.[38]

Katherine's mother was seriously alarmed when the news of her marriage—and perhaps her separation—reached New Zealand. She sailed immediately for London and arrived on May 27 to find her daughter destitute and pregnant. As Katherine wrote, with justified self-pity, at the end of April: 'I can't rest. That's the agonizing part. . . . My *body* is so self-conscious. Je pense of all the frightful things possible—"all this filthiness". Sick at heart till I am physically sick—with no home, no place in which I can hang up my hat and say here I belong, for there is no such place in the wide world for me.'[39] Her fashionable mother's first words of greeting to Katherine, who appeared at the train station in her cheap black wedding hat, were: 'Why child! what are you wearing? You look like an old woman in that. As if you were going to a funeral!'[40]

The meeting with her cold, conventional and disdainful mother must have been agonizing, for Annie lacked both sympathy and understanding. Katherine later wrote: 'I often long to lean against Mother and know she understands things . . . that can't be told . . . that would fade at a breath . . . *delicate needs* . . . a feeling of fineness and gentleness.'[41] And on January 21, 1922, her grandmother's birthday, she tenderly recalled an old photograph of Margaret Dyer: 'my dear love leaning against her husband's shoulder', and then adds: 'Mother gave it to me at a time when she loved me.'[42] The last sentence implies that Katherine had *lost* her mother's love, probably when she was pregnant in 1909, and that this loss reinforced the memory of her grandmother's affection.

George Bowden says that after Katherine left him he had an interview with Mrs. Beauchamp at the Bank of New Zealand which 'turned chiefly on the state of K.'s health.' When it became clear to her mother that Garnet would not marry Katherine and that Katherine would not return to Bowden, she decided to conceal the scandal by taking her daughter to a convent in Germany and leaving her there. By June 10 Annie was on the way back to New Zealand. Their trip to Bavaria is described in Katherine's story, 'The Little Governess' (1915), which concerns the sexual guilt of a vulnerable heroine who is cruelly deceived by a lecherous older man.

Katherine stayed only briefly at the convent, and in June moved to Wörishofen, a cheap and conveniently obscure spa, fifty miles west of Munich and 2000 feet high in the Bavarian Alps. In 1909 the town had 3000 permanent residents, and 9000 visitors who endured the famous hydrotherapy cure of hosings with ice-cold water, which had been invented and popularized by Pastor Sebastian Kneipp. Katherine, who used the names Käthe Beauchamp-Bowden and Käthi Bowden, had four different addresses in six months. She spent the first week (June 4 to 11) at the Hotel Kreuzer (which still exists) on Kneippstrasse, and probably left when she found a cheaper room. She lived for the next seven weeks (June 12 to July 31) in the Pension Müller on Türkheimerstrasse, and after meeting Fraulein Rosa Nitsch, who owned the lending library in the post office building on Kasino-weg, stayed in her house for another seven weeks (August 1 to September 22). Possibly because of her miscarriage, Katherine moved in with the family of Johann Brechenmacher on Kauf-beurerstrasse on September 23 and remained there until January

1910.[43] She used the actual name of that family in her story, 'Frau Brechenmacher Attends a Wedding'.

Soon after she arrived Katherine caught a severe chill while walking barefoot in the woods (though this was part of the Kneipp 'cure') and found herself in what would later become a painfully familiar situation: abandoned, alien and alone in a strange country, and prey to tormenting thoughts: 'I think it is the pain that makes me shiver and feel dizzy. To be alone all day, in a house where every sound seems foreign to you, and to feel a terrible confusion in your body which affects you mentally, suddenly pictures for you detestable incidents, revolting personalities, which you only shake off to find recurring as the pain seems to diminish and grow worse again.'[44] She may have recalled these feelings when she wrote her early sketch, 'Tales of a Courtyard', (*Rhythm*, August 1912), in which a pregnant Russian girl, who lives with two male students, defies the jeers of her malicious neighbours. Katherine's loneliness and misery, and the 'heart and soul coldness' of the Germans, drove her once again to barbiturates, and in June 1909 she recorded her struggle against them: 'Now I know what it is to fight a drug. Veronal was on my table by my bed. Oblivion—deep sleep—think of it! But I didn't take any.'[45] In the summer of 1909, in the late months of her pregnancy, after attempting to lift a heavy trunk, Katherine gave birth to a premature and stillborn infant.

In the wretched circumstances of her convalescence, as she realized that her guilt, humiliation, mental agony and physical pain had all been for nothing, Katherine wrote the bitter, cynical and satiric stories, *In A German Pension* (1911). This book again emphasized her role as outsider in a hostile world, and expressed her fastidious revulsion against the vulgar, snobbish Germans, and the gross physical details of their crude, commonplace lives. By this time, if not before, she had certainly become familiar with Chekhov, perhaps in a German translation, for her first story, 'The Child Who Was Tired', is a virtual plagiarism of Chekhov's 'Sleepyhead'. Katherine's stories concern the struggle of the spirit against the flesh, the vulnerability of women threatened by brutal men and, in 'At Lehmann's' and 'A Birthday', the gruesome details of childbirth. At the end of the former a young man attempts to seduce a serving girl, whose name recalls a famous rape and who is described as 'a frightened little animal'.

But he is interrupted by the piercing shriek of a woman in labour
—the painful result, perhaps, of another male assault:

> He pulled her closer still and kissed her mouth.
> 'Na, what are you doing?' she whispered.
> He let go her hands, he placed his on her breasts, and the room
> seemed to swim round Sabina. Suddenly, from the room above,
> a frightful, tearing shriek.[46]

In order to compensate Katherine for the loss of her baby, Ida
found a poor, eight-year-old boy named Walter, who lived in a
London slum, suffered from malnutrition, had just recovered
from pleurisy and was in delicate health. Ida sent him to
Wörishofen, with Katherine's approval, to convalesce for
several weeks with her. Though she nursed Walter back to
health, she used the boy (as she had used Bowden) in a rather
selfish manner. After showering him with maternal love and
establishing his emotional dependence upon her, she sent him
back to the slums and never saw him again. Walter, who was the
model for the grandson Lennie in 'Life of Ma Parker', was the
first of Katherine's surrogate children. Though she often
dreamed of having a child of her own, she never had one.

Katherine, using the German she had learned from Walter
Rippmann, soon became acquainted with a group of literary
émigrés who planned journals that would publish translations of
her stories. She was intimate with 'S.V.', an Austrian journalist
who sent her love letters and spoke of kissing her breasts, and
had an affair with a charming but completely untrustworthy
critic, Floryan Sobieniowski, who was seven years her senior.[47]

When Floryan had to leave Wörishofen he arranged to meet
Katherine in Munich, and perhaps travel with her to Poland and
Russia. She looked forward to seeing him and wrote him
enthusiastic and loving letters. Ida states that when Katherine
arrived in Munich in January 1910 and discovered that Floryan,
like Bowden, planned to share her bed, she left him and returned
to England. But it is doubtful that Katherine, who was very fond
of Floryan, could have been so naive about his intentions. Though
they quarrelled in Munich, their separation was not final, and her
friendship with Floryan would later lead to some unpleasant and
ugly incidents.

Katherine's reckless sexual adventures had had disastrous

results. The ardent disciple of the doctrine of living dangerously, who believed in sacrificing her life in order to enrich her art, now felt that the experience of her 'inexplicable past' had been destructive: 'I've *acted* my sins, and then excused them or put them away with "it doesn't do to think about these things" or (more often) "it was all experience". But it hasn't ALL been experience. There IS waste—destruction, too.'[48]

Katherine ruthlessly destroyed nearly all her 'huge complaining diaries' for 1909–12, but sometimes made revealing references to her years of obscurity in her later *Journal*. In January 1920 she referred to Christ's agony in the garden of Gethsemane and asked: 'When will this cup pass from me? Oh, misery! I cannot sleep. I lie *retracing* my steps—going over all the old life before. ... The baby of Garnet Trowell.' And in June 1919 she chastized herself for the self-destructive adventures of her youth: 'Often I reproach myself for my "private" life—which, after all, were I to die, *would* astonish even those nearest me.'[49] She felt guilty about the sordid squandering of her 'inward purity', and while 'doing her stunts' (as the painter Mark Gertler called it), 'she wept and threw herself about wailing: "I am a soiled woman".'[50] Though her first adult year in Europe had been disastrous, she had written most of her first book. But she still had much more suffering to endure, and when she left Munich she had nowhere to go.

CHAPTER FIVE

Orage and *The New Age*, 1910–1911

WHEN KATHERINE returned to England in January 1910, physically weak and psychologically depressed by her wretched experiences in Germany, she needed protection and security even more than she did after Garnet's desertion. George Bowden writes that Katherine (who was staying at the Strand Palace Hotel) sent him a desperate and urgent summons to return to conjugal life: 'While at a house party at Easton Hall in Lincolnshire, the butler brought me in quick succession on his salver two or three open telegrams—received over the telephone. With a crescendo of urgency and signed Your Wife, they insisted on an immediate meeting in London. Now the misgivings were mine, and it was with apprehensive reluctance that I made the journey to town. . . . For her own reasons K.M. urgently insisted on our living together normally as man and wife.'[1] The kindly and accommodating Bowden seems to have recovered from his anticlimactic wedding night and was still sufficiently in love with Katherine to respond to her impulsive demands. The last sentence of Bowden's letter suggests that he did not understand nor inquire about Katherine's activities in Bavaria or her reasons for resuming their marriage, and that Katherine agreed to have sexual relations with him.

Katherine moved into Bowden's bachelor flat in Gloucester Place, Marylebone, in February, welcomed by the tall manservant, Charles. But after several weeks of domestic life, when Katherine sang with Bowden and took part in his concerts, he was forced to admit: 'Though we were the best of friends as ever, the venture proved short-lived, and only on the surface a success.'[2] Ida Baker provides an insight into Katherine's marital motives and reports she 'told me that, partly for the sake of the family, she would go back to her husband and try to make it work . . . meaning to write when he was out singing or teaching, but she was not happy and was much distressed by his lack of delicacy.'[3]

Katherine, who was probably thinking more about herself than about her family, treated Bowden callously and left him in March, as soon as she had published her first important story and established a more secure foothold in London. Ida's reference to Bowden's 'lack of delicacy' is a euphemism for his sexual desires, which Katherine tolerated for the briefest possible period. It is important to recognize that she did not escape without wounds from her dangerous experiments with Bowden, for she was less tough and more idealistic than she imagined. The failure of her marriage and collapse of her security did more harm than she realized, and intensified her reckless behaviour with men.

In *Between Two Worlds* (1935) Murry flatly states that after Katherine left Bowden he 'refused to take divorce proceedings against her. They were begun and dropped', and Ida agrees with Murry that 'there was much talk; but in the end he did nothing'.[4] Bowden, however, gives quite a different account of the divorce proceedings and objects to Murry's statement, 'Had Katherine been free, we would have married the next day.' Bowden quotes Katherine's letter of May 23, 1912, when she was living with Murry: 'I should very much like to see you if it can be arranged and discuss your project with reference to an American divorce', and he says that this plan was abandoned when they discovered the American divorce would not be valid in England.

Bowden saw Katherine for the last time later in 1912 when he and his solicitor visited the flat in Gray's Inn Road that she shared with Murry and found 'She did not seem to be concerned with any proceedings that would make remarriage possible for her'. Katherine, playing the role of the good hostess, asked Bowden to sing for them and he graciously complied. Since she expressed no desire for a divorce after the American idea fell through, Bowden continues: 'It was not until I wished to re-marry myself [in 1918] that the proceedings which had been initiated before I left London were completed. . . . There was never at any time the suggestion from either K.M. herself, or Mr. Murry, that the divorce should be proceeded with or concluded.'[5] Though there is no definite proof, Bowden's version of these events seems more convincing. After two humiliating experiments in marriage, he would have no desire to remain tied to her. And Katherine, after all her betrayals by men, must have been somewhat wary of marriage during her first months with the impoverished, passive and insecure Murry.[6]

Bowden, who took a great interest in Katherine's literary career and provided one valuable service for her, writes: 'I had the satisfaction of bringing the "New Age" to her attention as a likely medium for her German sketches.'[7] At Bowden's suggestion, Katherine personally took the manuscript of 'The Child Who Was Tired' to the office of the controversial Fabian weekly, the New Age; she impressed the editor, A. R. Orage, who immediately published it in the issue of February 24, 1910, and asked to see more of her work. Katherine's tempestuous association with the New Age, which published nine of her stories between February and August 1910, was a significant breakthrough and marked her liberation from Bowden and the beginning of her literary career in England. (She also published 'A Fairy Story' in the December 1910 issue of the Open Window, a whimsical magazine edited by Vivian Locke-Ellis.)

The attractive and talented Katherine was immediately taken up by Orage and his fiery mistress, Beatrice Hastings. She was often invited to their Sussex cottage, and was delighted to become part of a circle of serious artists. On July 29, 1910, Ida proudly wrote to Garnet Trowell that Katherine was busy with literary friends from the New Age, might soon take a flat by herself, would never return to George Bowden and did so earlier in the year only because of her duty to her family.[8]

A. R. Orage—a tall and formidable looking Yorkshireman of Huguenot ancestry, a shambling bear of a man with a hypnotic eye—had an enormous influence on Katherine's life.[9] Orage always cultivated conversation with his contributors—T. E. Hulme, Richard Aldington, Herbert Read and Edwin Muir—and held court in the afternoons at the ABC restaurant near his office off Chancery Lane. Shaw called Orage 'the most brilliant editor for a century past',[10] and Katherine's publication in the New Age, the most distinguished weekly of the time, was a very considerable achievement. In November 1921 she expressed her profound gratitude for the literary criticism and personal encouragement of Orage in a letter that recalls her earlier tribute to Thomas Trowell: 'I want to tell you how sensible I am of your wonderful unfailing kindness to me in the "old days". And to thank you for all you let me learn from you. I am still—more shame to me—very low down in the school. But you taught me to write, you taught me to think; you showed me what there was to be done and what *not* to do. My dear Orage, I cannot tell you how often I call to mind your conversation or how often, in *writing*, I remember my master.'[11]

Katherine was frequently ill during 1910–11, and the serious decline of her health began at this time. In March 1910 she finally left Bowden in order to have an operation for peritonitis which caused permanent injury and, according to Murry, made it unlikely that she would ever bear a child. After the operation Katherine asked Ida to carry her away from the nursing home in Marylebone, 'as the surgeon was taking an unprofessional interest in her body'.[12] She convalesced with Ida from April to August in a room above a grocer's shop in Rottingdean, on the Sussex coast, where Bowden, Orage and Beatrice Hastings came down to visit her. In May Katherine's illness was complicated and her recovery delayed by an attack of rheumatic fever. In photographs taken by Ida at Rottingdean just after the operation Katherine, who wears a long buttoned skirt with spectacles demurely fastened to her white frilly blouse or sits on a couch draped in her silver and black Egyptian shawl, looks pale, wasted, sickly and unhappy.

F. A. Lea writes of Katherine that 'One "adventure" had ended in a miscarriage, another in an abortion, a third in an operation for peritonitis',[13] and though his sequence is incorrect (the peritonitis came before the abortion), he does suggest (from evidence in Murry's journals) that a sexual experience caused the peritonitis. Ida Baker also writes rather cryptically: 'After a long time she was patched up, although the trouble was not correctly diagnosed nor was she fully cured until many years later in 1918 when Dr. Sorapure took charge of her. He told her then that the pains that she had suffered from almost continuously since this time in Rottingdean, and had always called her "rheumatiz", were the result of a disease that she had contracted before she was taken to the nursing home.'[14] Though Ida does not name the disease that was neither diagnosed nor cured until 1918, Katherine probably contracted gonorrhea—a venereal infection that can affect the peritoneum, can be unsuspected in a female and can cause pain similar to rheumatism—just before the operation for peritonitis.

In August, after Katherine had recovered from her illnesses, the painter Alfred Bishop, whom she had met through Orage, went to Morocco and lent her his two-room flat at 131 Cheyne Walk until December. Katherine's friend William Orton, who admired her *fin de siècle* preciosity, observes: 'She had made the place look quite beautiful—a couple of candles stuck in a skull, another between the high windows, a lamp on the floor shining through yellow chrysanthemums, and herself accurately in the centre, in a patterned pink kimono and white flowered frock, the one cluster of primary brightness in the room.'[15] Katherine bought a grand piano, paid for it in instalments, and was visited by Queen's College friends and by her old teacher Walter Rippmann.

Ida says that in the autumn of 1910: 'A frequent visitor was a young man, hardly more than a boy in appearance, and very handsome. He brought her lovely presents and I remember particularly a tiny painted Russian village. . . . Katherine was much attracted by him, and he fell in love with her. They were young and happy, intended to marry and soon became lovers. However, the affair was short-lived: his family disapproved. They looked on Katherine as a potential danger, a married woman who was living alone.'[16] Alpers adds that Katherine's lover was 'a good-looking, gay, and charming young man, with an attractive way of lying on his back on the floor and waving his legs in the air while the conversation went its airy way'.[17] (Katherine must have found it extraordinary that Murry, whom she described as 'a little boy playing with his toys', did precisely the same thing—'I raised both my legs in the air and waved them about'—when in April 1912 he refused Katherine's offer to become his mistress.[18]) Though Katherine's lover has never been named in print, Ida identified him as 'F.H.', the nephew or cousin of Lawrence's publisher.[19]

In January 1911, when Bishop returned from Morocco, Katherine moved to a top-floor flat in 69 Clovelly Mansions, Gray's Inn Road, a large and barrack-like building with trams below the windows and heavy traffic all day and night, which cost £52 a year, more than half her allowance. She put bamboo matting on the floor, brought in the grand piano and consecrated one room to an Indian Buddha which always had a dish of flowers before him.

Soon afterwards Katherine realized she was pregnant again, wrote several emotional letters to her lover, begged him to return to her, but received no reply. Katherine, who had been deserted for the second time and had had more than her share of painful experiences, felt she could not repeat the nightmare of Bavaria. In April, two months before her parents were due to arrive in England, Katherine enlisted the help of Beatrice Hastings, who was a rabid feminist and thought childbirth was 'the ugliest fact of human life', and had an abortion. It may have been this operation, rather than the earlier one for peritonitis, that prevented her from having the children she always wanted. In 'Juliet', written five years earlier in 1906, Katherine foreshadows her later abortion when a crass lover asks the plucky heroine: ' "How about those complications?" "O they're quite gone thank you. I . . . I took your advice." "That's fine, that's fine. I knew you would, my dear girl. I always said you had the grit in you." '20

Katherine may also have had two other lovers. In the autumn of 1910, she met the aesthetic young schoolmaster, William Orton, who portrayed his friendship with Katherine and published parts of her diary in his autobiographical novel, *The Last Romantic* (1937). Though Orton was unhappily in love with another woman, who is called Lais in the novel, Katherine's diary reveals that she was attracted to Orton and even discussed the possibility of marriage with him. He too might have been her lover during their year of friendship.

Katherine was also recklessly and passionately involved with a third man in 1911. In her diary of September 6, she vividly describes their sexual encounters as a kind of vicious and violent bestiality, which recalls the extreme emotions of her fierce masochistic combats with Maata and Edie Bendall: 'The Man came to see me. He gathered me up in his arms and carried me to the Black Bed. Very brown and strong was he. . . . It grew dark. I crouched against him like a wild cat. . . . How vicious I looked! We made love to each other like two wild beasts. . . . He tore my clothes from my shoulders. I laughed—bent forward—graceful and lithe—blew out the candle and stood naked to the waist in the moon-lit room. . . . I crushed him against me—shook back my hair and laughed at the moon. I felt mad with passion—I wanted to kill. . . . By and by he left me.'21

Apart from the sketchy autobiographical accounts of Orton and Ida, no first-hand records, journals or letters concerning Katherine's life in 1911 have survived. The bare facts remain, but there is no documentary evidence to bring them to life. We know that Katherine attended the brilliant and influential exhibition of Post-Impressionist paintings by Cézanne, Van Gogh, Gauguin and Matisse, organized by Roger Fry in November 1910, for in 1921 she told Dorothy Brett that Van Gogh's *Sunflowers* and *The Postman Roulin* (both painted in 1888) suggested a new way to capture bright splashes of colour and to make her writing more visually vivid:

> Wasn't that Van Gogh shown at the Goupil [i.e., the Grafton], ten years ago? Yellow flowers, brimming with sun, in a pot? I wonder if it is the same. That picture seemed to reveal something that I hadn't realized before I saw it. It lived with me afterwards. It still does. That and another of the sea-captain in a flat cap. They taught me something about writing, which was queer, a kind of freedom—or rather, a shaking free. When one has been working for a long stretch one begins to narrow one's vision a bit, to fine things down too much. And it's only when something else breaks through, a picture or something seen out of doors, that one realizes it.[22]

Katherine published six more stories in the *New Age* between May and October, and this must have impressed her parents, younger sister and brother when they came to England for the Coronation of King George V in June 1911. Though the Beauchamps stayed in England until March 1912, when Katherine saw her mother for the last time, they were unaware of her personal difficulties and financial problems. In July Katherine had a serious attack of pleurisy, an inflammation of the lung membrane which is a well-known early sign of tuberculosis. In the summer she recuperated in Bruges and Geneva, and had a pleasant reunion with a Pole called Yelski, who had been her friend in Wörishofen and had settled in Switzerland with his little boy, a musical prodigy. Katherine wrote three sketches about Geneva: 'Pension Séguin', 'Violet' and 'Bains Turcs', which were all published in the *Blue Review* in 1913. She returned to London in September, and spent most of her time with her family and with Ida.

December 1911 was one of the great turning points of Katherine's life. In that month Stephen Swift gave her an advance of £15 and published *In A German Pension*. Katherine's first book

3*

presented a bitter and satiric rather than a romantic and idealized view of Germany, as her cousin Elizabeth had done. It received favourable reviews in the *Morning Post*, *Daily Telegraph*, *Manchester Guardian* and *Athenaeum*, which praised her 'decided originality and liveliness', and went into a third printing. In December Katherine also met John Middleton Murry, with whom she lived for six years and married in 1918. Though she would have some agonizing times with Murry and one last love affair with Francis Carco, she now based her emotional life on her husband and ended her destructive liaisons with Floryan, Bowden, 'F.H.' and 'The Man'.

In 'Juliet', Rudolf tells the heroine: ' "You are afraid of everything, and you suspect everybody. Dieu! how afraid you are!" "I am *not*" said Juliet, shaking her head, but the colour rushed into her cheeks'—as if to confirm his accusation.[23] Many years later in 1920, when she was seriously ill, Katherine, quoting the first Epistle of St. John, wrote to Murry that the impulsive and destructive behaviour of her early years had been inspired by fear, which she had finally overcome with love and replaced with courage: 'I believe the greatest failing of all is *to be frightened*. Perfect Love casteth out Fear. When I look back on my life all my mistakes have been because I was afraid. . . . Was that why I had to look on death? Would nothing less cure me?'[24]

CHAPTER SIX

Murry, *Rhythm* and Bohemia, 1912

KATHERINE'S BIZARRE relationship with John Middleton Murry was the most important experience of her life. When Murry first met Katherine she was a beautiful, brave, talented, witty and caustic woman, who had been through some painful sexual experiences and wanted to annihilate her past. Katherine, who had just published her first book, had a promising literary reputation and a talented circle of friends. Her great strength of character and belief in her artistic vocation had enabled her to break away from her New Zealand life and values, and create a new destiny in England.

A wonderful transformation took place in Katherine around the time she met Murry: suddenly, at the age of twenty-three, she changed from a dumpy and unattractive girl into a beautiful young woman. She had lost weight during her numerous illnesses, but now regained her strength and vivacity. She completely altered her appearance by cutting her hair short years before it became fashionable and by dressing in elegant and striking clothes. These changes reflected the modern style of her artistic friends and her new self-confidence.

Murry's brother Richard, a young artist who adored Katherine, writes: 'In those days Katherine was a head-turner. The mode from Paris; the brown velvet jacket with silver buttons, the short skirt, the coloured stockings, the Spanish-Japanese hair-do, the high heels, the immaculate turnout.'[1] The painter Dorothy Brett synthesizes several points that recur in descriptions of Katherine: her fine features, intense dark eyes, clear skin, even white teeth, bobbed hair, boyish body, unusual dress, quiet movements, mask-like composure and defensive bearing: 'A little later Katherine Mansfield and Murry appear. Katherine small, her sleek dark hair brushed close to her head, her fringe sleeked down over her white forehead; she dresses nearly always in black with a touch of white or scarlet or a rich, deep purple. This evening she is dressed in black. Her movements are quaintly restricted; controlled, small, reserved gestures. The dark eyes glance about much like a bird's, the pale face is a quiet mask, full of hidden laughter, wit and gaiety. But she is cautious, a bit suspicious and on her guard.'[2]

All the young men acquainted with Katherine were attracted to her. David Garnett writes in a recent letter: 'At the age of 23 I thought her extremely attractive—the dark lively intelligent face under the dark fringe. I was aware also that she was a "copycat", a very good mimic.'[3] Frank Swinnerton, who met Katherine before World War I and wrote sketches of her in several books, mentions her reserve, her delicacy and, unlike most others who saw only the harsher side of Katherine's character, her gentleness: 'She was not very tall, and was very slim and dark; and she spoke, without moving her lips, in a very mysterious little murmur. She had a porcelain delicacy which invariably made others gentle when they spoke to her. . . . I had never [known] any young woman who talked so frankly or who looked so distinguished in her prettiness.[4] . . . I thought I had never met so mentally-attractive a young woman. It was not a powerful mind, or even a very quick one; but she had great sweetness and great sympathy. I still recall her with affectionate respect, not quite as a real woman, but as a being charmingly remote and tender, speaking chiefly of art, but thinking all the time of delicious secrets, with a half-smile upon her lips.'[5]

Many of these personal traits are described in the fictional portraits of Katherine by D. H. Lawrence and Aldous Huxley. In *Women in Love* (1920), Katherine appears as Gudrun Brangwen: 'so *charming*, so infinitely charming, in her softness and in her fine, exquisite richness of texture and delicacy of line. There was a certain playfulness about her too, such a piquancy or ironic suggestion, such an untouched reserve.'[6] And in *Those Barren Leaves* (1925), where Katherine is characterized as Mary Thriplow, 'A female novelist of good repute,' Huxley uses the metaphor of an oriental mask to suggest the depth of character beneath the surface: 'The features were small and regular, the eyes dark brown; and their arched brows looked as though they had been painted on to the porcelain mask by an oriental brush. Her hair was nearly black. . . . Her uncovered ears were quite white and very small. It was an inexpressive face, the face of a doll, but an exceedingly intelligent doll.'[7]

Though everyone agrees that Katherine was an attractive woman, the accounts of her character are extremely diverse. This confusion is caused by her acting ability, her fondness for role-playing, her deliberate projection of contradictory selves and her defensive mask-like *persona*. In 1919 it seemed to Katherine that no one could discover her true and hidden self—perhaps because she would never reveal it to anyone: 'One's own life—one's own secret private life—what a queer positive thing it is. Nobody knows where you are—nobody has the remotest idea *who* you are, even.'[8]

Aldous Huxley understood the connection between Katherine's role-playing, acting and contradictory selves, while Lytton Strachey noticed her defensive mask. Huxley, who believed that Katherine lacked a secure sense of self—'She was an unhappy woman, capable of acting any number of parts but uncertain of who, essentially, she was'[9]—portrayed both the bourgeois and the bohemian side of her personality in *Those Barren Leaves*: she 'was at once old fashioned and tremendously contemporary, school-girlish and advanced, demure and more than Chelsea-ishly emancipated. . . . He liked her combination of moral ingenuousness and mental sophistication, of cleverness and genuineness.'[10] Strachey, who agreed with Huxley that it would be a difficult but rewarding experience to penetrate Katherine's passive façade, called her 'an odd satirical woman behind a regular mask of a face. . . . She was very difficult to get at; one felt it would take years of patient burrowing, but that it might be worth while.'[11]

Victor Pritchett, misled by the qualities that Katherine often chose to emphasize rather than conceal, quite mistakenly calls her 'the exquisite colonial, the prim exile, who belongs neither to England nor New Zealand'.[12] Though illness gave Katherine a frail and delicate appearance, her character was more tough than exquisite, more like Simone Weil's than like Camille's. She was rebellious and daring, not prim, and belonged very much to New Zealand as well as to England.

Katherine, who could be irritable, suspicious and demanding, admitted that she had a ferocious temper—'I think the only thing which is really "serious" about me, really "bad", really incurable, is my temper'[13]—though she did not fully realize that her black rages were frequently provoked by the constant pain of her disease. Her sudden transition from feline withdrawal to caustic anger made many people fear her; Murry explains that her satire seemed to flash like lightning from her gentle countenance: 'There is no doubt that she was regarded by many of her acquaintances as a rather icily perfect, remote and forbidding figure. Undoubtedly, people tended to be "afraid" of her.'[14] The kindly Dorothy Brett, who adored Katherine but was frequently the victim of her satire, mentions her savage changes of mood and her cruel speeches: 'Her reputation of brilliancy, of a sort of ironic ruthlessness toward the small minds and less agile brains, simply terrified me. . . . She had daring, courage and a tremendous sense of humour. She was like a sparkling brook—like quicksilver. Her changes of mood were rapid and disconcerting; a laughing joyous moment would suddenly turn through some inadequate remark into biting anger. . . . Katherine had a tongue like a knife, she could cut the very heart out of one with it.'[15] Joyce Cary, who had known Murry at Oxford and met Katherine in 1912, later recalled: 'He had not liked her, he had thought her hard, selfish, and a little sordid. Later, he realized he had been wrong.'[16]

Writing to a friend in New Zealand, Frances Cornford, the poet and grand-daughter of Charles Darwin, also refers to Katherine's odd mixture of vulgarity, vanity and bitterness, which later seemed to be purged by her suffering and disease: 'My sister Fredegond described to me once meeting KM in her earlier Bloomsbury days at a tea party [c. 1917]. KM came in late & described most brilliantly how she'd been shopping—acting the whole conversation with the shopwoman. But yet it was just a little vulgar, a little vain & strung up, a little unkind. Later F. saw her again,—though once more only at a party, at the house in Hampstead. KM was much thinner & coughing, but something lively shone out of her, & something else seemed to have been washed away.'[17] The central conflict in Katherine's character and work was between the remote, restrained, forbidding and frightening woman and the lonely, isolated, and often helpless girl who was herself frightened of life and of death; between the savage satirist of German crudity and marital cruelty, and the nostalgic sentimentalist of childhood life in New Zealand.

Murry, who was ten months younger than Katherine, was born in London in 1889, the son of a poor copy-clerk at the War Office and a petty tyrant at home. Murry's biographer writes that his repressive childhood led to 'an atrophy of the sensuous, a hypertrophy of the intellectual, from which he never recovered';[18] and Murry's aunt told his son, Colin: 'Your dad was never a *real* boy at all. He was just a little old man.'[19] D. H. Lawrence, who had a complex love-hate relationship with Murry and was fond of diagnosing his weaknesses, agreed: 'Spunk is what one wants, not introspective sentiment. The last is your vice. You rot your own manhood at the roots, with it.'[20]

Murry's highly-developed intellect won him scholarships to Christ's Hospital and Brasenose College, Oxford, where he formed friendships with the novelist Joyce Cary and the biographer and critic, Michael Sadler. Murry spent the Christmas vacation of 1910 in Paris where he first encountered Left Bank bohemianism and Fauvism, and conceived the plan for his *avant-garde* magazine, *Rhythm*; and had his first love affair with a Parisian *demi-mondaine*, Margueritte.

Dorothy Brett described Murry as a handsome and dreamy young man who 'rolls in with the gait of a sailor, his curly dark hair is getting a bit thin on top. He is nervous, shy, a small man. The eyes are large and hazel, with a strange unseeing look; the nose is curved one side and perfectly straight the other, due to its having been broken. His lips are finely cut, the mouth sensitive, the chin determined. A fine and beautiful head.'[21] And Murry accurately characterized himself as 'Part snob, part coward, part sentimentalist',[22] as if the confession justified the faults.

Murry's fatal combination of intellectuality and sentimentality weakened his rational thought and also made him distrust his own feelings. This in turn led to a moral ambiguity, for his intellectualism allowed him to escape from emotional dilemmas. He was able to understand this quality in himself and even condemn it, yet he was also disingenuous enough to believe that he could dispose of his defects by acknowledging them. His extreme subjectivity and the admission of his own inadequacy led to a belief in his own greatness, but an inability to do anything more than editing and criticism.

Murry met Katherine through the novelist and critic Walter Lionel George, whom Swinnerton describes as a French Jew who 'was small, black-moustached, brisk, and opinionated; an early enthusiast for Katherine Mansfield's work'.[23] In the autumn of 1911 George sent a rather bitter 'fairy story' by Katherine to Murry, who was editing *Rhythm* from his Oxford college. Murry was intrigued but puzzled by the story, asked for another one and received the New Zealand tale 'The Woman at the Store'. He accepted it at once, told Katherine that it was the best story ever sent to his magazine and published it in the spring of 1912 (with two of her poems, 'translated from the Russian of Boris Petrovsky', which had been rejected by Orage).

In December 1911 Katherine was introduced to Murry at W. L. George's house at 84 Hamilton Terrace, St. John's Wood—the same street where she had first met George Bowden. George had warned Murry that Katherine was a mysterious and formidable creature, and Murry was excited about the prospect of meeting her. In his autobiography, *Between Two Worlds*, Murry relates that he found Katherine impressive in appearance, sophistication and intellect, and that he felt awkward in the clever and rather precious social milieu that inspired the setting of 'Bliss':

Katherine Mansfield arrived in a taxi, late. She wore a simple dove-grey evening frock with a single red flower, and a gauze scarf of the same dove-grey colour. She was formidable, though not at all in the way I had been made to fear. She was aloof and reserved; and beside her I felt clumsy. In other ways, too, I felt subtly out of it. W. L. George always addressed her, Russian fashion, as 'Yékaterina', beside which my 'Miss Mansfield' sounded very provincial. In honour of her newly published book there was red plum-soup for dinner—a German gourmet's dish quite unknown to me, and equally unknown were Artzibashef and his book, *Sanine*, on which the conversation turned.[24]

When they parted that evening Katherine invited Murry to tea but forgot to give him her address. They corresponded briefly about reviewing for *Rhythm*, and in January Katherine left for a brief holiday in Geneva, probably paid for by her parents, who went back to New Zealand in March. From Switzerland Katherine wrote to Murry offering Russian cherry jam for tea when she returned to London, and their second meeting at her Clovelly Mansions flat in February 1912 was momentous. The 'little Colonial' and the lower middle-class student, who were both socially *déraciné* and outsiders in London and Oxford, were immediately attracted to each other. Katherine served tea sitting on the floor of the sparsely furnished room and urged Murry, who was weary of Oxford and wanted to leave before taking his degree, to give up the University and come to London. Murry gladly took her advice, moved into his parents' house in South London and began to review for J. A. Spender's *Westminster Gazette*.

Two months after this first meeting Katherine invited Murry to live in her flat, and he moved in on April 11. The next morning, Murry writes, 'I was awakened by a knock at the door. "I've finished with the bathroom," said Katherine's voice. "And your breakfast is in the kitchen." There I found the table laid, and a kettle boiling. Brown bread and butter and honey, and a large brown egg in an egg-cup. Fixed between the egg and the egg-cup, like a big label, was a half-sheet of blue notepaper, with this inscription: "This is your egg. You must boil it. K.M." ' When *Rhythm* began to lose money they became desperately poor and ate at a meat-pie shop where they could have dinner for two-pence. They also frequented the *Duke of York* pub in Theobald's Road, where the maternal landlady took them for an unemployed music-hall couple and insisted on standing them free drinks.

After several rather formal weeks during which they always shook hands before going to sleep in separate rooms, Katherine asked Murry: 'Why don't you make me your mistress?' He waved his legs in the air and primly replied: 'I feel it would spoil—everything.' And when she added: 'So do I,' he missed her bitter irony.[25] Murry may have been restrained by his fear of infecting Katherine with the gonorrhea he had contracted at Oxford in the autumn of 1911,[26] as well as by Katherine's passionate assurance and his own fearful repression, but after she told Murry: 'I *love* you. Doesn't that make any difference?'[27] she was finally able to seduce him.

The sophisticated Hugh Kingsmill, who was less responsive to Katherine's theatrical poses and lyrical affectations than the landlady or Murry, relates that one day in the spring of 1912: 'Katherine Mansfield suddenly sprang to her feet and ran to the window, overlooking Gray's Inn Road. "Oh, wouldn't you love to be running by the sea," she cried, "with the sand trickling

between your bare toes!" I muttered "Rather!" and with a
weary shrug she sat down again.'²⁸

In May 1912 Katherine and Murry had a brief honeymoon in
Paris. Murry introduced her to his friend, J. D. Fergusson, and
through him they met the American Fauve painter and follower
of Matisse, Anne Estelle Rice. Anne, who became Katherine's
intimate friend and correspondent, was the mistress and model of
Fergusson, who painted Anne's stunning portrait. Katherine
described Anne, who brought out the best in her, as '*bronze*-
coloured with light periwinkle eyes'; and in 1918 contrasted
Anne's warmth and vitality with her own illness: 'You know she
IS an exceptional woman—so gay, so abundant—in full flower
just now and really beautiful to watch. She is so healthy. . . .
There are certain people who do make me feel *loving*, warm-
hearted, tender, and—like children feel. Anne is one.'²⁹

In the spring of 1912, after Murry's 'respectable' family had
greeted Katherine with icy disdain, his mother and aunt invaded
Clovelly Mansions in order to rescue him from the perilous
clutches of a married woman, but they failed in their mission and
did not see Murry again for three years. In a passage deleted by
Murry from Katherine's *Journal*, she wrote with considerable
justice: 'I don't like Jack's family. I could never *bear* to have
them live with us. . . . We'll come to blows about them one
day.'³⁰

Katherine and Murry lived in Clovelly Mansions until August
1912 when the landlord discovered they were not married and
forced them to leave. They then rented a country cottage at
Runcton, near Chichester, and were visited at weekends by Ida
Baker, Edward Marsh and Rupert Brooke. After a year and a
half in the Gray's Inn Road, Katherine began her itinerant life of
poverty and squalor with Murry; they had nearly a dozen
addresses—in London, Buckinghamshire, Kent, Cornwall and
Paris—during their first two years together.

Katherine, who wrote about childhood and cultivated childishness, sought refuge from the ugly reality of poverty and
illness in a fantasy world of pet names (Bogey, Tig and Wig),
favourite cats and dolls (Wingley and Ribni), unreal plans for a
permanent home (The Heron), baby-talk based on New Zealand
working-class accents ('Dozzing' and 'Kitching' for dozen and
kitchen) and dreams of a baby of her own, who she believed

would solve all their problems. The adoption of 'Bogey', which was also the familiar name of Katherine's brother, and 'Heron', which was Leslie's second name, reinforced Katherine's maternal role with Murry. The novelist Gilbert Cannan ironically called Katherine and Murry 'The Two Tigers' (one of their pseudonyms in *Rhythm*), after an illustration in the first number of that magazine of a tiger treading on a monkey's tail, which was soon softened to the more intimate 'Tig' and 'Wig'. The name of Katherine's cat came from one of her favourite music-hall songs: 'Wing Lee bought a clock the other day—Just because it kept rag-time'; Ribni, her Japanese doll, was taken from the Japanese spy, Captain Ribnikov, the eponymous hero of Kuprin's story. As Murry observes: we were 'prey to a subtle sense of our own unreality, as though we were only a kind of dream-children'.[31]

Murry, who was inept as a lover, writes with surprising naiveté: 'It was only when we were settling in at Runcton, and I happened to read one or two passionate love-letters from S.V., an Austrian journalist . . . in which he spoke of kissing her breasts, that I plucked up courage and dared to kiss them. . . . Beyond that I never made love to her—right to the end.' And his biographer adds: 'There were no caresses, no preliminaries; their love-making (such as it was) was a climax without a crescendo.'[32] When they finally realized they could not have a child, Katherine, who was anxious to conceal her unhappy sexual experiences, put the blame on Murry. He gallantly accepted it, and did not find out about her abortion in 1911, which may have led to her sterility (he later had four children), until after her death.

The husband in Katherine's 'A Married Man's Story' (1923) says: 'Though one might suspect her of strong maternal feelings, my wife doesn't seem to me the type of woman who bears children in her own body.'[33] But the dream—and the symbol— of the baby persisted. In 1915 Katherine dreamed of having a dead baby, and two years later she told Murry that, for security: 'we shall have to have all our babies in pairs so that we possess a complete "set" in either place.'[34] In April 1919 she told Virginia Woolf (who was also childless): 'I could get on without a baby— but Murry, I should like to give him one'; in November 1919 Katherine insisted, 'We *must* have children—we *must*'; when Murry sent one of his cruellest letters the following month, the deeply wounded Katherine translated it into the metaphor of a dead child: 'I'd say we had a child—a love-child and it's dead. We may have other children, but this child can't be made to live again. J. [her cousin] says: Forget that letter! How can I? It killed the child—*killed* it *really* and *truly* for ever as far as I am concerned.'[35] As late as 1922, during the terminal phase of her disease, she combined her fantasies about Russia, Chekhov (her literary father) and babies into an impossible but revealing wish: 'I want to adopt a Russian baby, call him Anton, and bring him up as mine, with Kot for a godfather and Mme. Tchehov for a godmother. Such is my dream.'[36] Throughout her life Katherine felt that a child would help ease the anguish of disease and solitude.

Despite their upheavals, *Rhythm* remained the centre of their intellectual and artistic life, and in July Katherine replaced Michael Sadler, who had financed the magazine, as co-editor. The handsome quarto—which began as a quarterly, became a monthly after the fourth issue and had a total of fourteen numbers between the summer of 1911 and March 1913—had a dove-grey and then a deep blue cover, was printed in Caslon type on good paper, and had full-page reproductions of paintings, drawings and woodcuts by Picasso (for the first time in England), Derain, Gaudier-Brzeska, Augustus John and Jack Yeats as well as J. D. Fergusson and Anne Rice. Though *Rhythm* showed a cosmopolitan interest in French art and literature, it printed only 250 to 750 copies per issue and had a very limited influence on contemporary taste. It had stories, poems, essays and reviews by Katherine and Murry in nearly every issue as well as contributions by their circle of friends: Floryan Sobieniowski, William Orton, Michael Sadler, Francis Carco (who wrote a '*Lettre de Paris*'), W. L. George, Raymond Drey, Frank Swinnerton, Rupert Brooke, Walter de La Mare (whom Murry met at the *Westminster Gazette*), Gilbert Cannan and, in the last issue, D. H. Lawrence on 'The Georgian Renaissance'. From July 1912, when Ida Baker was no longer needed by Katherine and had opened a beauty salon in South Molton Street, the magazine regularly ran an advertisement for 'Lesley Moore and Rebecca Rinsberry, Specialists in Scientific Hair-Brushing and Face Massage'.

Despite the handsome format and considerable talent of the contributors, *Rhythm* was cliquish, naive and only mildly revolutionary, and it rarely published first-class work by any of the authors. Murry, who was frequently carried away by temporary enthusiasms, declared that James Stephens was not only 'the greatest poet of our day' but one of those 'whom we consider the greatest poets the world has ever known'.[37] And in their didactic editorial, 'The Meaning of Rhythm', Murry and Katherine propagated their lively but rather muddled tautological doctrine: 'Art and the artist are perfectly at one. Art is free; the artist is free. Art is real; the artist is real. Art is individual; the artist is individual. Their unity is ultimate and unassailable. It is the essential movement of Life. It is the splendid adventure, the eternal quest for rhythm.'[38]

The vitality and immaturity of *Rhythm* provoked some heated opposition and several nasty incidents. On March 28, 1912, the *New Age*, which Katherine had temporarily left to join Murry and publish in *Rhythm*, printed a full-page denunciation of its new rival; a later anonymous attack on April 18 condemned the latest volume as 'stupid, crazy and exceedingly vulgar', and claimed the authors of *Rhythm* 'were running after sensationalism; dancing with seals in delirium, dreaming of murderous hags and degenerate children [in 'The Woman at the Store'], playing with sadism and devil-worship, gazing at drunken tramps amid daffodils until they lost all sense of decency.'[39] Yet on July 4 Katherine, who published her work wherever she could, reappeared in the *New Age* as the author of a Russian pastiche which began: 'The servant girl, wearing a red, sleeveless blouse, brought in the samovar. "But it is impossible to speak of a concrete ideal," thought Dimitri Tchernikofskoi. . . .'[40]

Many contributors to *Rhythm* frequented Dan Rider's bookshop off St. Martin's Lane, where Katherine met Alfred Knopf, who later became her American publisher. Just after the appearance of the June issue of *Rhythm*, in which Murry published his exaggerated praise of James Stephens and called a passage from the Irish poet greater than Milton, the fiery Frank Harris entered the bookshop and vehemently condemned Murry. According to Hugh Kingsmill, 'Murry burst into tears and ran out of the shop. "Good God!" Harris stared round in amazement. "Oh, he'll kill himself!" Katherine Mansfield cried, and rushed after Murry.'[41] When Murry recovered himself, he regretted that he had already given the printers the July issue in which, with typical hyperbole, he called Harris 'the greatest writer of short stories that England has ever possessed' and said his commonplace, plagiarized works were 'among the supreme creations of art'.[42]

In about June 1912, at the time of the contretemps with Harris, Katherine and Murry met the artist Henri Gaudier-Brzeska and asked him to contribute some drawings to *Rhythm*. Gaudier, an exceptionally gifted sculptor, had a slender build, an ascetic-looking face with thin lips and nose, and long dark hair. He spoke with a heavy French accent and had a great deal of nervous energy. Gaudier was, like both Katherine and Murry, an impoverished artist and unmarried lover; he joined the name of his older Polish mistress to his own. But the Gaudier-Brzeskas were real bohemians and the Murrys middle-class rebels who hated poverty and still believed in marriage, family and home. The reserved Katherine disliked the intensity of Sophie Brzeska's revelations and gauche gestures of friendship, and feared she would be strangled by Sophie's tentacles. In September the extremely sensitive Gaudier, who had made the unwelcome suggestion that they all share the cottage at Runcton (which Katherine called 'our wedding house'), came down there unexpectedly and overheard Katherine slandering his beloved Sophie:

M.M.: 'I think she should come down here now, there is plenty of room. Just let us speak to Gaudier about it.'

K.M.: 'Oh, no. I don't want to see her here—she's too violent—I won't have her.'

M.M.: 'But, Tiger, look here, she's not like that—I don't see why—'

K.M.: (violently): 'Leave me alone, I don't like her and I don't want to see her—she'll make me ill again.'[43]

Gaudier, who was deeply wounded by this conversation, left unseen, swore never to meet them again, and sent Murry an emotional and incoherent letter which defended Sophie and condemned the 'fiendish' Katherine: 'Your acquaintance has been for me one long suffering—not only for me but also for the object of my love, which is twice worse. I met you at a dangerous turning, the brains burned by the recent summer, thirsty for good friendship, only with one drawback: poverty. Being then freshly strong, promising all kinds of things and favours, you behaved stupidly, thinking I was lashed to you, and that I would not mind any dirt. I was confirmed into my thought of the wickedness of Katherine Mansfield by a conversation I overheard when at Runcton. . . . K.M., with a fiendish jealousy, upheld to the end that Zosik [Sophie] was too *violent*.'⁴⁴ In May 1913, when Murry was in the *Rhythm* office on Chancery Lane, Gaudier suddenly rushed into the room, threatened to throttle him, demanded payment that had never been promised, snatched two drawings from the wall, slapped Murry in the face and disappeared. After Gaudier was killed in the War, at the age of twenty-three, Sophie became insane.

Another incubus of this period was the penniless Floryan Sobieniowski. He suddenly reappeared at Runcton with two big black trunks filled with books and manuscripts, entertained the Murrys with his melancholy Slavic songs, and moved in with them—against their will—from August to November 1912. He became the 'Polish Correspondent' of *Rhythm*; the drawing of Floryan that appeared in the magazine portrays him as an attractive and pensive man with dark wavy hair, a high forehead, broad nose and thick moustache. Floryan also contributed an essay on his .compatriot, Stanislaw Wyspianski, whom he described as: 'Poet and dramatist, painter and sculptor, architect and creator of new values for the Polish consciousness . . . his literary creation had two "Leitmotiven"—one, the necessity for close connection with national tradition; the second, the awakening of independence.'⁴⁵

Floryan, 'who by this time appeared to regard himself as [their] dependent for life',⁴⁶ turned up again as soon as they had settled in the *Rhythm* office-flat in Chancery Lane, and his financial extortions from Katherine and Murry anticipated his less successful attempts with Shaw. He 'borrowed' more than £40 from them at a time they were deeply in debt and had just had their furniture repossessed, and when they refused to support him any longer, had to 'lend' him another £15 before he would leave. Floryan remained the 'Polish Correspondent' until the last issue of *Rhythm* in March 1913, when Katherine's poem 'Floryan Nachdenklich' (Floryan Pensive) appeared in the *Dominion*, published in Wellington. His sinister power over Katherine and Murry was probably based on his sexual relations with her in Germany in

1909. Since Floryan threatened Katherine, and Murry (who never suspected that she had been Floryan's mistress) was passive by nature, they were forced to tolerate him until they could pay what he demanded. After her final break with Floryan in the summer of 1913 Katherine called him 'a rather dangerous fraud'; her story, 'A Dill Pickle' (1917), describes an awkward encounter with a former lover, who is pompous, fussy and unduly concerned with money, and has been to Russia, where Katherine had planned to travel with Floryan.

The final disaster occurred when Katherine's publisher, Stephen Swift, who began to finance *Rhythm* in June 1912 and paid them a joint salary of £10 per month, went bankrupt in October. Swift's real name was Charles Granville and his office was next door to Martin Secker's at 7 John Street, Adelphi. His career as a publisher came to a dramatic end when, at a dinner party in Hampstead, Swift met a magistrate who remembered that he had jumped bail on a charge of bigamy. Swift left for the Continent the next morning, but was later arrested in Algiers and brought back to serve his sentence.[47] Before taking the cash and disappearing from England, Swift had increased the printing order and placed it in the name of Murry, who was now held legally responsible for a debt of £400. At this point Edward Marsh, Winston Churchill's secretary at the Admiralty, editor of *Georgian Poetry* and patron of the arts, offered a guarantee of £150 and Katherine agreed to pay the printers her entire allowance of £100 for the next four years. Marsh later recalled 'the *Rhythm* luncheons at Treveglio's in Soho, where the brilliant contributors met and resourcefully plotted to keep the brave little paper going for another month'.[48] *Rhythm* came out on schedule in November under the imprint of the publisher Martin Secker, who commissioned Murry's book on Dostoyevsky to help pay off the debt. It continued for five more months and, influenced by the French *Revue bleu*, reappeared for three more numbers during May–July 1913 as the *Blue Review*. The final issue of the magazine contained Katherine's slight story of Geneva, 'Bains Turcs', Lawrence's review of Mann's *Death in Venice*, poetry by Rupert Brooke, essays by H. G. Wells and Ford Madox Hueffer, and other contributions by Murry, Hugh Walpole, Frank Swinnerton, Raymond Drey and Gilbert Cannan.

The bankruptcy of Stephen Swift, which cost them Katherine's

book royalties as well as their monthly salary and burdened them
with an enormous debt, forced them to leave Runcton. Their
servant, an incredibly dirty and drunken ex-soldier, confessed
that he had been constantly stealing from them; he had sold their
watches for a few pounds and then squandered the money on
gambling and drink. Murry had to tell the hire-purchase company
to reclaim the furniture they could no longer afford to keep. In
November they took a cheap room in Chancery Lane, and
furnished it with a single camp bed, two chairs and a packing
case. They soon exchanged this for a gloomy little three-room
flat at 57 Chancery Lane, which also served as the editorial office
of *Rhythm*, whose name was boldly painted on the door. But the
light was poor, the view depressing and the canary given to
Katherine promptly died.

Though Katherine and Murry were an attractive and exciting
couple who managed to survive numerous disasters, many of her
friends thought he brought out the worst side of her character.
Murry was afraid of life, tended to withdraw from people and
admitted: 'I knew I was her inferior in many ways, but I could
have accepted them all save one. She had immediate contact
with life which was completely denied to me.' And in 1919 he
told her: 'It's your sheer courage more than anything else that
sets you on a higher plane altogether than me.'⁴⁹ Katherine
agreed: 'We are both abnormal: I have too much vitality—
and you not enough.'⁵⁰ Katherine was brave, Murry cowardly;
she was reserved, he wore his heart on his sleeve; and from
the beginning she took the active male role and he became
the passive female. Katherine liked to identify herself with
George Sand and Colette, who were independent, impulsive, and
imaginative women, proud of their desire for love and passion
for art.

Edward Marsh relates that in June 1913 Katherine, provoked
by an attack on suffragettes, was turned out of an omnibus for
calling a woman a whore.⁵¹ Ottoline Morrell recounts an amusing
anecdote that also conveys the odd mixture of the ethereal and
the earthy in Katherine's character, and suggests why Ottoline
thought her friend was slightly common. After attending a
balalaika concert in 1917: 'We seemed to be still floating over
wild country. Katherine was as much moved as I was. Just as we
were parting to go our several ways home, she said, "My corns

are hurting. I must go to my old corncutter tomorrow. Good night, darling." '52 But Dora Carrington, who shared a house with Katherine in 1916, admired her unconventional qualities: 'She was an extraordinary woman, witty and courageous, very much an adventuress and with the language of a fish-wife in Wapping. But Middleton Murry ate the soul out of her.'53

Enid Bagnold, the author of *National Velvet*, met Katherine in Dan Rider's bookshop. She reveals in a recent letter that Katherine was frequently impatient and angry with Murry: 'None of us liked her much (though we were impressed). . . . Whenever I saw her she was a bit out of temper: not with me but about some recent row with Murry.'54 And Ottoline Morrell accurately attributes Katherine's irritation to Murry's egoism and selfishness: 'She seemed often as if she would like to shake him. She called him "a little mole hung out on a string to dry". She felt, I think, that he was not really alive or aware of her as a woman. I was rather surprised by the way she talked of him, as if she really did not care much for him, but I have since seen how little he ever did to help her, or provide for her.'55

Ottoline, like Frank Swinnerton and other friends, also noted that Katherine and Murry made a religion of art: 'She takes great pride in being an "artist", and she speaks as if she and Murry belonged to some sacred order of artists superior and apart from ordinary people like myself.'56 Swinnerton, who also thought Katherine 'was a little too literary and perhaps even a little insincere', was attracted to her nevertheless and saw that her mysterious reserve was another form of role-playing. As he recently wrote: 'I liked K.M. very much. She was quite unlike the suburban girls I knew; and I found her enigmatic silence most attractive. . . . We thought her fragile and lost in a dream. . . . I think [Murry] and K.M. were genuinely fond of each other, and that they were in a way affectionate conspirators. In the light of what I have since read or been told, I think K.M.'s enigmatic silence may have been protective, and that, being at bottom quite conventional, she had played at being something else.'57

At the end of December 1912 Katherine and Murry were invited to a grand Christmas party given by Anne Rice in her large Montparnasse studio and travelled to Paris with two couples who had recently become their friends. Katherine had met the Irishman, Gordon Campbell, who had a long lugubrious face, an inseparable umbrella and a rich, forlorn voice, at the house of W. L. George late in 1911.[58] The following year Campbell married the striking-looking blonde, Beatrice Moss, whom Katherine described as 'a queer mixture for she is really loving and affectionate, and yet she is malicious'.[59] Their other friend was the popular novelist Gilbert Cannan, a tall, exceptionally handsome and moody man with a bitter sense of humour, 'a martyr to his own good looks and the emotional complications they invariably led him into'.[60] His beautiful wife, the former actress Mary Ansell, was seventeen years older than Gilbert and had been previously married to the playwright Sir James Barrie, who still gave her a generous allowance on their wedding anniversary.[61]

Soon after they returned from Paris the Cannans, who had bought the Mill House on the edge of the common at Cholesbury in Buckinghamshire, suggested that the Murrys should rent the small semi-detached red brick villa next door. Katherine, who was glad to leave the depressing flat, eagerly accepted the offer and Murry, who had to work in the *Rhythm* office during the week, came down at weekends. Mark Gertler's painting, *Gilbert Cannan at his Mill, Cholesbury* (1915), gives a stylized view of the wooden windmill just behind the house and portrays Gilbert with the famous sheepdog that was said to be the original of Nana in *Peter Pan*.

Though their first year together in various lodgings had been disastrous, and they were still impoverished, unsettled and unrecognized, Katherine and Murry had made *Rhythm* a *succès d'estime* and remained undaunted and optimistic. They had formed some valuable friendships and in 1913 met D. H. Lawrence, who would have a profound emotional impact on their lives.

CHAPTER SEVEN

Friendship with D. H. Lawrence, 1913–1923

D. H. LAWRENCE and Katherine Mansfield had a good deal in common. Both were outsiders in English society: Lawrence because of his working-class background, Katherine because of her colonial origins. Though they left their birthplaces, they were strongly influenced by them and frequently recreated them in their work. They revolted against the conventional values of the time, and had considerable sexual experience in early life, though Lawrence had been strengthened and Katherine hurt by it. They spent many impoverished years on the Continent and maintained a European rather than an insular outlook. They had intuitive and volatile personalities, experienced life with a feverish intensity, were highly creative and passionately committed to their art, and achieved a posthumous fame far greater than their contemporary reputations. Most important of all, they were both physically sterile and seriously ill for a great part of their adult lives, and made their pilgrimage from country to country in search of a warm climate and good health. They were subject to sudden fits of black rage, suffered the constant pain of disease and the fearful threat of death, and died of tuberculosis at an early age.

During their ten years of friendship, in which Lawrence and Katherine twice lived in neighbouring houses, they oscillated between profound attachment and extreme hostility. When they did not see each other, they kept in touch through letters and news from their close mutual friends—S. S. Koteliansky, Mark Gertler, Dorothy Brett and Ottoline Morrell—and read each other's books. Katherine was attracted to Lawrence's vitality, but was repulsed by his passionate enthusiasms and dogmatic obsessions, which intensified her natural inclination to retreat into her private world. Because their temperaments were radically different in this respect, Katherine frequently appeared negative, cowardly, pallid and sickly to Lawrence, who blamed her for being ill; while to Katherine, Lawrence's extreme affirmations and condemnations seemed almost insane in their manic egoism. Their most serious estrangement occurred in February 1920 when Lawrence sent Katherine what Murry justly called a 'monstrously' and 'inhumanly cruel' letter. If we can understand why Lawrence sent this letter and how Katherine was able to forgive him after he had (as she said) 'spat in my face and threw filth at me', we will be able to perceive the essence of their friendship.

The history of their relationship is a record of affection given and received, for both Lawrence and Frieda said the Murrys were their most intimate friends. But Lawrence had a tendency to quarrel with the people closest to him, and Katherine's response to his temperamental extremism inevitably caused a breach, with harsh letters and bitter recriminations. Though both Lawrence and Katherine recognized that he was the greater writer, she became more of a personal threat to him as her literary reputation increased.

Lawrence had great insight into the characters of his friends, yet was intransigent about his prescriptions for their behaviour. He could demonstrate, in long letters or personal harangues, his love for them and concern about what they should do with their lives. But if they chose to ignore his advice, Lawrence felt wounded and betrayed, and harshly rejected them. This conflict accentuated his sense of isolation and self-righteousness, and gave him licence to abuse them viciously. In his essay on Lawrence, Bertrand Russell (who is satirized as the elderly sociologist, Sir Joshua Mattheson, in *Women in Love*) says that when he received one of Lawrence's violent letters in 1915 he actually felt like committing suicide for twenty-four hours—until common sense reasserted itself. If Lawrence could make Russell feel suicidal, then the effect on Katherine must have been even more devastating.

Like Gaudier, whom he resembled in many ways, Lawrence was emotional and impulsive, demanded an intense and absolute friendship, and seemed to have the quality of genius. Both Lawrence and Frieda were extremely responsive, and derived great pleasure from ordinary things: 'I believe the chief tie between Lawrence and me was always the wonder of living,' Frieda wrote, 'every little or big thing that happened carried its glamour with it.'[1]

Frieda von Richthofen, the beautiful and passionate daughter of a German baron, was born in Metz in 1879 and grew up in the society of the Prussian Imperial Court. Violet Hunt called her a charming, 'handsome, golden-haired, tall woman with a magnificent figure, like a Teutonic goddess.'[2] And Brigit Patmore wrote that Frieda shone 'in a sun-drenched way, wild, blonde hair waving happily, grey-green eyes raying out laughter, her fair skin an effulgent pale rose'.[3]

In 1898 the rather wild Frieda blundered into marriage with Ernest Weekley, whom Aldous Huxley called 'possibly the dullest Professor in the Western hemisphere',[4] and went to live in the gloomy industrial city of Nottingham, where he had been appointed Lecturer at the University. Though Frieda had three children and numerous lovers she was extremely bored, after fourteen years of stifling marriage, when Lawrence, her husband's former pupil, was invited to their home in April 1912. Three weeks after their first meeting they left England together, travelled in Germany and then lived on Lake Garda, where Lawrence worked on *Sons and Lovers*, until the spring of 1913.

In December 1912, after Lawrence (who was three years older than Katherine) had published *The White Peacock* (1911) and *The Trespasser* (1912), and Katherine *In A German Pension* (1911), he asked Edward Garnett if *Rhythm* would publish any of his stories; the following month she sent him a copy of *Rhythm* and asked for a contribution. Lawrence replied from Gargnano on January 29 offering several stories, and in February he told a friend: 'You should find some of my stuff in March *Rhythm*. It's a daft paper, but the folk seem rather nice.'[5] When the Lawrences returned to England in June 1913, they looked up Katherine and Murry and liked them immediately. Both Lawrence and Murry came from poor families and were extremely conscious of their origins, and when they discovered that neither couple was married and both women were waiting for a divorce, it seemed they were made for each other. Frieda felt 'theirs was the only spontaneous and jolly friendship that we had. . . . I fell for Katherine and Murry when I saw them quite unexpectedly on the top of a bus, making faces at each other and putting their tongues out.'[6] This was a charming but characteristically childish aspect of their relationship. Frieda was then estranged from her young children, and Katherine was far more understanding than

Lawrence about Frieda's maternal feelings. Katherine visited the children and took them letters, and Frieda 'loved her like a younger sister'. Later in the summer the two couples bathed naked on the deserted sands of Broadstairs, and Lawrence gave Katherine and Murry a copy of *Sons and Lovers*.

The Lawrences returned to Italy in September, described their lonely life in Lerici as one long enchantment, and passionately urged their friends to join them. The great problem was lack of money, for Murry's small income depended on reviewing in London. If he had followed Lawrence's advice he would have had to live on Katherine's allowance of £100 a year (which was then being paid to the printers), but that seemed 'quite intolerable' to him. When Murry refused to live in Italy on Katherine's money, he received and ignored Lawrence's well-intentioned and perceptive harangue, which exposed Murry's hypocrisy and weakness: 'When you say you won't take Katherine's money, it means you don't trust her love for you. When you say she needs little luxuries, and you couldn't bear to deprive her of them, it means you don't respect either yourself or her sufficiently to do it. . . . She must say, "Could I live in a little place in Italy, with Jack, and be lonely, have a rather bare life, but be happy?" If she could, then take her money. If she doesn't want to, don't try. But don't beat about the bush. In the way you go on, you are inevitably coming apart. She is perhaps beginning to be unsatisfied with you.'[7]

Lawrence discussed and dismissed this financial problem in a long letter to Murry written in the autumn of 1913, in which he also analysed the essential defect in Murry's marriage and, unlike his later letters, was both shrewd and reasonable.

It looks to me as if you two, far from growing nearer, are snapping the bonds that hold you together, one after another. I suppose you must both of you consult your own hearts, honestly. . . .

You must rest, and you and Katherine must heal, and come together, before you do *any serious* work of any sort. It's the split in the love that drains you. . . .

If you want things to come right—if you are ill and exhausted, then take her money to the last penny and let her do her own housework. Then she'll know you love her. You can't blame her if she's not satisfied with you. . . . But, you fool, you squander yourself, not for *her*, but to provide her with petty luxuries she doesn't really want. You insult her. A woman unsatisfied must have luxuries. But a woman who loves a man would sleep on a board. . . .

You've tried to satisfy Katherine with what you could earn for her, give her: and she will only be satisfied with what you *are*.[8]

Lawrence saw that trust and love could overcome Murry's scruples about money, and that Katherine's 'need' for luxuries was merely a false and insulting excuse. Lawrence, like Katherine, also understood that a true marriage would strengthen her art. 'I believe in marriage', Katherine told her fair-haired Irish friend, Sylvia Lynd. 'It seems to me the only possible relation that is really satisfying. And how else is one to have peace of mind to enjoy life and to do one's work?'[9]

When Lawrence states that 'a woman who loves a man would sleep on a board', he is alluding to Frieda, who abandoned her security, her comfort and even her children to run off with an impoverished writer. Murry, who could never satisfy Katherine's material or emotional needs, knew that she was *not* satisfied with what he was. But Murry's own career was just as important to him as Katherine's; he did not love her enough to make this sacrifice, or have sufficient faith in his own talents to believe that he could write while abroad or start afresh later on. Murry, who was insecure, had a wife whom he had to support emotionally and also nourish as a writer (as Frieda nourished Lawrence). Since Murry was self-absorbed and had high literary ambitions, he was particularly unsuited to this sacrificial role.

Murry was a kind of rancid Rousseau: his thought was equivocal and confused, he had an endless capacity for self-deception, he disguised a total egocentricity behind his mock-saintliness and was always eager to display his stigmata before the public. Katherine, who loathed his self-pity, accused him of being 'just like a little dog whining outside a door', and impatiently exclaimed: 'When you know you are a voice crying in the wilderness, *cry*, but don't say "I am a voice crying in the wilderness".'[10] Katherine also condemned his high moral tone and pretentious philosophy, called him 'a monk without a monastery' and said he 'couldn't fry a sausage without thinking

1 (a) The Beauchamp
Children, Wellington,
c. 1898: *Standing*,
Kathleen, Vera;
Centre, Leslie,
Jeanne; *Front*,
Charlotte Mary

1 (b) Maata
Mahupuka,
Wellington, 1901

2 (a) The Beauchamp Family at Las Palmas, 16 March 1903: *Back row (left to right)*, Kathleen, Harold, W. Crow, B. J. Dyer, Vera; *2nd row*, Charlotte, Mrs Beauchamp, Captain Fishwick, Jeanne, Miss Dyer; Leslie seated in front

2 (b) Katherine, Vera, Charlotte and Belle Dyer at Queen's College, London, c. 1906: *Standing, extreme left*, Katherine; *fourth from left*, Vera; *seated, extreme left*, Charlotte; *second from right*, Belle Dyer

3 (a) Thomas Trowell
in middle age

3 (b) Arnold, Dolly, and Garnet Trowell, Wellington, 1901

4 (a) Arnold Trowell,
Brussels, 1905

4 (b) George Bowden, 1948

5 (a) A. R. Orage, 1928

5 (b) William Orton, c. 1925

6 (a) Anne Estelle Rice, 1919

6 (b) Katherine and Murry, London, 1913

7 The Lawrences:
left, Frieda as a girl;
below, D. H. Lawrence,
1913

8 (a) S.S. Koteliansky
by Mark Gertler

8 (b) Katherine, 1913

about God'.[11] Like Orage, he was a self-made intellectual and a talented editor, who had a crippling strain of mysticism and was clever but not creative.

Katherine agreed with Lawrence and later criticized Murry for his unwillingness to leave his literary career in London and live modestly with her in the Mediterranean until her health improved. As she wrote in her *Scrapbook* in December 1919: 'We were not *pure*. If we had been, he would have faced coming away with me. And that he would not do. He would not have said he was too tired to earn enough to keep us here. He always refused to face what it meant—living alone for two years on not much money.'[12] When poor health forced Katherine to leave England every winter, she found it difficult to bear the solitude during the separation from her husband, although she had temporarily replaced him with Ida Baker.

Murry must have resented the invidious comparison between Lawrence's marriage and his own (a comparison which Lawrence was very fond of making) as well as the attempt to direct his life, and he rejected Lawrence's argument as graciously as possible. Though Lawrence could rarely refrain from giving good, if tactless, advice, he understood Murry's feelings, was grateful for his forbearance, and wrote rather apologetically in April 1914: 'I thought that you and Katherine held me an interfering Sunday-school superintendent sort of person who went too far in his superintending and became impossible: stepped just too far, which is the crime of crimes. And I felt guilty. And I suppose I am guilty. But thanks be to God, one is often guilty without being damned.'[13] Lawrence's 'impossible' interference in their lives frequently went too far and was a major cause of their most bitter quarrels.

Katherine and Murry (who could not marry until 1918) were witnesses at the Lawrences's wedding in July 1914, when Frieda impulsively gave her friend her old wedding ring, which Katherine took to the grave. In October 1914, Katherine and Murry stayed with the Lawrences in Buckinghamshire for two weeks while they prepared Rose Tree Cottage, an hour's walk away. During this stay, Lawrence introduced Katherine to the Russian law clerk and translator, Koteliansky, and began to expound his plans for the island community of Rananim, named after one of Kot's Hebrew psalms. Unlike the passive and dependent Murry,

4

Katherine was too sceptical and individualistic to become a disciple of Lawrence, and she proceeded to deflate his idealistic dreams. Catherine Carswell reports that 'when Katherine, not without realistic mischief, went and obtained a mass of detailed, difficult information about suitable islands, Lawrence fell sadly silent. . . . Hiding her fun behind a solemn face, [Katherine] proved by time-tables and guide-books that Rananim was impossible.'[14] Murry remarks that Katherine 'had, moreover, a lightly mocking but ruthless way of summing up various people over whom [Lawrence] was temporarily enthusiastic, which made him smile rather crookedly. At such a moment he was a little afraid of her'.[15]

Katherine's *Journal* entries for January 1915 suggest the difficulties of living in close proximity with the exciting yet exasperating Lawrences, and the extreme variations of her attitude towards them:

In the evening Lawrence and Koteliansky. They talked plans; but I felt *very* antagonistic to the whole affair. (January 9)

In the morning, Frieda suddenly. She had had a row with Lawrence. She tired me to death. . . . [At night:] L. was very nice, sitting with a piece of string in his hand, on true sex. (January 10)

In the evening we went to the Lawrences'. Frieda was rather nice. (January 15)

Walked to the Lawrences'! They were horrible and witless and dull. (January 16)

Lawrence arrived cross, but gradually worked around to me. (January 19)[16]

After a quarrel with Lawrence about her children a few months after their marriage, Frieda sent Katherine to threaten her husband that she would not come back. ' "Damn the woman," shouted Lawrence in a fury, "tell her I never want to see her again".'[17]

In February 1915, Katherine left Murry for her lover Francis Carco, who resembled Lawrence in his ardent self-confidence and warm, high-spirited life, and was then in the French army near Besançon. The abandoned Murry came to see Lawrence, who had moved to Greatham in Sussex, and during the long walk from the station his cold turned to influenza. Lawrence devoted himself to nursing Murry and enjoyed the opportunity to give strength and comfort to his ailing friend, a gratifying reversal of his weaker and dependent role with Frieda. This episode inspired the passage in *Aaron's Rod* when Lilly nurses the sickly Aaron back to health. Murry's letters about his visit to Lawrence are extremely dull, and if he was not trying to hide his feelings from Katherine, the experience apparently meant much more to Lawrence than to Murry. Lawrence's new bond of intimacy with Murry alienated him from Katherine, who spent most of that spring in France, disillusioned and wounded by the selfishness of Carco and the indifference of Murry. In March Katherine stayed briefly with the Lawrences at Greatham, and in May Lawrence wrote to Kot: 'Does Katherine depress you. Her letters are as jarring as the sound of a saw.'[18]

In September, when Lawrence was living in Hampstead and Katherine and Murry in nearby St. John's Wood, they started a new little magazine, *Signature*. It had a brown cover, octavo format and published Lawrence's 'The Crown' and Katherine's 'The Wind Blows' and 'The Little Governess' as well as a story by Murry. Lawrence recalled that the group held weekly meetings near Red Lion Square 'up a narrow stair-case over a green-grocer's shop. ... We scrubbed the room and colour-washed the walls and got a long table and some windsor chairs from the Caledonian market. And we used to make a good warm fire: it was dark autumn in that unknown bit of London. Then on Thursday nights, we had meetings of about a dozen people'[19] during October and November 1915. *Signature* was printed in the East End by I. Narodiczky, who had a Hebrew sign on his shop front in the Mile End Road, and had printed Isaac Rosenberg's first book of poems in 1912. But the war had a fatal effect on *Signature* which, like the *Blue Review*, died after only three issues. By December Lawrence had revived his plans for Rananim and wrote about his hopes for a harmonious and purposeful life: 'My dear Katherine, you know that in this we are sincere friends, and what we want is to create a new, good, common life, the germ of a new social life together.'[20]

Katherine and Lawrence were drawn together that autumn by a tragic event. Her younger brother, Leslie, had come to England for training in 1915 *en route* from New Zealand to the battlefields of France, and they had spent some happy days together recollecting and idealizing their childhood. In October, a week after Leslie reached the front, he was killed. 'Do not be sad', Lawrence wrote with an optimistic compassion that anticipates his poem, 'The Ship of Death': 'It is one life which is passing away from us, one "I" is dying; but there is another coming into being, which is the happy, creative you. I knew you would have to die with your brother; you also, go down into death and be extinguished. But for us there is a rising from the grave, there is a resurrection, and a clean life to begin from the start, new and happy. Don't be afraid, don't doubt it, it is so. . . . Get better soon and come back, and let us all try to be happy *together*, in unanimity, not in hostility, creating, not destroying.'[21] In an attempt to bring Katherine out of her misery, Lawrence offered his friendship and understanding, and the opportunity to join him in an idealistic and creative community. By contrast Murry (to whom Katherine had returned after her brief affair with Carco) was reduced to insignificance by Katherine's morbid love for her dead brother and felt more cut off from her than ever.

After Leslie's death Katherine and Murry moved to Bandol, near Marseilles, and when Murry saw Lawrence on a brief trip to England, he wrote to Katherine: 'I think that Lawrence was really and truly pleased to see me back again. I feel that he is very fond indeed of you and me—and that he feels that we are the only two people who really care for him in the way he wants to be cared for. Our going away had depressed him very much.'[22]

In February 1916 Lawrence, who was then living in Cornwall, intensified the campaign, begun in Lerici, to get his friends to live with him and wrote to them in the guise of a courting lover: 'I've waited for you for two years now, and am far more constant to you than ever you are to me—or ever will be.'[23] And in March he pleaded: 'Really, you must have the other place. I keep looking at it. I call it already Katherine's house, Katherine's tower. There is something *very* attractive about it. It is very old, native to the earth.'[24] Though Katherine was strongly opposed to Cornwall and distrusted the very idea of a community, Katherine and Murry allowed themselves to be persuaded by Lawrence's desperate pleas: 'No good trying to run away from the fact that we are fond of each other. We count on you two as our only two *tried* friends, real and permanent and truly blood kin.'[25]

Murry gives two different accounts of their departure from

Bandol, where they had spent the happiest months of their lives. In his *Reminiscences of D. H. Lawrence*, Murry suggests that they left France reluctantly: 'The personal appeal was not to be resisted. Without it, I suppose, Katherine Mansfield and I would have stayed where we were, at Bandol.'[26] And in a note to Katherine's letters, written twenty years later, he says with greater accuracy that they were quite willing to return to England and would have left Bandol even if Lawrence had not called them to Cornwall: 'We might have stayed at the Villa Pauline longer than we did: but we knew from the beginning that our felicity must have an end; and when we had finished our respective pieces of writing [Katherine's 'The Aloe' and Murry's *Dostoyevsky*] it did not seem to make much difference whether we anticipated by a month or two the end that was certain.'[27] Katherine, who was dubious about the plan of rejoining the Lawrences after the *débâcle* in Buckinghamshire, wrote an ironic letter to Ottoline Morrell and accurately predicted that their stay would be short: 'We are going to stay with the Lawrences for ever and ever as perhaps you know; I daresay eternity will last the whole summer.'[28]

The Lawrences were overjoyed at their arrival in April. 'I see Katherine Mansfield and Murry arriving sitting on a cart', Frieda later remembered, 'high up on all the goods and chattels, coming down the lane to Tregerthen.'[29] And Lawrence, who loved to do manual work, wrote enthusiastically to Ottoline Morrell: 'The Murrys have come and we are very busy getting their cottage ready: colouring the walls and painting and working furiously. I like it, and we all enjoy ourselves. The Murrys are happy with each other now. But they neither of them seem very well in health.'[30] Though the couples were irresistibly drawn to each other, they could not live together; and their second communal experience, like the first, ended in failure.

Though Lawrence yearned for a starlike 'equilibrium, a pure balance of two single beings', Frieda recognized that what he really wanted was a satellite, a woman submissive to his absolute will. As he later explained to Katherine: 'I do think a woman must yield some sort of precedence to a man, and he must take this precedence. I do think men must go ahead absolutely in front of their women, without turning round to ask for permission or approval from their women. Consequently the women must follow as it were unquestioningly. I can't help it, I believe this. Frieda doesn't. Hence our fight.'[31] Another problem, as Katherine explained to Beatrice Campbell, was Lawrence's obsession with man's animal nature and omnipresent sexual symbolism: 'I cannot discuss blood affinity to beasts for instance if I have to keep ducking to avoid the flatirons and the saucepans. And I shall *never* see sex in trees, sex in the running brooks, sex in stones and sex in everything. The number of things that are really phallic from fountain pen fillers onwards! I suggested to Lawrence that he should call his cottage The Phallus and Frieda thought it was a very good idea.'[32]

Though Lawrence had his own problems with Frieda, he was still highly critical of his friends' relationship and prescribed a radically new foundation for their friendship. As Murry writes in *Between Two Worlds*: 'Lawrence believed, or tried to believe, that the relation between Katherine and me was false and deadly; and that the relation between Frieda and himself was real and life-giving; but that his relation with Frieda needed to be completed by a new relation between himself and me, which I evaded. . . . By virtue of this "mystical" relation with Lawrence, I participate in this pre-mental reality, the "dark sources" of my being come alive. From this changed personality, I, in turn, enter a new relation with Katherine.'[33] The emotional yet abstract language does not explain precisely why Lawrence needed a completion he could not get from Frieda nor how Katherine and Murry recharge themselves on Lawrence's marital battery; but it is not difficult to see how these ideas offended Katherine, who naturally resented Lawrence's assaults on Murry. Their friendship inevitably degenerated as Katherine reacted against Lawrence's powerful influence on Murry and his attempt to revitalize their existence through a passionate attachment to her lover. When Murry turned towards Lawrence, Katherine's unhappy feeling of isolation engulfed her completely. 'I am very much alone here', she wrote to Kot in May 1916, after a few gloomy weeks in Cornwall. 'It is not really a nice place. It is so full of huge stones. . . . I don't belong to anybody here. In fact, I have no being, but I am making preparations for changing everything.'[34]

Katherine's phrase 'ducking the flatirons and saucepans' alludes to the most striking aspect of Lawrence's marriage: his violent battles with Frieda and his humiliating dependence upon her, which astounded and repelled the rather reserved Katherine far more than the bleak and rocky landscape, and soon drove her away. Katherine described her reaction in a letter to Kot: 'I don't know which disgusts me worse, when they are loving and playing with each other, or when they are roaring at each other and he is pulling out Frieda's hair and saying "I'll cut your bloody throat, you bitch".'[35] And she gives a lively and thorough account of one explosion that took place in Cornwall in May 1916:

> Frieda said Shelley's Ode to a Skylark was false. Lawrence said, 'you are showing off; you don't know anything about it.' Then she began. 'Now I have had enough. Out of my house. You little God Almighty you. I've had enough of you. Are you going to keep your mouth shut or aren't you.' Said Lawrence: 'I'll give you a dab on the cheek to quiet you, you dirty hussy.' Etc. Etc. So I left the house. At dinner time Frieda appeared. 'I have finally done with him. It is all over forever.' She then went out of the kitchen & began to walk round and round the house in the dark. Suddenly Lawrence appeared and made a kind of horrible blind rush at her and they began to scream and scuffle. He beat her, he beat her to death, her head and face and breast and pulled at her hair. All the while she screamed for Murry to help her. Finally they dashed into the kitchen and round and round the table. I shall never forget how L. looked. He was so white, almost green and he just hit, thumped the big soft woman. Then he fell into one chair and she into another. No one said a word. A silence fell except for Frieda's sobs and sniffs. In a way I felt almost glad that the tension between them was over for ever, and that they had made an end of their 'intimacy'. L. sat staring at the floor, biting his nails. Frieda sobbed. . . . And the next day, whipped himself, and far more thoroughly than he had ever beaten Frieda, he was running about taking up her breakfast to her bed and trimming her a hat.[36]

Despite the passion and violence, their operatic playlet contains an element of slapstick and self-parody. Act One begins with Lawrence's destruction of Frieda's aesthetic evaluation, leads to her verbal abuse of his assumed omniscience, and ends with his colloquial threat of punishment and Katherine's exit. Act Two opens with Frieda's absolute judgment ('It's all over forever') which is absolutely unconvincing, and leads to her exit and Lawrence's sudden reappearance as an avenging Fury. But the brutality of his attack is alleviated by the burlesque chase around the table and softened by the description of a green Lawrence thumping a pillow-like Frieda. The curtain falls on this act as both protagonists collapse with physical exhaustion, sobbing and biting nails, and as Katherine, acting as Chorus, makes another absolute pronouncement ('the tension was over for ever'). Act Three reveals a comic reversal of sexual roles, with the defeated male aggressor serving and wooing his lady love.

In May, Katherine gave Beatrice Campbell another precise and vivid description of Lawrence's rages, which embroiled her emotions, exhausted her and made it impossible to concentrate and to work: 'Once you start talking, I cannot describe the frenzy that comes over him. He simply *raves*, roars, beats the table, abuses everybody. But that's not such great matter. What makes these attacks insupportable is the feeling one has at the back of one's mind that he is completely out of control, swallowed up in an acute, *insane* irritation. After one of these attacks he's ill with fever, haggard and broken. It is impossible to be anything to him but a kind of playful acquaintance.'[37]

And in a letter to Ottoline Morrell, Katherine emphasizes Lawrence's madness, which could only be controlled by friends or cured by laughter, and blames Frieda, who has him 'completely in her power', for his irrational behaviour: 'Left to himself, Lawrence goes mad. When he is with people he expands to the warmth and the light in them, he is a darling and often very wonderful, but left to himself he is [like Cornwall] cold and dark and desolate. Of course Frieda is at the bottom of it. He has chosen Frieda and when he is with real people he knows how false that choice is. . . . I am *sure* there is only one way to answer him. It is very cruel, but it's the only weapon to prick his sensitive pride. It is to laugh at him, to make fun of him, to make him realize that he has made a fool of himself.'[38] Katherine continues to condemn Frieda in other letters to Ottoline. She portrays Frieda as a German organ-grinder who deifies—without understanding—the Nietzschean influence on Lawrence's ideas, claims that she has swallowed up and defeated Lawrence, and feels absolutely no sympathy for the woman who brutalized and buried him, and then took masochistic pleasure in being beaten:

Sooner or later all Frieda's friends are bound to pop their heads
out of the window and see her grinding it before their door,
smoking a cigarette with one hand on her hip and a coloured
picture of Lorenzo and Nietzsche dancing together 'symbolically' on the front of the barrel organ.[39]

It is really quite over for now, our relationship with L. The
'dear man' in him whom we all loved is hidden away, absorbed,
completely lost, like a little gold ring in that immense German
christmas pudding which is Frieda. . . .
Though I was dreadfully sorry for L. I didn't feel an atom of
sympathy for Frieda. . . .
I think it's horribly tragic, for they have degraded each other
and brutalized each other beyond Words, but, all the same, I
never did imagine anyone to thrive upon a beating as Frieda
seemed to thrive. I shall never be persuaded that she did not
take some Awful Relish in it. . . . Lawrence has definitely
chosen to sin against himself and Frieda is triumphant.[40]

Katherine was frightened by the insane quality of Lawrence's
outbursts, and felt that she had to humour him if she wanted to
avoid the rages that had such a disastrous effect on his health.
Though these eruptions were embarrassing and unpleasant,
Katherine was most disturbed by the fact that they closely
resembled the kind of behaviour she hated and feared in *herself*:
'My fits of temper are really terrifying. I had one this . . . morning
and tore up a page of the book I was reading—and absolutely
lost my head. Very significant. When it was over J[ack] came in
and stared. "What is the matter? What have you done?" "Why?"
"You look *all dark*." He drew back the curtains and called it an
effect of light, but when I came into my studio to dress I saw it
was not that. I was a deep earthy colour, *with pinched eyes*. I was
green. Strangely enough these fits are Lawrence and Frieda all over
again. I am more like L. than anybody. We are *unthinkably* alike,
in fact.'[41]
After Lawrence's violent behaviour with Frieda, attempt to
possess Murry and mad ravings when he screamed at his friend:
'I hate your love, *I hate it*. You're an obscene bug, sucking my life
away',[42] the break between the couples was inevitable. When
Katherine and Murry left, with suitable excuses, at the end of May,
Lawrence wrote defensively to Ottoline Morrell and ironically

4*

suggested the proper setting for their unrealistic child-love: 'Unfortunately the Murrys do not like the country—it is too rocky and bleak for them. They should have a soft valley, with leaves and the ring-dove cooing.'[43] In June, after Lawrence had visited them in Mylor, on the south coast of Cornwall, Katherine spoke of him affectionately to Ottoline: 'Lawrence has gone home again. We walked with him as far as the ferry and away he sailed in a little open boat pulled by an old, old man. Lawrence wore a broad white linen hat and he carried a rucksack on his back.'[44] But in July Lawrence sent Kot his usual depressing diagnosis: 'I think— well, she & Jack are not very happy—they make some sort of contract whereby each of them is free. . . . Really, I think she & Jack have worn out anything that was between them. I like her better than him. He was rather horrid when he was here.'[45] In his autobiography, Murry responds to Lawrence's criticism and quite reasonably states that 'he appeared to think that we, simply because we had nothing to correspond with his intense and agonizing sexual experiences, were flippant about sex. . . . It struck us as quite exorbitant that Katherine should be regarded as a butterfly and I as a child, merely because our sex-relation was exempt from agony.'[46]

Lawrence's friendship and affection for Katherine were justified by a famous incident that took place in the Café Royal in September 1916. Katherine was sitting with Kot and Gertler when she heard the novelist Michael Arlen and composer Philip Heseltine, both of whom had been friendly with Lawrence, maliciously reading and publicly ridiculing his new volume of poems, *Amores*. Though Katherine was still feeling hostile towards Lawrence, she was nevertheless loyal to his work and outraged that it should be mocked by the *canaille*. So she snatched the volume from their hands, bore it triumphantly out of the café and symbolically rescued her friend from their scorn—exactly as Gudrun does in 'Gudrun at the Pompadour', a chapter that was added to *Women in Love* just before Lawrence completed it in November 1916. Katherine also used this incident in her story 'Marriage à la Mode' (1921). When William, the husband whose wife had abandoned him for a corrupt set of 'bohemian' admirers, returns to the city, he sends his wife a love letter to set things right. But Isabel reads it aloud to her friends who mock the letter and become hysterical with laughter.

Murry and Katherine played a significant role in Lawrence's fiction, for the three satiric stories: 'The Border Line' (1924), 'Jimmy and the Desperate Woman' (1924) and 'The Last Laugh' (1928), concern his jealousy and posthumous revenge for Murry's love of Frieda, and 'Smile' (1926) portrays Murry after the death of Katherine, who 'had always wanted her own will. She had loved him, and grown obstinate, and left him, and grown wistful, or contemptuous, or angry a dozen times, and a dozen times come back to him.'[47] Katherine also appears as Anabel Wrath in Lawrence's play *Touch and Go* (1920) and as Gudrun Brangwen in his novel *Women in Love* (1920). Murry states that when he read and reviewed the novel in 1921 he did not see any biographical similarities and 'was really astonished when, one day, Frieda told me that I was Gerald Crich'.[48] Katherine, who shared Murry's hostility and is supposed to have called it a 'filthy rotten book',[49] criticized the element of madness in the novel and denied the biographical resemblances. As she wrote in a letter to Ottoline, who was another victim of Lawrence's fiction and appeared, thinly disguised, as Hermione Roddice: 'It is so absurd that one can't say anything; it after all is almost purely pathological, as they say. But it's sad to think what might have been. Wasn't it Santayana who said: Every artist holds a lunatic in leash. That explains L. to me. You know I am Gudrun? Oh, what rubbish it all is.'[50]

In *Women in Love*, which he wrote while living with Katherine and Murry in 1916, Lawrence uses Katherine as an inspiration rather than as a precise model for Gudrun, expresses his resentment about the failure of their friendship in Buckinghamshire and Cornwall, and triumphs over his friends in the novel in a way that he never did in actual life. Gudrun and Gerald's intense struggle of wills reflects the extreme violence of Lawrence's own marriage, and represents his very subjective conception of Katherine's mistress-love-relationship with Murry: the violent, destructive and disintegrating 'union of ecstasy and death' which provides a powerful contrast to the healthy and vital marriage of Ursula and Birkin.

Gudrun really represents Lawrence's gross exaggeration of the negative aspects of Katherine's character: her self-destructive quest for experience and the bitterness of her *early* work, for she had published only the satiric *In A German Pension* before

Lawrence completed his novel in 1916. Lawrence transforms Katherine's delicate art into attenuated preciosity, her satire into corrosion, her reserve into negation, her detached and determined resistance to his demands into arrogance and insolence, her insecurity and loneliness into infantile dependence, her quest for love into destructive sterility, her restless search for health into a rootless outcast life, her illness into evil.

Katherine makes her last appearance in Lawrence's late story, 'Mother and Daughter' (1929), an allegory of her seduction by the mysticism of George Gurdjieff. Lawrence's characterization of Virginia Bodoin expresses his feelings about Katherine's personality, her work, her relationship with Murry, her disease and her fatal submission to Gurdjieff, which is symbolized by exchanging her deadly existence with her mother for a kind of death-in-life with the horrible yet attractive suitor, Arnault. Lawrence is much more perceptive about and sympathetic to Katherine in this story than in *Women in Love*. After Katherine had died and was no longer a literary rival and disappointing friend, Lawrence came to understand that her unhappy marriage to Murry and her terrible disease made her especially susceptible to Gurdjieff's ideas.

Katherine's gallant gesture at the Café Royal did not prevent relations with Lawrence from deteriorating for the third time—perhaps because Lawrence had found out more about their reasons for leaving Cornwall—and in November he wrote angrily to Kot: 'I have done with the Murries, for ever—so help me God.'[51] In February 1917 Lawrence voiced his first direct, if ambiguous criticism of Katherine and told Kot, who was her staunchest friend and must have resented Lawrence's attack: 'Only for poor Katherine and her lies I feel rather sorry. They are such self-responsible lies.' And he repeated this charge, but much more violently, in a letter to Mary Cannan in February 1921: 'The *Nation* said K's book [*Bliss*] was the best short story book that could be or had been written. Spit on her for me when you see her, she's a liar out and out. . . . Vermin, the pair of 'em. And beware.'[52] Katherine had published only a few stories between 1916 and 1920, and *Bliss* was her first book in nine years and her first important collection. Lawrence's *Rainbow* had been suppressed in 1915 and *Women in Love* (though completed in 1916) was not published until 1920. He thought Katherine had only a minor talent, and must have been angry to see his own novels attacked and delayed while her stories received rave reviews in the leading weeklies.

Catherine Carswell's account of Lawrence's criticism of Katherine's work in 1918 gives some indication of what he meant by her lies: 'It was his opinion that the author of *Prelude* would come in time to find a certain falseness so closely entwined with the charm in her literary fabric that she would herself condemn even the charm and write nothing further until she had disentangled herself from the falseness.'[53] In *Women in Love* Lawrence also condemns Gudrun's criticism of Birkin as a lie: 'Gudrun would draw two lines under him and cross him out like an account that is settled. There he was, summed up, paid for, settled, done with. And it was such a lie. This finality of Gudrun's, this dispatching of people and things in a sentence, it was all such a lie.'[54] Lawrence seems to be suggesting that the 'self-responsible' lies in Katherine's personal life—her 'ruthless mockery', subtle malevolence, cynicism and negativism—were related to the falseness in her art, and that she would have to be more seriously self-critical of her character if she hoped to improve her work.

Katherine agreed with the truth of Lawrence's criticism, for (unbeknown to him) she had recognized the element of falsity in her art and analyzed her faults in a surprisingly similar way. She was aware, for example, of her tendency towards detachment from life and escapism, and wanted to learn to live a far more truthful existence and to establish a deeper contact with people. In December 1919 she compared her own lack of enthusiastic response to experience with Lawrence's vital engagement in life: 'Lawrence wrote from Florence. He said Florence was lovely and full of "extremely nice people". He is able to bear people so easily. Often I long to be more *in life*—to know people—even now the desire comes. But immediately the opportunity comes I think of nothing but how to escape.'[55] Katherine also felt, at the end of her life, that she had to undergo a personal purification and 'cure her soul' before she could clarify and perfect her artistic vision. Though she wrote 'At the Bay', 'The Voyage', 'The Garden Party', and 'The Doll's House' in a feverish burst of creativity between July and December 1921, a fundamental self-distrust made her lose faith in her work and abandon writing in July 1922.

Despite Lawrence's criticism in February 1917, he was

certainly not done with Katherine 'for ever' for he still believed in her fundamental integrity. Their friendship revived once again, in August 1917, when Katherine told Murry: 'I have read a long letter from Lawrence. He has begun to write to me again and in quite the old way. . . . I am so fond of him for many things. I cannot shut my heart against him and I never shall.'[56] In the autumn of 1918, when Lawrence came to London from the Midlands and saw Katherine for the last time, they forgot their quarrels and remembered their love for each other: 'For me, at least, the dove brooded over him, too. I loved him. He was just his old, merry, rich self, laughing, describing things, giving you pictures, full of enthusiasm and joy in a future where we become all "vagabonds"—we simply did not talk about people. We kept to things like nuts and cowslips and fires in woods and his black self *was* not. Oh, there is something so loveable about him and his eagerness, his passionate eagerness for life—that is what one loves so.'[57]

The following month, Lawrence sent Katherine a book by Jung and analysed their marriages in terms of its mother-incest idea: 'At certain periods a man has a desire and a tendency to return into the woman, make her his goal and end, find his justification in her. In this way he casts himself as it were into her womb, and she, the Magna Mater, receives him with gratification. This is a kind of incest. It seems to me it is what Jack does to you, and what repels and fascinates you. I have done it, and now struggle all my might to get out.'[58] Lawrence recognized that Katherine was both repelled and fascinated by Murry's passive dependence and sentimental idealization of her because he himself had some of Murry's tendencies. But he could not resist the temptation to exalt his own marriage at Murry's expense. Lawrence, who shared Katherine's bravery and was stoic about his disease, later condemned Murry's cowardice and self-pity, which had caused Katherine so much anguish. As he wrote to Dorothy Brett in March 1926: 'The greatest virtue in life is real courage, that knows how to face facts and live beyond them. Don't be Murryish, pitying yourself and caving in. It's despicable. . . . I do loathe cowardice, and sloppy emotions. My God, did you learn *nothing* from Murry, of how NOT to behave.'[59]

In January 1919 Murry became the editor of the *Athenaeum* and loyally asked Lawrence to write for the magazine. But he was very nervous about the vitriolic prose of Lawrence, who was angry at England and likely to shock Murry's respectable readers. Murry published Lawrence's first article under a pseudonym, but when he rejected Lawrence's 'embittered and angry' essay 'Adolf' in March, Lawrence became doubly angry and embittered. In April Katherine attempted to make a joke of the quarrel and told Kot: 'F[rieda] writes me that there is a "rumpus" between me and—them, I suppose. . . . But I refuse to have anything to do with it. I have not the room now-a-days for rumpuses.'[60]

Writing to Katherine from Derbyshire in March 1919, Lawrence returned to the marriage theme, realized that he had often offended her, reaffirmed his belief that some day they would all be harmoniously united, stated that the stormy months in Cornwall had brought him *closer* to her and illustrated this by means of a dream-parable:

Frieda said you were cross with me, that I *repulsed* you. I'm sure I didn't. The complication of getting Jack and you and F. and me into a square seems great—especially Jack. But you I am sure of—I was ever since Cornwall, save for Jack—and if you must go his way, and if he will *never* really come our way—well! But things will resolve themselves.

I dreamed such a vivid little dream of you last night. I dreamed you came to Cromford, and stayed there. You were not coming on here because you weren't well enough. You were quite clear from the consumption—quite, you told me. But there was still something that made you that you couldn't come up the hill here.[61]

Katherine, who had her first hemorrhage in February 1918, was warned in October that she would die in a few years if she did not submit to the discipline of a sanatorium. In Lawrence's dream she is cured of consumption, but is not well enough to come up the hill to him. They do meet, however, go outside together to look at the brilliant sky, and are momentarily 'pierced' and 'possessed' by a 'star that blazed for a second on one's soul'. The blazing star unifies their souls in a moment of epiphany that transcends the common battle of their bodies against consumption. Two weeks before Lawrence told Katherine his encouraging dream he wrote sympathetically to Kot: 'Poor Katherine—I'm afraid she is only just on the verge of existence.'[62]

In December 1919 Katherine's life was seriously undermined by the gravest crisis of her marriage. Katherine, who was ill and living unhappily with Ida Baker in Ospedaletti, sent Murry a desperate plea for security and love. When he responded with selfish indifference, she sent him her most moving poem, 'The New Husband', in which she portrays herself as a helpless child abandoned by her husband and 'rescued' by death. When Lawrence sent his cruel letter to Katherine in February 1920, she was still separated from Murry, living in a clinic in Menton, in extremely bad health, and emotionally dependent on letters from her husband and friends. On February 4 she recorded in her *Journal*: 'Horrible day. I lay all day and *half* slept in this new way—hearing voices', and the following day she noted: 'Couldn't work: slept again. Dreadful pain in joints. Fearfully *noisy* house!'[63] In February 1920 Lawrence was living in Capri near Compton Mackenzie and Norman Douglas, embroiled in the unsavoury affairs of the journalist and swindler, Maurice Magnus, and very much the 'black self' that Katherine so dreaded. On February 5 Lawrence wrote to Catherine Carswell: 'I am very sick of Capri: it is a stewpot of semi-literary cats. . . . I can't stand this island. I shall have to risk expense and everything and clear out: to Sicily, I think.'[64] In early February, then, Katherine was extremely vulnerable and Lawrence extremely angry.

On about February 7 Katherine, deeply wounded and embittered about the betrayal of their friendship, complained to Murry: 'Lawrence sent me a letter today. He spat in my face and threw filth at me and said: "I loathe you. You revolt me stewing in your consumption. . . . The Italians were quite right to have nothing to do with you" and a great deal more.'[65] According to Murry, Lawrence also said: 'You are a loathsome reptile—I hope you will die.'[66] On February 10 Katherine, who was horrified by Lawrence's allusion to the fact that she had recently been forced to leave a hotel in San Remo because of her disease, told Murry: 'I wrote to Lawrence: "I detest you for having dragged this disgusting reptile across all that has been." When I got his letter I *saw* a reptile, *felt* a reptile—and the desire to hit him was so dreadful that I knew if I ever met him I must go away *at once*. I could not be in the same room or house, he is somehow filthy. I never had such a feeling about a human being.'[67] Murry told Lawrence that 'he had committed the unforgivable crime', and wrote to Katherine with unusual ferocity: 'may God do so unto me & more also if I ever enter into any communication whatever with him. If I ever see him, no matter when or where, the first thing I shall do is to hit him as hard as I can across the mouth.'[68] But Katherine doubted Murry's adamancy and asked him at the end of March: 'Will you one day forget and forgive Lawrence— smile—give him your hand?'[69]

E. M. Forster, who speaks with the authority of a victim, asserts, 'There is a vein of cruelty' in Lawrence.[70] But F. R. Leavis, who is blind to Lawrence's faults, attempts to justify and excuse Lawrence's violent letter to Katherine and states that it 'was no more to be called "cruel" than medicine would be. Lawrence's genius manifested itself in *sympathetic* insight and an accompanying diagnostic intelligence, and cruelty was not in him.'[71] But it is far more useful to explain than to excuse the motives behind Lawrence's terrible letter, which are intimately connected with the fact that he refused to recognize his own disease and saw Katherine, as his dream suggests, 'clear from the consumption'.

In January 1930, Dr. Andrew Morland, the tuberculosis specialist who came from London to Bandol to examine Lawrence, stated he 'had obviously been suffering from pulmonary tuberculosis for a very long time—probably 10 or 15 years.'[72] After Lawrence's death Huxley said that for the last two years of his life Lawrence had been like a flame that miraculously burned on though it had no fuel to feed it. Lawrence admitted that he was seedy, sick, inflamed; had colds, coughs and bronchitis; and defensively joked about his death. But he would never admit that he had tuberculosis—even after his near fatal hemorrhage in Mexico in 1925—and would never allow himself to be treated for the disease until the very end of his life in Vence. Despite his disease, he restlessly drove himself about the world and, like Katherine, would never enter a soul-destroying clinic.

In 1920 Lawrence was not, like Katherine, in the terminal phase of tuberculosis, and he never really believed in her illness any more than he did in his own. He preferred to ignore the disease and pretend it would go away, and (as Huxley suggests) his amazing vitality allowed him to do so for many years. But by 1920 Katherine had admitted her tuberculosis and feared she might die: 'Life is—getting a new breath. Nothing else counts.'[73]

Lawrence felt threatened by Katherine's admission and terrified that the same thing would happen to him (just as Katherine had been terrified by Lawrence's 'black rages'), and he irrationally lashed out at what he considered to be Katherine's weakness. His savage remark about Katherine was really about himself.

In March 1921, a year after this letter, Lawrence again refused to face the reality of Katherine's disease, characterized her as a hypocritical Camille and told Kot: 'I hear [Murry] is—or was—on the Riviera with K.—who is doing the last-gasp touch, in order to impose on people—on Mary Cannan, that is.'[74] And in November he wrote, 'I see Murry and the long-dying blossom Katherine have put forth new literary buds. Let 'em.'[75] It is ironic that at the end of her life, after many unsuccessful medical treatments, Katherine (like Lawrence) turned away from the reality of her grave disease and assumed it was non-existent. Neither Lawrence nor Katherine could give up freedom and endure (as she wrote) 'being alone, cut off, ill with the other ill'.[76] This tragic refusal to submit to the regime of a sanatorium obviously hastened their deaths.

Katherine and Lawrence did not meet again after the autumn of 1918, but his novels continued to evoke a powerful response in her. Katherine intended to review *The Lost Girl* for Murry's *Athenaeum* in December 1920, and when she became too ill to do so she sent Murry her notes on the novel:

> Lawrence denies his humanity. He denies the powers of the Imagination. He denies Life—I mean *human* life. His hero and heroine are non-human. They are animals on the prowl. . . . They submit to the physical response and for the rest go veiled —blind—*faceless*—*mindless*. This is the doctrine of mindless-ness. . . .
>
> Take the rotten rubbishy scene of the woman in labour asking the Italian into her bedroom. All false. All a pack of lies! . . .
>
> Don't forget where Alvina feels 'a trill in her bowels' and discovers herself with child. A TRILL—What does that mean? And why is it so peculiarly offensive from a man? Because it is *not on this* plane that the emotions of others are conveyed to our imagination. It's a kind of sinning against art.[77]

Though Katherine had formerly praised Lawrence's vital response to life, she now felt he denied life and had descended into mindless animalism. Katherine, who had portrayed the gruesome details of childbirth in her *German Pension* stories, had been through a miscarriage and an abortion that prevented her from having the children she so desperately wanted. She therefore had little tolerance for Lawrence's male ignorance, and condemned as false the description of Mrs. Tuke in labour and of Alvina's discovery that she is pregnant.

Katherine also criticized Lawrence's concept of love in a letter to Dorothy Brett in August 1921: 'What makes Lawrence a *real* writer is his passion. Without passion one writes in the air or on the sand of the seashore. But L. has got it all wrong, I believe. . . . It's my belief that nothing will save the world but love. But his tortured, satanic demon love I think is all wrong.'[78] She alludes to Keats's ironic epigraph—'Here lies one whose name was writ in water'—and praises Lawrence's passion. But Katherine—who had rarely slept with Murry since her hemorrhage in February 1918—rejects Lawrence's demonic physical love. In October 1921 she again praised Lawrence's vitality and responsiveness: 'I thought Lawrence was good this month, so warm, so living. In spite of everything Lawrence's feeling for life is there.'[79]

As the years passed and Katherine mellowed she forgot the old quarrels with Lawrence, recalled only the pleasant memories and was even inclined to forgive the Teutonic lamentations of Frieda. In December 1921 she remembered a Christmas party of 1914 in a letter to Kot: 'Wasn't Lawrence awfully nice that night? Ah, one must always *love* Lawrence for his "being". I could love Frieda too, tonight, in her Bavarian dress, with her face flushed as though she had been crying about the "child*er*en". It is a pity that all things must pass. And how strange it is, how in spite of everything there are certain people, like Lawrence, who remain in one's life forever, and others who are forever shadowy.'[80]

In August 1922 Katherine read *Aaron's Rod*, found it honest and convincing, admired Lawrence's maturity and integrity, and told Ottoline: 'I did feel there was growth in Aaron's Rod— there was no desire to please or placate the public. I did feel that Lorenzo was profoundly moved. Because of this perhaps I forgive him too much his [personal] faults.'[81] And Katherine's final judgment of Lawrence was positive: 'He is the only living writer whom I really profoundly care for,' she wrote to Kot in

July 1922. 'It seems to me whatever he writes, no matter how much one may "disagree", is important. And after all even what one objects to is a *sign of life* in him. He is a living man.'[82]

In August 1922 she also emphasized their intuitive understanding despite some differences in their ideas: 'I do not go all the way with Lawrence. His ideas of sex mean nothing to me. But I feel nearer L. than anyone else. All these last months I have thought as he does about many things.'[83] The influence of his beliefs is apparent in Katherine's journal and letters of 1921 and 1922, where many of the entries sound more like Lawrence than Katherine; Lawrence, with Murry, Orage and Gurdjieff, had the strongest contemporary influence on her ideas.

One passage from Katherine's journal of August 1921 reflects Lawrence's belief that the complementary union of masculine and feminine elements represents a return to an original wholeness that unifies man and woman in marriage: 'We are neither male nor female. We are a compound of both. I choose the male who will develop and expand the male in me; he chooses me to expand the female in him. Being made "whole".'[84] A second passage, from Katherine's letter to Murry in January 1922, quotes Lawrence's concept of friendship, which he felt was as solemn as marriage. Though Katherine found this idea fanatical when Lawrence expounded it, first in Cornwall and then in a letter of November 1918, she now recognized the importance of Lawrence's belief and thought it much more convincing: 'I remember once talking it over with Lawrence and he said "We must swear a solemn pact of friendship. Friendship is as binding, as solemn as marriage. We take each other for life, through everything—for ever. But it's not enough to say we will do it. We must *swear*". At the time I was impatient with him. I thought it extravagant—fanatic. But when one considers what this world is like I understand perfectly why L. (especially being L.) made such claims.'[85] In a third passage, written in December 1922, Katherine explains her mystical reaction against intellectual life in purely Lawrentian terms: 'I can see no hope of escape except by learning to live in our emotional and instinctual being as well, and to balance all there.'[86]

The final phase of Lawrence and Katherine's friendship took place in the spring and summer of 1922 when he travelled to Australia and New Zealand and in May told Kot: 'If you were here you would understand Katherine so much better. She is *very* Australian! or New Zealand. Wonder how she is.'[87] Katherine realized that Lawrence's rather frenetic travels were very like her own and closely related to his disease. As she told Kot, who rarely left London, in August: 'It is a pity that Lawrence is driven so far. I am sure that Western Australia will not help. The desire to travel is a great, real temptation. But does it do any good? It seems to me to correspond to the feelings of a sick man who thinks always "if only I can get away from here I shall be better".'[88] That same month Katherine left Lawrence a book in her will, as a token of remembrance, forgiveness and love; and Lawrence, who had not communicated with her since the cruel letter of February 1920, pleased her very much by sending a postcard from Wellington with just one word: '*Ricordi*'. 'Yes, I care for Lawrence', Katherine told Murry in October. 'I have thought of writing to him and trying to arrange a meeting after I leave Paris—suggesting that I join them until the spring.'[89] And the following month, when the Lawrences had settled in New Mexico, she asked Murry: 'Do you ever feel inclined to get in touch with Lawrence again, I wonder? I should very much like to know what he intends to do—how he intends to live now his *Wanderjahre* are over.'[90]

But Katherine's desperate wanderings ended seven years before Lawrence's. When in February 1923 they heard of her death, Frieda told Adele Seltzer: 'It grieved us both deeply— She was such an exquisite creature and we had real fun with them'[91] and Lawrence wrote Murry one of his most moving letters, which recalls the letter to Katherine on the death of her brother: 'Yes, it is something gone out of our lives. We thought of her, I can tell you, at Wellington. Did Ottoline ever send on the card to Katherine posted from there for her? Yes, I always knew a bond in my heart. Feel a fear where the bond is broken now. Feel as if the old moorings were breaking all. . . . I asked Seltzer [his publisher] to send you *Fantasia of the Unconscious*. I wanted Katherine to read it. She'll know, though. The dead don't die. They look on and help.'[92]

In the autumn of 1923, a few months after Katherine's death, Frieda quarrelled with Lawrence, left America without him and, after being rejected by her children, turned to Murry, who was the most serious threat to the Lawrences's marriage—both in 1916 when Lawrence was attracted to him and in 1923 when Frieda was. Murry writes that Frieda arrived in England completely out of love with her husband: 'She had had enough of Lawrence in his Mexican "moods", and in fact she had left him. She felt—rightly enough—no more loyalty to him.' Since Katherine had died and Lawrence was in America, Frieda and Murry decided to travel to Germany together. According to Murry: 'On the journey, we declared our love to each other. She was sweet and lovely, altogether adorable, and she wanted us to stay together in Freiburg for a few days anyhow, and I wanted it terribly. The idea of our sleeping together, waking in each other's arms, seemed like heaven on earth. I was worn out with the long strain of Katherine's illness, and Frieda's love was the promise of renewal. And Lawrence had been horrible to her in Mexico—something really had snapped between them. So I felt free to take Frieda, or thought I did; but when it came to the point, I didn't. . . . "No, my darling, I mustn't let Lorenzo down—I can't".'[93] The loyalty of Murry (who did not live with Katherine during the last six months of her life) seems unconvincing, for in his confusion of grief and love it is doubtful that he could have resisted the desires of the impulsive aristocrat. Murry probably slept with Frieda but did not take her away from Lawrence.

In March 1929 chance brought the seriously ill Lawrence to the Hôtel Beau Rivage in Bandol, where Katherine had had her first hemorrhage in 1918. ('How I *loathe* hotels,' she once wrote. 'I know I shall die in one.'[94]) As usual, Lawrence kept up a brave front, tried to disguise the gravity of his illness and felt a certain morbid comfort from the association with Katherine. As he told Murry: 'I'm pretty well, but a scratchy chest and cough as ever—sickening—but pretty well in spite of it all. I believe Katherine once stayed here, so perhaps you know the place.'[95] Frieda relates that in July 1927, when Lawrence had his second hemorrhage: 'He called from his room in a strange, gurgling voice; I ran and found him lying on his bed; he looked at me with shocked eyes while a slow stream of blood came from his mouth.'[96] Lawrence survived that hemorrhage and lived for nearly three more years, but in March 1930 he finally succumbed to the same disease that had killed Katherine.

CHAPTER EIGHT

Koteliansky and Carco, 1913–1915

LAWRENCE'S SEVERE but just criticism characterized Murry's chaotic, itinerant and impoverished life with Katherine from the time they left Cholesbury in July 1913 until she returned to him after two visits to Paris in May 1915: 'You don't know what you are. You've never come to it. You've always been dodging round, getting *Rhythms* and flats and doing criticism for money.'[1] During these two years of emotional and artistic frustration Katherine met S. S. Koteliansky, experienced her first serious crisis with Murry and had a brief affair with the French writer, Francis Carco.

When the *Blue Review* came to a depressing end after only three issues, they gave up the gloomy flat in Chancery Lane and the cottage at Cholesbury, with its muddy path to the outside lavatory and its blocked sink that reduced Katherine to tears. In July 1913 they moved into a small but comfortable flat, with communal gardens and tennis courts at the back, at 8 Chaucer Mansions, Barons Court, off the Cromwell Road. Murry, as usual, took the best room for his own study, and began to earn a decent income by reviewing. They planned to save money and then live abroad, as the Lawrences had done.

The following month Katherine and Murry visited the Campbells at their summer cottage on the Hill of Howth outside Dublin, and went swimming, sailing, fishing and kite-flying. Katherine persuaded Ida Baker to come with them and take a room at a private house so that they could meet every day for a walk and a talk. When Beatrice Campbell saw Ida and invited her to stay with them, Katherine insisted that Ida would 'hate it'. She preferred to keep her companion separate from her other friends.

In December 1913, a year after their visit to Anne Rice's Christmas party in Montparnasse, Katherine and Murry raised a bit more money by selling their piano and paid £25 to send the rest of their furniture to Paris. After a few days in a modest hotel in the Rue Gay-Lussac, they found a flat at 31 Rue de Tournon in a shabby building with a cobblestone courtyard near the Place de l'Odéon and the Luxembourg Gardens. They explored the dance halls and night clubs of the city with Murry's friend, Francis Carco, who sometimes kept them out until dawn; late one night at the Café Weber they caught a glimpse of the pallid, shadowy figure of Marcel Proust.

Katherine, who had ordered Ida to accompany her to Ireland, was now glad to free herself from the emotional burden of her friend: 'The strongest reason for my happiness in Paris was that I was safe from her.'² Katherine wrote 'Something Childish But Very Natural' in Paris, but Murry's plan to review French books for the *TLS* and the *Westminster Gazette* was a total failure, and his income suddenly fell from twelve pounds to thirty shillings a week. Since they had almost no money to live on they stopped paying Katherine's allowance to the printers. Murry was forced to declare himself bankrupt, and remained insolvent until 1921. Just before their ignominious return to London in February 1914, the fastidious Katherine, who had been used to luxury for most of her life, complained to Ida about their squalid existence: 'Yes, I *am* tired, my dear, a little,—but it's mostly mental. I'm tired of this disgusting atmosphere of eating hard-boiled eggs out of my hands and drinking milk out of a bottle.'³ Since they could not afford to send their furniture back to London, Carco (in return for an English armchair he coveted) sold it to various brothels for less than £10. Katherine also asked Ida to send £5 and since the money could not be insured, Ida tore the notes in half and mailed them in separate envelopes. When the letters arrived by different posts and the desperate Katherine received the torn halves, she thought Ida had gone completely mad.

When Katherine and Murry returned to London in March they borrowed money from Gordon Campbell and a furnished flat from Richard Curle (a contributor to *Rhythm*) in Beaufort Mansions, Chelsea, which had a view of a timber yard and a cemetery. That same month Murry became the art critic of the *Westminster Gazette*, they found another cheap but grim two-and-a-half room flat at 102 Edith Grove, off the Fulham Road in Chelsea, and grandly furnished it with two chairs, two tables and a mattress on the floor. Both Katherine and Murry became seriously ill with pleurisy, and when the Lawrences visited them in July Katherine again confessed 'how much she detested the dirty stair-case, the common w.c., the smell of unwashed socks and cabbage-water that clung perpetually about the dark unvarnished hall'.[4]

In July, when Katherine could no longer bear the smells, they were delighted to find two attic rooms and a kitchen in the top half of a charming house in Arthur Street (now Dovehouse Street), Chelsea, which had a fine tree in the back garden. But they were immediately besieged by armies of ferocious bugs, and though Katherine bravely suggested: 'let's imagine that we are Russians', they were soon driven out. When World War I broke out in August, Murry, seized with patriotic fervour, im-mediately enlisted with Hugh Kingsmill in a cycle battalion, but he was promptly rejected by a medical officer who thought his pleurisy might be tuberculosis. Shortly after the war began, two publishers made attractive offers for the right to reprint *In A German Pension*, but though desperately poor, Katherine refused the money because she thought the book immature and was unwilling to profit by the current hatred of Germany.

In September, weary of city life, Katherine and Murry took a brief recuperative holiday in a cottage at St. Merryn, near Padstow, on the north coast of Cornwall; and then retreated to the country village of Udimore near Rye and lived in a rather primitive wooden shack which would be uninhabitable in the winter. At the end of October, when the temperature began to drop, they moved to Rose Tree Cottage, at The Lee, near Great Missenden in Buckinghamshire, three miles from the Lawrences's cottage at Chesham and the Cannans's house at Cholesbury. But the cottage, like the flats, was small, ugly and cold. The squalor once again made Katherine miserable, and when the roof leaked and every-thing became damp she suffered from fibrositis, arthritis and rheumatism, which may have been symptoms of gonorrhea.

Katherine and Murry saw the Lawrences, who helped them clean and paint the cottage, nearly every day. They sang folk songs, dreamed of Lawrence's ideal community, Rananim, and witnessed their friends' ferocious quarrels. They were caught up in the Lawrences's emotions and tried to find a way to make peace without taking sides or expressing their own feelings. But they were not always able to do this, and in May 1915 Katherine, who sympathized with Lawrence, wrote bitterly to Murry about

Frieda, wished she were dead, and said that Lawrence was nearly blind to her faults.[5]

Katherine escaped to London whenever she could and saw Ida, the Dreys and the Campbells. During a shopping expedition with Katherine, who could not afford the clothes she wanted, Beatrice Campbell was shocked by her friend's eccentric behaviour: 'One day in some big store [Katherine] tried on about a dozen blouses; it went on and on for so long that she finally became exhausted, so did the shop-assistant. . . . Suddenly I heard her make a decision and give a completely fictitious name and address for it to be sent, saying it would be paid for on delivery. . . . She said, "I couldn't think of any other way of getting out of that shop. We might have been there for ever".'[6]

In October 1914, at the Lawrences's cottage in Chesham, Katherine met Samuel Solomonovich Koteliansky, who was immediately attracted to the unconventional side of her character. Kot, a Russian Jew, was born in the Ukraine in 1882, and after enduring years of poverty, persecution and pogroms, came to England on a scholarship from the University of Kiev in 1911, and stayed for the rest of his life. In 1914 Kot was working at the Russian Law Bureau, a pretentious name for a law office run by his compatriot R. S. Slatkowsky at 212 High Holborn. The hideous office, where Katherine like to smoke handrolled cigarettes and drink Russian tea in glasses, was dark, filled with dreary furniture, and incongruously decorated with pictures of kittens playing in a basket of flowers and Christ surrounded by little children. Despite Mark Gertler's claim that Kot's job was 'to black his boss's beard', he actually worked as a secretary and translator.

Gertler's portrait of Kot, painted in 1917, captures his unusual combination of hieratic integrity, moral authority and gentle benevolence. Murry writes that Kot 'looked like some Assyrian king . . . with an impressive hooked Semitic nose, a fine head of coarse curly black hair, and massive features: very dark eyes with pince-nez.'[7] Dorothy Brett remembers him as 'so broad-shouldered that he looks short, his black hair brushed straight up "en brosse", his dark eyes set perhaps a trifle too close to his nose, the nose a delicate well-made arch, gold eye-glasses pinched on to it. He has an air of distinction, of power, and also a tremendous capacity for fun and enjoyment.'[8]

Kot's friend Leonard Woolf provides the most thorough perceptive description of him:

In 1914 he met D. H. Lawrence on a walking tour in the Lakes and they took to each other at once. Kot's passionate approval of what he thought good, particularly in people; his intense hatred of what he thought bad; the directness and vehemence of his speech; his inability to tell a lie—all this strongly appealed to Lawrence. When Kot approved of anyone, he accepted him absolutely; he could do no wrong and Kot summed it up always by saying of him: 'He is a real person.' . . . Lawrence liked this kind of thing in Kot, just as he liked Kot's ruthless condemnation of people like Murry. . . .

If you knew Kot well, you knew what a major Hebrew prophet must have been like 3,000 years ago. If Jeremiah had been born in a ghetto village in the Ukraine in 1882, he would have been Kot.[9]

Woolf said Kot's vehement denunciation: 'It is hor-r-r-ible' was like the roll of thunder on Mount Sinai, and Katherine liked to quote Kot's dreadful promise to deal with irritating people by 'beating them simply, but to death'. Kot, who later became a reader for the Cresset Press and worked on the *Adelphi* under Murry, would say in a deep voice, 'All men are scoundrels, but Murry is a great scoundrel.' Kot loved to give Katherine cigarettes, chocolates, cakes and embroidered Russian shirts with high collars, and to perform his impressive trick of howling like a dog; his melancholy howl was so penetrating and convincing that real dogs howled back from far away. Katherine respected and trusted him absolutely. 'Yes, Koteliansky, you are really one of my people', she wrote in March 1915, '—we can afford to be quite free with each other—I know.'[10] Kot, who thought Katherine was 'a real person' and fell in love with her, told Ruth Mantz: 'If Kat'run ever wanted a greater relationship with me, she had only to indicate it.'[11] Kot moved into Katherine's Acacia Road house when she left for Bandol in November 1915, and lived there until his death in 1955.

Kot collaborated on superb translations of Tolstoy, Dostoyevsky, Chekhov, Gorky, and Bunin with Katherine, Lawrence, Murry, Cannan and the Woolfs. He first made a literal translation into his own picturesque English, and Katherine then corrected, polished and perfected his prose. They translated Chekhov's letters and diary (published in the *Athenaeum* in 1919–1920), Gorky's *Reminiscences of Leonid Andreyev* (published in the *Adelphi* and the *Dial* in 1924, and as a book in 1928), and Dostoyevsky's letters to his wife (which Murry completed and published as a book in 1923 without acknowledging Katherine's work).

Though Kot provided a soothing and stabilizing influence, illness, poverty, squalor, emotional upheavals and artistic frustration intensified Katherine and Murry's first emotional crisis in December 1914. During a lively Christmas party at Gilbert Cannan's Mill House the guests performed a play that dramatized the difficulties of Katherine and Murry. The handsome, vital and talented Mark Gertler was cast as Murry's rival, and when they reached the moment when Katherine was supposed to leave Gertler and return to Murry (who played himself with grim conviction), she refused to follow the script and remained with Gertler. As the painter wrote, with some exaggeration, to Lytton Strachey and to Dora Carrington: 'I got so drunk that I made violent love to Katherine Mansfield! She returned it, also being drunk. I ended the evening by weeping at having kissed another man's woman and everybody trying to console me. . . . No one knew whether to take it as a joke or scandal.'[12]

Their essential problem was that Katherine felt Murry did not love her—or did not love her enough—so she made love to Gertler as she would soon do with Carco. The more love Katherine demanded, the less Murry gave, and tormented by his self-consciousness and self-distrust, he felt the need to withdraw into a protective 'citadel of the soul'. Late in 1914 Katherine, who overheard his conversation, expressed her resentment of Murry's selfishness and her habitual submission to *his* needs rather than to her own: 'One night when Jack was with [his Oxford friend Frederick] Goodyear and I had gone to bed, he said that what he really wanted was a woman who would keep him—yes, that's what he really wanted. And then again, so much later, with Campbell, he said I was the one who submitted. Yes, I gave way to him and still do—but then I did it because I did not feel the urgency of my own desires. Now I do and though I submit from habit now it is always under a sort of protest which I call an *adieu* submission. It always *may* be the last time.'[13]

Murry also antagonized Katherine by indulging his 'queer kind of intellectual sensationalism' during endless, egoistic conversations with Gordon Campbell. Lawrence actually told Murry that Katherine had gone away because his friendship with Campbell made him 'unaware' of her and 'left her out in the cold'; and in March 1915 Katherine wrote to Murry from Paris: 'I hope C[ampbell] was decent. I feel that I dislike him utterly—that he is a fool and no end of a beggar.'[14]

On December 18, 1914, Katherine recorded that Murry had rather brutally stated she was 'hardly anything except a gratification and a comfort',[15] and he admitted: 'I did not need Katherine in the way she then believed she required to be needed.'[16] Though Katherine was at least a 'gratification' to Murry, he did not satisfy her. She was an emotional woman who had had a number of affairs before she met Murry and he was a rather inept lover who did not fully recognize her sexual needs. A passage omitted from her journal of 1916, which recalls her adolescent confessions, reveals that her passionate longings distracted her thoughts and interfered with her work: 'My head is full of only one thing. I can't begin writing or even thinking because all my thoughts revolve around le seul sujet. It is a real vice avec moi au présent. I keep thinking round and round it, beating up and down it and still it stays in my head and won't let me be.'[17] In January 1915 Katherine dreamed of Carco while in bed with Murry, and wrote in her Journal: 'I deliberately drugged myself with Jack and made it more bearable by talking French. . . . I feel I betrayed F[rancis] and slept hardly at all.'[18] As Murry later explained: 'She wanted me to remain an innocent lover: and then she got bored with me for being an unexciting one. Hence her stupid and deeply disappointing affair with Carco.'[19] By February 1915 Katherine felt that Murry was freezing the warm life in her, and turned away from him. She wanted money, luxury, adventure and the excitement of a city, and thought her three years with Murry had been merely a charming but irrelevant idyll.

Francis Carco (1886–1958), the son of Corsican parents, was born Carcopino-Tusoli on the French Pacific island of New Caledonia. He was a popular poet and novelist who wrote about the bohemians and criminals of Montmartre, and published his first novel, Jésus-la-Caille in 1914. Murry had met Carco during

his student days in Paris in December 1910, and introduced him
to Katherine during their brief, disastrous stay in that city in the
winter of 1913. In Katherine's story, 'Je ne parle pas français'
(1919), Raoul Duquette (Carco) smugly describes himself as
fleshy and epicene: 'I am little and light with an olive skin, black
eyes with long lashes, black silky hair cut short, tiny square teeth
that show when I smile. My hands are supple and small. . . . I
confess, without my clothes I am rather charming. Plump,
almost like a girl, with smooth shoulders, and I wear a thin gold
bracelet above my left elbow.'[20]

Though Carco was ugly and had a sinister character, Katherine
was nevertheless attracted to his confidence, vitality and sensuality: 'he is so rich and so careless—*that* I love.' Frieda Lawrence
felt Katherine was attracted to peculiar men and had odd attach-
ments; Anne Rice thought Carco was repulsive and could never
understand why Katherine wanted to sleep with him.[21] But Carco
reminded her of Gaudier, Gertler and Lawrence, and provided a
powerful contrast to the handsome but priggish Murry. Katherine
carried on a highly charged correspondence with Carco during
the winter of 1914 when she was desperately unhappy with
Murry, who refused to take his rival seriously. Carco had joined
the French army when war broke out and wrote Katherine
passionate letters from Gray, between Dijon and Besançon, where
he was living in barracks, drinking heavily and serving ignobly as
postman in a bakery unit. In December he warned Katherine that
he might soon be sent to the front, declared his love, urged her to
visit him and wrote a stream of letters filled with the kind of
flattering Gallic banalities that Katherine wanted to hear. Carco
claimed that he loves her more each day, that as he falls asleep and
takes her in his arms he feels a terrible sadness, that he wants only
her, and that she is and will be his entire life: 'He said "Je vous
aime chaque jour davantage"; and he told me that all the while
we had been in Paris he had loved me. Well, he thinks so, *now*.
And that he would like to live in a little hut on the edge of the
world, where no one would ever come, and that at times now he
has merely an awful sensation of emptiness. He would like to lie
in the road and let the world pass over him "et quand je m'endors,
je vous prends dans mes bras—et j'éprouve une tristesse affreuse"
—and ever so much more. . . . "Chère Katherine, je ne veux que
vous. Vous êtes et vous serez toute ma vie".'[22]

When Katherine's brother Leslie arrived in London to join a
British regiment, he gave her the money to go to Carco. Murry,
who knew that Carco was untrustworthy and was shocked by her
infatuation, remained passive and did not protest, and on
February 16, 1915 she made her way to Paris and into the war
zone, where women were forbidden. Frieda Lawrence over-
simplified matters when she later told Murry: 'Katherine went to
Carco because he had told her: "*Ah, Madame, vous devrez être au
soleil*", that's how it began'²³—for there was very little sun in
south-eastern France in February 1915. Katherine's motives for
leaving Murry were really quite complex. She wanted to have an
adventure, find sexual satisfaction, achieve artistic inspiration,
assert her independence, provoke Murry, draw him away from
Campbell and Lawrence, and test his love.

Katherine's expedition to France was very characteristic, for it
revealed her impulsiveness, passion, courage and willingness to
take chances for the sake of 'experience'. She had no assurance
that she would reach Carco, for the risk of being turned back
was considerable, and no guarantee that she would be anything
except 'a gratification and a comfort' to the sexually starved
soldier. Beatrice Campbell reports that Katherine's incredibly
naive 'plan to get permission to visit Carco was to pretend she
was his wife, about to have a child, and she wanted to borrow a
maternity dress of mine and wear a pillow under it'.²⁴

Katherine's journey through France was agonizing, for the
cold train passed slowly through the stations where the wounded
men were waiting to be rescued. In 'An Indiscreet Journey'
(1915) and her *Journal* of February 1915, Katherine gives a vivid
account of her examination by two French colonels whose
'heads rolled on their tight collars, like big over-ripe fruits'²⁵
and her three-day fling with Carco: 'We arrived at Gray, and one
by one, like women going in to see a doctor, we slipped through a
door into a hot room completely filled with two tables and two
colonels, like colonels in a comic opera, big shiny grey-whiskered
men with a touch of burnt red on their cheeks, both smoking, one
a cigarette with a long curly ash hanging from it.'²⁶

Katherine's good looks must have helped her much more than
her dubious explanations. When she slipped out of the examining
room she found Carco standing near the station looking terribly
pale. He greeted her, whispered 'follow me as though you were

not following', and led her to a cab. As they drove to a nearby village they kissed each other and clutched at the banging doors that would not stay shut. Her room was in a large white house and was furnished with a bed, a wax apple and an immense flowery clock. Katherine then mentions Carco's feminine looks and braceleted wrist, and refers to their sexual intimacy: 'In the most natural manner we slowly undressed by the stove. F. slung into bed. "Is it cold?" I said. "Ah, no, not at all cold. Viens, ma bébé. Don't be frightened. The waves are quite small." With his laughing face, his pretty hair, one hand with a bangle over the sheets, he looked like a girl. . . . The act of love seemed somehow quite incidental, we talked so much. It was so warm and delicious, lying curled in each other's arms, by the light of a tiny lamp.'[27] Carco adds, in his curt account, that since Katherine could not be seen with him, 'she spent most of the time confined within the four walls of her room and took her meals, with me, in her landlady's house'[28]—where there was a suffocating smell of onion soup and boots and damp cloth.

Katherine had some brief but ecstatic moments with Carco, and on February 20 wrote a suggestive passage in her *Journal*: 'And F. quite naked making up the fire with a tiny brass poker—so natural, so beautiful. . . . Then just for a moment I saw him passing the window—and then he was gone. That is a terrible moment for a woman.'[29] Whether the terrible moment was caused by the girlish Carco's 'tiny poker' or by Katherine's profound feeling 'that he does not love me at all' and 'I don't really love him now I know him',[30] Carco, whom she imagined would be her 'deliverer', turned out to be as selfish as Murry. Two days later she returned home, deeply disillusioned and bitterly hurt by the callous egoism of both lovers.

In Carco's novel *Les Innocents* (published in 1916 and still in print), Winnie (Katherine) is portrayed as a 'high-class chick' with pink cheeks and hair cut short above the nape of her neck, who has a lesbian affair with Béatrice (Hastings). Winnie lives with the tough street-urchin Milord (Carco), pays for everything and parasitically uses him as raw material for her writing: 'She did not love Milord, but she felt in love, for the sake of her book, with everything that formed his mysterious life. She lived what she wrote, and perhaps was jealous of everything that detached Milord from her unhealthy curiosity.'[31] At the end of the violent and sensational novel Milord's mistress Savonette strangles Winnie, who has disturbed her precarious relationship with her lover. Milord then takes Savonette to a hotel, shoots her and kills himself. Carco later softened and romanticized his description of Katherine in *Mémoires d'une autre vie* (1942) in order to fit the rather sentimental French legend that had developed after her death: 'I can loyally affirm that the most important thing in our friendship was the profound and natural taste Katherine Mansfield and I shared for the poetry of the night and of the rain, of an absurd and dangerous existence; in a word, for a certain plaintive romanticism where exoticism blends with the marvellous, not without a touch of humour and of disenchantment.'[32]

Katherine's bitter story of personal betrayal, 'Je ne parle pas français', expresses her profoundest fears, and settles some scores with both Carco and Murry. The first-person narration is essentially a revelation of the loathsome character of Raoul Duquette who is, by his own admission, impudent and cheap, cynical and calculating. Dick Harmon (Murry) has a 'dreamy half smile on his lips' that barely disguises his weak and treacherous character. He runs away to Paris with the frail and exquisite, childlike and terribly vulnerable Mouse (Katherine), and is met at the station by Duquette, who takes them to their hotel. Dick then abandons Mouse, leaving a letter that feebly explains: 'I can't kill my mother! Not even for you.'[33]

When Mouse tells Raoul that it is impossible to go home because all her friends think she is married, he ambiguously promises to come back the next morning to 'take care of you a little'. But he thinks better of it when he realizes how little he can get out of it for himself. Mouse, abandoned by both men and quite helpless—'je ne parle pas français'—is in a desperate state and may even be forced to surrender her virginity to some 'dirty old gallant' whose promises and protection would match those of Raoul and Dick. This story, which was privately printed by Katherine, originally had a deliberately disgusting conclusion (deleted from the edition later published by Constable) which hints at Raoul's homosexuality and portrays his revulsion for the proprietress of a café: 'I'd rather like to dine with her. Even to sleep with her afterwards. Would she be pale like that all over? But no. She'd have large moles. They go with that kind of

5

skin. And I can't bear them. They remind me somehow, disgustingly, of mushrooms.'[34] After their affair was over, both Carco and Katherine justified themselves and expressed their hostility by alluding to each other's sexual depravity. 'Je ne parle pas français', as Katherine told Murry, is '*a cry against corruption* . . . I mean corruption in the widest sense of the word'[35]—a protest against moral perversion that leads to personal betrayal. Harold Beauchamp's characteristically philistine response to his daughter's story was: 'I chucked the thing behind the fireplace. It wasn't even clever.'[36]

Katherine was, of course, not able to write during her gypsylike quests for a place to live and her continuous moving, unpacking and settling into her temporary and often dreary dwellings. A *Journal* entry of April 1914 reveals that she had not yet resolved the conflict between her sentimental and satiric literary modes, nor learned to use her cruel eye and ruthless judgment in a *positive* way: 'If I try to find things lovely, I turn pretty-pretty. And at the same time I am so frightened of writing mockery for satire that my pen hovers and won't settle. . . . I've decided to tear up everything that I've written and start again.'[37] She continued to destroy her work until the following spring.

After her return from Gray in March 1915 Katherine once again became dissatisfied with both Murry and her surroundings. Murry writes that 'From the Carco folly she reacted violently; and I was made the paradigm of innocence and fidelity'[38]—an unrealistic role which he apparently failed to sustain. She informed Kot, from Rose Tree Cottage: 'I cannot write my book living in these two rooms. It is impossible—and if I do not write this book, I shall die.'[39] And on March 18 she left for Carco's empty flat at 13 Quai aux Fleurs, near Notre Dame on the Île de la Cité, in order to escape from Murry and find the necessary solitude and material comfort. Though she eventually completed two minor stories, 'Spring Pictures' and 'The Little Governess', and began 'The Aloe', which later became 'Prelude', her life in Paris was as tumultuous as ever. She was caught in the Zeppelin raids of March 1915 and became deeply involved with the manic and vitriolic Beatrice Hastings. In *Les Innocents* Carco portrayed Beatrice as the ruthless alter-ego of Winnie, and as a woman who had strangled her lover in order to discover how it felt to be a murderer. Beatrice had left Orage in 1914, had been the mistress

of Modigliani and had recently replaced him with the equally
handsome though less talented Italian sculptor, Alfredo Pina.

On March 21 Katherine, who was scrupulously observing the
signs of decay in her friend, told Murry: 'Strange and really
beautiful though she is, still with the fairy air about her and her
pretty little head still so fine, she is ruined. There is no doubt of
it. I love her, but I take an intense, cold interest in noting the
signs.'[40] And in subsequent letters Katherine described her calm
superiority in the face of Beatrice's violent alcoholic fury:
'B. was very impossible—she must have drunk nearly a bottle of
brandy and then at 9 o'clock I left and refused either to stay any
longer or to spend the night there. She flared up in a *fury* and we
parted for life again. . . . B. I have not seen since her famous
party. It's an ugly memory. I am glad it happened so soon. I
think next morning she must have felt horribly ashamed of herself, for she was drunk and jealous and everybody knew it. I am
thankful that I stood firm. I feel so utterly superior to her now.'[41]

But Katherine's clinical objectivity and cool disdain did not
protect her from the filthy abuse of the friend she once had loved.
As she later explained to Murry: 'Yes, it is true, I *did* love B.H.
but have you utterly forgotten what I told you of her behaviour
in Paris—of the last time I saw her and how, because I refused to
stay the night with her, she bawled at me and called me a *femme
publique* in front of those filthy Frenchmen? She is loathsome and
corrupt and I remember very very well telling you I had done
with her, explaining why and recounting to you how she had
insulted and abused me.'[42] Beatrice struck the last blow, as she
had struck the first. In her savage pamphlet about the *New Age*
group, published in 1936, she referred to Katherine's sexual
adventures and described her as a woman who ' "twittered" her
way out of a world she had fouled wherever she went'.[43]

On March 31, when Katherine had had enough of Beatrice,
who was as bitterly disappointing as Carco had been, she returned
to Murry and moved into a top-floor flat at 95 Elgin Crescent in
Notting Hill. She lived there for just over a month, and then went
to Paris for the third time and spent three more unhappy weeks in
Carco's empty flat. She wrote Murry love letters nearly every day
but, unlike Carco, he never said that he longed for her and was
desolate without her. Katherine insisted that she 'needed' to be
happy and rather petulantly combined a memory of New Zealand

with her constant but frustrated wish for a child: 'Why haven't I got a real "home"—a real life—why haven't I got a Chinese nurse with green trousers and two babies who rush at me and clasp my knees? I'm not a girl—I'm a woman. I *want* things. Shall I ever have them?'[44] Though Murry obviously could *not* give Katherine what she wanted, she finally realized that she was better off discontented with him than writing well by herself: 'Yesterday was simply hellish for me. My work went very well, but all the same, I suffered abominably. I felt so alien and so far away, and everybody cheated me, everything was ugly and beyond words cruel.'[45]

Katherine returned to Elgin Crescent at the end of May and stayed with Murry for the next two years, but was unable to resolve the basic conflict between her life as a writer and as a woman: between her quest for artistic independence and her desire for emotional support. She accommodated herself to the disappointing reality of life with Murry and convinced herself: 'There is something wonderfully sustaining and comforting to have another person with you, who goes to bed where you do and is there when you wake up—who turns to you, and to whom you turn.'[46] But Katherine's best work evolved directly from the major crises of her life; and the only time she ever enjoyed good health, artistic creativity *and* Murry's love and companionship was when, after her brother's death in October 1915, they lived together in Bandol.

CHAPTER NINE

Leslie, Bandol and 'Prelude', 1915–1916

IN JULY 1915, after three months at Elgin Crescent, Katherine and Murry found their first really attractive house at 5 Acacia Road, St. John's Wood, her favourite part of London, near the Trowells's old home in Carlton Hill. The white stucco house had a long garden where they played badminton and a tall pear tree that later appeared in 'Bliss'; from Katherine's beautiful attic-study, they watched the first Zeppelin sailing over the city. The Lawrences lived close by in Hampstead, and they all spent the summer planning and writing the short-lived *Signature*, which expired in November.

Katherine's younger brother Leslie (who was born in 1894) had joined the British Army in New Zealand and come to England for training in February, *en route* to the war in Europe. A photograph of Leslie in uniform, taken in the autumn of 1915, shows a boyish and handsome face, with regular features and a clipped martial moustache. They had not been close as children, for Leslie was only nine years old when Katherine sailed for England in 1903 and was at boarding school when she returned to New Zealand three years later. But Edie Bendall recalls that Katherine was 'always devoted to Chummie'[1] (as he was called by the family) and Beatrice Campbell agrees that Leslie 'seemed to be the one member of her family with whom she was absolutely in tune'.[2]

In her *Journal* of October 1915 Katherine remembers Leslie as a little boy: 'Bogey with his scratched knees pressed together, his hands behind his back, too, and a round cap on his head with "H.M.S. Thunderbolt" printed across it.'[3] In a letter of 1908, written during her last months in Wellington, Katherine expressed her love for Leslie, praised his sympathetic qualities and spoke of her plans to share a house with him when he grew up: 'He and I mean to live together—later on. I have never dreamed of loving a child as I love this boy. Do not laugh when I tell you

I feel so maternal towards him. He is intensely affectionate and sensitive.'[4] In the summer of 1911 Leslie came to England with the Beauchamps, remained in London for a time after the family left and saw a good deal of his sister.

Leslie frequently visited Katherine in Acacia Road during the summer of 1915. Their meetings were happy and largely nostalgic, and they spent most of the time reminiscing about their early life in New Zealand. Her younger sister recalls that Katherine preferred to keep her own life private but loved to stimulate her imagination by remembering the past: 'She didn't want to disclose—it was always: "Jeanne, shall we go back and talk about the old days? Do you remember, do you remember. . . ?" '[5] In her dialogue with Leslie, Katherine attributes their profound understanding to their early life together:

> [Leslie:] 'But isn't it extraordinary how *deep* our happiness was —how positive—deep, shining, warm. I remember the way we used to look at each other and smile—do you?—sharing a secret. . . . What was it?'
> [Katherine:] 'I think it was the family feeling—we were almost like one child. I always see us walking about together, looking at things together with the same eyes.'[6]

Katherine received the news of the death of Leslie, who was absolutely confident that he would return safely from the War, while dining in Acacia Road with Anne and Raymond Drey. On October 7, only a week after Leslie had arrived at the Ploegsteert Wood front in Belgium, a grenade went off in his hand while he was instructing trainees, and both he and his sergeant were killed. A fellow officer later tried to comfort Katherine by idealizing Leslie's death: 'after it happened he said over and over "God forgive me for all I have done" and just before he died he said, "Lift my head, Katy, I can't breathe".'[7]

Leslie's horrible and even ludicrous death had a profound effect on Katherine. She created a fanatical cult of her brother, longed to join him in death, felt that *she* had died, and developed mystical yearnings that finally led her to Gurdjieff:

> I welcome the idea of death. I believe in immortality because he is not here, and I long to join him. First, my darling, I've got things to do for both of us, and then I will come as quickly as I

can. Dearest heart, I know you are there, and I live with you,
and I will write for you. . . .

I am just as much dead as he is. The present and the future
mean nothing to me. I am no longer 'curious' about people; I
do not wish to go anywhere; and the only possible value that
anything can have for me is that it should put me in mind of
something that happened or was when we were alive.[8]

Katherine also carried her posthumous adoration to the
pathological extreme of rejecting Murry for Leslie, as if it were
impossible to love both men. In the frequent *Journal* entries
addressed to her dead brother she confesses that his memory
makes her frigid with Murry, and pledges Leslie her profoundest
spiritual love: 'You are more vividly with me now this moment
than if you were alive. . . . The night before, when I lay in bed, I
felt suddenly passionate. I wanted J. to embrace me. But as I
turned to speak to him or to kiss him I saw my brother lying fast
asleep, and I got cold. This happens nearly always. . . . You know
I can never be Jack's lover again. You have me. You're in my
flesh as well as in my soul. I give Jack my 'surplus' love, but to
you I hold and to you I give my deepest love. Jack is no more
than . . . anybody might be.'[9] Murry, who now had sexual rivals
among the dead as well as the living, was reduced to trivial
insignificance by Leslie's ghost, became more confused and
helpless than ever, and admitted that her brother, 'though dead,
was far more real and near to her than I was now; and that was
anguish to me.'[10] Murry, who could neither compete with Leslie
nor comfort Katherine, was completely alienated and tormented
by jealousy and frustration.

Though Katherine's grief was profound, it was to a certain
extent false as well as morbid. Katherine's adoration of Leslie—
whose second name, Heron, she adopted as the name of their
private press and never-to-be-found dream house—really exemplified the way she wanted Murry to love *her*, just as her capacity for
suffering reflected the contrast between Murry's coldness and her
own delicacy of feeling. As Aldous Huxley shrewdly writes of
Katherine in *Those Barren Leaves*: 'She was proud of being able to
suffer so much; she encouraged her suffering. This sudden
recollection of Jim [Leslie] when he was a little boy . . . was a
sign of her exquisite sensibility. Mingled with her grief there was

a certain sense of satisfaction. After all, this had happened quite by itself, of its own accord, and spontaneously. She had always told people that she was sensitive, had a deep and quivering heart. This was a proof. Nobody knew how much she suffered, underneath.'[11] It is ironic that Katherine made, or pretended to make, a greater emotional commitment to her dead brother than she had ever made to Carco, to Ida (who was also called Lesley) or even to Murry (who was known as Bogey). Her attachment to Leslie, which seemed much stronger *after* his death, was rooted in her nostalgic and sentimental longing for childhood and adolescence, and was used by Katherine as a sexual and psychological defence.

A month after Leslie's death, in November 1915, Brett, who had been a student at the Slade School of Art with Mark Gertler and Dora Carrington, invited Katherine and Murry to a party at her studio off Earl's Court Road. There they first met Lytton Strachey, who was amused and intrigued by Katherine, and later introduced her to Virginia Woolf. The Honourable Dorothy Brett, daughter of Viscount Esher and sister of the Ranee of Sarawak, was born in 1883. She became deaf at an early age, which made her extremely sensitive and vulnerable, and was both ignored and humiliated by her father, a covert homosexual, who had married 'when he would have preferred to live with another man. In fact, he almost always had some young man living in the house with them as secretary or chauffeur. He never showed any interest in his own daughters, and made them both feel quite stupid and unwanted.'[12] In *The Boy in the Bush* (1928) Lawrence portrays Brett as Hilda Blessington, a rather eccentric woman with a tyrannical father, who had been persecuted because of her harmless peculiarities. There were 'brothers who had bullied her and jeered at her for her odd ways and appearance, and her slight deafness. [There was] the governess who had mis-educated her, the loneliness of the life in London, the aristocratic but rather vindictive society in England, which had persecuted her in a small way, because she was one of the odd borderline people who don't and *can't*, really belong.'[13]

Katherine's friendship with Brett really began in July 1916 when the writer slyly put bread crumbs in the painter's pocket during lunch at Garsington.[14] Both artists were a bit afraid of the Bloomsbury group, and were cautious and withdrawn. Later that night Katherine came to Brett's room and asked for a pledge of friendship, just as she had done with Ida Baker at Queen's College in 1903. Brett writes that 'she asked me to be her friend. We made a secret pact of friendship which was never broken for the rest of her life. . . . She gave me the encouragement I needed badly. Katherine really started me doing serious painting in England.'[15] Like Ottoline Morrell and Bertrand Russell, Brett was wealthy and aristocratic, but she was also, like Ida and Kot, reliable, supportive and something of an outsider.

Though Brett, in fact, later betrayed their friendship and aroused Katherine's bitter jealousy, Katherine was eventually able to forgive her. In May and August 1922 Katherine wrote to Kot with great insight and compassion about Brett's secret self, and discussed the early neglect, humiliation, loneliness and unhappiness that had caused her weakness, her dependence and her fear:

> It has been strange to see Brett. There is something very real and true in her. Her secret self is too deeply buried, though. I wish I could make her happier. I feel she has been ignored, passed by. No one has ever *cherished* her. This is sad. . . .
>
> I do not think she will ever be an adult being. She is weak; she is a vine; she longs to cling. She cannot nourish herself from the earth; she must be fed on the sap of another. . . . She is seeking someone who will make her forget that early neglect, that bullying and contempt. But the person who would satisfy her would have to dedicate himself to curing all the results of her unhappiness—her distrust, for instance, her suspicions, her fears.[16]

About ten days after Brett's party, in the middle of November 1915, Katherine found she could not bear the painful memories of Leslie that were inevitably associated with Acacia Road. So she and Murry, who had been exempted from military service, took their first journey to the south of France. They stayed for a few days in Marseilles where 'everybody cheated Murry *at sight*. Even before he bought anything they put up the price.'[17] Katherine caught 'Marseilles fever' (possibly viral enteritis), and suffered from loss of appetite, shivering fits and dysentery. When she recovered they travelled westward along the coast to Cassis, and spent two weeks in a cold hotel room while the mistral blasted against the sunless windows. When Katherine became depressed and began to weep uncontrollably for her brother, Murry felt rejected and was furious. Finally, at the beginning of December, they moved to the Hôtel Beau Rivage in Bandol, a picturesque fishing village between Marseilles and Toulon. Murry could not deal with Katherine's grief nor she with his morbid jealousy, and on December 7 he returned to England to seek the friendship and consolation of Lawrence.

Katherine, alone at the hotel, took long walks along the bays to Sanary and St. Cyr, and admired the splendid sub-tropical scenery, filled with exotic flowers, that reminded her of New Zealand. She felt her observation was more acute and 'detailed' in France, and wrote to Murry: 'Once I found myself right at the very top of a hill and below there lay an immense valley—surrounded by mountains—very high ones—and it was so clear you could see every pointed pine, every little zig-zag track—the black stems of the olives showing sooty and soft among the silvery green.'[18] Katherine visited the market and the crèche in the church, watched the fishermen on the quay mending their nets and hauling in their catch, sat outside in a sunny café and observed the African soldiers, listened to the sea and fed the hotel fire with pine cones. She read the Bible, Shakespeare, Dickens, Dostoyevsky, Victor Hugo, Jules Laforgue and the Oxford Book of English Verse as well as Le Radical and The Times. She also thought about her brother, recorded her dreams and wrote daily letters to Murry that combined maternal solicitude with passionate longing. She made characteristically satiric observations on the French, and linked their sexual licence with domestic discomfort: 'what appalling furniture—and never one comfortable chair. If you want to talk the only possible thing to do is to go to bed. . . . I quite understand the reason for what is called French moral laxity. You're simply forced into bed—no matter with whom.'[19]

About a week after Murry had left, Katherine again caught Marseilles fever and was tormented by rheumatic pains that prevented her from walking and had a pernicious effect on her heart. These illnesses threw her into the destructive mood that characterized all her lonely months in foreign countries—from Germany in 1909 to Switzerland and France in 1922. Her sickness and solitude led to bitterness and depression that made the

Mediterranean sunset look 'horribly like a morsel of tinned apricot'. She began sending Murry a series of letters filled with self-pity and angry reproach about correspondence that had been delayed by the War, and also made invidious comparisons between her husband and her father, a much busier and more important man who 'always had time to write every single day to my Mother'.[20] Her ultimate salvation was her brave spirit, for when she became dreadfully anxious and felt 'cut off from all human kind', she put on her favourite perfume, *Genêt Fleuri*, looked straight into the mirror, and said 'Courage, Katherine'.

Fortunately, she was befriended by an elderly gentleman, F. Newland-Pedley, the head of Guy's Dental Hospital, who gave her an effective ointment for rheumatism. Katherine remarked that the old-fashioned, courteous and reliable man was 'a queer delightful good-natured person and he has certainly been a comfort to me'—partly because he had condemned Murry and asked: 'What did he marry you for if it wasn't because he wanted to look after you?'[21] Murry confessed to Katherine that he had received the same criticism from Lawrence, who rightly blamed Katherine's illness on Murry's weakness and selfishness: 'He said that it was all my fault, that I was a coward, that I never offered you a new life, that I would not break with my past, that your illness was all due to your misery, and that I had made you miserable by always whining and never making a decision; that I should never have left you there.'[22] Yet as soon as Murry had gone to England they both realized how desperately they needed each other; when Katherine was not accusing him, she was investing Murry with a spiritual aura and confessing her love: 'It is strange. I feel that I only really know you since you went back to England. I feel as though a miracle had happened to you and you are rich and bathed in light. While I sit here writing to you time is not. I am one with our love for ever.'[23]

Murry encouraged Katherine to look for a house, and in a joyous letter of December 29 she described the tiny four-room Villa Pauline, which had pink walls, blue-grey shutters and a graceful almond tree that brushed against the window, and was perched on a hill overlooking the sea: 'It stands alone in a small garden with terraces. It faces the "midi" and gets the sun all day long. It has a stone verandah and a little round table where we can sit and eat or work. A charming little tiny kitchen with pots and pans and big coffee pot, you know. Electric light, water downstairs and upstairs too in the cabinet de toilette. A most refined "water-closet" *with* water in the house. . . . The salle à manger is small and square with the light low over the table. It leads on to the verandah and overlooks the sea. So does the chambre à coucher. It is very private and stands high on the top of a hill.'[24] Katherine ordered wine, wood and coal from the friendly shopkeepers, and the next day the landlady, Mme. Allègre, promised to provide a tea-pot and cups, since her tenants were English. Katherine then signed the lease, took the key, and bought roses and violets in the flower market. Murry arrived suddenly in Bandol on New Year's Day, before he had even received her letters.

Katherine and Murry's three-month stay at the Villa Pauline from January to April 1916 was the only time they had no serious problems and were really happy. They were together in a lovely place, experienced mutual self-surrender, enjoyed good health and warm weather, worked well, and lived modestly on Katherine's money—as Lawrence had advised them to do in the autumn of 1913. They got up each morning at six, finished their shopping by eight, began to write at eight-thirty, sat on opposite sides of a tiny table and interrupted each other constantly. By eleven they began to feel hunger pangs, and Katherine would sneak two slices of bread and secretly push the clock ahead so that they could have lunch, with dates and honey, before the appointed hour of noon. They spent the evenings of one entire week sitting at the kitchen table and writing poetry on a chosen theme. The result was Katherine's seven 'Poems at the Villa Pauline: 1916', including the moving elegy on her brother: 'To L.H.B.(1894–1915).' (Leslie's death also influenced two late stories: 'Six Years After' and 'The Fly.') In March Katherine went alone to Marseilles to meet her elder sister Charlotte, who was coming to England from India. When Katherine was startled by a nocturnal intruder who knocked at her door in the Hôtel Oasis late one night, she reacted with her usual courage: 'I leapt out of bed, threw my kimono on and, arming myself with a pair of scissors, I opened the door. There stood a horrid creature in his night-shirt who began mumbling something about the wrong door—but he *leered*. Oh I *slammed* the door in his face, and walked up and down my room—furious—I was not at all frightened.'[25]

Though Katherine criticized Virginia Woolf's *Night and Day* (1919) for ignoring the War, she too was oblivious to the cataclysm until it affected her personal life—and even afterwards. Though the battle of Verdun was raging while Katherine and Murry lived blissfully in Bandol, they felt the War was merely a personal inconvenience and never mentioned it. Once Katherine accepted the death of her brother, she transformed her private tragedy into a literary triumph. The exotic landscape of Bandol and the memories of Leslie turned her thoughts back to childhood, dissolved the hostility to her family and country, and inspired the finest stories about New Zealand: 'I want to write about my own country till I simply exhaust my store. Not only because it is "a sacred debt" that I pay to my country because my brother and I were born there, but also because in my thoughts I range with him over all the remembered places. I am never far away from them. I long to renew them in writing. . . . I want for one moment to make our undiscovered country leap into the eyes of the Old World.'[26]

By the time Katherine wrote 'The Aloe' she had fully understood and assimilated the techniques of her Russian master, Anton Chekhov. In 1919 she wrote to Kot about Constance Garnett's translations of Chekhov's stories: 'She seems to take the nerve out of Tchekhov before she starts working on him, like a dentist takes the nerve from a tooth.'[27] But two years later she sent Mrs. Garnett a letter of extravagant praise and revealed how Chekhov, whose work she had known since her teens, stimulated her imagination and even transformed her life:

[I can] no longer refrain from thanking you for the whole other world that you have revealed to us through those marvellous translations from the Russian. Your beautiful industry will end in making us almost ungrateful. We are almost inclined to take for granted the fact that the new book is translated by Mrs. Constance Garnett. Yet my generation (I am 32) and the younger generation owe you more than we ourselves are able to realize. These books have changed our lives, no less. What could it be like to be without them!

I am only one voice among so many who appreciate the greatness of your task, the marvel of your achievement. I beg you to accept my admiration and deepest gratitude.[28]

Several critics have suggested the direct influence of Chekhov's works on Katherine's stories: of 'Sleepyhead' on 'The Child Who Was Tired', 'Misery' on 'The Life of Ma Parker', 'The Grasshopper' on 'Marriage à la Mode', and 'Small Fry' on 'The Fly'.

In Katherine's stories the emphasis is not on plot and character, the traditional concerns of fiction, but rather on the presentation of a quintessential event, a summary of human life in a single significant scene. Like Watteau and Chopin, Katherine's works contain subtle detail, precise phrasing, delicate observation and concentrated emotion. She is an intensely visual and essentially impressionistic artist who expresses character through symbolic use of objects, distillation of atmosphere and poetic evocations of mood; the fragmentary and casually linked episodes obliquely convey the theme through suggestion rather than statement. Katherine's themes, which are sharpened by a certain cynicism and bitterness, are those of a sensitive and introspective invalid who fears solitude and death, and tries to escape from the false-ness of society and the oppressions of adult reality into the idyllic memories of childhood.

'Prelude', the longest and most memorable of Katherine's stories, and the first significant achievement of her literary career, begins the family saga that continues in 'At the Bay', 'The Doll's House' and 'The Garden Party'. 'Prelude' ostensibly concerns the family's move from Wellington to Karori at Easter 1893, but the title also suggests that the autobiographical child, Kezia, is moving to new experience ('Now everything familiar was left behind') and to greater perception. Like Wordsworth's long poem of the same title, the story portrays an imaginative awaken-ing and the 'growth of a poet's mind'. The most striking aspect of the story is the vivid portrayal of the family and their servants: Stanley Burnell, the physical and energetic *paterfamilias*; Linda Burnell, the delicate and sensitive invalid; Mrs. Fairfield, the gentle, loving and almost Proustian grandmother; Beryl Fair-field, an antipodean Blanche Dubois, vain, restless and dreamy; and the rough Trout cousins, the servant Alice, and the Irish handyman Pat, who fascinates the children by killing a duck as the kings of Ireland once did. The symbolic details: the blossom-ing aloe, Stanley's luxurious delicacies, Pat's earrings and Beryl's guitar; the episodic structure with its shifting views of the various characters; and the deliberately vague ending, all contribute to the rich and complex story. They express the moving themes of the 'real' and the 'other self' and of poignant solitude within the complicated relationships of the family.

In mid-April 1916, when Katherine had finished her story and Murry his book, they realized their idyll had to end, reluctantly responded to Lawrence's insistent invitation, and went to Cornwall with predictably disastrous results. In May they left the Lawrences and moved to Sunnyside Cottage in Mylor, near Falmouth in south Cornwall. A man with a horse and cart carried away their possessions, and Murry, who felt the separation was final, writes: 'It would have been unlike Lawrence, even at such a moment, not to have lent a hand; and he did. But our hearts were sore. When the last rope was tied, I said good-bye and hoped they would come over to see us. Frieda, who took such incidents lightly, said they would; but Lawrence did not answer. I wheeled my bicycle to the road and pedalled off, with the feeling that I had said good-bye to him for ever.'[29]

In July Murry, who was again in danger of being called-up as the need for recruits became more urgent, joined Military Intelligence as a civilian translator and after six months became editor of an abstract of enemy newspapers, the *Daily Review of the Foreign Press*. During that month Katherine rather mysteriously wrote to Kot from Cornwall that she was thinking of leaving Murry and going to Denmark in the autumn. In August, just before Katherine returned to London from Mylor, she once again became 'prostrate with misery' and lamented her estrangement from Murry, which she felt had been only briefly alleviated by their ephemeral happiness in Bandol: 'Are we *never* to be happy—never, never? We haven't had any "life" together at all yet—in fact it's only on the rarest occasions that we have any confidential intercourse.'[30] They had completed an emotional cycle and were back to where they had been just after Leslie's death.

CHAPTER TEN

Garsington and Bloomsbury, 1916–1917

IN 1916 KATHERINE formed three new friendships at
Garsington and in Bloomsbury with Lady Ottoline Morrell,
Bertrand Russell and Virginia Woolf. But their rank and wealth,
confidence and security, aloofness and reserve, prevented
Katherine from establishing that profound intimacy she had with
her closest friends: Ida Baker, Anne Rice, Lawrence and Kot.
Ottoline had met Murry at the Lawrences's cottage at Greatham
in Sussex in February 1915, when Katherine was in France, and
Lawrence had asked her to invite the lonely Murry for Christmas
at Garsington, when Katherine was grieving for her brother in
Bandol. Murry sought the advice of Ottoline (as well as of
Lawrence) about whether he ought to go back to Katherine,
and she gave him £5 for the fare and told him to return to
France.

While living in Mylor, Katherine made several summer visits
to Ottoline's home at Garsington, an Elizabethan manor house
with mullioned windows and a steep-pitched roof, built on the
slope of a hill and surrounded by an estate of 500 acres. Dons and
undergraduates, artists and writers, poets and young bohemians
as well as aristocrats and distinguished politicians gathered in the
luxurious mansion and magnificent garden, embellished with a
swimming pool and peacocks. The interior of the house—which
Lytton Strachey described as 'very remarkable, very impressive,
patched, gilded and preposterous'[1]—was sumptuously decorated
with silk curtains and Persian carpets, precious knick-knacks and
strange scents; the large oak-panelled rooms were painted over in
bright colours and adorned with works by Duncan Grant, Mark
Gertler and Augustus John. 'Is the sunlight ever normal at
Garsington?' Virginia Woolf once asked. 'No I think even the
sky is done up in pale yellow silk, and certainly the cabbages are
scented.'[2]

Ottoline Morrell, the daughter of a General, half-sister of a

Duke and wife of the M.P. Philip Morrell, was described by
Osbert Sitwell as an 'over-size Infanta of Spain'.[3] She was
extremely tall and striking, with dyed red hair and jutting jaw,
nasal voice and neighing laugh, and extravagant costumes that
resembled the exotic plumage of an enormous bird. She was a
baroque and flamboyant, eccentric and even a grotesque personality, with a malicious sense of humour and an exalted though
indiscriminate devotion to the arts. She was also an encouraging
patron and generous hostess who provided a pleasant atmosphere,
comfortable surroundings and good food, and allowed artists to
work quietly all day and enjoy stimulating conversation in the
evenings and at weekends, which were characterized by high
spirits and high-mindedness, pacificism, poetry and all that was
ultra-modern in the arts.

Ottoline's hospitality to novelists was often accepted un-
graciously and repaid with ridicule, and she was satirized as
Priscilla Wimbush in Huxley's *Crome Yellow* (1921) and as
Hermione Roddice in *Women in Love* (1920), in which Lawrence
describes the extraordinary effect of her hypnotic bearing and
chromatic clothing:

> She drifted forward as if scarcely conscious, her long blanched
> face lifted up, not to see the world. She was rich. She wore a
> dress of silky, frail velvet, of pale yellow colour, and she
> carried a lot of small rose-coloured cyclamens. Her shoes and
> stockings were of brownish grey, like the feathers on her hat,
> her hair was heavy, she drifted along with a peculiar fixity of
> the hips, a strange unwilling motion. She was impressive, in
> her lovely pale-yellow and brownish-rose, yet macabre, some-
> thing repulsive. . . . Her long, pale face, that she carried lifted
> up, somewhat in the Rossetti fashion, seemed almost drugged,
> as if a strange mass of thoughts coiled in the darkness within
> her.[4]

Lawrence, who quarrelled with Ottoline before Katherine visited
her home, was ambivalent about the traditional and artificial
aspects of Garsington, a model for Breadalby in *Women in Love*.
In November 1915 he wrote from Garsington to Edward Marsh:
'Here one feels the real England—this old house, this countryside—so poignantly'; but in February 1921 he warned Mark
Gertler, who was ill with tuberculosis: 'I should beware of

Garsington—I believe there is something exhaustive in the air there, not so very restful.'[5]

Ottoline was an old friend of John Adam Cramb, who had been Katherine's history teacher at Queen's College, and the two women had heard a great deal about each other from mutual friends. They were both guarded and uneasy at first, for Ottoline writes that Katherine 'was suspicious of me and thought I was just a grand lady patronizing artists for my own glory. . . . I think Katherine feels unsure of her position, partly because she is a New Zealander and is not yet very easy or natural in England and she is constantly playing different parts. . . . She told me lately that she and her brother had been so much in the habit of acting parts together that she doesn't now know what is her real self and what is the part she is acting.'[6]

But Ottoline, who wished she had met her before Katherine had been hurt by life, understood and sympathized with her far more than the snobbish Virginia Woolf. Virginia later emphasized the contrast between the impoverished existence of Katherine, who had been used to luxury, and her lively response to the splendours of Garsington (which Katherine recaptured in her poem 'Night Scented Stocks'): 'Katherine Mansfield describes your garden, the rose leaves drying in the sun, the pool, and long conversations between people wandering up and down in the moonlight. It calls out her romantic side; which I think rather a relief after the actresses, A.B.C.'s [teashops] and paint pots'.[7]

Though she came from a wealthy family, Katherine was déclassé in England, lived in poverty and, like Murry, Lawrence, Kot and Gertler, must have been extremely self-conscious about the difference between her own modest and Ottoline's magnificent circumstances. The relations of patron and artist were inevitably difficult, and it was impossible for Katherine to achieve with the regal Ottoline that sense of equality which is essential for friendship. The aristocratic Frieda Lawrence, who was banned from Garsington after her husband's satiric portrayal of his hostess, envied Ottoline's wealth and was jealous of her friendship with Katherine. She emphasized their difference in class and appearance, and mocked their relationship by insisting: 'You look like a maid going out with a grand lady when you are with her.'[8] Though Katherine sometimes quarrelled with Ottoline and made spiteful remarks about her, she also confided in her, told her a great deal about her childhood, early life and marriage to Murry, continued to see her at Garsington and in London, and wrote her many warm letters between 1916 and 1922.

After Katherine's death Ottoline adopted Virginia Woolf's condescension and wrote to Rosamund Lehmann that Katherine could be affectionate but not loyal, and that the satiric triumphed over the sympathetic side of her character: 'She had rather a cheap taste, slightly Swan and Edgar, she was like a strange flower with a perfume that was almost too unreal. I think she was fond of me. She came to Garsington at first to take copy I think, but she was moved and went away with a good deal of affection for me—for we got on well. But then she could never be stable or loyal. She always ebbed or flowed. She was also very envious and jealous. And I know she made fun of me, and said all sorts of things about me. But that, after all, is a common habit, isn't it?'⁹

Ottoline's daughter Julian, who was ten years old when she first met Katherine in 1916, remembers her affectionately and writes: 'She was always very nice to me as a child—I think she had great sympathy for children. She had a soft voice and quiet ways.'¹⁰ Katherine entertained Julian and the Garsington guests —Maynard Keynes, Clive Bell and Mark Gertler—with ragtime dances and successful impersonations of Yvette Guilbert and of Hollywood stars. Brett recalls that she 'fetched her guitar and sang quaint old folk songs, Negro spirituals, ballads of all kinds. She sang in a low whispering voice, all caution momentarily forgotten, her quick expressive face rippled with light and fun, her humour bubbling over.'¹¹

Katherine returned to Garsington for Christmas 1916 and wrote a short play, 'The Laurels', for the occasion. Aldous Huxley told his brother Julian that the Christmas party had been lively and amusing: 'We performed a superb play invented by Katherine, improvising as we went along. It was a huge success, with Murry as a Dostoevsky character and Lytton as an incredibly wicked old grandfather.'¹² The formal cast of characters slyly reflected the personalities of the actors: Strachey played Dr. Keit (a bird of prey), Carrington was his grandchild Muriel Dash (who rushed frantically between her male and female lovers), Katherine was Florence Kaziany (a zany Kezia), Huxley was Balliol Dodd (his Oxford college), Maria Nys, who later married Huxley, was

Jane, and Murry was the arch-Russian, Ivan Tchek(ov). A few lines of dialogue between the innocent Muriel and the working-class Jane suggests the mood and tone of the playlet:

Jane. I'm a love child, I am.

Muriel (*claps her hands*). A love child, Jane? How divine. What is it? How pretty it sounds. (*dreamily*) A love child.

Jane (*leaning towards her curiously*). Do you mean to say you *don't know*, Miss? It means I haven't got no Father.

Muriel. But oh, Jane, how perfect. Just like the Virgin Mary.

Jane (*furious*). You ought to be ashamed of yourself, Miss Muriel, that you ought. Don't you know it's the most horrible thing that can happen to anybody, not to have a Father? Don't you know Miss, that's the reason what [makes] young girls like me jump off buses and in front of trains and eat rat poison and swoller acids and [kill] themselves. Just because they 'aven't got a Father, Miss.[13]

Another frequent guest at Garsington was Bertrand Russell, whose brother married Katherine's cousin Elizabeth in 1916. Russell first met Katherine and Murry in Kot's office in July 1915 and was appalled by their apparent indolence and cynicism: 'They were all sitting together in a bare office high up next door to the Holborn Restaurant, with the windows shut, smoking Russian cigarettes without a moment's intermission, idle and cynical. I thought . . . the whole atmosphere of the three dead and putrefying.'[14] But they met a year later at Garsington, and in December 1916, when Katherine was looking for a London flat and had been refused a reference by the barrister St. John Hutchinson because she was 'living in sin' with Murry, she turned to Russell, who obliged her and saw her frequently for the next two months. Though Katherine had asked herself 'Is there another grown person as ignorant as I?'[15] the brilliant Russell was impressed by her intelligence as well as her conversation. But he reassured Ottoline (who had once been his mistress) that their relationship was entirely platonic: 'I want to get to know her really well. She interests me mentally very much indeed—I think she has a very good mind & I like her boundless curiosity.'[16]

Ottoline notes that during Christmas 1916 at Garsington: 'Bertie and Katherine had long talks together, so late into the night in the red room, which was under my bedroom. . . . I made

them look uncomfortable next day by telling them that I had
heard all their conversation, which of course wasn't true.'[17]
Katherine's flattering and flirtatious letters to Russell, written
during December 1916 and January 1917, hint at sexual intimacy:
'I have just re-read your letter and now my head aches with a kind
of sweet excitement. . . . It is such infinite delight to know that
we still have the best things to do and that we shall be comrades
in the doing of them. But on Tuesday night I am going to ask
you a great many questions. I want to know more about your
life—ever so many things. There is time enough perhaps, but
I feel definitely impatient at this moment. . . . You have already,
in this little time, given me so much—more than I have given
you, and that does not satisfy me.'[18] Russell later explained that
the tone of their correspondence was misleading and their
friendship innocent: 'They read as if we were having an affair,
but it was not so. She withdrew, possibly on account of Colette
[O'Neil: Lady Constance Malleson], though I never knew. My
feelings for her were ambivalent; I admired her passionately, but
was repelled by her dark hatreds. Her talk was marvellous, much
better than her writing, especially when she was telling of the
things that she was going to write, but when she spoke about
people she was envious, dark and full of alarming penetration in
discovering what they least wished known and whatever was bad
in their characteristics.'[19]

It is significant, in view of Katherine's belief that she and
Lawrence were *unthinkably* alike', that Russell admired and
criticized them in precisely the same terms. For Russell, despite
his immense egoism, assumed a compassionate and philosophic
persona, preferred reason to emotion, and wrote: 'I liked
Lawrence's fire, I liked the energy and passion of his feelings';
but he was repelled by Lawrence's 'passionate hatred' of his
Cambridge and Bloomsbury friends, who were condemned as
'dead, dead, dead'.[20] Russell told Ottoline that Katherine spoke
very maliciously about her, and suggested their friendship broke
off because he disliked Katherine's envy—though he also
admitted that she withdrew from him. Ottoline reports: 'He said
that she was by nature so jealous that she would try and alienate
me from all my friends, so as to be the only one left in possession.
Whether this was true I don't know. Bertie certainly seemed to
mistrust her after a time.'[21]

The third and most important friendship Katherine made during 1916 was with Virginia Woolf, who often visited Garsington. In July 1916 Strachey, who had met Katherine first at Brett's party and then at Garsington, wrote Virginia a long letter which, despite its sneering tone, reveals that Katherine had made a strong impression on him:

> She wrote some rather—in fact distinctly—bright storyettes in a wretched little thing called the Signature, which you may have seen, under the name of Matilda Berry. She was decidedly an interesting creature, I thought—very amusing and sufficiently mysterious. She spoke with great enthusiasm about the Voyage Out, and said she wanted to make your acquaintance more than anyone else's. So I said I thought it might be managed. Was I rash? I really believe you'ld find her entertaining. But just now she's in the recesses of Cornwall, so it must be later on, if at all. I may add that she has an ugly impassive mask of a face—cut in wood, with brown hair and brown eyes very far apart; and a sharp and slightly vulgarly-fanciful intellect sitting behind it.[22]

Strachey's description of Katherine's 'ugly' face was probably meant to disguise his attraction to her, and his churlish charge of 'vulgarity', was undoubtedly intended to prejudice Virginia against Katherine. Yet Strachey had clearly aroused Virginia's interest, and a week later she replied that he had not been rash and that his new discovery was indeed worthy of her attention: 'Katherine Mansfield has dogged my steps for three years—I'm always on the point of meeting her, or of reading her stories, and I have never managed to do either.'[23] She asked Strachey to arrange a meeting, which finally took place in London late in the year.

The precarious, delicate and ethereal quality of Virginia's mind was reflected in her striking beauty, in what Christopher Isherwood calls her forlorn eyes, her high-shouldered and strangely tense figure, and 'the eggshell fragility of her temples'.[24] Dora Carrington, the painter and companion of Strachey, agreed that 'few women since the beginning of the world have equalled her for wit and charm, and a special rare kind of beauty'.[25] And Carrington's lover, Gerald Brenan, observed that Virginia's facial 'bones were thin and delicately made and her eyes were large, grey or greyish blue, and as clear as a hawk's. In conversation they would light up a little coldly while her mouth took an ironic and challenging fold, but in repose her expression was pensive and almost girlish.'[26]

Katherine, though six years younger than Virginia, had published her first book of stories in 1911, four years before the appearance of Virginia's first novel, *The Voyage Out*. Both women shared a passionate devotion to their 'precious art' and knew the anguish of creation, for as Katherine wrote: 'We have got the same job, Virginia, and it is really very curious and thrilling that we should both, quite apart from each other, be after so very nearly the same thing.'[27] They were both sensitive, poetic, impressionistic and lyrical writers, concerned with visual details and subtle nuances of emotion, who relied on their 'inner voices' to achieve stylistic purity and perfection. Katherine was the first to use the 'stream of consciousness' technique that was later masterfully employed by Virginia.

Katherine and Virginia were certainly friends, but they were also rivals as women and artists, and deeply distrusted each other. Though Virginia could be bitchy and terrifying, her cold irony, sharp wit, spiteful sarcasm and malicious jealousy were essentially a defence against her own fearful sensitivity. Both women were highly strung and delicate invalids who, though married, committed themselves to lesbian relationships, and both were childless, lonely, bitter and caustic. But Katherine, the insecure Colonial, was frightened of Virginia, the haughty intellectual, and pretended to be hard and tough. Leonard Woolf perceptively related her defensiveness to her fear: 'She had a masklike face and she, more than Murry, seemed to be perpetually on her guard against a world which she assumed to be hostile', and which frequently was.[28] Influenced perhaps by the extreme antagonism of Lawrence, Katherine was hostile to Bloomsbury's sneers and snobbery, and felt excluded from that charmed circle of friends. Never afraid to express her emotions, she wrote to Ottoline in July 1919: 'I confess that at heart I hate them because I feel they are enemies of Art—of real true Art. The snigger is a very awful thing when one is young and the sneer can nearly kill. They profess to live by feeling—but why then do they never give a sign of it—and why do they do their very best to ridicule feeling in others? It is all poisonous.'[29]

Katherine, sometimes the victim of Bloomsbury malice, was nearly as sensitive as Virginia to criticism. Ottoline, who thought Katherine was 'like a strange flower with an unreal perfume', relates how in 1916 Katherine's preciosity and sensibility were spitefully ridiculed: 'We were playing a game after dinner when [Katherine] was here, describing people by symbols, such as pictures and flowers and scents; unfortunately Katherine was described by some rather exotic scent such as stephanotis or patchouli, and although her name was not mentioned, we all knew and she knew who was meant. It was dreadful. The spite that was in the company maliciously flared out against her and hurt her.'[30] Ottoline was always cautious when speaking to Virginia about Katherine, and in September 1917 Virginia quarrelled with her brother-in-law Clive Bell, who rightly believed she had told Katherine the unkind remarks that he and Desmond MacCarthy had made about her.

Virginia, who repressed her sexual desires and stopped sleeping with Leonard a few weeks after their marriage in 1912, was truly shocked by Katherine's self-conscious bohemian life and reckless sexual adventures. Though Dorothy Brett calls Katherine 'petite and beautiful, *not* vulgar and common',[31] the jealous Virginia thought Katherine 'dressed like a tart and behaved like a bitch',[32] and found her lack of sexual scruples both fascinating and abhorrent. After a dinner party where Katherine had been illuminating about Henry James, Virginia wrote in her diary with characteristic bitchiness: 'We could both wish that our first impression of K.M. was not that she stinks like a—well, civet cat that had taken to street walking. In truth, I'm a little shocked by her commonness at first sight; lines so hard and cheap. However, when this diminishes, she is so intelligent and inscrutable that she repays friendship.'[33] This passage reveals much more about Virginia than about Katherine, for the *ad feminam* attack, the superficial judgment and the assumption of moral superiority reflect the rigid and intolerant response of Virginia, who could only appreciate people of her own class and kind. She felt seriously threatened by Katherine and disturbed by the possibility that someone who was not from her background could be intelligent, sensitive and, perhaps, a finer artist.

Despite her curious probings, Virginia never really knew about Katherine's poverty and illness, her deeply wounding love affairs, and the miscarriage and abortion that were responsible for her 'hard and cheap' appearance. Though Katherine responded to Virginia's criticism with suspicion and hostility, her 'commonness' was redeemed, as Strachey had suggested, by her wit and intelligence; and an intense if guarded relationship developed rapidly in 1917 when Katherine introduced the Woolfs to Koteliansky. Leonard explains: 'A curious friendship, with some deep roots, did spring up between them. When they did not meet, Katherine regarded Virginia with suspicion and hostility and Virginia was irritated and angered by this, and supercilious towards Katherine's cheap scent and cheap sentimentality. But when they met, all this as a rule fell away and there was a profound feeling and understanding between them.' Even the kindly Leonard was infected by Virginia's snobbishness when he described her attitude towards Katherine and punned on 'cheap scent and sentimentality', but he was not envious or afraid of Katherine, did not (despite the editorial 'We could both wish') share Virginia's feelings about her, and found Katherine gay, witty and 'extraordinarily amusing'.[34]

The difference in Virginia's and Katherine's beliefs about vulgarity and feeling is also reflected in their attitudes about contemporary novelists. Virginia refused to recognize the greatness of Lawrence's works and condemned *Ulysses*, which she considered 'underbred', as 'merely the scratching of pimples on the body of the bootboy at Claridge's';[35] while Katherine admired Lawrence's works and when she first read *Ulysses*, which was submitted to the Hogarth Press in 1918, overcame her initial hostility and recognized its significance. Virginia records: 'She began to read, ridiculing: then suddenly said, But there's something in this: a scene that should figure I suppose in the history of literature.'[36] Similarly, Virginia respected E. M. Forster more than any contemporary novelist, while Katherine condemned his lack of emotion and vitality (qualities that Lawrence had in abundance) in her *Journal* in May 1917: 'I came across a copy of *Howards End* and had a look into it. But it's not good enough. E. M. Forster never gets any further than warming the teapot. He's a rare fine hand at that. Feel this teapot. Is it not beautifully warm? Yes, but there ain't going to be no tea.'[37]

Virginia liked to question Katherine about the kind of life she herself had never known, and Katherine, who liked to remain inscrutable, misled Virginia by disguising and by exaggerating her adventures (which began when she was nineteen), and by telling Virginia anything that came into her head. In February and June 1917 Virginia expressed her ambivalent mixture of scorn and admiration for Katherine in letters to her beloved sister Vanessa, and said that though Katherine was 'unscrupulous', Vanessa (who was also a sexual adventuress) would like her: 'I have had a slight rapprochement with Katherine Mansfield; who seems to me an unpleasant but forcible and utterly unscrupulous character, in whom I think you might find a "companion". . . . I had an odd talk with K. Mansfield last night. She seems to have gone every sort of hog since she was 17, which is interesting; I also think she has a much better idea of writing than most. She's an odd character.'[38] And in June 1918 Virginia, who was clearly intrigued by Katherine's extraordinary experiences, repeated Katherine's quite fantastic tales (an elaboration of her operatic days with Garnet) and described her to Violet Dickinson as 'a woman from New Zealand, with a passion for writing, and she's had every sort of experience, wandering about with travelling circuses over the moors of Scotland'.[39]

Katherine, who remained entirely faithful to Murry after her brief liaison with Carco in February 1915, eventually had to reassure Virginia that her wild days were over and she was now dedicated to her art: 'Don't let THEM ever persuade you that I spend any of my precious time swopping hats or committing adultery. I'm far too arrogant and proud.'[40] Though Katherine warned Virginia against the malicious enemy, it appears that Virginia believed THEM rather than Katherine, for she wrote of the posthumously published Dove's Nest in June 1923: 'She said a good deal about feeling things deeply: also about being pure, which I won't criticize, though of course I very well could.'[41] This judgment was entirely unworthy of Virginia, who must have been aware that it was quite possible for Katherine to strive for purity without being entirely 'pure'.

The friendship of the two gifted and beautiful women deepened, despite Katherine's illness and absence, as Virginia overcame her initial repugnance, realized that they had a great deal in common, and was more understanding and responsive. Although, as Brett observes, everyone knew Virginia had been mad,[42] Katherine gradually gained insight about the quality of her mind and perceived (without knowing that Virginia's older half-brother, George Duckworth, had sexually molested her during her childhood and adolescence) that her spiritual innocence had been irreparably wounded. In a letter of July 1917 Katherine told Ottoline: 'I do like her tremendously, but I felt then for the first time the strange, trembling, glinting quality of her mind, and quite for the first time she seemed to me to be one of those Dostoevsky women whose "innocence" has been hurt. Immediately I decided I understood her completely.'[43]

Virginia, who had suffered serious mental and physical illness, was also able to sympathize with Katherine as few others could. In March 1918, when Katherine was stranded in Paris just after her first hemorrhage, Virginia wrote compassionately to Strachey: 'Katherine Mansfield has been dangerously ill, and is still pretty bad, so that Murry was sunk in the depths, what with that and overwork, poor wretch.'[44] When Katherine returned to England after three disastrous months in wartime France, Virginia was delighted with their relationship: 'I had a most satisfactory and fascinating renewal of my friendship with Katherine Mansfield. She is extremely ill . . . [and] is the very best of women writers—always of course passing over one fine but very modest example.'[45] And when Katherine's mother died after a dangerous operation in August 1918, Katherine confessed her grief to Virginia, who had had a mental breakdown when she was thirteen years old and tried to kill herself after *her* mother's death: 'My mother has died. I can't think of anything else. Ah, Virginia, she was such an exquisite little being, far too fragile and lovely to be dead for ever more.'[46]

In the spring of 1919 Virginia noted the queer mixture of amusement and annoyance in her attitude towards Katherine, and after Katherine was hurt when Roger Fry did not invite her to his party, Virginia recognized that Katherine's 'hard composure is much on the surface'.[47] In May 1920 Virginia wrote in her diary that: 'She is of the cat kind; alien, composed, always solitary—observant. And then we talked about solitude and I found her expressing my feelings as I never hear them expressed. . . . A queer effect she produces of someone apart, entirely self-centred; altogether concentrated upon her "art": almost fierce to me about it. . . . Once more as keenly as ever I feel a common understanding between us—a queer sense of being "like", not only about literature and I think it's independent of gratified vanity. I can talk straight out to her.'[48]

Though Katherine's intense observation and egoistic concentration alarmed Virginia, they were absolutely essential to Katherine's art. In a letter of August 1919, Katherine responded warmly to the more cautious and reserved Virginia and eagerly sought her friendship: 'My God, I love to think of you, Virginia, as my friend. Don't cry me an ardent creature or say, with your head a little on one side, smiling as though you knew some enchanting secret: "Well, Katherine, we shall see." . . . But pray consider how rare it is to find some one with the same passion for writing that you have, who desires to be scrupulously truthful with you.'[49]

Virginia's admiration of Katherine's work produced tangible results. When the long story that Katherine worked on throughout 1917 was rejected by publishers, she submitted it to the Woolfs who printed and bound 'Prelude' by hand, and published it in July 1918 as the second pamphlet of the Hogarth Press. In October 1917 Katherine wrote joyfully to Brett about the Woolfs's response to her work: 'I couldn't help feeling gratified. I did not think they would like it at all and I am still astounded that they do.'[50] In July 1918 Virginia explained to Vanessa: 'I can't do anything just now except fold and staple 300 copies of K.M.'s stories. It takes a good deal of time by hand, but we hope to send out some copies on Thursday'.[51] She noted in her *Diary*: 'I myself find a kind of beauty about the story; a little vapourish I admit, & freely watered with some of her cheap realities; but it has the living power, the detached existence of a work of art.'[52] When the volume finally appeared, it was almost completely ignored.

Though Virginia liked 'Prelude', she was seriously disappointed in 'Bliss', a satiric story of lesbianism and adultery that appeared in August 1918. She rather harshly condemned Katherine's superficiality, limited vision and poor style—and then attempted to relate her literary to her personal weaknesses:

> I threw down *Bliss* with the exclamation, 'She's done for!'
> Indeed I don't see how much faith in her as a woman or writer can survive that sort of story. I shall have to accept the fact, I'm afraid, that her mind is a very thin soil, laid an inch or two deep

upon very barren rock. For *Bliss* is long enough to give her a chance of going deeper. Instead she is content with superficial smartness; and the whole conception is poor, cheap, not the vision, however imperfect, of an interesting mind. She writes badly too. And the effect was as I say, to give me an impression of her callousness and hardness as a human being. . . . Or is it absurd to read all this criticism of her personally into a story?[53]

But Virginia, whose opinion of the story contradicted her earlier view of Katherine's intelligence, realized she was being unfair. In November she wrote to Vanessa about Katherine's futile plans for a Swiss cure and modified her ideas about Katherine's character and commitment to art: 'Poor Katherine Mansfield seems very bad, though I don't like to ask her how bad, and she says she's going to Switzerland with Murry and will be cured. I can't help finding her very interesting, in spite of her story ["Bliss"] in the English Review; at least she cares about writing, which as I'm coming to think, is about the rarest and most desirable of gifts.'[54] Virginia repeated this idea, and expressed a far more generous opinion of Katherine's mind and art, in her 1927 review in the *Nation and Athenaeum* of Katherine's posthumously published *Journal*: 'No one felt more seriously the importance of writing than she did. In all the pages of her journal, instinctive, rapid as they are, her attitude towards her work is admirable, sane, caustic, and austere. There is no literary gossip; no vanity; no jealousy.'[55] It is significant that Virginia praised Katherine's freedom from the vices frequently associated with Bloomsbury: gossip, vanity and jealousy.

Katherine's criticism of Virginia's works repeats Virginia's pattern of private censure and public praise. In a letter to Murry of November 1919 Katherine, who had direct contact with the War during her long months in France, criticized Virginia for coldly ignoring the War and the radical changes in English society, and for expressing herself in a traditional novel, *Night and Day*, rather than in a new mode of art:

My private opinion is that it is a lie in the soul. . . . The novel can't just leave the war out. There *must* have been a change of heart. . . . I feel in the *profoundest* sense that nothing can ever be the same—that, as artists, we are traitors if we feel otherwise: we have to take it into account and find new expressions, new moulds for our new thoughts and feelings. . . . It positively frightens me—to realize this *utter coldness* and indifference. But I will be very careful and do my best to be dignified and sober. Inwardly I despise them all for a set of *cowards*. We have to face our war. They won't.[56]

Katherine's sober and dignified review, which appeared eleven days later in Murry's *Athenaeum*, subtly conveyed her fundamental criticism of the long and rather lifeless novel, and drove her knife home under a cloak of bland praise:

The strangeness lies in her aloofness, her air of quiet perfection, her lack of any sign that she has made a perilous voyage—the absence of any scars. . . . It is extremely cultivated, distinguished and brilliant, but above all—deliberate. There is not a chapter where one is unconscious of the writer, of her personality, her point of view, and her control of the situation. . . . 'Night and Day' [is] fresh, new and exquisite, a novel in the tradition of the English novel. In the midst of our admiration it makes us feel old and chill: we had never thought to look upon its like again![57]

Katherine believed that Virginia's quiet perfection, absence of scars and deliberate control of the situation actually concealed her cowardly indifference to the War that had killed Katherine's brother; and that Virginia's exquisite traditional novel, referred to in Hamlet's words of praise for his dead father, revealed that the realistic tradition from Jane Austen to John Galsworthy was finished. Virginia, of course, understood Katherine's oblique and muted criticism and 'felt her acid'. In her *Diary* she recorded: 'K.M. wrote a review which irritated me—I thought I saw spite in it. A decorous and elderly dullard she describes me.'[58] But she later agreed with Katherine that her early novel, *Night and Day*, 'is dead'.[59] Writing in September 1921 to Sylvia Lynd, Katherine repeated her criticism and identified the essential weakness in Virginia's work—the aloofness from life that made Katherine's range of emotional experience so fascinating: 'I've only just read Virginia Woolf's Monday and Tuesday stories. I didn't care for them. She's detached from life—it won't do, will it? Nothing grows.'[60] Though there was a certain admiration and respect on both sides, Virginia and Katherine's jealousy, pride and self-esteem prevented the generous recognition of each other's genius.

The difference between the artistic achievement of Virginia and Katherine derived from the contrast between the selfish Murry and the devoted Leonard as well as from the fact that Virginia had greater genius and reached her artistic maturity. Katherine, who wrote her finest stories in the last two years of her life, died at thirty-four while Virginia, whose writing career spanned twenty-eight years, killed herself when she was fifty-nine. Katherine, who was frustrated in motherhood, craved an orthodox and secure marriage with a strong and intelligent husband, an equal partnership like that of George Eliot and George Henry Lewes. Though Katherine tried to pretend, a few weeks after her marriage to Murry in May 1918, that their relationship was not important to her, she envied Virginia, who was sustained in her work and her phases of madness by the devotion and constant companionship of her husband. Virginia saw through this transparent pose and wrote to Ottoline: 'I saw Katherine Middleton Murry the other day—very ill, I thought, but very inscrutable and fascinating. After a good deal of worrying by me, she confessed that she was immensely happy married to Murry, though for some reason she makes out that marriage is of no more importance than engaging a charwoman. Part of her fascination lies in the obligation she is under to say absurd things.'[61]

Just after Murry had been appointed editor of the *Athenaeum* (to which she contributed), Virginia recorded in her diary of April 1919: 'I respect M. I wish for his good opinion.'[62] But her good opinion changed radically when she became more familiar with Murry's character, his confessional novel, *The Things We Are* (1922), and his embarrassing poetry which Katherine may have praised to Virginia. (Katherine, who was caustic and austere about her friends' work and her own, wrote rapturously to Murry of *Cinnamon and Angelica* in December 1917: 'Your poem— ah, your poem is simply wonderful. Yes, it is really great. Don't hesitate to believe that. It is simply thrillingly good.')[63] In the spring and summer of 1922, just after Murry's novel had been published, Virginia treated her friends to a savage but accurate dissection of his character, which was 'full of spite and back-biting and gush and high-mindedness': 'Middleton M[urry] is a posturing Byronic little man; pale, penetrating: with bad teeth; histrionic; an egoist; not, I think, very honest; but a good journalist, and works like a horse, and writes the poetry a very old hack might write. . . . He has a mania for confession. I suppose his instinct is to absolve himself in these bleatings and so get permission for more sins.'[64]

Gerald Brenan spoke for most of Bloomsbury when he said: 'Everyone detested Middleton Murry'; and Bertrand Russell also 'thought Murry *beastly*'.[65] People disliked Murry because he was a pretentious and ambitious self-made man who, though shy and diffident, conveyed an impression of condescension and learned superiority. He lived in a world of ideas rather than of people, and often adopted and then abandoned untenable beliefs, which made his followers feel deceived and betrayed. He also used an unfashionable self-confessional mode of writing to blacken his own image.

Though Katherine found Leonard overcautious and dull—he 'is so extremely worthy, but I find him terribly flattening'[66]—she always envied Virginia's happy and secure marriage much more than her artistic achievement: 'I used to feel like Virginia but she had Leonard. I had *no one*.'[67] Katherine lamented to Murry in November 1919, when she was isolated in Italy and in the depths of despair: 'You know it's madness to love and live apart. That's what we do. Last time when I came back to France do you remember how we *swore* never again? Then I went to Looe—and after that we *swore*: never again. Then I came here. Shall we go on doing this? It isn't a married life at all—not what I mean by a married life. How I envy Virginia; no wonder she can write. There is always in her writing a calm freedom of expression as though she were at peace—her roof over her, her possessions round her, and her man somewhere within call.'[68] Virginia never realized the agony Katherine suffered when poor health frequently forced her to live apart from Murry; and though Virginia had a secure home and devoted husband, Katherine certainly exaggerated the superficial calm that disguised Virginia's internal chaos.

Virginia saw Katherine for the last time in August 1920, and noted the contrast between the bright and tidy 'doll's house' in Hampstead and the terrible disease of her friend: 'She looked very ill—very drawn, and moved languidly, drawing herself across the room like some suffering animal.'[69] And when Katherine died in January 1923, Virginia's (perhaps defensive) reaction was insensitive, envious and malicious. In a three-page diary passage of January 16, she compared herself to Katherine (as she had always compared herself to Vanessa), egoistically judged Katherine by coldly calculating her fidelity, and confessed she had been guilty of gossip and treachery—for there is no evidence that Katherine had ever personally attacked Virginia:

> One feels—what? A shock of relief?—a rival the less? . . . When I began to write, it seemed to me there was no point in writing. Katherine won't read it. Katherine's my rival no longer. . . . I was jealous of her writing—the only writing I have ever been jealous of. This made it harder to write to her; and I saw in it, perhaps from jealousy, all the qualities I dislike in her. . . . Hers were beautiful eyes—rather dog-like, brown, very wide apart, with a steady slow rather faithful and sad expression. Her nose was sharp, a little vulgar. Her lips thin and hard. . . .
> Did she care for me? Sometimes she would say so—would kiss me—would look at me as if (is this sentiment?) her eyes would like always to be faithful. She would promise never never to forget. That was what we said at the end of our last talk. . . . For our friendship was a real thing, we said, looking at each other quite straight. It would always go on whatever happened. What happened, I suppose, was faultfindings and perhaps gossip. . . . The small lies and treacheries, the perpetual playing and teasing, or whatever it was, cut away much of the substance of friendship. One was too uncertain. . . . Yet I have the feeling that I shall think of her at intervals all through life. Probably we had something in common which I shall never find in anyone else.[70]

Virginia understood that she and Katherine shared a painful but creative conjunction of imagination, isolation and illness. The last observation she made about Katherine and herself, which synthesized all the references to her friend's disease, was also the most perceptive: 'I never gave her credit for all the physical suffering and the effect it must have had in embittering her.'[71]

The year after Katherine died Virginia met Vita Sackville-West and established a lesbian relationship with her, for Vita did not have Katherine's profound commitment to her art and to her husband. Quentin Bell's comparison of Virginia's feelings for Katherine and Vita reveals that her friendship with Katherine,

6

though not as passionate as her relationship with Vita, had touched her heart, and was more intimate and important to Virginia than her diaries and letters suggest: 'Virginia felt as a lover feels—she desponded when she fancied herself neglected, despaired when Vita was away, waited anxiously for letters, needed Vita's company and lived in that strange mixture of elation and despair which lovers—and one would have supposed only lovers—can experience. All this she had done and felt for Katherine.'[72] Virginia's later judgment of Vita applies with equal force to Katherine: she is 'in short (what I have never been) a real woman. There is some voluptuousness about her.'[73]

CHAPTER ELEVEN

Chelsea and Return to Bandol, 1916–1918

IN SEPTEMBER 1916, when Katherine came back to London from Mylor, she and Murry rented the ground floor of a house owned by Maynard Keynes at 3 Gower Street, which had Brett on the second floor and Carrington in the attic. In December and January Katherine visited Garsington, acted in films and tried to find a suitable flat, which for an unmarried couple in wartime London was both difficult to locate and expensive to rent. Ida and Ottoline both state that Katherine disliked the atmosphere of the Gower Street house and the proximity of Carrington, who spied on Katherine's friends, watched her movements and made her feel uncomfortable. In January 1917, when the strain of Gower Street became intolerable, Katherine wrote to Murry (though they were still living together) about all the horrible and depressing places they had found and left: 'Do you remember as vividly as I do ALL those houses, ALL those flats, ALL those rooms we have taken and withdrawn from. My valiant little warrior, have you forgotten the horrors? In their time they have broken me and I must live from week to week and not feel bound. . . . I'd far rather sit in a furnished room in an hotel and work than have a lovely flat and feel that the strain of money was crippling us again.'[1] Their relationship was always precarious and they were frequently forced to re-establish it without the conventional foundations of marriage, a supportive family and a secure home and income. Except for Ida Baker, whom she could always depend on, Katherine was alone in all her undertakings.

Murry, who was working very hard at the War Office, also wrote regular reviews of French literature for the *TLS* and contributed political articles to the *Nation*. But his overwork and concern about the War threw him into a profound depression that became a terrible burden to Katherine. When they failed to find a flat and Katherine wished to be alone, she took a studio in February at 141a Old Church Street, in Chelsea, and Murry rented rooms a few streets away at 47 Redcliffe Road. This was the first of their voluntary separations, and it established a pattern that recurred from May to July 1918 when Katherine was in Cornwall and Murry in London, and from July 1922 to January 1923 when they lived separately in Switzerland, in London and Fontainebleau. Murry later wrote rather fatalistically and inhumanly about their Chelsea separation: 'That Katherine went to live apart from me seemed to me only natural. In my own way, I had also passed beyond the personal.'[2]

Just as Murry, when alienated from Katherine, had previously turned to male friendship and 'intellectual ecstasy' with Gordon Campbell and D. H. Lawrence, so he once again turned to intimate and introspective speculations with a new Irish friend, John William Navin Sullivan. To a certain extent, Sullivan also replaced Murry's close Oxford friend, Frederick Goodyear, who had died of wounds in France in 1917. Sullivan had been enthusiastic about Murry's book on Dostoyevsky (which was published in 1916) and they met through Dan Rider, whose bookshop had been a centre for Frank Harris and the *Rhythm* group. Sullivan served under Murry in the Censorship Department during the War, reviewed for the *TLS* and the *Athenaeum*, wrote books on science and a biography of Beethoven, and married 'Mimi' Bartrick-Baker, Katherine's Queen's College friend. Aldous Huxley, who found Sullivan a cultured and lively man, told his father: 'He has a very clear, hard and acute intelligence and a very considerable knowledge, not merely on his own subjects— mathematics, physics and astronomy—but on literature and particularly music. A stimulating companion.'[3] Katherine, who resented Murry's friendship with the chain-smoking Sullivan, agreed with Huxley about his intelligence but criticized his lack of sensibility, which she considered far more important. 'A queer fish, a true Bohemian', she told Sydney Schiff. 'He has written a Life of Beethoven and a book about Einstein. He likes beer, a lot of it. . . . Sullivan has brains but no intuition, no sensibility. I like him but he sets my teeth on edge.'[4]

Though they lived separately, Murry saw Katherine every evening when she resumed her wifely role and prepared dinner for him. Ida Baker gives a precise description of the Old Church Street studio, which often had a damp and ominous air: 'The rectangular room which [a single window] lighted went right through to the glass doors at the back of the house, which opened on to a communal garden, and on sunny days it was rather lovely with the large leaves of a tree tapping on the window. Half way through the main room, on the right, a bedroom was curtained off, with a bathroom to the left of it. Above this was a staircase leading to a deep balcony, like a minstrels' gallery, which stuck out over the bedroom into the studio. Behind this was a small kitchen. Katherine slept in the big main room on a wide settee'.[5] Katherine's charwoman was the model for the grief-stricken heroine of the 'Life of Ma Parker' which, like 'The Garden Party' and 'The Doll's House', expresses her understanding of and sympathy with the realities of working-class life.

Katherine and Murry now seemed to be testing their capacity for self-destruction and were desperately unhappy without each other. Murry, who was deeply depressed and even contemplated suicide, describes how he walked through the streets during air-raids and hoped for death. And in May 1917 Katherine told him that she was frequently engulfed by loneliness and overcome by fear: 'When dusk came, flowing up the silent garden, lapping against the blind windows, my first and last terror started up. . . . It was so violent, so dreadful I put down the coffee pot—and simply ran away—*ran ran* out of the studio and up the street.'[6] Katherine roamed the dark streets rather than remain alone in the queer oblong room; when she was attacked by her dreaded 'night fears', Ida—who had returned to England in the autumn of 1916 after spending two years caring for her father in Rhodesia—moved into the studio and discreetly slept in the high 'minstrels' gallery': 'If there happened to be a visitor I lay on my bed very silently, since, though Katherine and I were content, it might have been inhibiting for the visitor to know that an unseen third person was present.'[7]

One rather disconcerted visitor was Aldous Huxley, who saw Katherine in December 1917 and was struck (like Virginia Woolf) by her 'mysterious' bohemian life. As he wrote to his future sister-in-law: 'Last Sunday I looked in on Katherine in her curious little kennel in Chelsea: all very mysterious, particularly when she suddenly gave a shout in the middle of our conversation and was answered by the sleepy voice of somebody who was in bed behind a curtain and whose presence I had never realized.'[8] Two months earlier, after a dinner party with Katherine, Virginia met Ida (who had a wartime job as tool-setter in an aeroplane factory) and described her as an uprooted woman: 'A munition worker called Leslie Moor came to fetch her—another of those females on the border land of propriety and naturally inhabiting the underworld—rather vivacious, sallow skinned, without any attachment to one place rather than another.'[9]

Katherine, who had had difficulty publishing her work since the demise of *Signature* in November 1915 and had accumulated a number of satiric stories, began in the spring of 1917 to send her work to Orage—who had parted from Beatrice Hastings in 1914. Between April and October, Katherine published in the *New Age* a pastiche, a translation of Alphonse Daudet's 'M. Séguin's Goat' and nine stories.[10] During her eleven months in Chelsea Katherine saw many of her friends, including the painter J. D. Fergusson, who had returned from Paris when the War began and made a drawing that was used in a few early copies of 'Prelude'. In her *Journal* of August 21 Katherine recorded a happy meeting with the sympathetic Fergusson, who assuaged her loneliness, seemed to understand her almost as well as Kot, and gave her the warmth and security that Murry failed to provide:

This man is in many ways extraordinarily like me. I like him so much; I feel so *honest* with him that it's simply one of my real joys, one of the real joys of my life, to have him come and talk and be with me. I did not realize, until he was here and we ate together, how much I cared for him—and how much I was really at home with him. A real understanding. We might have spoken a different language—returned from a far country. I just felt all was well, and we understood each other. Just that. And there was 'ease' between us. There is a division: people who are my people, people who are not my people. He is mine.[11]

In the summer of 1917 Katherine and Murry also met Siegfried Sassoon, who was then making a pacifist protest against the War while still on active duty. Sassoon writes of Murry in his auto-biography: 'With him and Katherine Mansfield (of whose great talent as a story-writer I was still unaware) I spent a self-conscious sultry evening in a candle-lighted room in [Redcliffe Road] South Kensington. He was sympathetic and helpful in clarifying my [pacifist] statement and reducing it to a more condensed form. Katherine Mansfield was almost silent. The only thing I can remember her saying was "Do you ever think about anything except the war?" '[12] It is not surprising that the War obsessed Sassoon, who had endured many months of trench warfare, and Katherine's single remark suggests that she was irritated by his impassioned conversation, which must have stirred memories of Leslie's death.

Katherine's perennial problems—poverty, illness and Murry— also plagued her during the summer and winter of 1917. In August she complained to Ottoline about the minor expense of a window cleaner and about the cheap and ugly furniture in her studio. In the same month Katherine told Virginia she was ill with 'Rheumatics plus ghastly depression *plus* fury'.[13] Her fury was intensified that summer by Murry's foolish and egoistic attempt to arouse her jealousy and win her love. He asked Ottoline, who was quite unprepared for any emotional intimacy, if he might 'come into her heart', and then told Katherine that Ottoline had 'fallen deeply and passionately in love with him',[14] which made Katherine bitterly angry and hurt her friendship with Ottoline.

Despite this quarrel, Ottoline invited Murry to recuperate at Garsington when his health broke down from overwork in November 1917 and he was—ironically—suspected of tuberculosis. Ottoline begged Katherine to come and care for him, but Murry failed to prepare for her arrival and she caught a severe chill on a bitterly cold night while being driven from the station to the manor house in an open dog-cart. She arrived frozen, and then asked Murry: '*must* you look so ill?'[15] When Katherine returned to Chelsea, her 'bit of a chill' turned to high fever and she collapsed, suffered her third attack of pleurisy and was ill in bed for three weeks. The following month she apologized to Murry for the cost of her illness and promised to reimburse him promptly for her medical bills. Katherine also saw the connection between her sickness and her terrible temper, which reminded her of Lawrence's black rages and accounted for a great deal of her harsh criticism of Murry, Ida, Brett, Ottoline and Virginia: 'A funny feature about this sort of illness is one's temper. . . . If many people start talking I just lose my puff and feel my blood getting black.'[16]

At the end of December Katherine consulted a New Zealander, Dr. Ainger, the first in a long series of physicians who failed to cure her disease. He told her she ought to recuperate in 'Teneriffe or Madeira, but as you can't go there, Spain or the South of France *will do*'. 'If I stay in England', she explained to Anne Rice, after quoting the doctor's advice, 'he says I may become consumptive.'[17] Katherine could not go to the warm Spanish and Portguese islands off the west coast of Africa (where she had briefly stopped *en route* to England) because of the danger of submarine warfare, the considerable cost of travel and her reluctance to live so far from Murry, but she could have gone to Algiers or Málaga, which are much warmer than Bandol.

Katherine also told Murry of the terrible sentence that had been pronounced by Dr. Ainger and would affect the rest of her life: 'There is a SPOT in my right lung which "confirms him in his opinion that it is absolutely imperative that I go out of this country and keep out of it through all future winters".' Katherine, who was no longer able to work, also asked Murry to write to the Hôtel Beau Rivage: 'But don't mention LUNGS, or they will take fright: you know the French. They'd imagine I had come there to gallop away.'[18] Despite the (increasingly common) attempt to joke about galloping consumption, Katherine and Murry must have been terrified by the lung spot, for it meant that her pleurisy had become tuberculosis.

Murry could have taken control of Katherine's life at that point and commanded her to stay at home, for his job was to read the foreign press and he must have known about the austere conditions in wartime France. Instead of acting decisively, Murry, whom Mark Gertler described in September 1917 as pathetic, 'shifty, backboneless, fearful, and ill',[19] blamed his personal weakness on the inhumanity of the world: 'Oh, why did she ever go so far away?' he asked in his diary of January 15, a week after Katherine's departure, 'I do not believe that anyone ever had, more than we, the sense of the vastness and inhumanity of the world and of our own frailness and smallness.'[20] Though Murry was introspective and analytical about his relations with Katherine, he never really understood either her or himself. And though he knew her plan to return to Bandol was impractical and dangerous, he later admitted: 'Because she believed that [it would help], I came to believe it, too.'[21] Murry's

fatal acquiescence in Katherine's self-deception was repeated
when Katherine refused to enter a sanatorium in October 1918,
when she left a healthy life in Switzerland to take Dr. Manoukhin's
treatments in February 1922 and, finally, when she entered
Gurdjieff's Institute in October 1922. In all four cases Murry
refused to assert himself, to care for Katherine and to prevent
her from propelling herself into destruction, for her decision
to journey—for the fifth time—into war-torn France was one of
the most disastrous of her entire life. On January 8, 1918, she
set out for Bandol and became an exile from England as well
as from New Zealand; and though she left London to avoid
consumption, she returned after three months in the grip of the
deadly disease.

Murry and Ida, who were doing vital war work, were refused
permission to leave the country and saw Katherine off at Waterloo
Station. Though Katherine crossed the Channel in a rough sea
and snow storm, and the windows were broken in the unheated
Paris train, she was struck by the good French food and (like
Lawrence) contrasted the vitality of the Continent with the
stolidity of the English. There is, she wrote to Murry, 'a wonderful spirit here—so much humour, life, gaiety, sorrow one cannot
see it all and not think with amazement of the strange cement-like
state of England.'[22] But her happiness was short-lived, and she
was quickly overcome by the sense of fear and insecurity that
always threatened to envelop her when she travelled by herself and seemed to be at the mercy of every stranger and servant.
As she wrote in a revealing *Scrapbook* passage in 1917, 'Even
when she was feeling her happiest, at her freest, she would
become aware, quite suddenly, of the "tone" of the waiter
or the hotel servant, and it was extraordinary how it wrecked
her sense of security. It seemed to her that something malicious
was being plotted against her, as though everybody and everything—yes, even to inanimate objects like chairs and tables
—was secretly "in the know"—waiting for that ominous,
infallible thing to happen to her which always did happen, and
which was bound to happen to every woman on earth who
travelled alone.'[23]

The inevitable yet unendurable hardships began as soon as
Katherine reached Paris, where she began to suffer the discomfort and exasperation of a country at war. The trains were

6*

cold, late and packed to overflowing, without food, hot drinks or lavatories that worked. She had a burning pain in her 'wing' (a euphemism for lung) and was almost knocked over by a blow in the chest from a French pimp who was trying to board the train at Marseilles. Her greatest adventure occurred in that town, and her vivid description of the battle between soldiers and civilians, in which she portrays herself as a defenceless yet stoical heroine protected by strong men—a signal example to Murry—captures the sense of drama and romance in the ugly incident:

There were 8 Serbian officers in the compartment with me and their 2 dogs. Never shall I say another word against Serbians. They looked like Maiden's Dreams, excessively handsome and well cared for, graceful, young, dashing, with fine teeth and eyes. But that did not matter. What *did* was that after shunting for 2 hours, five yards forward, five yards back, there was a free fight at the station between a mob of soldiers and the civilians. The soldiers demanded the train—and that *les civils* should evacuate it. Not with good temper, but furious—very ugly—and VILE. They banged on the windows, wrenched open the doors and threw out the people and their luggage after them. They came to our carriage, swarmed in—told the officers they too must go, and one caught hold of me as though I were a sort of packet of rugs. I never said a word for I was far too tired and vague to care about anything except I was determined not to *cry*—but one of the officers then let out— threw out the soldiers—said I was his wife and had been travelling with him five days—and when the *chef militaire de la gare* came, said the same—threw *him* out—banged the door, took off their dogs' leads and held the door shut.[24]

When Katherine finally reached Bandol she was struck by the ironic contrast between her consummate happiness in 1916 and her desperate condition exactly two years later. At the Hôtel Beau Rivage a strange woman appeared in the smoky hall wiping her mouth with a napkin, and Katherine suddenly realized that she was not expected, that the hotel had new owners, and that it was very cold and expensive. She tried to look up her old acquaintances in the town, who had been so friendly on her last visit, but because of the change in her appearance and the distractions of war nobody recognized or remembered her. It was bitterly cold, with the moaning wind like an iced knife and a strange grey light over the boiling sea, which reminded her of the storm that killed Shelley. She was weak and depressed after the exhausting journey and felt 'like a fly who has been dropped into the milk-jug and fished out again'[25]—an image that would recur in her letters and in one of her finest stories. After a disenchanting visit to the Villa Pauline she found her mood reflected in a rain-storm and in a football that was transformed into an image of despair: 'Big soft reluctant drops fell on my hands and face. The light was flashing through the dusk from the lighthouse, and a swarm of black soldiers was kicking something about on the sand among the palm trees—a dead dog perhaps, or a little tied-up kitten.'[26]

Katherine's letters to Murry from Bandol reflect the emotional extremes of her solitary life. At first she describes minor dis-tractions like the warships in the bay and her devoted maid Juliette who was strong and gay, her daily activities, her food, her reading of Shakespeare and the Romantics, her work or attempt to work, and she sends endless salutations to her Japanese doll, Ribni. But she soon becomes gloomy about having to remain indoors during the cold spells of the Mediterranean where one counts on good weather, where the whole way of life depends on being outside and where the heating is inadequate and the houses damp. She complains of delays in the mail (threatening to buy and train a pigeon to obtain better service), financial problems, physical discomforts (including cigarettes that taste like 'the most infernal camel-droppings'), poor health and unbearable loneli-ness. She worries about the air raids in London and about Murry's health (as she had worried about Garnet's), longs for her lover, and impatiently counts the months, weeks and days until she can return to him. She thinks of their happy reunion, loving reconciliation with his 'darling little Mother' (who had been so hostile to her in Clovelly Mansions), plans of marriage (for she was finally getting divorced from Bowden), and she dreams of the future and The Heron—'the fortress and hiding place of our love'—which she hoped would be a kind of English Villa Pauline, with children and a printing press. Towards the end of Katherine's stay her moods fluctuate wildly, she fears the War will isolate her indefinitely in France, and she feels homesickness, anxiety and panic: 'I suffer so frightfully from insomnia here and from night terrors. . . . There is a great black bird flying over me, and I am so frightened he'll settle—so terrified. I don't know exactly what *kind* he is. . . . Not to sleep, and to be alone, is a very neat example of HELL.'[27]

When Murry was isolated in London during the spring of 1913, editing *Rhythm* from Chancery Lane and visiting Katherine in Cholesbury at weekends, he found the separation very hard to bear. He now wrote often, tried to respond to Katherine's feelings by discussing Ribni and The Heron, and by counting the days, and was genuinely concerned about her welfare. But he failed to understand the agony of Katherine—who swore they would never part again—when she was ill and separated from him in Bandol.

Whereas Murry's letters are prosaic and dull, filled with clichés and self-pity, Katherine's letters, by contrast, are perceptive and poignant. They are especially witty when she is satirizing the sexual habits and physical vulgarity of the French and defensively attempting to find humour in degrading circumstances. In a passage omitted from the *Journal* of January 1918 she rather primly remarks: 'With them it is always rutting time. See them dancing and sniffing round a woman's skirts.'[28] And writing to Murry the following month she describes the unfortunate effects of occupying a room near the hotel lavatory: 'Another thing I hate the French bourgeoisie for is their absorbed interest in evacuation. What is constipating or what not? That is a real *criterion*. . . . At the end of this passage there is a W.C. Great Guns! they troop and flock there . . . and not only that . . . they are all victims of the most amazing Flatulence imaginable. Air raids over London don't hold a candle to 'em.'[29] Despite its humorous aspect, flatulence must have been revolting to the fastidious Katherine, who had to concentrate in order to write and often suffered from insomnia. Her isolation made her extremely vulnerable, for she was frustrated in her desire for Murry and only her courage, her reserve and her illness prevented her from becoming the sexual prey of the French.

On the voyage to the salubrious climate of Bandol Katherine had overheard a morbid conversation between two French women who insisted the coast was a deadly spot, and this irrational but fearful idea became firmly embedded in her mind: 'The big [woman], rolling about in the shaking train, said what a *fatal place* this coast is for anyone who is even threatened with lung trouble. She reeled off the most hideous examples, especially one which froze me finally, of an American "belle et forte avec un simple bronchite" who came down here to be cured and in three weeks had had a severe haemorrhage and *died.* . . . I knew the woman was a fool, hysterical, morbid, *but I believed her*; and her voice has gone on somewhere echoing in me ever since.'[30] Katherine, who noticed her first grey hairs in Bandol, did not regain the weight she had lost when she first arrived, and on January 20 she confessed to Murry the gravity of her illness: 'It is quite true. I have been *bloody ill.* . . . I really *did*, at one or two times, think I would "peg out" here.'[31] But two days later she apologized for the admission that had caused him pain and anxiety, and tried to reassure him about her solitary and restful routine: 'I will just tell you, so that you know how I am taking care of myself. I stay in bed every day until lunch. Then I dress by a fire. If it is fine I go for a small walk in the afternoon, then I come back to my fire. After dinner, at about 8.30 I go to bed.'[32]

Despite mental depression and physical illness Katherine forced herself to write and to achieve a 'break through', and by February she was totally absorbed in her stories: 'My work excites me so tremendously that I almost feel *insane* at night, and I have been at it with hardly a break all day.'[33] She wrote 'Je ne parle pas français' (her response to Carco's *Les Innocents*, which was published in 1916), 'Bliss' and 'Sun and Moon' between January and March; and she explained to Murry in a letter of February 3 that two contrary impulses, which she associated with her first and second trips to Bandol, inspired her writing. The first impulse derived from the joy of being in love and inspired her mature works, and the second, which dominated her early adult life, was rooted in her profound sense of tragic despair and inspired her satiric stories:

I've two 'kick-offs' in the writing game. *One* is joy—real joy— the thing that made me write when we lived at Pauline, and that sort of writing I could only do in just that state of being in some perfectly blissful way at *peace*. . . . The other 'kick-off' is my old original one, and (had I not known love) it would have been my all. Not hate or destruction (both are beneath contempt as real motives) but an *extremely* deep sense of hopelessness, of everything doomed to disaster, almost wilfully, stupidly.[34]

When Ida heard about Katherine's illness and loneliness, she instinctively understood the situation, realized that Katherine needed her, obtained leave from her factory and, without being summoned, left for Bandol. When Katherine heard she was coming, she had the irrational fear that her friend was bringing news of Murry's illness—the only reason that would justify her journey in Katherine's eyes. Ida relates that when she reached Bandol on February 12 with some squashed *babas au rhum*—frightened, exhausted and without the disastrous news of Murry—Katherine, who feared Ida would interrupt her work, was extremely hostile and immediately challenged her by asking: ' "What *have* you come for?" My heart sank to the uttermost depths', Ida relates. 'All that struggle and effort and anguish of mind and body was wasted.'[35]

Brett says that Ida, who was also called the 'dragoon', was devoted to Katherine, who in fact despised her.[36] But their relationship was much more complex than she suggests. Ida joyfully served the object of her love, and Katherine extinguished Ida's other interests and prevented her from developing a life of her own. Ida had to be, or chose to be, always available when Katherine needed her, yet able to continue her own existence when she became superfluous during Katherine's brief and intermittent periods of health and happiness. Ida, who was timid and humble, felt awkward with intellectuals and cultured society. She found her vocation in service, not only with Katherine, but also as a hairdresser and factory worker in England and (when she followed Katherine from country to country) as a nurse in Menton and Switzerland, and a farm worker in France. Katherine, who was fiercely independent but often helpless, both needed and resented Ida, because of her own illness and Murry's failure as a husband. Katherine was cruel to Ida because she hated to lean on her yet had to do so, and also because Ida unintentionally provoked and encouraged Katherine to treat her that way. Katherine's work and disease dominated the last five years of her life; and Murry, whose own work was equally important to him and who felt her disease robbed him of his emotional support, could not really help her. Most of Katherine's intense frustration and anger about her disease and Murry was channelled into aggression against Ida, who was literally starved of affection and ate huge quantities of food to compensate for her lack of sex and love. Murry liked to hear Katherine's criticism of Ida, who was his main rival for her affection; and Ida, always a willing victim, was extremely objective and understanding about Katherine's abuse, and returned her bitter cruelty with self-abasement.

Katherine, who called Ida the albatross, ghoul, lunatic attendant, great monster and fiend guardian, felt guilty about selfishly devouring Ida's life and failing to respond to her emotional needs. In a *Journal* passage called 'The Toothache Sunday', her code word for depression, Katherine alludes to God's relation to the faithful in Psalm 101:6 in order to describe Ida's selfless devotion, and wishes she could comfort and cherish Ida, as she had hoped to do with Brett: 'Have I ruined her happy life? Am I to blame? When I see her pale and so tired that she shuffles her feet as she walks when she comes to me—drenched after tears; when I see the buttons hanging off her coats and her skirt torn—why do I call myself to account for all this, and feel that I am responsible for her? She gave me the gift of herself. "Take me, Katie. I am yours. I will serve you and walk in your ways, Katie." I ought to have made a happy being of her.'[37] Katherine probably portrayed her relationship to Ida in 'Psychology' (1918), in which the heroine fails to re-establish an intimate rapport with her all-too-'spiritual' lover and has the unsatisfactory compensation of a 'virgin, a pathetic creature who simply idolized her (heaven knows why) and had this habit of turning up and ringing the bell and then saying, when she opened the door: "My dear, send me away!" She never did.'[38]

The patronizing tone of Katherine's letter to Murry in November 1917, which refers to the foreman in Ida's factory and mocks her timidity and lack of response to men, suggests that Katherine believed Ida's adoration allowed her to daydream about men but precluded any serious relationship: 'L.M. is still in bed—dreaming of Webb, I expect, and saying that she never, never could be kissed on the mouth but did not mind the cheek.'[39] In June 1918 Katherine urged Ida (who remained a spinster) to marry the foreman or the South African gunnery officer she had met on the ship from Rhodesia to England so that Ida could successfully

bear and nurture the children Katherine was unable to have: 'I
wish you would marry Webb or Gibson and have some children.
We seem so *very* short of children, don't we? I simply pine for
some but they don't want me (small wonder). Now I feel you
would be superbly successful.'[40]

Katherine's letters during February 1918 express the full range
of her feelings for Ida, who infuriated Katherine and led her
to believe that Ida's docility and submission masked her deceit
and insincerity. Katherine described Ida, who was intensely
jealous of Murry, as 'gross, trivial, dead to all that is alive for me,
ignorant and *false*'.[41] She felt that Ida wanted to prey upon her
weakness and destroy her relationship with Murry, and portrayed
Ida as a cannibal who fed on her wasted flesh:

> If I didn't put up a fight, she'd ruin all our life. That's what she
> wants to do. 'If there wasn't Jack'—that is what she says,—and
> that I really CANNOT STAND from anybody. . . . What she
> can't stand is you and I—*us*. You've taken away her prey—
> which is me. I'm not exaggerating. . . .
> She's a revolting hysterical ghoul. She's never content except
> when she can eat me. My God!! . . . She'd *like* me to be
> paralyzed of course—or blind—preferably blind. . . . I even go
> so far as to feel that she has pecked her way into my lung to
> justify her coming, which *is* cruel, I know. . . . I always feel
> her dream is to bury me here and bring back a few bulbs from
> Katie's grave to plant in a window-box for you.[42]

Katherine also told Murry that she thought Ida had devoured and
swallowed her up, just as the powerful Frieda had done to the
delicate Lawrence: 'I felt exactly as L. must have felt with F.—
exactly. You remember the feeling L. had (before he was so mad)
that F. wanted to destroy him; I have—oh, just that!!!'[43]

We have seen, from Katherine's fastidious account of her
father's 'blatantly vulgar manner' of feeding while sailing back to
New Zealand in 1907, that she considered eating a gauge of
morality, and her caustic but hilarious descriptions of Ida's
eating habits reveal her resentment of her friend's health and
strength:

> [She has] an Appetite which makes the hotel *tremble*, and after
> having devoured the table-cloth, glasses and spoons, says,

'What I miss is the puddings.' . . . L.M. is also exceedingly fond of bananas. But she eats them so slowly, so terribly slowly. And they know it—somehow; they realise what is in store for them when she reaches out her hand. . . .

Meal times and walk times are quite enough to exasperate me and lash me into fury beyond measure. 'Katie mine, who is Wordsworth? Must I like him? It's no good looking cross because I love you, my angel, from the little tip of that cross eyebrow to the *all* of you. When am I going to brush your hair again?' I shut my teeth and say 'Never!' but I really *do* feel that if she could she'd EAT me.[44]

In 'The Aloe', which was written in the spring of 1916 and reflects Katherine's ambivalence towards Ida, Beryl cannot suppress her contempt and curious attraction for Nan Fry, whom she repeatedly allows to brush her hair: '[Nan] would snatch up Beryl's hair and bury her face in it, and kiss it, or clasp her hands round Beryl's head and press it back against her firm breast, sobbing: "You are so beautiful!" . . . At these moments Beryl had such a feeling of horror, such a violent thrill of physical dislike for Nan Fry. . . . She didn't even try to suppress her contempt and her disgust. . . . The curious thing was that Beryl let her brush her hair again, and let this happen again.'[45]

In the last year of her life, after expressing considerable hostility towards Ida—much of it displaced from Murry—Katherine, exhausted by illness, finally accepted her dependence upon Ida, recognized her as a distinct alternative to Murry and used the word 'share' which in the Georgian era had a suggestive meaning: 'Now my *idea* is that we should spend the foreign months together, you and I. You know by that I mean they will be my working months but apart from work—walks—tea in a forest, cold chicken on a rock by the sea and so on we could "share".'[46] Two months later Katherine openly declared their implicit relationship: 'But try and believe and keep on believing without signs from me that I do love you and want you for my wife.'[47] Though Katherine took the dominant role with men as well as with women, she rarely had a successful relationship with a man and desperately needed Ida's emotional support, physical help and devoted nursing. And Ida, who willingly adopted the passive role, always felt guilty about her friendship with Katherine and confessed: 'I never gave her the buoyant, unfettered love that she needed, and was often a responsibility which, for a sick woman, must have been exasperating. . . . Leaving her entirely for an indefinite period was always a most bitter anguish for me, physically as well as in my heart.'⁴⁸

Though Ida unintentionally threatened Katherine, her intuition about the dangerous state of Katherine's health was sound, and Ida capably cared for her during the long periods of sickness and separation from Murry. In order to prove how well she was, Katherine took a long and thoroughly exhausting walk the day before her tubercular hemorrhage. The next morning, February 19, 1918 (a week after Ida arrived), Katherine got up to open the shutters and, as she writes in a moving passage in her *Journal*: '[I] bounded back into bed. The bound made me cough—I spat—it tasted strange—it was bright red blood. Since then I've gone on spitting each time I cough a little more. Oh yes, of course I'm frightened. But for two reasons only. I don't want to be ill, I mean "seriously", away from Jack. Jack is the first thought. 2nd, I don't want to find this is a real consumption, perhaps it's going to gallop—who knows?—and I shan't have my work written. *That's what matters*.'⁴⁹ Katherine's hemorrhage was induced by the strenuous coughing which brought up the bright blood from the lung whose tissues had been destroyed by tubercle bacilli. On the day of her hemorrhage Katherine also wrote a restrained and very brave letter to Murry, which tried to reassure him by blaming Ida and admitting that it was useful to have her as a nurse: 'I have not been so well these last few days. Today I saw a doctor. . . . I've got a bit of a temperature and I'm not so fat as when I came—and, Bogey, this is *not* serious, does *not* keep me in bed, is absolutely easily curable, but I have been spitting a bit of blood. . . . It's not serious. But when I saw the bright arterial blood, I nearly had a fit. But he says it's absolutely curable. . . . So it's a good thing L.M. came (even though I feel in some mysterious way *she has done it*. That's because I *loathe* her so. I do.) Still I'll use her as a slave.'⁵⁰

Though Katherine's English exit permit stipulated that she could not return for three months, the longing for Murry, the irritation with Ida, the gravity of her disease and the ineffective treatment by the disreputable and drunken English doctor—'a little sot with poached eyes who bites his fingers'—made her attempt to return to England in mid-March, before that time had elapsed. She had planned to get Murry to send a telegram announcing that her mother was ill, but when she discovered that everyone on the Riviera had already tried that obvious ploy, she had to obtain a note from the shady doctor that quite honestly stated it was essential that she should return to England for medical reasons. This was not so easy, for the doctor was lecherous and had behaved offensively during his physical examination of Katherine. But she was cynically determined to get what she needed and use the 'toad' for her own ends. She dressed elegantly in a new frock, lit the fire in her room, flattered and charmed the doctor—who must have reminded her of the ones who had taken an unprofessional interest in her body and performed her abortion 'with a dirty button-hook'—until he agreed to write the note: 'I dictated it *and* had to spell it *and* had to lean over him as he wrote *and* hear him say—what dirty hogs do say. I am sure he is here because he has killed some poor girl with a dirty button-hook. He is a maniac on *venereal* diseases and *passion*. Ah, the filthy little brute! There I sat and smiled and let him talk. I was determined to get him for our purpose—any way that didn't involve letting him touch me.'[51] Katherine then bought sleeping pills that were 'the same things that good old Doctor Martin gave Mother to give me when I was 13 and knew myself a woman for the first time'.[52] The memory of Dr. Martin replaced the disgusting abortionist with the kindly physician of her childhood and helped to obliterate the unpleasant experience in Bandol.

Katherine and Ida stayed in the Hôtel de Russie in Marseilles on March 18 and 19 while making arrangements with the British Consul and the travel agent. The next day they returned to Bandol to pack and check out of the hotel, returning to Marseilles, *en route* to Paris, on March 21, just as rumours of a great German offensive spread through France. When they arrived in Paris the following day Katherine was shocked to discover that she could not proceed to London without explicit permission from the English authorities in Bedford Square. She had to cancel her ticket, arrange formalities with the police and military permit office, which had tightened restrictions against foreigners, and search for a reasonably priced hotel room. She waited in vain for letters from Murry, for postal and telegraph communication with England were suspended during the bombardment of Paris, which began just after Katherine arrived, and marked the last great German offensive of the War and final attempt to break through the front at Amiens.

Katherine and Ida found attic rooms with armchairs 'very like pug-dogs' in the Select Hôtel at 1 Place de la Sorbonne, in the student quarter near the Rue de Tournon where she had lived with Murry in the winter of 1913. 'It is very quiet—trees outside, you know, and an extremely pleasant chiming clock on the Sorbonne *même*', Katherine wrote to Murry on her first day in Paris. She had a rather ornate and large 'square room with 2 windows, a writing table, waste-paper basket, two armchairs, de l'eau courante, a low wooden bed with a head piece of two [symbolic] lions facing each other, but separated for ever'.[53] Every night Ida crept into Katherine's room with blankets and pillow, and slept at her feet on the floor.

Murry found Katherine's *bulletins du front*, written during her three weeks in Paris from March 22 to April 10, when she was feverish, seriously ill and trapped against her will during the bombardment, too painful to publish in the 1928 edition of her letters, though they did appear in the 1951 edition. Katherine's hotel was pleasant, but she was soon overwhelmed by her agonizing situation, and by what she called the waste of love and the cruel trick that life had played on her: 'The spring this year seems to me *hateful*—cruel—cruel like pigeons are cruel—all the leaves burst into claws.'[54] The loud and ominous sound from the firing of the German super-*Kanon*, which bit huge chunks out of the houses, took place regularly every eighteen minutes, and Katherine was forced to descend into the icy bomb shelter where 'ugly and horrible' people smoked in the fetid air of the cellars.

On March 29 Katherine learned that all civilian traffic and letters to England had been cancelled for eight days. Two days later, in order to pass the time and earn some money for her protracted stay, Katherine got a job at an underground canteen for soldiers and refugees at the Gare du Nord, but was forced to abandon this foolish project after only one day of exhausting work. On April 1 Katherine dreamed that Murry would suddenly appear and carry her home: 'Every taxi that stops at this hotel, stops my heart, too. I know how utterly absurd that is. But I feel—by some miracle.'[55] This miracle, like others that Katherine later hoped for, never occurred, but she finally received her permit to return to England on April 3, and devoted her remaining energy to a futile search for letters from Murry and a reservation on the Channel ferry. Katherine, burdened by Ida, felt like Mouse, the terrified heroine of 'Je ne parle pas français': '*alone* in a *foreign* country, with absolutely *nobody* to talk to—*no* influence—a woman dependent on you who can't speak the tongue.'[56] Ida relates that in a final, desperate effort Katherine re-enacted her fiction, summoned up her courage and sought out Francis Carco, whom she disliked and feared, and returned with enough money for their tickets home.

By the time Katherine arrived in London on April 11 she had lost fourteen pounds and looked as if she had just come out of prison. A passport photograph taken in April 1918, two months after her hemorrhage and during a period of extreme psychological and physical strain, provides a strong contrast to the 1917 picture of Katherine wearing a velvet suit. The passport photograph marks the beginning of her physical decline and shows a haggard and wasted woman, with deep pouches under her eyes and hard lines creasing her young face. Though only twenty-nine, her appearance had radically deteriorated since 1913 when she was at the height of her beauty. Katherine's return to London marked the completion of another emotional cycle which would recur again and again in her marriage: anger with Murry, separation in England, winter abroad with Ida, longing for Murry, dreams of return, and extreme disillusionment—followed by a recurrence of anger and separation, longing and disillusionment.

CHAPTER TWELVE

Cornwall and Hampstead, 1918–1919

KATHERINE'S DIFFICULTIES in living *with* Murry when she had tuberculosis were as great as those when living apart from him. She was acutely aware of her own physical decay and said she understood Shakespeare's line 'To *rot* itself with motion': 'better than I care to. I mean—alas!—I have proof of it in my own being.'[1] Despite this self-disgust, she tried to reassure Murry by quoting a doctor who said that tuberculosis transferred from a wife to a husband 'was so rare as to be absolutely left out of account. It is perhaps the rarest form of contagion. This may reassure you in a mauvais moment.'[2] This opinion runs counter to all modern medical evidence, for husbands and wives who are exposed to tuberculosis become infected five times as often as people who have had no contact with the disease.

In the 1920s patients followed the regimen described in Thomas Mann's *The Magic Mountain* (1924), which consisted of rest cure, proper diet, open air and lung-collapse therapy. X-rays were not widely used for diagnosis until the thirties, and advanced techniques in pulmonary surgery and chemotherapy were not employed until the late forties. Though the sanatoria prevented many carriers from infecting other people, taught the patients hygienic discipline, decreased their mental and physical strain, and allowed the disease to be studied by doctors, a recent book on tuberculosis states: 'The importance attributed to prolonged rest, to a change in climate, or to special diets is no longer warranted. . . . No locality or climate specifically prevented the development of tuberculosis or caused its cure.'[3] In 1934, 36,000 people died of the disease in Britain.

Though there was no specific cure for tuberculosis during Katherine's lifetime, she did not take any of the prescribed treatments of the time: neither rest in a sanatorium, nor consistent medical supervision, nor strict regimen, nor healthy diet—and she did not even stop smoking, though it provoked coughing fits.

Katherine's extreme psychological stress further weakened her resistance to tuberculosis, for her frequent separation from Murry intensified her financial worries, marital problems, lack of security and craving for protection. During the last five years of her life her very existence was precarious, and she was haunted by the nearness and the inevitability of death.

Ida Baker suggests in a recent letter that tuberculosis was likely to attack Katherine, who had been used to the pure air of New Zealand, and had moved to a difficult and impoverished life in the rain and fog of London.[4] Dr. Lewis Moorman is probably correct when he suggests that her pleurisy 'represents an extension of pulmonary tuberculosis to the pleura, which covers the lungs and lines the chest cavity' and that she 'had slightly or moderately active tuberculosis long before she was overwhelmed by the acute attack of pleurisy'.[5] Another doctor adds that Katherine's fever with aches and pains, which she called rheumatism, 'may have been active periods of her tuberculosis.'[6] Katherine was not actually diagnosed as tubercular until November 1917 but, like Lawrence, had been suffering from the disease since 1911.

In April 1918 Katherine admitted she had tuberculosis, rejected the idea of a sanatorium and warned Ida of the highly contagious disease in a childishly light-hearted, heart-breaking tone that was more painful than tears or lamentations: 'Yes there is no doubt I have definitely got consumption. He [Dr. Ainger] appreciates that a sanatorium would kill me *much* faster than cure me. (It's a 2nd lunatic asylum to me.) I am to try a "cure" at home. . . . I must not borrow a handkerchief (this is serious Betsy, for you know how they fly from me) or drink out of loving cups or eat the little bear's porridge with a spoon. And so on. But you see I am ever so gay. . . .'[7]

It is therefore understandable that Murry was frightened and even disgusted by Katherine. She was quick to perceive this and wrote, while separated from him in Cornwall: 'Do you remember when you put your handkerchief to your lips and turned away from me? . . . You are always pale, exhausted, in a kind of anguish of set fatigue when I am by. Now I feel in your letters this is lifting and you are breathing again. "She's away and she's famously 'all right'. Now I can get on." '[8] Murry's fourth wife testifies to the 'lack of any physical expression of their love which her illness imposed upon them',[9] and Ida records that when he came to

Ospedaletti in December 1919 she was surprised to discover that he spent the night in the spare room. Katherine, who had a terrible fear of death, was exhausted by pain, loneliness, insecurity, and the hopelessness of trying to get better while gradually getting worse.

When she was trapped during the bombardment of Paris, Murry addressed her as 'Mouse' and rather pitifully expressed his impotence, his longing and his despair: 'Oh, Wig, my mouse, my secret soul: you are there suffering and I am dead without you. Surely life can't be so awful not to bring us together again quickly now. It's getting desperate. I feel that I had come to the top of the water for the last time. Of course, it can't be the last. Just as I never come to the end of my despair, I shan't come to the end of my hope either.'10 Though Katherine had been dreadfully lonely in Bandol, counted the days until she could come home, and then went through agony in Paris for three more weeks, Murry could neither understand her emotions nor satisfy her expectations when she finally returned to England for their long-awaited marriage.

Katherine was divorced by Bowden on April 29; and on May 3 she married Murry—after living together, more or less, for six years—in the South Kensington registry office with Fergusson and Brett as their witnesses. Katherine tried to be optimistic, but Murry felt it was tragically ironic that their marriage and hopes for happiness coincided with the beginning of Katherine's fatal disease: 'In 1918, deep in my heart I could feel no joy at all. Katherine had returned from France now desperately ill after all the fantastic shattering of our hopes. She knew, just as well as I, how ill she was; yet she expected our marriage to work the miracle, and was bitterly disappointed in me because I could not behave as though it were so. . . . The memory of my wedding to Katherine is a memory of the *anguish*, not the happiness of love.'11

Murry states that his two dark ground floor rooms at 47 Redcliffe Road were cramped and unhealthy, that he worked all day at the War Office and was unable to look after Katherine, and that he persuaded her to go to Cornwall against her will (though he could never persuade her to enter a sanatorium). But he does not explain why he failed to find a decent flat so that they could continue to live together. Katherine, who was terribly unhappy at the idea of another separation, was suspicious of his motives, felt Murry was 'trying to get rid of her' and realized 'he has not this same great devouring need of me that I have of him. He *can* exist apart from me.'[12] She tried to explain to him—when the sea stank, and grey crabs scuttled on the rocks and the paths had been fouled by human excrement—that he was too absorbed in his anguished brooding to be really aware of her feelings and need for love: 'Our marriage. You cannot imagine what that was to have meant to me. It's fantastic—I suppose. It was to have shone—apart from all else in my life. And it really was only part of the nightmare, after all. You never once held me in your arms and called me your wife. In fact, the whole affair was like my silly birthday. I had to keep on making you remember it.'[13]

On May 17, after living with Murry for five weeks, Katherine moved to Looe on the Cornish coast, where Anne Rice Drey, who was painting there, had found her a comfortable place to stay. While Ida returned to work in the aeroplane factory and tried to take care of Murry, Katherine enjoyed the warm weather and the expensive but luxurious Headland Hotel. She had a room with French windows that faced south to a fine view of the sea, good food (despite wartime shortages) and the devoted service of her aged chambermaid, Mrs. Honey: 'She's got only one tooth, and she's small with those rose cheeks and big soft blue eyes and white hair, but how fond I am of her!'[14] Katherine had her doll Ribni, drives through the countryside in an open carriage and the companionship of her friend, Anne Rice, who was pregnant and more radiant than ever. She thought Katherine looked 'touching and alarming', and the contrast of their lives and health was painfully obvious to both of them.

After sketching for two hours, Anne painted Katherine in a scheme of vivid reds, and portrayed her friend seated three-quarter length in a soft chair with her hands folded over a thick volume. Katherine wears a straight low fringe across her forehead and hair piled high on the back of her head. Her face is boldly modelled with planes of colour, and she has a rather severe expression and stares intensely past the viewer. Her closely fitting yoke-collared persimmon dress reveals the contours of her thin chest and body, and sets her solid form against the painted floral background. Anne's portrait successfully captures Katherine's love of bright colours, and her extraordinary mixture of serenity and vivacity, intelligence and beauty.

Despite the pleasant aspects of the hotel, Katherine could hear the sound of gunfire in France and was kept awake by a neighbour coughing through the night. She still worried about money, still missed Murry desperately, still wanted a baby, still suffered sharp pain in her spine and lungs, still lost weight and spat blood, and was often overcome by fits of weeping as her first days of joy turned—as they always did when she was isolated and ill—into gloomy bitterness. Though Murry had promised not to leave her alone, he had abandoned her once again. His somewhat premature belief that her love was actually a morbid *Liebestod* reinforced all her suspicions and fears, and he relates that her letters to him had a devastating effect: 'The ecstasy of love, which she required, was not health, but only a hectic hastening to death. Yet if I stood my ground against her fatal desire, she tore me to pieces by her suffering and her despair.'[15] Katherine wounded Murry by condemning his well-meaning but insensitive 'betrayal' and insisted that she preferred death to solitude:

All my longing, all my desires, all my dreams and hopes had been just to be with you, and—to come back to my home. Bien! I came. Heard how ill I was, scarcely seem to have seen you, except through a mist of anxiety, felt that *all* your idea was for me to get away into the country again. Well, I understood that —although, please try to realize the appalling blow it was to me to uproot again—and so soon—with hardly a word spoken. Please do try and realize that. . . .

What—of all other things—seems so hard is how we swore *not* to let each other go again . . . and then how soon . . . we were gone. Yesterday, thinking of all this in the afternoon, I wept so. I could not bear it: I thought I must come back and *die* there rather than always this living apart.[16]

When Katherine was living in Cornwall she had time to reflect on the gravity of her disease, and felt, like Lear, stretched out 'upon the rack of this tough world'. In June 1918, she wrote to Ottoline of her immense longing for 'a body that isn't an enemy— a body that isn't fiendishly engaged in the old, old "necessary" torture of—breaking one's spirit'.[17] That summer she also poured out her soul to Ida, who would be certain to understand the knife-like pain of her cough if not the morbid symbol of Chekhov's seagull: 'One wants to weep; one thinks of death; the seagulls fly into the infinite—and one wonders why on earth one should be cursed with this perpetual ill-health! . . . You see I am never for one single hour without pain. If it is not my lungs it is (far more painful) my back.'[18]

Because of her illness and profound unhappiness in Cornwall, Katherine wrote only one slight story, 'Carnation', about a boring French class at Queen's College. But she expressed her belief in the compensatory and even redemptive value of art to Ottoline Morrell: 'My secret belief—the innermost "credo" by which I live is—that *although* Life is loathsomely ugly and people are terribly often vile and cruel and base, nevertheless there is something at the back of it all—which if only I were great enough to understand would make *everything*, everything indescribably beautiful.'[19] Katherine's most important and technically brilliant work, 'Prelude', fell stillborn from the Hogarth Press in July. But in August she published 'Bliss' in Austin Harrison's *English Review* and received six guineas for her first appearance in an important literary journal.

Murry and Katherine spent the last week of June together in Cornwall, and then shared the dreariness of Redcliffe Road until the end of August. Just as Katherine's marriage had been ruined by her disease, so the pleasurable prospect of having, for the first time in her life, a husband, a home of her own, her possessions, a great many books and a 'passion for writing', was extinguished by the death of her mother on August 8, after a long illness and a dangerous operation. Katherine had not seen her mother since March 1912 when Annie returned to New Zealand after visiting England to see the Coronation, and her mother's death seemed to threaten her own existence. In two letters to Ottoline Morrell (who was only nine years younger than her mother) she portrayed Annie as an intensely natural being, described her own sense of loss and recalled the vivacious invalidism which she shared with her: 'She was the most exquisite, perfect little being—something between a star and a flower—I simply cannot *bear* the thought that I shall not see her again. . . . Yes, my mother's death is a terrible sorrow to me. I feel—do you know what I mean—the *silence* of it so. She was more alive than anyone I have ever known.'[20]

On August 26, two weeks after her mother's death, the Murrys moved into a tall grey brick house overlooking Hampstead Heath, at 2 Portland Villas, East Heath Road, which they called The Elephant. When Katherine became mistress of The Elephant (now commemorated by a blue plaque) she had to take care of Murry, who was terribly overworked, assume the domestic burdens of a large household, and become responsible for the four women in her establishment—the maids Violet and Gertie, a difficult and drunken cook, and Ida. Ida, who was both a hindrance and a help, served as an emotional buffer between Katherine and Murry and kept them at 'one remove from each other'. But Ida's fanatical and sacrificial solicitude grated on Katherine's nerves and she complained about her in witty letters to her more sophisticated friends. She told Anne Rice: 'The Faithful One changed the hot water bottles so marvellously often that you never had a hot water bottle at all. It was always being taken or brought back'; and to Ottoline she described 'L.M. bringing my lunch with a "Take, eat, this is my body" air'.[21] Katherine was again ambivalent about the irritating but indispensable Ida, whom she sometimes saw as a jealous and philistine enemy and sometimes as a devoted and sympathetic friend. In May 1918 she told Murry: 'My love for her is so divided by my extreme *hate* for her that I really think the latter has it. I feel she'll stand between us—that you and she will be against me'; and in November she recorded in her *Journal*: 'L.M. and I are really the bitterest enemies imaginable. I stand for all she *hates* in Life, and she for all that I *detest*. When I leave her this time, we must see each other no more.'[22] But Katherine could never leave Ida; and Ida, whom Katherine 'flew to with bad tempers, worries, depressions, money troubles, wants, rages, silences',[23] would never leave her. When Katherine attacked and insulted Ida she accepted her friend's right to be abusive and blamed herself for being passive and dull: 'An angry letter never *hurt* me—just depressed me. It must have been dreadful for the poor darling, banging away on putty.'[24] Though Ida could not meet Katherine's exacting standards and thought herself worthy of punishment, her passivity—like Murry's—was both disarming and infuriating, and Katherine was reduced to complaining about one to the other.

Katherine's friendship with Murry's younger brother Arthur (born in 1902), whom she soon renamed Richard, was much happier. Katherine first met Richard at the Murrys's home in Wandsworth in the spring of 1912, and she saw a good deal of

him during the summer of 1917 when he worked with the pacifist
farmers at Garsington. Leonard Woolf states: 'Katherine seemed
to be always irritated with Murry and enraged with Murry's
brother, who lived with them and, according to Katherine, ate
too much. Every now and then she would say sotto voce something bitter and biting about the one or the other.'[25] But Katherine
was extremely fond of Richard, who did not live at The Elephant,
and her letters to him are playful, loving and kind. Many of
Katherine's friends—Fergusson, Brett, Gertler, Carrington and
Anne Rice—were painters, and their achievement and Katherine's
encouragement inspired Richard to become an artist. Richard
helped Murry print his poems and Katherine's story, 'Je ne parle
pas français', on the Heron Press at The Elephant in December
1919. After Leslie was killed in 1915 Katherine transferred a great
deal of her maternal love to Richard, and she saw him frequently
in November 1918 when the end of the War brought back
memories of her brother's death.

Murry states that in October 1918 an English specialist told
Katherine the truth, recommended the only possible treatment
that might save her life, and warned her about what would
happen if she did not follow his advice: 'There's one chance for
her—and only one. If she goes into a *strict* sanatorium immediately. Switzerland is not one atom more good to her than England
is. Climate means nothing. Discipline everything. If she will go
somewhere for a year and submit to discipline, then she has about
an even chance. If not, she has two or three years to live—four at
the outside.' Murry then relates the subsequent conversation with
Katherine:

'He says I must go into a sanatorium', she said. 'I can't. A
sanatorium would *kill* me.' Then she darted a quick, fearful
glance at me. 'Do *you* want me to go?'
'No', I said dully. 'What's the good?'
'You do believe it would kill me?'
'Yes, I do', I said.
'You do believe I shall get well?'
'Yes', I said. . . .
Did I really believe that she would get well? I did not know.
What I did know was that I must say so, again and again—for
ever.[26]

Though Katherine was very stubborn and strong-willed and would not tolerate contradiction, Murry's acquiescence in her self-deception undoubtedly hastened her death.

The fastidious and elegant Katherine, who was constantly inspired by her dream of The Heron—an idyllic home in a lovely setting—was particularly disgusted by the prospect of sharing the squalid details of her illness with vulgar people in a huge hospital-hotel. She was not comforted and sustained, like Elizabeth Barrett or Marcel Proust, by an invalid existence, and believed that the sterile regimen of a sanatorium would not only kill her, but would also extinguish her creative inspiration. Though she was temporarily persuaded to enter a sanatorium, she soon convinced herself that she could not tolerate the exclusive company of consumptives and would be able to establish her own regime at home: '[I] consented to do what has always seemed to me the final intolerable thing, i.e. to go into a sanatorium. To-day, finally thinking it over, and in view of the fact that it is not, after all, so much a question of *climate* as of *regime* (there are very successful sanatoria in Hampstead and Highgate), I am determined, by my own will, to live the sanatorium life *here*. . . . Anything else, any institutional existence, would kill me—or being alone, cut off, ill with the other ill.'[27]

Katherine's mental strain and physical weakness forced her into an irrational decision, and the perceptive analysis of Dr. Andrew Morland, the specialist who examined Lawrence in Bandol just before his death in March 1930, applies with equal force to Katherine: 'His sad story illustrates the incompatibility between a certain type of genius and the ordered way of life necessary for recovery from tuberculosis. Those very qualities which gave Lawrence such keen perception and such passionate feeling made it quite impossible for him to submit for any length of time to a restricted sanatorium existence; the ingredients for tragedy were therefore present from the start and its course, although slow, was inexorable.'[28]

The only physician Katherine both liked and trusted, and who treated her for several years, was Dr. Victor Sorapure. Ida Baker, who resented Murry, Kot, and most of Katherine's friends, gives Sorapure warm—if undiscriminating—praise: 'He was wonderfully kind and imaginative. He seemed to understand both her illness and the way in which she, with her character, could best come to terms with it. She told me once, when the treatment he was giving her proved almost unendurably painful, he helped her over it by quietly talking of the immensity and wonder of the universe and the incomprehensibility of space. He showed real and deep understanding in all her troubles, and even eventually discovered the infection that was the true cause of the "rheumatiz" which had persisted and increased ever since 1910.'[29] In December 1920 Katherine dedicated the manuscript of 'The Daughters of the Late Colonel': 'To Doctor Sorapure. Were my gratitude to equal my admiration, my admiration would still outstep my gratitude.'[30] She returned to England in August 1922, after an absence of two years, to consult Sorapure, and left him a book in her will.

Though Katherine was extremely fond of the sympathetic Sorapure, her *Journal* entry of June 1919 (like Ida's eulogy) suggests the significant difference between his theory and practice, and his inability to cure her disease: 'His point of view about medicine seems to me *just completely right*. . . . Quite the right man to have at one's dying bedside.'[31] For the 'incomprehensibility of space' had nothing to do with Katherine's illness, and Sorapure's idea of how she could best come to terms with it was to disagree with the specialist and definitely advise, on psychological grounds, against the 'highly dangerous experiment' of a sanatorium—Katherine's only hope of survival.

As Katherine's health inexorably deteriorated, she made a desperate and pathetic search for a medical, a 'miraculous' and finally a mystical cure for tuberculosis. The 'mild' winter climate of the French and Italian Riviera, where a doctor told her 'a chill in your case would be a fatal disaster', was often bitterly cold with pouring rain, high wind, thick fog and air like acid. In Bandol in January 1918 her ineffectual daily 'regime' was to stay in bed until lunch, take a walk in the afternoons and go to bed at 8.30. By December 1919, when her illness forced her to eliminate the walk and retire several hours earlier, she would rise at noon, lie down on a sofa till six, and then take a hot-water bottle to bed. She was exhausted by the slightest exertion, tried to fight an overwhelming depression and was desperately lonely. She weighed 105 pounds when she escaped from the German bombardment of Paris in April 1918, and by November 1919, when Sylvia Lynd noticed she was so thin that 'her rings slid up and down her finger as she made tea',[32] she weighed only ninety-seven pounds.

Katherine's disease also had a profound influence on her creative life, for her hemorrhage of February 1918 reaffirmed her emotional and artistic bonds with the significant number of writers, artists and musicians who had died of tuberculosis since the beginning of the nineteenth century. Katherine believed in the influential Romantic idea that the artist is ill, and his illness gives him the power to see and to tell the truth. As Nietzsche stated: 'Sickness itself can be a stimulant to life.'[33]

Katherine saw herself as part of the moribund yet creative tradition: 'I, being what I am, had to suffer *this* in order to do the work I am here to perform. . . . The more I suffer, the more fiery energy I feel to bear it. . . . I do not see how we are to come by knowledge and love except through pain.'[34] In June 1922 Katherine romanticized a disappointing hotel in a Swiss *Kurort* by associating it with Stevenson and Chekhov: 'I decided to accept it as a kind of picnic: "the kind of place R. L. Stevenson might have stayed at"—or "some little hotel in Russia" ';[35] and she specifically related the tubercular tragedies of Bashkirtseff, Keats and Chekhov to her own condition and fate.

Like the Russian painter and diarist, Marie Bashkirtseff, whom she had read as a girl in New Zealand, Katherine sensed the first flowering of her mature talent (she published 'Prelude' and 'Bliss' in 1918) at the very moment she was threatened by death. Marie had written in the last months of her life: 'I have spent six years working ten hours a day to gain what? The knowledge of all I have yet to learn in my art—and a fatal disease. . . . The fact is not to be disguised; I have consumption. The right lung is far gone, and the left lung has been affected for a year past. Both lungs, then. . . . I may linger for a while, but I am doomed. . . . Here it is at last, then, the end of all my miseries! So many aspirations, so many hopes, so many plans—to die at twenty-four at the threshold of everything.'[36] In 1919 Katherine, with less self-pity, bravely faced the truth at the same time that she tried to avoid it: 'I *must* know from somebody how I am getting on and what is the state of my left lung, *i.e.*, I must be cheered up. Ten years passed this morning as I sat in my darkish little room. [It seems as though] I am now 41 and can't lose a moment. I must know.'[37]

Katherine also saw Keats's tragedy reflected in her own life, and compassionately recorded: 'These letters written during his fatal illness are terrible to one in my situation. It is frightening that he

9 (a) Leslie Beauchamp, 1915

9 (b) Francis Carco as a student aviator, 1917

10 (a) Virginia
and Leonard
Woolf

10 (b) Lady Ottoline at
Garsington, c. 1922

11 Katherine Mansfield, portrait by Anne Estelle Rice, 1918

12 Katherine and Murry, 1918

13 Elizabeth Bibesco

14 (a) Katherine (*right*) with Connie Beauchamp (*front*), Mrs Dunare (*next to KM*) and Jinnie Fullerton (*back*) at the Villa Flora, Menton, 1920

14 (b) Katherine (*centre*), with Dorothy Brett (*left*) and Ida Baker (*right*) at Sierre, 1921

15 (a) Violet Schiff, portrait by Wyndham Lewis

15 (b) Sydney Schiff, caricature by Max Beerbohm, 1925

16 (a) Katherine at
the Isola Bella,
Menton, 1920

16 (b) George Gurdjieff

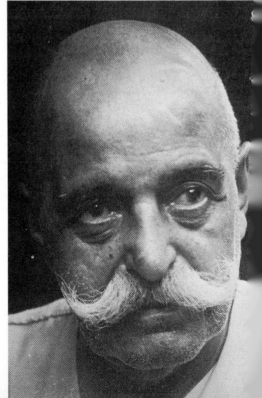

too should have known this mental anguish.'[38] Her letters to Murry quite consciously echoed Keats's last letters to Fanny Brawne about the effect of tuberculosis on the nerves, the tenuous line between life and death, and the relation between love and health, disease and creativity:

A person in health as you are can have no conception of the horrors that nerves and a temper like mine go through. (Keats)
I get so irritable, so nervous that I want to *scream*. (Mansfield)

How horrid was the chance of slipping into the ground instead of into your arms. (Keats)
That's the fearful part of having been near death. One knows how easy it is to die. The barriers that are up for everyone else are down for you and you've only to slip through. (Mansfield)

They talk of my going to Italy. 'Tis certain I shall never recover if I am to be so long separate from you. (Keats)
[Murry] will never realize that I am only WELL when we are 'together'. (Mansfield)

How astonishingly does the chance of leaving the world impress a sense of its natural beauty upon us! (Keats)[39]
My fever makes everything 100 times more vivid, like a nightmare is vivid. (Mansfield)[40]

Katherine was morbidly fascinated by Keats's and Chekhov's striking descriptions of their hemorrhages and by Chekhov's beautifully objective statement (written on the day of Katherine's birth and translated by Katherine and Kot): 'there is something ominous in blood running from the mouth: it's like the reflection of a fire.'[41] Katherine's comments on Chekhov apply to herself as well as to her Russian master who, like Keats, was frequently separated from his love (Olga Knipper) because his health forced him to live in the Crimea and her career as an actress kept her in Moscow. Katherine felt, on her last birthday, that Chekhov's final letters resembled those of Keats: 'He has given up hope. If you de-sentimentalize those final letters they are terrible. There is no more Tchehov. Illness has swallowed him.'[42] She also explains the difference between her artistic aspirations and achievement when discussing the effect of disease on Chekhov's art: 'For the last 8 years he knew no *security* at all. We know he felt his stories

7

were not half what they might be. It doesn't take much imagination to picture him on his death-bed thinking "I have never had a real chance. Something has been all wrong." [43] In March 1922, when she had less than a year to live, she told Richard Murry: 'I'm 33; yet I am only just beginning to see now what it is I really want to do. It will take years of work to really bring it off.' [44] In Chekhov and in Mansfield, the self-protective cynicism of an over-sensitive artist scarcely had sufficient time to ripen into compassion.

Murry, like Katherine, was also infatuated with Keats and Chekhov, with the Romantic concept that tuberculosis endowed its victim with a quality of spirituality and of creative genius, and with the Keatsian idea of 'Beauty that must die'. He was more than half in love with *Katherine*'s 'easeful death', and dispassionately regarded it not only as inevitable but also as a necessary part of his education. 'You see Jack "accepts" it', Katherine told Ida with bitter resentment, 'it even suits him that I should be so subdued and helpless. And it is deadly to know he NEVER tries to help.' [45]

Katherine felt that Murry did not give her either practical assistance or emotional support. The compassionate Ida relates that in the winter of 1918, when Katherine needed an oxygen cylinder in order to breathe, Murry would 'bemoan how terrible it all was, how dreadfully he was suffering, and how he could hardly bear it. He was too full of self-pity to give any help.' [46] In her *Journal* Katherine describes Murry's ostentatious suffering while she was gasping for the very breath of life: 'I cough and cough and at each breath a dragging, boiling, bubbling sound is heard. I feel that my whole chest is boiling. I sip water, spit, sip, spit. I feel I must break my heart. And I can't expand my chest; it's as though the chest had collapsed. . . . And J. is silent, hangs his head, hides his face with his fingers *as though* it were unendurable. "This is what she is doing to me! Every fresh sound makes *my* nerves wince." I know he can't help these feelings. But, oh God! how wrong they are. If he could only for a minute, serve me, help me, give *himself* up. . . . It's like having a cannon-ball tied to one's feet when one is trying not to drown.' [47]

Katherine condemned Murry's self-pity, his lack of love and understanding, and his 'Romantic' feeling that she was doomed to die—so that he could 'learn'. Katherine felt Murry treated her as posthumous while she was still alive, dug 'the garden as though he were exhuming a hated body or making a hole for a loved one',[48] and was pained by the belief that he wished her dead and was killing her.[49] Murry, who was suspected of tuberculosis in 1914 and again in 1917, had accepted Lawrence's devoted nursing during his attack of influenza in 1915, but when Katherine became ill in 1918, he could not bear the reversal of roles and his attractive qualities suddenly became liabilities.

Murry states that after 1918 the idea that Katherine would get well seemed like 'a childish dream', and their child-love was prolonged by their childlessness. Though Katherine, who was extremely independent, felt guilty about imposing herself on Murry and denying him a normal married life, she never abandoned her (now vicarious) desire for children; in June 1922 she admitted to her cousin Elizabeth: 'My only trouble is John. He ought to divorce me, marry a really gay young healthy creature, have children and ask me to be Godmother. He needs a wife beyond everything. I shall never be a wife and I feel such a fraud when he still believes that one day I shall turn into one.'[50]

Katherine summarized their unhappy relationship in her *Journal* of December 15, 1919—after the most serious crisis of their marriage—and emphasized Murry's inability to help her and his unwillingness to live abroad with her so that she could recover: 'This illness—getting worse and worse, and turning me into a woman and asking him to put himself away and to *bear* things for me. He stood it marvellously. It helped very much because it was a romantic disease (his love of a "romantic appearance" is immensely real) and also being "children" together gave us a practically unlimited chance to play at life, not to live. It was child love. . . . He said and three-quarters of him believed: I couldn't stand the strain of it with you ill. But it was a lie and a confession that all was not well with us.'[51]

The cold weather in the autumn of 1918 confined Katherine to The Elephant, and she was so weak that she had to use a cane. In December she wrote to Brett: 'I am hardly alive. I have not been out for months and cannot walk up and down the stairs with any success.'[52] Virginia Woolf, who came to Hampstead to see Katherine nearly every week from November 1918 to the following August, was alarmed by the effects of her friend's disease and wrote that at the beginning of the winter: 'Katherine was up, but husky & feeble, crawling about the room like an old woman. How far she is ill, one can't say. She impresses one a little unfavourably at first—then more favourably. I think she has a kind of childishness somewhere which has been much disfigured, but still exists. Illness, she says, breaks down one's privacy, so that one can't write.—The long story ["Bliss"] she has written breathes nothing but hate. Murry and the Monster watch & wait on her, till she hates them both. She trusts no one; she finds no "reality".'[53]

Though Murry recognized that Katherine was his moral, artistic and intellectual superior, he was totally egoistic and self-absorbed. He scarcely realized that he always took the best room for himself, and (like his father) expected his wife to do most of the housework. In October 1918, for example, Katherine recorded: 'Finding no towels in his room to-night, [he expressed] his indignation, sense of injury, desire so to shut the door that it would bring the house down. . . . It's like his *Why is lunch late?* as though I had but to wave my hand and the banquet descended.'[54] The following June she wrote that Murry 'ought not to have married. There never was a creature less fitted by nature for life with a *woman*'; and he confirmed: 'I don't know what a Woman is: and never shall.'[55] Murry could not understand people except through books, was incredibly naive and saw in life only what he wanted to see. He constantly praised the genius of Katherine, yet she had to support him for many years, perform the domestic duties, and then write her stories with the little time that remained. In Hampstead she wrote 'See Saw', 'This Flower', 'A Suburban Fairy Tale' and the unfinished 'Second Violin', but these were minor works and the year was not a productive one.

Murry, meanwhile, was having a very successful career. He became Chief Censor at the War Office in 1919 and was awarded an O.B.E. for his work the following year. And when Arthur Rowntree, the Quaker and chocolate tycoon, bought the *Athenaeum*, Murry was offered the editorship—a very considerable position which carried a salary of £800 a year. In January 1919 Murry moved into the editorial office at 10 Adelphi Terrace, on the floor below Bernard Shaw's flat, hired Aldous Huxley and J. W. N. Sullivan as assistant editors, and published his first issue in April. The *Athenaeum* contributors included Russell and Santayana, Eliot and Valéry, Forster, Strachey, Leonard and

Virginia Woolf and (very briefly) Lawrence, as well as writers like Frank Swinnerton who had contributed to *Rhythm* and whom Murry wanted in order 'to escape the stranglehold of Bloomsbury'.[56] But the magazine, which published almost nothing but reviews, was intended for an elite audience and doomed to failure. It first lost momentum and then a great deal of money (Lawrence told Kot: 'I hear the *Athenaeum* lost £5000 a year under our friend the mud-worm'[57]), and eventually merged with the *Nation* in February 1921, when Murry resigned and joined Katherine in Menton.

During the two years that Murry edited the *Athenaeum* Katherine published her translation of Chekhov's letters, eight poems (half of them under the pseudonym of Elizabeth Stanley), two essays, and seven stories (including 'Sun and Moon' and 'Miss Brill'), and established her reputation as a regular reviewer of fiction in that magazine. (Her 112 reviews were posthumously collected in *Novels and Novelists*, 1930.) When in London Katherine was sometimes angry at Murry for failing to consult her about editorial policy or even to show her a copy of the *Athenaeum*, and when abroad she felt the three editors reviewed the best books themselves and sent her the inferior ones. In February 1920, while living in Menton, she justly complained to Murry: 'The books are rather difficult to do: they are SO BAD!'[58]

But Katherine was amused in April 1919 when her black and white cat Charles Chaplin turned out to be female and suddenly gave birth to two kittens: Athenaeum and Wingley. She helped him through this trying period and told Virginia: 'He would only lie still when I stroked his belly and said, "It's all right, old chap. It's bound to happen to a man sooner or later." '[59]

The most vivid and perceptive description of Katherine and Murry's rather theatrical ambience—with its strange combination of invalidism, adoration, affection, aestheticism and courage—has been written by the shrewd and sceptical Enid Hilton, who met Katherine in Hampstead in the autumn of 1918 when Enid 'was very young, very raw and in the process of being dragged by Lawrence out of the narrow world of Eastwood and exposed to a wider if not better world he knew':

I remember a fairly large room with quite a number of people who must be nameless in case my memory of them is confused.

Middleton Murry was there, and of course Lawrence. Katherine was 'draped' on a couch (it was one of her not-so-good days) and *draped* seemed to me to be the correct word. She was dressed in a long, very full gown, carefully arranged to give the appearance of drapery. People stood around, adoring her, talking quietly to her. I was not prepared for this adoration and the whole picture, to my provincial down-to-earth view, was utterly artificial, all affectation. Even now I remember steeling myself against exposing Katherine.

As an outsider and a nobody I was ignored, leaving time to study and rearrange my thoughts. Gradually the picture changed. Katherine was lovely, quite exquisite, her sickness giving her an ethereal quality and great appeal. I remained critical of the contrived 'show' but fell under her spell. I compared her with her stories. These always attracted me and I read them with enjoyment of their perfection. Yet always I regretted the excessive *polishing*—they were polished until the *guts* were eliminated, little but the perfection remaining. And here was this woman, the writer, 'draped', polished to a delicate perfection. I wondered about the 'guts'. She had courage—to die!

There was something to drink, whether coffee or liquor I do not remember, and delicate little cakes. Whether the cakes were *so* delicate I am not sure, or whether they reflected everything about Katherine, seeming ethereal. I thought about this when I left.

I never met Katherine again but the picture remains so vivid [after fifty years]. As I write to you I see the room, adoring crowd, the lovely, almost evaporated woman, frail, polished, the star performer in a show that was nevertheless a part of her. Was Murry the producer, director, of these admiration performances? Other people who knew them may know. I do not, but am suspicious.[60]

In August 1919, Katherine, who had grave doubts about her plans and her future, told Anne Rice that she would rely on the strength and practical wisdom of her father, who was devastated by the loss of his son and his wife, and had arrived in London after an absence of six years: 'He seems to me a kind of vast symbolic chapeau out of which I shall draw the little piece of

paper that will decide my Fate. But that is absurd. For my plans
are to go abroad in about three weeks' time and there to remain.
We are on the track of several different places, and not decided
yet, but c'est tout.'[61] Since Katherine's health had noticeably
deteriorated during the English winter of 1918–19, she considered
living in Switzerland, Majorca and Corsica, and finally decided on
the Italian Riviera. On September 14, 1919 she left England for
San Remo with Ida and Murry. After two weeks, he returned to
England to edit the *Athenaeum* and continue the eternal search for
The Heron, the frail symbol of their faith in the future.

CHAPTER THIRTEEN

Ospedaletti and Menton, 1919–1921

I

THE MURRYS chose the hotel in San Remo because it was owned by an Englishman whom they hoped would be sympathetic, but they encountered difficulties within two weeks. When Katherine, exhausted by the journey, began to cough a great deal, the guests discovered she had tuberculosis, the manager asked her to leave because of her disease, and she had to pay to have her room disinfected.

Katherine, who felt like a pariah and feared she would have no place to go, was glad to rent a three-room villa, Casetta Deerholm, from the manager of the hotel. The whitewashed, red-roofed house was located in Ospedaletti, three miles west of San Remo, near the French frontier. At that time the village had nothing but a laundry, a flower market and a wine shop, and the people seemed pleasant and self-contained. The Casetta, which was high above the deep bay and the curving coastal road, and seemed to tremble in the late sun and shadows, had a splendid view of the village and the Mediterranean. Katherine was enthusiastic about the site and the lush flora, which once again reminded her of New Zealand, and wrote to Kot just after she moved in: 'It is on a wild hill slope, covered with olive and fig trees and long grasses and tall yellow flowers. Down below is the sea—an entire ocean—a huge expanse. It thunders all day against the rocks. At the back there are mountains. The villa is not very small. It has a big verandah on one side where one can work and an overgrown garden.'[1]

But by the time of Katherine's thirty-first birthday on October 14, which always made her feel nostalgic, she had fallen into the familiar phthisical pattern of ecstasy and disillusionment. In her daily letters to Murry she began to create plans for The Heron and expectations for the future that could not possibly be fulfilled. She felt the present was less important than the future and immediately started to count the days until she could return, sending emotional greetings to her cats and discussing her weekly *Athenaeum* reviews and her writing—or inability to write. She was tormented by bloodthirsty mosquitoes, the wind tugged at the trees and the waves, and made the draughty house paralyzingly cold, and snow appeared on the mountains behind the villa. She always worried about money, was constantly cheated by the local people and gave a detailed account of the petty but intensely irritating 'swins' of her laundress, woodman, gardener, postman, landlady and watchman. She frequently complained about the lack of mail, especially during the postal strike of January 1920, and told Murry how to resurrect her: 'When I die, just before the coffin is screwed up, pop a letter in. I shall jump up and out.'[2]

Katherine, isolated with Ida, had very little intellectual stimulation and was often bored and lonely, for she deliberately cut herself off from other people so that she could write and rarely made new friends while living abroad. The arrival of a magazine or book was a major event. She experienced depression, sexual frustration and maternal longings, and dreamed of adopting a child. Her constant nervousness, anxiety and raging temper were disastrous for her disease, and she suffered from nightmares, insomnia, high fever, sharp pain and loss of weight. Her doctors, who were either brutally honest or patently deceptive, were extremely expensive but could neither cure nor comfort her. Foster told her she could not get a maid because of her tuberculosis: 'they won't come because they *know* about me. . . . Very nice! But "can't be helped".' Bobone, who had the inexpressive red eyes of an ox, reassured her: 'So long as you have not the fevers you do not die. It is de fevers which kills.' When she was feverish and terribly depressed the 'charlatan' Ansaldi admitted that the encouraging 'reports he gave me were because "I saw dis lady wants vot you call sheering up". . . . When I told him of my melancholia, he said it was part toxin poisoning and part because you are alone wiz nobody near to love and sherish you. . . . Then he went away and I . . . REALIZED how I had been taken in again.'[3]

In December 1919, Dr. Foster pronounced his frank but brutal verdict: 'There is serious disease in your left lung of long

7*

standing. The right is at present quiescent. You stand a reasonable chance.'⁴ Afterwards Katherine felt she had transcended the intolerable fear of death and wrote in her *Journal*: 'All these two years I have been obsessed by the fear of death. This grew and grew *gigantic*, and this it was that made me cling so, I think. Ten days ago it went, I care no more. It leaves me perfectly cold. . . . Life either stays or goes.'⁵ Yet the obsessive fear could not be so easily dismissed; a few days later her wasted body, exposed in the bath, reminded her of a corpse: 'This is how I shall look, this is how they will arrange me in my coffin.'⁶

Katherine's bodily suffering changed the appearance of things and cast a black shadow on the world. During one profound depression—'like great black birds dashing at one's face'—she saw 'a little boat, far out, moving along, *inevitable* it looks and *dead silent*—a little black spot, like the spot on a lung.'⁷ As the weeks passed and winter approached her solitude intensified and she felt frightened, imprisoned, trapped; and she even longed for the 'comforts' of England: porridge and coal. She bravely kept a small loaded revolver in her room near the front door, practised firing in the garden and once she had learned to handle it felt 'like a new being'. But an English neighbour tormented her, during a phase of postwar revolutionary violence, by insisting (she told Murry) that 'even at 3 o'clock in the afternoon no one could hear my screams if I were attacked, and that a revolver for a person like me was ridiculous. *They'd* knock it away in no time.' He also suggested that 'navvies will break in and "slit your throat" while L.M. is in San Remo.'⁸

In her isolation and fear Katherine subjected Ida, her most convenient and immediate victim, to a merciless scrutiny, focused on her faults and forced Ida to bear the brunt of her own unhappiness. Katherine's letters frequently mentioned the irritating Ida, a poor housekeeper and cook, and dreary companion. As soon as they moved into the Casetta Ida broke three dishes and a thermometer, and Katherine, who called her 'stupidity personified', felt Ida thought it was 'so nice and homey' to smash a thing or two. She refrained from shooting Ida only because it would be so difficult to dispose of a body that was too huge for a parcel and would never burn. But Katherine told Murry she dreamed Ida had 'died of heart-failure and I heard myself cry out "Oh, what heaven! what heaven!" ' She also blamed Ida for her artistic sterility: 'Worst of all is that I can't write a book while I live with her.'[9]

Katherine felt there was absolutely no escape from the ever-present Ida, for if she stirred in the night her friend would offer to help, unintentionally emphasizing Katherine's weakness and total dependence: 'If I do absolutely nothing then she discovers my fatigue *under* my eyes. There is something profound and terrible in this eternal desire to establish contact.'[10] Their relationship, which was then at its worst, must have been horrifying for Ida, who desperately tried to maintain her intimacy with Katherine while her friend became more ill, more reclusive and more angry. Katherine, who felt Ida's passion fed perversely on hatred, hinted that their friendship seemed to threaten and contaminate her love for Murry: 'This *awful relationship* living on in its secret corrupt way beside my relationship with you is very extraordinary; no one would believe it. I am two selves —one my true self—the other she creates in me to destroy my true self.'[11] Katherine reached the peak of bitterness against Ida at the end of November when, in a letter to Murry, she attempted to free herself from Ida's stranglehold by emphasizing her physical disgust for Ida's large but infantile body and her moral revulsion for Ida's gluttony: 'Her great fat arms, her tiny blind breasts, her baby mouth, the underlip always wet and a crumb or two or a chocolate stain at the corners'.[12]

A visit from Katherine's father, who was travelling from England to New Zealand in November 1919, disappointed her expectations and intensified her unhappiness. Katherine wrote in 'Prelude' that the sensitive Stanley Burnell 'was the soul of truth and decency and for all his practical experience he was awfully simple, easily pleased and easily hurt'.[13] When she learned that her father's wallet had been stolen by a pickpocket in Boulogne, she was extremely sympathetic about his attachment to money, his loneliness and his rather pathetic need to maintain a worldly image: 'If he does mind so terribly about money, it must have been so *ghastly* to be *alone* among foreigners, having to keep it up and be a man of the world and look out of the railway windows as though it hadn't happened. I really literally nearly fainted when this swept over me and I "saw" him with a very high colour "putting on" a smile.'[14] But Harold, unfortunately, could not give Katherine this kind of intuitive understanding, and she guessed, when he first wrote that he was only coming as far as Nice or Cannes, that he was frightened by her disease.

Katherine described, in an early letter to Murry, her father's subtle mixture of rich and attractive odours: 'He would smell of fine cloth with a suspicion of cigar added, eau de Cologne, just an atom of camphorated chalk, something of fresh linen and his own particular smell.'[15] And when her father finally came to visit her (two hours early), with friends and a luxurious car and chauffeur, she wrote at length to Murry about her longing for the wealth and luxury she had abandoned to become a writer, her desperate craving for affection (which she failed to get from her mother and husband), and her father's astonishing indifference to her illness, discomfort and poverty:

> I was, I am, just a little corrupted, Bogey darling. That big soft purring motor, the rugs and cushions, the warmth, the delicacy, all the uglies so far away. . . . Father at the last was wonderfully dear to me. I mean, to be held and kissed and called my precious child was almost too much—to feel some-one's arms round me and someone saying, 'Get better, you little wonder. You're your mother over again.' It's not being called a wonder, it's having *love* present, close, warm, to be felt and returned. . . .
>
> Pa did not like this place, neither did they. They were horrified by the cold. Pa said that at Menton they have had *none* of this bitter wind, that it has never been cold like today. He seemed to think I had made a great mistake to be in such a thin house and so exposed.[16]

Though Katherine contrasted her father's liveliness and spontaneity with her husband's deadly passivity, noted that money did not save Harold from 'pits of depression' and counted on his generosity, he criticized her villa, complained of the cold, and left her five cigarettes and some daisies. Two months later Harold married Laura Kate Bright, a widow and Annie's best friend in Wellington.

The annual winter separations from Murry put an almost intolerable strain on Katherine, for she could not bear either the sickening solitude or the essential companionship of Ida. She quoted Marlowe's 'Lone women like to empty houses perish' and Keats's letters to Fanny Brawne, and reminded Murry of her invalid mother whose illnesses were palliated by family, friends, home and possessions: 'Mother, of course, lived in this state for years. Ah, but she lived *surrounded*. She had her husband, her children, her home, her friends, physical presences, darling treasures to be cherished—and I've not one of these things. I have only my work.'[17] Katherine emphasized the agony of solitude and begged Murry never to abandon her again: 'The *strain* we have lived under! No one will ever know. Isn't it queer, my little brother, what a cold indifferent world this is really? Think of the agony we've suffered. Who cares? . . . Oh, God, let us try to make this our last separation. At any rate it will be. I'd never bear another. They are too terrible.'[18]

Murry, who understood poems much better than people, later wrote of Keats and Fanny Brawne: 'The first separation at the end of June 1819, after a period in which they had come closer and closer together, was the real beginning of Keats's torments. It is important to realize this, for it has a direct bearing on our understanding of Keats both as man and poet.'[19] But he did not realize the extent of Katherine's suffering. Murry, who was frequently separated from Katherine after 1919, when she searched for health and lived abroad with Ida, remembered 'the days, the months rather—when Katherine and I were parted from one another and held apart'.[20] But he ignored the fact that he *chose* to remain apart and could have been with her if he had wanted to. Murry's fourth wife, Mary, attempted to answer one of the crucial questions of his marriage—why Murry (like Annie and then Harold Beauchamp) left Katherine alone and ill in a foreign country—by explaining: 'It was of paramount importance that her lover should earn some money.'[21] But since Murry gave Katherine very little money (which was of paramount importance to *him*), it would be more accurate to say that though he was devoted to her and recognized her genius, he was unaware of her fears, hopes and moods, and was unwilling to leave his editorial work and make the sacrifices that were necessary to sustain her.

There was also an irrational paradox at the heart of Katherine's behaviour, for as Frieda Lawrence later told Murry: 'She wants to be alone; when she *is* alone, she complains about loneliness.'[22] As Christmas 1919 approached Katherine asked Murry to come to Italy and then begged him not to do so, and Murry's inevitably confused and rather clumsy responses determined, to a great extent, the extreme variation of her daily moods. They tortured each other with a strange combination of love and wrath, and experienced one of the gravest crises of their marriage. She condemned Murry's complaints about *his* suffering and lack of money, his attraction to her 'romantic' disease, his inability to sustain a male role and bear the burden of her illness, his unwillingness to live abroad with her and his belief that he would be liberated by her death. She sank into a morbid gloom, insisted that (like her mother) she no longer cared about people, claimed she was not afraid of death and thought about how she would look when she was dead. She thought of the dying Chekhov and of Garnet Trowell's dead baby, and felt that Murry's cruelty had killed their (non-existent) 'love-child'. She described her loneliness, her invalid routine, her ineffectual doctors, her fever and the deterioration of her lungs. She longed for her mother's security and Lawrence's friendship, swore she did *not* want Murry to live with her, and then anatomized the faults of his character and criticism, his meanness about money and the lamentations of his letters.

Since there is no sign of crisis or specific provocation in Murry's letters of November 1919, it would seem that Katherine, under the stress of constant pain and anxiety, finally reached the breaking-point, and forced Murry to recognize her torment and come to her rescue. After only two months in Ospedaletti, on December 4, 1919, when Katherine felt Murry had responded with characteristic indifference to her desperate *cri de coeur*, she confessed: 'It's pretty frightful—the loneliness, the noise of one's heart pounding away—and the feeling that this is ALL there is. I can't master it.' She wished her mother were alive to rescue her and 'make miracles happen'; stated their insoluble dilemma: 'If you were to leave there our future is wrecked; if I came there, I'd die'; and sent him her most bitter and moving poem, a ballad called 'The New Husband', in which she is a helpless child abandoned by Murry and 'rescued' by death:

> Someone came to me and said
> Forget, forget that you've been wed.
> Who's your man to leave you be
> Ill and cold in a far country?

> Who's the husband—who's the stone
> Could leave a child like you alone? . . .
> Ha! Ha! Six months, six weeks, six hours
> Among these glittering palms and flowers
> With Melancholy at my side
> For my nurse and for my guide
> Despair—and for my footman Pain
> —I'll never see my home again.[23]

On December 9, before Katherine had received Murry's reply, she denied his accusations and condemned his stinginess and weakness:

> I will not receive your dreadful accusations into my soul for they would kill me. But here is your letter and you tell me I have driven you nearly insane—ruined you, it seems—quenched your hopes even of getting your money affairs straight. You tell me again that you are a bankrupt. . . .
> You are not a pauper. You have £800 a year and you only contribute to my keep—not more than £50 a year at most now. You write as though there were me to be provided for—yourself—and all to be done on something like £300. I know you have paid my doctor's bills and that my illness has cost you a great deal. IT WILL COST YOU NO MORE. . . . I leaned on you—and *broke you*. The truth is that until I was ill you were never called upon 'to play the man' to this extent—and it's NOT your rôle. When you said you ought to be kept you spoke the truth.[24]

Murry was crushed by Katherine's epistolary barrage and her 'New Husband' poem, overwhelmed by his responsibility for her and frozen into impotence: 'I don't think that at any time *I've* had a bigger blow than that letter and these verses. . . . *I feel that everything depends upon me; that I have to do something quite definite, very quickly.* But I don't know what it is, and *my* faculty for doing anything has been suddenly paralyzed.'[25] He complained pitifully about his financial problems, apologized for his 'horrible letter' that had sparked her extreme reaction and promised to put the *Athenaeum* in order and come to Ospedaletti for two weeks. When Murry arrived at the Casetta on December 16 he had, for the first time in his life, an acute and protracted attack of neuralgia

—as if to gain sympathy and defend himself against Katherine's emotional demands. Though Ida claims that Murry's visit brought no happiness, Katherine stated that her cough nearly stopped and her appetite improved when he was with her.

Just after Murry left, on January 2, 1920, Katherine had a serious relapse. She was unable to eat or sleep, felt frightened, fell into fits of crying and suffered from acute nervous exhaustion. On January 8 her courage broke and she recorded in her *Journal*: 'BLACK. A day spent in Hell. Unable to do anything. Took brandy. Determined not to weep—wept. Sense of isolation frightful. I shall die if I don't escape. Nauseated, faint, cold with misery. Oh, I *must* survive it somehow.'[26] On January 20 she confessed, in a letter to Ottoline Morrell, that Murry neither understood nor loved her:

My heart has been affected by—they say—the fever. It isn't that. It's by misery. Really, I have simply wept for days. The appalling isolation, deathly stillness, great wind and sea, and this feeling that I had consumption and was tainted, dying here. If I moved—even to the door-step—my heart beat so hard that I had to lean against the door, and then no sleep—nothing but going over and over one's whole past life, as one will do when one is dead, I suppose. I tried to explain this to M. but—he did not understand at all. Not in the very slightest. . . .

I thought, until even now, that 'one' understood, that superficially perhaps I was alone but that really it wasn't so. And I find out I was wrong. For nearly six years I have felt *loved* (you know that feeling?). Now it is gone.[27]

Katherine also expressed these feelings in her *Journal* on January 11: 'I love him but he rejects my *living* love. This is anguish. These are the worst days of my whole life.' She praised the act of selfless surrender as the most difficult and highest form of human behaviour, truthfully told Murry that he lacked her capacity to love and insisted he did not want her love: 'you only want an "idea".'[28] Murry later admitted: 'I've had enough love, for I feel that the kind of unearthly love I'm inclined to ends inevitably in disaster.'[29] Though he was a practical and efficient editor and writer, he confessed his fatal mixture of ineptitude and immaturity; 'Even if I had realized your loneliness, I don't see what I could have done. It's that—not knowing what to do, or what I could have done that has knocked the bottom out of me. . . .I wish to God I were a man. Somehow I seem to have grown up, gone bald even, without ever becoming a man; and I find it terribly hard to master a situation.'[30]

Katherine and Murry's emotional problems were exacerbated by their impoverished life, for Katherine earned only £21 for her writing between December 1911, when she received £15 for her first book, and August 1918 when she earned six guineas for 'Bliss' (the *New Age* did not pay contributors); and Murry had no adequate salary until he became editor of the *Athenaeum* in January 1919. Murry, who grew up in poverty and was always stingy, had Harold Beauchamp's miserliness without his impressive strength and character. He insisted they keep their money in separate banks and rarely contributed anything to his wife's support: they shared expenses and kept strict accounts.

When Katherine was seriously ill in 1920 and wired Murry for £10, he ungenerously replied: '*Though things are tight*, I will send you a cheque for £20 tomorrow, *if* you will repay me when you get the money for your book.'[31] Katherine was naturally furious with the 'if', scorned his meanness, made a pathetic reference to her illnesses (as she had done with her father) and an ironic allusion to Murry's self-pity: 'Let me tell you what I "imagined" you would do on receipt of my first letter from Menton. I imagined you would immediately wire me £10. . . . Perhaps I did not make clear that I ASKED you for the £10 a month—I mean, not as a loan. I am afraid from this note you may advance it to me and take the book money. But I am afraid that will not do. . . . I would perfectly understand your *money is tight* had I NOT consumption, a weak heart and chronic neuritis in my lower limbs. . . . But this is all rubbish beside your sore throat and your remark about breaking your neck househunting.'[32] The following spring she wrote another exasperated yet witty letter to Ida and compared Murry's stinginess and lack of decent feelings with her father's: 'Just now—making out the week's bills he asked me for 11 francs for the carriage—half—plus a 2 franc tip! I think it's awful to have to say it. But fancy not paying for your wife's carriage to and from the surgery! Is that simply extraordinary or am I? I really am staggered. I think it is the meanest thing I ever heard of. It's not the fact which is so queer but the lack of fine feeling. I suppose if one fainted he would make one pay 3d for a 6d glass of salvolatile and 1d on the glass. That really does beat Father.'[33]

Katherine's allowance was raised after several years from £100 to £120 per annum, was increased to £156 in 1916, and reached £260 in 1919. But Harold enjoyed the power of money and could not give up his last vestige of control over Katherine, who was fiercely independent and deeply resentful of her subjugation. After borrowing £100 from her cousin Elizabeth (instead of from Harold) she ironically referred to her childish dependence and his paternal disapproval, and promised to repay the debt before it was due 'if in the meantime my Papa shakes a money bag at me—but it is far more likely to be a broomstick'.[34] And in a moving letter to her father in November 1921, Katherine mentions an unwelcome reminder of her financial obligation, Harold's irritation at Murry's inability to provide for her, and her fatal illness which consumed her money as well as her lungs. She subtly pleads for her father's sympathy and apologizes for having been a 'disappointing child':

> Connie and Jinnie made me understand how very much you considered you were doing for me. They made me realize that for you to give me £300 a year was an extreme concession and that as a matter of fact my husband was the one who ought to provide for me. Of course I appreciate your great generosity in allowing me so much money. And I know it is only because I am ill that you are doing so. But it is highly unlikely that I shall live very long and consumption is a terribly expensive illness. I thought that you did not mind looking after me to this extent. And to feel that you did—was like a blow to me—I couldn't get over it. I feel as though I didn't belong to you, really. . . . There is no reason, father dear, that you should go on loving me through thick and thin. I see that. And I have been an extraordinarily unsatisfactory and disappointing child.[35]

In February 1923, just after Harold was knighted for financial services to New Zealand, he gave £6000 (over twice the total amount he had given Katherine) to help establish a National Gallery of Art in Wellington. If Harold had been a true patron of the arts and shown the same generosity to his daughter as he had to his city, he could easily have eliminated her constant anxiety about money, improved her health and even prolonged her life.

Murry's weakness, insecurity, dependence and naiveté aroused Katherine's maternal feelings; she was attracted to Murry partly because of her revulsion against her aggressive and domineering father. But she did not realize that when she rejected masculine authority she also gave up the emotional support she rightly felt was essential for the development of her artistic gifts.

Though Katherine felt December and January were the worst months of her life, four positive events took place at that time. In December 1919 *Je ne parle pas français*, her satire on Carco, was published by the Heron Press; and in January 1920 she wrote 'The Man Without a Temperament', a grim projection of her relations with Murry. Also, the deterioration of her relations with her husband, whom she decided to treat as a visitor rather than as a person she could count on for advice and support, led to an extraordinary reconciliation with Ida. Instead of the familiar condemnation, she now told Murry—with bitter satisfaction—that she recognized her own dependence and Ida's devotion, and that her hate had finally turned to love:

> My feelings towards Lesley are absolutely changed. It is not only that the hatred is gone. Something positive is there which is very like love for her. She has convinced me at last, against all my opposition, that she is trying to do all in her power for me, that she is devoted to the one idea which is (please forgive my egoism) to see me well again. This time she has fed me, helped me, got up in the middle of the night to make hot milk and rub my feet, brought me flowers, *served* me as one could not be served if one were not loved. . . . It was only when I refused to acknowledge this—to acknowledge her importance to me—that I hated her.[36]

And in January 1920, Katherine's wealthy second cousin, Connie Beauchamp, who had accompanied Harold when he arrived for lunch at the Casetta, heard about Katherine's desperate situation and rescued her.

Connie, a stout, grey-haired matron, lived with her friend Jinnie Fullerton, who was a tall, slender, commanding woman, in the magnificent Villa Flora in Menton. Both ladies were sixty-four (two years older than Harold) and both were Catholic converts, and for many years they had run a large and expensive nursing home in Hampstead. Katherine may have seen in the friendship of the strong Jinnie and the dependent Connie an idealized image of what she and Ida would be like if they lived for thirty more years and inherited Harold's wealth: 'It's a queer queer relationship', she explained to Murry. 'C. obviously adores J. and refers everything to her, but she is not in the least a parasite or overshadowed. She is a complete creature who yet *leans* on J. as a woman may do on a man. One feels her happiness to an extraordinary degree. That is what is so restful about these two women.'[37]

Though both women were generous, lively and loving, they were much older, richer and more conventional than Katherine, and as absorbed in their religion as she was in her work. Katherine, as always, felt estranged from the Beauchamps, and confided to her sympathetic friend, Anne Rice: 'I am living here with "relations"—the dearest people *only* they are not artists. You know what that means? I love them, and they've been just too good and dear to me, but they are not in the same world as we are and I pine for *my own people*, my own wandering tribe.' When Connie, glancing at the *Oxford Book of English Verse*, said to Katherine: 'There are some quite pretty things here, dear. Who are they by?' she politely pretended not to hear.[38]

Like most of Katherine's journeys, the escape from Ospedaletti was a disaster. Katherine's only overcoat was stolen from the Casetta just before they left, she had to pay extortionate charges for the hire of a stove she had thought was a gift, and the taxi driver, who claimed they could not take the main road along the sea because of the current anti-British feeling, took them for a long detour through the mountains and made them pay £6 for the fare plus ten shillings for crossing the border. They knew they were being cheated, but Katherine was far too weak and Ida too frightened to argue with the Italians, and they reluctantly paid what was demanded. As Katherine told Murry: 'I have got away from that hell of isolation, from the awful singing at night, from the loneliness and fright. To tell you the truth, I think I have been *mad*, but really, medically mad. A great awful cloud has been on me. . . . It's nearly killed me. Yes. When J[innie] took me in her arms to-day she cried as well as I. I felt as though I'd been through some awful deadly strain, and just survived—been rescued from drowning or something like that.'[39]

When she reached Menton Katherine was disappointed to discover that Jinnie had decided *not* to place her in the Villa Flora—she was expecting a wealthy patient from London who might object to a tubercular guest—but in an expensive sanatorium. Katherine told Murry that her first impression of L'Hermitage (like that of the Headland Hotel) was enthusiastic: 'Here—after the journey—was this room waiting for me—exquisite, large, with four windows, overlooking great gardens and mountains, wonderful flowers—tea with *toast* and honey and butter—a charming maid—and these two dear sweet women to welcome me with papers, books, etc. This is really a superb place in every way.'[40] But, as usual, she was quickly disillusioned and extremely depressed by her fellow *moribundi*, whom she also described to Murry, two days after her arrival: 'They look exactly as though they were risen from the dead, stepped out of coffins and eating again *pour la première fois*. Their hair is thin and weak and poor; their eyes are cold and startled, their hands are still waxen—and THIN!'[41]

By the end of the first week in L'Hermitage Katherine noted in her *Journal* that the room was horrible, the food appalling and the noise intolerable, and she compared it to her depths of misery in Bavaria where she had been able to alleviate her despair with veronal. It was at this intensely unhappy moment of her life that Katherine suddenly received Lawrence's vicious letter about 'stewing in her consumption'. Then, when Murry asked Katherine to wire *if* she still loved him, she felt he no longer believed in their marriage and was killing her 'again and again' with every letter. It seemed that her health, friendships and marriage were simultaneously destroyed, and that everyone was betraying and abandoning her.

Katherine somehow managed to get a doctor to certify that she was not infectious, the rich London patient allowed her to move into her cousin's house, and Ida found a room in Menton and a job in a nursing home. Katherine arrived at the Villa Flora on February 15 and gratefully succumbed to the temptation of security and luxury, symbolized by her father's soft purring motor that kept 'all the uglies far away'. She wrote to Richard Murry about the 'great garden, lemon and orange groves, palms . . . and inside a very beautiful "exquisite" house with a spirit in it which makes you feel that nothing evil or ugly could ever come near';[42]

and she told Murry that the villa reminded her of a (philistine) version of Ottoline's mansion:

> Today she arrived with a carriage and fur rugs and silk cushions. Took me to their villa. It is really superb. . . . They had a *chaise longue* in the garden—a tiny tray with black coffee out of a silver pot, Grand Marnier, cigarettes, little bunch of violets, all ready. Then we went in to tea. Their villa is really—Boge—it's a dream. I mean even the furnishing is *perfect*—Spanish silk bed coverlets, Italian china, the tea appointments perfect, stillness, maids in tiny muslin aprons flitting over *carpets* . . . and so on. Then they showed me into a room, grey and silver, facing south, with a balcony—the only touch of colour a little rose brocade couch with gilt legs. . . . The villa is in style like Garsington. I mean that is the tone. It is very large—a huge hall lighted from above—a great double salon. It has delicate balconies and a tower.[43]

Katherine's two and a half months with Connie and Jinnie in the Villa Flora, which provided a powerful contrast to the thieves at the spartan Casetta and the half-resurrected skeletons at L'Hermitage, were generally happy, and a photograph of her seated under an umbrella in April 1920 reveals a thin but still extremely attractive young woman. But she could not entirely escape the 'black shadow' that seemed to hang over her world and darken her vivid letters to Murry. When they drove to Monte Carlo in the big chauffeured car Katherine was revolted by the decadence and avarice of the old men and young whores: '*Monte is real Hell*. To begin with it's the cleanest, most polished place I've ever seen. . . . All the shops are magasins de luxe, lingerie, perfumes, fat unguents and pawnbrokers and patisserie. . . . [The Casino has] a continual procession of *whores*, pimps, governesses . . . old, old hags, ancient men stiff and greyish, panting as they climb, rich great fat capitalists, little girls tricked out to look like babies. . . . Cruelty is there—and vultures hover.'[44] And when the waves washed a suicide on to the beach near their house, Katherine carefully studied the ugly but apparently fascinating details of the *memento mori* that seemed to threaten the security of the Villa: 'Yesterday the sea washed her up just opposite the Villa. She came rolling, rolling in with each wave and they waited till she was tumbled on the beach. All her clothes were gone except her corset. Her arms and feet were gone and her hair was bound round and round her head and face—dark brown hair. She doesn't belong to a soul. No one claims her. I expect they'll shovel her under today.'[45]

Connie and Jinnie had taken Katherine under their care to save not only her body but also her soul, for both women, who were ardent to win other converts to the Catholic Church, felt 'the Lord has delivered you into our hands'. Though Katherine had referred to 'the Lord who gave me consumption',[46] she had a profound need to believe in *something*, responded to their persistent propaganda and flirted with conversion for a couple of months. In March she confided to Ida, in deceptively solemn and simple words that sounded much more like Jinnie's than her own: 'One day (before I go back to England, I hope), I mean to be received into the Church. I'm going to become a Catholic. Once I believe in a God, the rest is so easy. I can accept it all *my own way*—not "literally" but symbolically: it is all quite easy and beautiful.'[47]

But the atmosphere of piety and incense, which may have recalled painful memories of the Bavarian convent where her mother had left her when she was pregnant in 1909, became oppressive, and Katherine found that science made it impossible for her to believe in God. In the end she had it her own way, and her letter to Murry in October 1920 suggests the struggle for her soul in the Villa Flora: 'Jinnie and Connie have been in several times. They are very tamed OR they are offended with me for not giving in about the Church. It's in their eyes every time they look at me. Very uncomfortable. Every pause in the conversation I hear Jennie silently saying: "Don't you think, dearest, you would like to see Father X?" And I have in consequence a kind of No Popery manner. What a bother!'[48] Though Katherine resisted the ladies' missionary zeal, their influence prepared the way for her final conversion to the mysticism of Gurdjieff.

In April 1920 Katherine first met Sydney and Violet Schiff, a wealthy and extremely intelligent English couple who were patrons of the arts and had a villa near Menton. Sydney Schiff had written a novel, *Richard Kurt*, which Katherine had admired in her review in 1919: 'It is an account of how Richard Kurt wasted, idled through several years of his life, now happily and now unhappily. He isnever more than a shadow; but Elinor and then Virginia, the second woman of the book, are amazingly real.'[49]

Sydney had been the friend and patron of the poet Isaac Rosenberg and was the publisher of *Art and Letters*, where Katherine's 'Pictures' and 'The Man Without a Temperament' had recently appeared. In 1922 he gave the famous party at which Joyce and Proust met and found they had absolutely nothing to say to each other. He also translated Proust's final volume, *Le Temps retrouvé*, after the death of Scott Moncrieff; and was savagely satirized in Wyndham Lewis's *The Apes of God* as Lionel Kein, 'the rich Jew who acts Proust'.[50] Proust's biographer, George Painter, describes Sydney as 'bald, thin, alarmingly brisk and slightly deaf, with piercing spectacled eyes and a bristling moustache. . . . Mrs. Schiff was tall and softly graceful, with brown doe-like eyes and slender hands, an unfading Edwardian beauty: "the angel Violet", Proust called her, "retiring, fragrant and miraculous flower".'[51]

Sydney first came to visit Katherine in Menton, and in early April invited her to lunch and took her in a victoria to the Villa Violet, where he showed Katherine his Gauguins and Picassos. Katherine was glad to escape from the proselytizing old ladies and to discover in the Schiffs her 'own wandering tribe'. She was immensely impressed by Sydney and Violet—who had wealth and taste, beauty and brains, sensitivity and sympathy—and praised them in a series of letters written to Murry in April 1920:

He attracts me *tremendously* and his great kindness—sensitiveness—almost childishness endear him to me. . . . He has had my disease and rather exaggerates the care one ought to take. But it's all in *more* than kindness. . . . She's one of the most attractive *women* that we have known, physically *and* mentally. You'd admire her—you'd like her and her mind. . . . You would certainly find her very beautiful, as I do. I want you to see her and to talk to her. She is extremely sympathetic. . . . Mr. Schiff is a kind of literary fairy godfather to one. He looks after one so perfectly and so gently, and Violet Schiff seemed to me the last time far more beautiful and more fascinating than before. She will *fascinate* you—the movement of her lips, her eyes, her colour—all her beauty.[52]

The Schiffs widened Katherine's circle of artistic acquaintances, and introduced her to the supercilious Osbert Sitwell and to Lytton Strachey's sister, Dorothy, who had married the French painter Simon Bussy and was the translator of Gide.

Katherine returned to Hampstead for four months at the end of April 1920, insisting that the diplomat Sydney Waterlow (who had once proposed to Virginia Woolf) move out of The Elephant, which he had been sharing with Murry. Katherine, who was in poor health during the spring and summer, complained of the cold and was often confined to the house. But she worked with Murry on the *Athenaeum* and prepared the manuscript of *Bliss* for publication. She visited Dr. Sorapure, sat in her garden with Kot, Brett, the Schiffs and Aldous Huxley, and in May invited the T. S. Eliots to dinner. She disliked Vivien intensely, but did not know she was close to madness; and wrote to Virginia about her objections to the cold façade of Eliot's poetry: 'The poems *look* delightful but I confess I think them unspeakably dreary. How one could write so absolutely without emotion—perhaps that's an achievement.'[53] In August Virginia told Roger Fry and Vanessa Bell that she was coming up to London from Sussex to say goodbye to her friend—for the last time. 'Katherine Murry goes away for 2 years. Have you at all come round to her stories? I suppose I'm too jealous to wish you to, yet I'm sure they have merit all the same. . . . I had one more farewell visit to Katherine yesterday, as she got ill, and had to put off coming here.'[54]

When Katherine returned to Menton with Ida on September 13, 1920, she rented Villa Isola Bella from Connie and Jinnie, and lived at the edge of their garden. Isola Bella was in Garavan, the village near Menton, and was just next to the local railway station and five minutes from the Italian frontier. The villa was built on a steep hill, with a wide terrace and stone balustrade, and had a garden with a tall palm tree on the lower level and a surpassingly beautiful view. Katherine felt fortunate to find a maid named Marie, the widow of a coachman, who had periwinkle blue eyes, spoke with sweeping gestures, and was sympathetic, attentive and a good cook. Ida was rather jealous of Marie, emphasized her sharp eyes and mentioned that she stole food and padded the bills.

In September, just before the publication of *Bliss* (her first book in nine years), Katherine wrote to Murry from Menton about

Floryan's threats of blackmail and confirmed that he had damaging letters (written when they were lovers) which she would pay anything to recover. She borrowed £40 from Ida and instructed Murry to buy the letters and burn them in a great fire:

> *It is true* that he does possess letters written during my acquaintance with him which I would give any money to recover. And it is true that especially if he is married [and needs money] he will never cease threatening. What I propose is this. I talked it over with Ida. She agreed to give me £40. I want you to go with F. to a solicitor, receive the letters, get his sworn statement [to leave me alone] and hand him my cheque for the amount. It's *not* a waste of £40. . . . I haven't worried an atom bit about F—— except in so far as it worried you and affects US. I won't have that Pole outside our door. Burn all he gives you—won't you. A bon fire.[55]

In Garavan Katherine once again settled into her familiar invalid routine: she got up at 11, remained downstairs till 2, rested in her room until 5 and then got back into bed. In October she saw Ottoline and her fourteen-year-old daughter Julian who were staying near the Schiffs in Roquebrune and may have told her that Mark Gertler now had tuberculosis. On October 10 Katherine asked Murry about her friend and recalled his insensitivity about *her* disease: 'Is Gertler really ill? Do tell me. I always remember him swaggering up to me when I was just back from the South: "Well, Katherine, I hear you've got it. Do you spit blood and so on? Do all the things in the books? Do you think you'll get over it?" And then he laughed out.'[56]

In March 1920 Katherine had hoped to achieve an acceptable invalidism, if not a complete recovery, by the following year; and she realized that her heart had to beat faster and pump more blood to oxygenate her system because (she could not bear to write it in clear English): 'Part of my *left* lung *n'existe plus*.'[57] In October 1920, when she was lonely, ill, suffering pain and aware that she was close to death, Murry—with editorial genius but appalling insensitivity—sent her a copy of Richard Prowse's *A Gift of the Dusk*, the journal of a tubercular patient in Switzerland, which she called: 'A simply terrible book—awful—ghastly!'[58] In her *Athenaeum* review Katherine echoed Stevenson's views in 'Ordered South' and stressed the conflict between psychological health and physical disease: 'The peculiar tragedy of the consumptive is that, although he is so seriously ill, he is—in most cases—not ill enough to give up the precious habits of health. . . . Thus the small stricken company, living its impersonal life together among the immense mountains, is for ever mocked by the nearness of those things which are forever out of reach.'[59]

That same month the vividly alive Dr. Bouchage, who had Katherine's disease and seemed like a plant touched by frost, recommended paraffin and iodine to combat infection (just as the drunken English doctor had ordered injections of strychnine in 1918), a procedure, writes a modern authority, 'to be condemned and never employed'.[60] No wonder, then, that Katherine wrote to Ottoline in May 1921: 'I've just paid little B[ouchage] 2,000 francs for looking after me and I'm 50 times worse than I was at Christmas.'[61] When she had an attack of pneumonia in December 1920, she bargained with God and generously conceded: 'If I manage to live for 10 years I don't think I'd mind dying at 42.'[62]

The winter of 1920–21 was in many ways a repetition of the previous year. Katherine's health continued to deteriorate and she was fearfully lonely and unhappy. She wrote to Murry: 'Life is terribly short. I know that, on my death bed, I shall regret the time we didn't have together.'[63] She again lashed out at him in a series of letters that led to an even more serious crisis, which was temporarily alleviated by his Christmas visit. In November, when Murry innocently supplied the editor of the *Sphere* with a lovely photograph of Katherine to be used as publicity for *Bliss*, she responded in four different letters with uncontrollable rage: 'I *detest* it. It's not me. It's a HORROR. If it's given to anyone please get it back. Fool I was not to have burnt it. . . . It's true I am hurt as I've never been. Perhaps it is your carelessness. But then carelessness in love is so dreadful.'[64] As late as 1951 Murry found the violence of her reaction incomprehensible, until he finally realized, Lea reports, 'that she might have had it taken for Carco',[65] and had been infuriated by the bitter memory.

When Murry, who was resigning from the *Athenaeum*, arrived with Sullivan for his second two-week visit on January 19, Katherine was moved by his emotional anxiety and told Violet Schiff: 'I feel *fearfully* sorry for him—overwhelmingly so. I did not realize myself until this morning, the extent of his need.'[66]

Though Katherine also told Sydney Schiff that Murry had been 'particularly graceless and argumentative and talked of nothing but money',[67] her health, which was clearly and closely connected to her emotional state, improved significantly when they were together. As soon as Murry went back to England, Katherine suffered a relapse, exactly as she had done in 1919. 'I have been in bed for six weeks with my lungs and heart', she wrote to Ottoline in March 1921, 'then "They" have decided that my heart trouble is caused by a very swollen gland which presses, with intense pain, on an artery. This the surgeon [Bouchage] tapped on Saturday and intends to tap 2 or 3 times again.'[68]

Katherine's greatest source of anxiety during her second winter in Menton was the infidelity of her handsome husband, who inspired affection in women, was starved for physical love and was thoroughly weary of Katherine's emotional onslaughts. On Christmas day 1915, when Katherine had concluded her affair with Carco and was alone in Bandol, and Murry was spending the holidays at Garsington, she warned him about festive flirtations and emphasized the importance of absolute loyalty: 'I hope you don't kiss anybody at Lady Ottoline's. After all I have said, it does sound absurd! But I minded you kissing even Anne [Rice] "seriously". I minded you *really* kissing. For this reason. If I wished to, I could not.'[69] And Ottoline reports that after another visit to Garsington in about 1919, Murry, who was then the important and influential editor of the *Athenaeum*, deliberately aroused Katherine's jealousy by telling her that Ottoline had fallen in love with him: 'When she told me this I really laughed. It was so absurd. But at the time to Katherine it was no laughing matter; for here in her eyes was another treachery.'[70]

Katherine was therefore outraged when she learned that Murry had betrayed her with her friend Brett, who was much less attractive and intelligent than she was. Though Lea stated in his biography of Murry: 'As long as Katherine lived, he never gave way to his inclinations beyond an occasional kiss or caress',[71] he has recently written: 'I was mistaken about Murry's not "giving way to his inclinations": he had an affair with Dorothy Brett. . . . This, among much else, [was] unknown to me in 1957.'[72] Lea's statement has been corroborated by Ruth Mantz, Brett's friend, Enid Hilton, and Brett's biographer, John Manchester.[73]

Katherine had been jealous of Brett—who was healthy and

played tennis with Murry in London while Katherine led an invalid's life abroad—since her days in the Villa Flora. In 1920 and 1921 she wrote two ironic passages, omitted from the published letters, about Murry's love for Brett and Katherine's feeling that he would marry Brett after she died, for Brett would never challenge her dogmatic but insecure husband in the way she did. She told Murry: 'I'm glad you love Brett so much. I used to feel in [Ospedaletti] Italy that if I died you'd marry Brett very soon after—I nearly wrote to you about it. She's wonderfully suited to you in a thousand ways';[74] and wrote to Ida: 'You know, he, Jack, will marry her one day. It would be an ideal marriage. She worships him and her flattery, reverence, adoration are just what he needs from a wife. Also he can lay down the law to her on art and life to his heart's desire. I *know* they will marry.'[75] In an unpublished passage from her journal of August 12, 1920, Katherine condemns Brett's maudlin relations with Murry, refers to her unhappy childhood, emphasizes disgusting physical details (as she had done with Ida) and criticizes the weaknesses in Murry's character that allowed him to succumb to Brett's hysterical adulation.[76]

A week later, while still in Hampstead, Katherine reported her shock and anger at Murry's flirtation with Brett, and his selfish and dangerous proposal that he should live in Brett's house in Pond Street when Katherine left for the Villa Isola Bella: 'J. let fall this morning the fact that he *had* considered taking rooms in [Brett's] house this winter. Good. Was their relationship friendship? Oh no! He kissed her and held her arm and they were certainly conscious of a dash of something far more dangerous than *l'amitié pure*. . . . I suppose one always thinks the latest shock is the worst shock. This is quite unlike any other I have suffered. The lack of sensitiveness as far as I am concerned—the selfishness of this staggers me.'[77] It was perhaps this incident that made Katherine accuse Brett of having an affair with Murry and then burst into tears of pain and rage. Though Brett had not slept with Murry in the summer of 1920, her response to Katherine was extremely disingenuous: 'I was appalled! It had never entered my head. I knew that there was only one woman in Murry's heart— that was Katherine. She upset the boiling water from the tea kettle on to her legs. She was crying and utterly miserable. I did all I could, but I don't think I convinced her.'[78]

Katherine and Ida were both certain that Brett was in love with Murry, and they did become lovers soon after Katherine returned to Menton. John Manchester, who has studied Brett's unpublished letters and private papers, states: 'Once [in September 1920], when Katherine had left the London winter for Southern France, she had said to Brett, "Take care of my boy". Now Brett found a duty and a meaning for her life. She not only took Katherine literally, she tried to take Katherine's place in Murry's life. He seemed quite willing to lean on her and they became lovers. Murry had his separate rooms in a house next door, but often spent the nights with Brett. However, it wasn't too many months before Murry found other nightly interests and Brett was left more and more alone.'[79]

Both Ida and Lea mention that Murry had another affair with Brett (as he did with Frieda) after Katherine's death in 1923 and that he actually considered marrying her, as Katherine had predicted. John Manchester has recently confirmed this: 'Yes, Brett was Murry's mistress for about a year after Katherine died. In fact she became pregnant by him though I've never been able to find out if she had an abortion or a miscarriage. I believe it was the latter—though an abortion was planned and she was already taking some pills from the doctor (Dr. [James] Young, I believe).'[80] In 1976, when Brett was ninety-three, she fondly recalled how handsome, charming and intelligent Murry was.[81]

Katherine, who scorned Brett, was contemptuous of her obsequious relationship with Murry and did not consider her a serious rival. But she was even more 'staggered' and alarmed by Murry's apparent affair with Princess Elizabeth Bibesco. Elizabeth, the daughter of the wartime Prime Minister, Herbert Asquith (whom Katherine had met at Garsington), was married to the rich and handsome friend of Proust, Antoine Bibesco, who had been First Secretary of the Rumanian Legation in pre-war London. Enid Bagnold, who was once in love with Antoine and knew Elizabeth well, writes in a recent letter: 'Antoine looked after Elizabeth tenderly. She drank, & eventually died of it. And he nursed her totally till her death, in Roumania I think. Antoine wasn't a man to be jealous, certainly not of Murry. It was a relief & an amusement on Elizabeth's part.'[82] Murry had met Elizabeth at The Wharf, the Asquiths' country house in Berkshire, and began 'philandering' (as he called it) in November 1920, when she became his 'other nightly interest'. While Katherine felt: 'I have to be physically faithful because my body wouldn't admit any one else—even to kiss *really*, you know', Murry explained to Elizabeth: '*How* one is starved for [feminine warmth] when one has spent years tending, and anxious for, a sick wife!'[83]

Elizabeth appears in a rather obscure photograph taken at Garsington as chic, dark, round-faced and wrapped in fur, and Wyndham Lewis describes her as 'very dark and handsome, reminding me of Mr. Augustus John's more aristocratic gypsies, very solemn and upright'.[84] Julian Vinogradoff and Juliette Huxley, who knew Elizabeth at Garsington, both described her as an extremely unhappy 'nymphomaniac',[85] and Ottoline wrote, 'She is like a quick ticker-tape machine, ticking out aphorisms and anecdotes, which are all neatly ready-made inside her box. There seemed no heart, or character inside and no understanding of tragedy or comedy. The mechanical clapping of her tongue went on in my brain like a tune on a barrel-organ. She seems merely a collector of celebrities. She has never been young and never will be. She isn't unkind and I feel has rather a nice tolerant nature, but she is too conceited and vain.'[86] Katherine's *Journal* entry of December 1920 once again uses greedy appetite as a metaphor for defective character and, like Ottoline, portrays Elizabeth as a mechanical woman with no independent life of her own: 'I thought also of the Princess [Bibesco]. . . . She has a quick rapacious look—in fact she made me think of a *gull*, with an absolutely insatiable appetite for bread. And all her vitality, her cries, her movements, her wheelings, depend upon the person on the bridge who carries the loaf.'[87]

Katherine's letters to Murry during late November and early December 1920 were, at first, apologetic, conciliatory and understanding, and she conceded that their way of life was completely unconventional and they had 'a relationship which is unique but it is not what the world understands by *marriage*'.[88] Even when she discovered his affair with Elizabeth she maintained an unusually objective and tolerant attitude, analyzed his relations with women, admitted that she was more interested in her art than in her husband, criticized his treacherous affair with her friend Brett and urged him to do whatever he pleased as long as he did not tell her about it: 'You're very attractive

to women, as you know, but as long as they don't interfere—
surely you like knowing them. . . . I think you ought to enjoy
them. There is even a strong dash of the lady-killer in you!
. . . I'm a writer first and a woman after . . . I can't give you *all*
you want—above all, a kind of easy relaxation which is essential
to you. . . . I was blind not to have understood the B[rett] affair
—but no—that *was* "wrong" as we say. However, *do feel free*.
I mean that. . . . I told you to be free because I meant it. What
happens in your personal life does NOT affect me.[89]

Despite her attempts to remain indifferent, Murry's personal
life had, of course, an intimate connection with her own. His
calm acceptance of her offer and Elizabeth's arrogant claim to
Murry (who, as usual, remained passive), made Katherine afraid
that he would leave her for the well-connected, wealthy and
elegant Princess, a realization which shocked her into an extreme
change of mood. In an entry in her *Journal* of December 9, at
the very moment she was urging Murry to feel free, Katherine
condemned Elizabeth's possessiveness, Murry's deceitful remark
that he was not attracted to the Princess and his 'selfish' boast
that Elizabeth loved him: 'And the horrible vulgar letters of
this woman about "John's fou rire" and so on. And his *cruel*
insulting letter about "no *physical attraction*" (!!) "I think she
is in love with me" and so on—were they necessary? He now
claims his right not to suffer on my account any more—oh god!
How base its selfishness.'[90]

Ten days later, on December 19, at about the time Murry
arrived in Menton, the jealous Elizabeth, in a frantic effort to
win Murry, wrote to Katherine, criticized her callous treatment of Murry and asked how 'a sick woman, away in France,
and quite unable to make any kind of life or happiness for
Murry, how dared she try to hold him'. Katherine replied in a
rather arch tone: 'I shall write to the silly little creature and
tell her I have no desire to come between them only she must
not make love to him while he is living with me, because that
is undignified.' But her attempt to appear indifferent merely
revealed the depths of her bitterness. After receiving Elizabeth's
letter Katherine told Ida that she 'must never, never forgive
Jack for what he had done to her'.[91]

Katherine also hated the tedium and guilt of reviewing
inferior books for a vital £10 a month, instead of writing her

own stories in the short time that remained. When Murry revealed that he planned to publish Elizabeth's story, 'An Ordinary Man', in the *Athenaeum* of January 14, 1921, Katherine announced the end of her own contributions. Katherine, who thought she had reached the extremes of despair in Ospedaletti, uttered a new *De profundis* on December 19: 'I thought last year in Italy: Any shadow more would be death. But this year has been so much more terrible that I think with affection of the Casetta!'[92]

Katherine seemed to have triumphed over Elizabeth when, in mid-February 1921, after two brief trips to Menton, Murry finally left London to live with Katherine in the Mediterranean for the first time since Bandol in 1916. But, Katherine told Ida, Elizabeth made her last offensive in March 1921 when she sent Murry a letter 'begging him to resist Katherine. "You have withstood her so gallantly so far how can you give way now". And "you swore nothing on earth should ever come between us". From the letter I feel they are wonderfully suited and I hope he will go on with the affair. He *wants to*.'[93] Katherine managed to maintain the condescending attitude she had taken with Brett and at the end of the month wrote Elizabeth an icily dignified letter that resembled her mother's haughtiest manner, banished Elizabeth from their lives and concluded the correspondence:

I am afraid you must stop writing these little love letters to my husband while he and I live together. It is one of the things which is not done in our world.

You are very young. Won't you ask your husband to explain to you the impossibility of such a situation.

Please do not make me have to write to you again. I do not like scolding people and simply hate having to teach them manners.[94]

By April Katherine, whose fever consumed her with a slow fire and seemed to drive her dark eyes deep into their sockets, felt infinitely worse than when she had left England. She thought the hot Riviera climate was enervating, yet could not face the prospect of returning to London because Murry had given up The Elephant. She decided, instead, to try the Alpine heights of Switzerland, where she would spend most of her last two years.

II

In the midst of these emotional upheavals, which depressed but also inspired Katherine, she continued to publish and to write in frantic spurts whenever her health would permit. As she told Murry in November 1920: 'I'm in such a queer state mentally—work excites me MADLY and fatigues me, too. I can't take it calmly. . . . When I do begin I begin to get into a fever.'[95] Though Heinemann, who was Lawrence's publisher, rejected her stories in April 1919, Katherine refused an offer from another publisher in February 1920 to reprint *In A German Pension*, which she considered juvenile and even dishonest. In January 1920 Katherine was negotiating with Grant Richards and was willing to sell *Bliss* outright for £20. But the more experienced Murry submitted the book to his old friend Michael Sadler, an editor at Constable, who gave Katherine an advance on royalties of £40. When she deposited this money in the London branch of the Bank of New Zealand, Alexander Kay proudly told her father, who temporarily stopped her allowance.

When *Bliss* appeared in December 1920, nine years after her first book, it received appreciative reviews. But most critics mentioned Katherine's tendency towards superficiality,[96] sentimentality and cynicism, and the *Saturday Review* and *Dial* took exception to the 'repellent' subject matter of her literary 'psychopathic ward'.[97] When Murry asked Sullivan and De La Mare to puff *Je ne parle pas français* and *Bliss* in the *Athenaeum*, the former said the story 'possesses genius', while the latter alluded to the conclusion to Keats's 'Grecian Urn' and wrote: 'The spirit that surveys its field is delicate yet intrepid, fastidiously frank. To her very finger-tips she is in love with beauty, and securely so because her love springs out of her devotion to truth.'[98] The critics in the *TLS* and the *New Republic* praised Katherine's sensitivity to beauty and artistry in fiction as well as her skilful use of detail to 'suggest the vital flame of life'.[99] The most intelligent review was by Conrad Aiken, who recognized her unique talent: 'Miss Mansfield is brilliant—she has, more conspicuously than any contemporary writer of fiction one calls to mind, a fine, an infinitely inquisitive sensibility; a sensibility indefatigably young which finds itself in the service of a mind often cynical, sometimes cruel, and always sophisticated.'[100]

These reviews helped to establish Katherine's reputation as a serious writer, and when J. B. Pinker became her literary agent in the winter of 1920 she began to place her stories more easily. Between October and December 1920, while Murry was having affairs with Brett and Elizabeth, Katherine wrote 'The Lady's Maid', 'The Young Girl', 'Poison', 'Life of Ma Parker' and three major stories: 'Miss Brill', 'The Stranger' and 'The Daughters of the Late Colonel'. Katherine completed this gentle satire on the Colonel's daughter, Ida *Constance* Baker, and her cousin and classmate, Sylvia Payne, on December 13 at three in the morning, and woke up Ida for a celebration with tea. Apart from the stories in the *Athenaeum* and in *Art and Letters*, Katherine published the compassionate story of a charwoman, 'Life of Ma Parker', in the *Nation* of February 1921 and 'The Stranger' and 'The Daughters of the Late Colonel' in the *London Mercury* of January (which also carried the review of *Bliss*) and May 1921.

A group of Katherine's most important stories—'Bliss', 'Marriage à la Mode', 'The Stranger', and 'The Man Without a Temperament' (all written between 1918 and 1921, and published in *The Garden Party*)—concern her relationship with Murry and provide a fictional portrait of their marriage that complements the grim reality of her *Journal* and *Letters*. 'Bliss' (1918) describes the destruction of Bertha's false euphoria about her too perfect marriage, complete with the baby, money and home that Katherine never possessed. The smugness and falsity of the dinner party merely intensify her self-deception, though she seems to experience an epiphany with her guest, Pearl Fulton, a beautiful woman who had 'something strange' about her. The spell is shattered when Bertha discovers that her husband, whom she really desires for the first time in her marriage, is having an affair with Pearl. This *dénouement*, like the pear tree which symbolizes deception (as in Chaucer's 'Merchant's Tale'), is too obvious. But the theme of the worm in the bud, what Katherine called 'the snail under the leaf', and her belief that one can never count on happiness, are basic to her life and work, for they were nurtured by her early unhappiness as well as by her insecurity with Murry.

'Marriage à la Mode' (1921) portrays the shell of a marriage in the modern, bohemian mode, after the core of meaning has been taken out of it. William, the rather plodding yet providing husband, disturbed by premonitions, comes home, like Ulysses, to a houseful of suitors and an indifferent Penelope. He is estranged from his wife and mocked by her arty friends who eat the fruit that he bought for his children, whom he barely manages to see. He is left isolated, with only the idyllic memories of their earlier life when 'he hadn't the slightest idea that Isabel wasn't as happy as he'. When poor William returns to the city and sends Isabel a love letter to set things right again, she reads it to her friends who become hysterical with laughter. Though Isabel suffers a moment of conscience, guilt and recrimination—'what a loathsome thing to have done'— she chooses to swim with her friends (who had previously excluded William from this pleasure) rather than answer his pathetic though well-meaning letter.

Though it is difficult to identify with—or even care about— either William or Isabel, and the satire is far too facile, the story does concern a significant conflict of loyalties between what really matters—her marriage and her family—and what (though she cannot see it) is essentially trivial and meaningless. Her friends' joking suggestion that William is 'sending you back your marriage lines as a gentle reminder', reminds the reader, if not Isabel, of the sacramental aspect of marriage in which Katherine deeply believed: 'To know *one other* seems to me a far greater adventure than to be on kissing acquaintance with dear knows how many.'[101]

In 'The Stranger' (1921)—Katherine's version of Joyce's 'The Dead'—John Hammond, wealthy, successful, self-important, pompous yet terribly insecure, waits impatiently for his wife's ship to dock in New Zealand. He is desperately eager to regain and possess Janey, and childishly jealous of her friends aboard ship, of the doctor and the captain, and even of his children's letters to their mother—of anything that distracts her attention from himself. Yet when he finally embraces his wife, 'again, as always, he had the feeling he was holding something that never was quite his—his. Something too delicate, too precious, that would fly away once he let go.'[102]

Katherine subtly conveys the intense strain on Hammond because of the difference in their feelings for each other—his wife responds coolly to his caresses—for he has great difficulty in re-establishing intimacy with her and 'never knew for dead certain that she was as glad as he was'. When he finally discovers (and all discoveries in these stories are shattering) the reason for the ship's delay and his wife's preoccupation—that a man has died in his wife's arms—he immediately understands that his wife has achieved an emotional connection with the stranger far stronger than he has ever had with her. Despite her half-hearted reassurance, 'It's nothing to do with you and me', he is destroyed by the recognition, and the story concludes: 'They would never be alone together again.' Hammond's jealousy of the emotional bond between his wife and the dead stranger—which may have been influenced by Murry's jealous rivalry with Katherine's dead brother—is stronger than anything he could feel about a living man, and reveals the superficiality and falsity of their marriage.

Katherine defended her technique and clarified her intention in this story in a letter to John Squire, the editor of the *London Mercury*, who had questioned the effectiveness of the final sentence:

> I agree with you that man will forget [the incident of the dead stranger]—almost immediately, really—it certainly won't be true of his future relations with Janey. But in the 'keyed up' state he was in, and remembering how it was natural to him to exaggerate everything—to take the most extreme view of everything, and remembering too, his *childishness*—his childish desire for everything to be all right and really his childish grief that it wasn't—I feel that nothing less than such an unqualified statement would fit. There in its glimpse of falsity, too, you had him. . . . It was all up with him, for ever. (Of course, it wasn't!)[103]

'The Man Without a Temperament' (1920), the most revealing and intimate of Katherine's marriage stories, describes her fears about how Murry would feel if he had given in to her pleas and followed the advice of her doctor—and of Lawrence, who urged him to 'save yourself, and your self-respect, by making it complete between Katherine and you'[104]—and lived abroad with her for the two years that she needed to recover her health. The boredom and trivial irritations of life *en pension* and the longing for a more meaningful existence in England are vividly evoked. Katherine lamented in her *Journal* that her 'typically English husband' (unlike Lawrence and Carco) seemed to lack a 'temperament' and was 'not warm, ardent, eager, full of quick response, careless, spendthrift of himself, vividly alive, [or] *high-spirited*.'[105] In this story, the invalid woman is far more intense and vital than the man, who is forced to suppress his temperament under an ox-like passivity and obedience, although he fails to conceal his bitterness and resentment about the inevitable sacrifice of his career and his independent life. Though the couple live in constant intimacy, they are divided by an abyss of unspoken hostility which she feels will lead to the dreaded separation.

This story is far more subtle than 'Bliss' or 'Marriage à la Mode', and succeeds because Katherine has understood Murry's needs and feelings as well as her own, and dramatized the central and insoluble dilemma of their marriage: 'It is *anguish* to be away from him but as my presence seems to positively torture him—I suppose it's the better of two horrors.'[106] And though she longed for Murry to stay with her, she also agreed: 'It would spell failure for you to live abroad with me—I absolutely fully realize that. I can imagine what hours we should spend when I realized and you realized the sacrifice.'[107]

Katherine's marriage stories reflect her own fear of abandonment and fear of betrayal, her self-destructive jealousy and guilt about being an invalid. They emphasize the isolated heroine who needs sympathy and love, and the lack of understanding and basic honesty in marital relations. As she told Murry in 1920: 'I have hiding places—so have you. They are very different ones. We do though emerge from them strange to each other, and it's only when the strangeness wears off that we are together. This must ever be so.'[108]

Until the last six months of her life Katherine's disease seemed to stimulate her creativity and she burned with a bright, if ephemeral, flame. But her illness inevitably intensified her egocentric introspection which limited both the range and the depth of her stories. Ottoline justly states: 'She did not see very deeply into the tragedy of human lives, and it was perhaps this want of insight that made her often so pitiless and scornful.'[109] For Katherine, who was caustic and austere about her own work, was aware of her lack of education and tendency to superficial smartness as well as her clinical rather than compassionate attitude towards the people who inspired her fictional characters. As she told Brett in December 1918: 'I am a writer who cares for nothing but writing—that's how I feel. When I am with people I feel like a doctor with his patients—very sympathetic—very interested in the case! very anxious for them to tell me all they can—but as regards myself—quite alone, quite isolated—a queer state.'[110] Katherine's themes, which evolved directly from her personal experience, are those of a lonely, frightened and sensitive invalid who wants to escape from the oppressions of adult reality into the memories of childhood, and concern abandonment, solitude and a profound fear of death.

CHAPTER FOURTEEN

Switzerland and Paris, 1921–1922

KATHERINE AND Ida took the train from Menton to Geneva on May 4, 1921 and then travelled around the Lake to the Hôtel Beau Site in Baugy, just above Montreux. Murry, who had published *The Evolution of an Intellectual* and *Aspects of Literature* in 1920 and was now an established critic, went to Oxford to deliver a series of lectures, later published as *The Problem of Style*, and rejoined them the following month. After her humiliating experience in the San Remo hotel, Katherine posed as a delicate lady with a weak heart.

She soon began to criticize Switzerland, a country—Scott Fitzgerald observed—'where few things begin, but many things end'.[1] Katherine found the place 'revoltingly clean' and thought the flowers looked as laundered as the linen: 'Every daisy in the grass below has a starched frill—the very bird-droppings are dazzling. . . . My bed—it's enough to unmake any man—the sight of it.'[2] She compared the hotel to a living cemetery, filled with 'deaders' of a bygone era, and wrote Ottoline two witty letters that contrasted the astonishing lack of taste in the country with her own personal possessions—which symbolized her art, her courage and her delicacy:

> Life in this hotel is a queer experience. I have two rooms and a balcony—so I am—thank Heaven—quite cut off. . . . But my balcony looks over Montreux and Clarens. Anything more hideous!! I think Switzerland has the very ugliest houses, people, food, furniture, in the whole world. . . . To me, though, the symbol of Switzerland is that large middle-class female *behind*. It is the most respectable thing in the world. It is Matchless. Everyone has one in this hotel; some of the elderly ladies have two. . . . On my bed at night there is a copy of Shakespeare, a copy of Chaucer, an automatic pistol and a black muslin fan. This is my whole little world.[3]

Katherine, who was still searching for an unorthodox cure, had come to Montreux to investigate the treatment of Henry Spahlinger, a Swiss bacteriologist whose method was first used in England in 1913 and became well known in the 1920s. For acute and severe cases Spahlinger employed serum taken from horses that had developed anti-bodies against tuberculosis. She drove up to Sierre to consult Dr. Stephani, an expensive but famous chest specialist and exponent of the Spahlinger treatment, who cautiously explained that he had known patients with tuberculosis in the second degree who had recovered and that she still had a chance. Though some doctors claimed that Spahlinger had great success in treating advanced cases, his cure was useless.[4]

At the end of May Katherine moved to a hotel in Clarens, just below Baugy on Lake Geneva, and in June she travelled through the countryside filled with ancient castles and solid towns, and met Murry at the Hôtel Château Belle Vue (now the Town Hall) in Sierre. The town, where Rilke lived from 1921 to 1925, is 1,700 feet high in the sheltered Rhône Valley and is known for its figs and white wine. After adjusting to the altitude for a month they took the winding little funicular railway through Randogne (3,250 feet) to Montana (5,000 feet), which is situated on a small plateau ringed by lofty mountains and was a centre of Swiss sanatoria. The dying poet, James Elroy Flecker, who had stayed in Montana in the summer of 1913, found the Alpine landscape depressing and wrote to his parents: 'This seems to be quite the place to come to—for health, but the desolation—the black fir trees again and the horrid snowy mountains are appalling.'[5]

Katherine at first thought her 'treacherous' heart was going to stop, felt nauseated, could not tolerate light, noise, heat or cold, and was afraid to speak for fear of provoking a spasm of coughing. She temporarily entered Dr. Stephani's luxurious Palace clinic which, she reassured herself, was 'not a real live-or-dead sanatorium', and once again had the doctor puncture her tubercular gland.

At the beginning of July the Murrys rented the Châlet des Sapins from the mother of the English Dr. Hudson and, after five moves in two months, finally settled into a house of their own. The large three-storey dark wooden building, with carved balconies and steep overhanging roof, was isolated among pine

8*

trees in a clearing of the forest. Katherine's bedroom was on the top floor and had wooden walls, a large square balcony and a magnificent view over the tree tops and across a long plateau to the glaciers and snowy peaks of the Alps. The snug, almost arcadian chalet had a bathroom, hot water, central heating, a piano, thick carpets and striped cotton blinds to shut out the mid-day glare. The air was pure and the weather was excellent, for even in winter the sun burned in the brilliant sky from early morning until mid-afternoon, and when Katherine sat outside she could hear the gentle sound of bells coming up the valley.

The house was run by a stolid servant called Ernestine, who always wore a peasant costume and succeeded Juliette in the Beau Rivage, Mrs. Honey in the Headland Hotel, Violet in The Elephant and Marie in the Villa Isola Bella as the last of Katherine's devoted maids. Ida, the 'official wife' of Katherine and Murry, took a job at a clinic in Montana. Like Ida, Ernestine was gentle and willing but also rather dim and incompetent, and by January 1922 the fastidious and ethereal Katherine began to express her familiar hostility to those who served her: 'My feeling about Ernestine is shameful. But there it is. Her tread, her look, the way her nose is screwed round, her intense stupidity, her wrists —revolt me.'[6]

Katherine's seven months in Montana, where she was relatively healthy, living with Murry in a beautiful place and working well, resembled their blissful period in Bandol during the early months of 1916. They soon established a regular routine: they wrote all morning, Murry walked and Katherine 'crawled' in the afternoon, they worked again from tea to dinner, and smoked, played cribbage and read Shakespeare aloud in the evening. They spent two entire weeks in the summer discussing Proust while Murry was writing about him, and he was immensely stimulated by Katherine's conversation. Ida brought their cat Wingley in September; and when the snow fell the following month Murry, who was a good athlete, went skating and skiing while Katherine took rides in a sleigh. Though Katherine felt content in 'remote and undisturbed' Montana, she was not especially attracted to the scenery, disliked the Swiss emphasis on food and money, and was repelled by the common people, who seemed to resemble Ernestine. As she told the sophisticated Sydney Schiff: 'I don't intend to live in Switzerland. In spite of the beautiful aspects one can't tolerate the peasants. They are so ugly, such bores, so heavy. Never have I imagined such ankles.'[7]

Katherine had a feverish attack of acute enteritis in August 1921; and by December her lungs were worse and her heart was strained: 'Both my lungs are affected; there is a cavity in one and the other is affected through. My heart is weak too. Can all this be cured. Ah, Koteliansky—wish for me.'[8] It is scarcely surprising —as Katherine became increasingly aware of the brevity of life— that she could rarely summon up the energy to write; the mornings were taken up by her cure and the afternoons with correspondence, and she was overcome by exhaustion in the evenings.

After several months Katherine's invalidism and their isolation began to get on Murry's nerves, and in late November the jealous Katherine complained in her *Journal*: 'It's a long time now since he started going out every evening. I can't stop him. I've tried everything but it is useless. Out he goes. And the horrible thing is I don't know where it is he goes to and who is he with? It's all such a mystery. That's what makes it so hard to bear. Where have you been? I've asked him and asked him that. But never a word, never a sign. I sometimes think he likes to torture me.'[9] Though Katherine also felt angry at Ida and noticed her friend's repressed hostility, she still turned to her, confessing: 'I take advantage of you—demand perfection of you—crush you', and asked rhetorically: 'Can I feel, payment apart and *slavery* apart and false pride apart—that you are mine?'[10]

Katherine had come to Montana not only because it was a health resort but also because her second cousin Elizabeth, who first told her about the village, had a large and luxurious villa in Randogne—half an hour's walk down the mountain. Elizabeth, whose maiden name was Mary Annette Beauchamp, was born in Sydney in 1866 and married Count Henning von Arnim (who was fifteen years older than she) in 1890. They had five children and lived on a large, bleak estate at Nassenheide in Pomerania, which she described in her first book, *Elizabeth and Her German Garden* (1898). Her pseudonym, Elizabeth (von Arnim), was probably based on the name of Goethe's famous mistress, Bettina Brentano von Arnim, and her charming and sentimental but trivial and snobbish memoir was phenomenally successful in Edwardian England, and went into twenty-one editions by 1899.

Elizabeth first came to Randogne after her husband's death in 1910, and used the royalties of her popular play, *Priscilla Runs Away*, to build the Château Soleil the following year. Elizabeth, who had a trying and tiring affair with H. G. Wells from 1911 to 1913, later described him as 'that coarse little man', and he said: 'when you've had her for a week you want to bash her head through the wall.'[11] In 1916 she married Bertrand Russell's elder brother Frank, the 2nd Earl Russell, but she left him three years later and, while retaining the title Countess Russell, wrote a novel, *Vera* (1921), about their unhappy marriage.

Though Elizabeth and Katherine were related, had the same background and shared similar tastes and interests, their lives had been very different. Elizabeth, who was Katherine's childhood heroine and literary inspiration, had a title, beauty, children, wealth and fame; she wrote for women's magazines and her readers were genteel. Katherine, who was a far greater artist, had led an impoverished and bohemian life, published mainly in *avant-garde* and high-brow magazines, was not well known, made very little money and was an invalid. The differences in their lives and personalities were reflected in their accents, for A. S. Frere (who knew them both in Switzerland) related that Katherine's speech was noticeably antipodean while Elizabeth's was distinctly upper-class English.[12] New Zealanders were not very interested in Katherine's career when she was alive, and some people resented being satirized in her stories,[13] while the Beauchamp family, who were not particularly proud of Katherine, were extremely impressed by Elizabeth's marriages to a Count and an Earl.[14]

Katherine and Elizabeth had scarcely met each other until the latter discovered that little Kathleen Beauchamp was, in fact, Katherine Mansfield and sought her out in London. In August 1920, when Katherine was living in Hampstead, she described Elizabeth to Violet Schiff with considerable condescension: 'A thousand devils are sending Elizabeth without her German garden to tea here tomorrow—her last time before she goes abroad into her Swiss chalet. I expect she will stay at longest half an hour— She will be oh, such a little bundle of artificialities—but I can't put her off.'[15] Their meeting was apparently a greater success than Katherine had anticipated, for in November she wrote to Murry from Menton: 'I am glad you are going to see Elizabeth. I confess

I've a great *tendre* for her really, more than I'd tell anybody. Perhaps it's just sentimentality.'[16]

Katherine had something of a personal and literary rivalry with Elizabeth, just as she had with Virginia Woolf. She reviewed Elizabeth's novel, *Christopher and Columbus*, about two Anglo-German children in wartime America, in the *Athenaeum* of April 1919 and diplomatically observed: 'She is, in the happiest way, conscious of her own particular vision, and she wants no other. . . . In a world where there are so many furies with warning fingers it is good to know of someone who goes on her way finding a gay garland, and not forgetting to add a sharp-scented spray or two and a bitter herb that its sweetness may not cloy.'[17] Katherine was really stating, without offending Elizabeth, that her success was based on a cheerful optimism that was extremely different from her own dark and cynical vision. But two years later, in a letter to Brett in October 1921, Katherine was genuinely impressed by the more serious novel, *Vera*, and described her cousin—who was only two years younger than Katherine's mother—as 'surrounded' and protected, just as Annie was, by her luxuries and friends: 'The point about her is that one loves her and is proud of her. . . . But no doubt Elizabeth is far more important to me than I am to her. She's surrounded, lapped in lovely friends. Read her last book, if you can get hold of it. It's called *Vera* and published by Macmillan. It's amazingly good!'[18]

Though Elizabeth admired Katherine's artistic integrity, sensitive style and technical skill, she tended to patronize, irritate and wound her. In January 1922 Katherine caustically recorded in her *Journal*: 'In the afternoon Elizabeth came. She looked fascinating in her black suit, something between a Bishop and a Fly. She spoke of my "pretty little story" ['At the Bay'] in the *Mercury*. All the while she was here I was conscious of a falsity. We said things we meant; we were sincere, but at the back there was nothing but falsity. It was very horrible. I do not want ever to see her or hear from her again.'[19] And in March 1922, a week after the appearance of *The Garden Party*, Elizabeth (in a letter to a friend) tempered her praise of the book with a faint note of proprietary condescension that suggested she did not entirely approve of Katherine's distasteful realism: 'I've just been writing to Katherine about her book—some of the things in it are marvellous—some less so, but still leave a queer, extraordinary impression on one—all are bleeding with reality. . . . I'm fearfully proud of her—just as if I had hatched her!'[20]

E. M. Forster, who had been her children's tutor in Germany and used her as the model for the worldly and malicious Mrs. Failing in *The Longest Journey* (1907), characterized Elizabeth as 'small and graceful, vivid and vivacious. She was also capricious and a merciless tease';[21] and Frank Swinnerton said that she was 'drawling, protrusive-eyed, and relentless, [and] frightened large numbers of people'—including himself—with her powerful and possessive personality.[22] Both Swinnerton and A. S. Frere recalled that when told about a man who had been wounded in seventeen places, Elizabeth replied: 'I didn't know a man had seventeen places'.[23] Though both women liked each other and became friends, Katherine's knowledge of Elizabeth's early life and colonial origins made her cousin uncomfortable. Elizabeth indulged, to a far greater extent than Katherine, in polite conventions and hypocrisies, while Katherine, who was more direct and honest with herself and others, wrote of her cousin's 'claw-like hands laden with jewels', had to restrain herself in conversation and was the one person Elizabeth really feared.

Elizabeth was the only person Katherine saw in Montana, and Murry probably went down to the Château Soleil when he mysteriously disappeared in the evenings. Katherine's letters and journal of this period reveal that she was extremely ambivalent about Elizabeth. Though Elizabeth had written a sentence in her *German Garden* which must have struck her cousin—'I never could see that delicacy of constitution is pretty, either in plants or women'[24]—Katherine recorded that she was hurt when Elizabeth said her art was inspired by her disease: 'Elizabeth came in the afternoon. She and I were alone. She wore a little blue hood fastened under the chin with a diamond clasp. She looked like a very ancient drawing. She suggested that if I did become cured, I might no longer write.'[25] Yet Katherine could not help admiring Elizabeth's apparent invulnerability to the emotional torment and physical disease that had devastated her own life. 'Elizabeth "fascinates" me', she told Sydney Schiff the following day, 'and I admire her for working as she is working now, all alone in her big châlet. She is courageous, very. And for some reason the mechanism of Life hardly seems to touch her. She refuses to be ruffled.'[26]

Katherine's final judgment of Elizabeth, which was inevitably influenced by a certain jealousy of her cousin's career, was expressed in her *Journal* of 1921-22:

> Elizabeth came, wearing her woolly lamb. A strange fate overtakes me with her. We seem to be always talking of physical subjects. They bore and disgust me. . . .
> [Katherine:] 'I have been writing a story about an old man.' She looked vague. 'But I don't think I like old men—do you?' said she. 'They *exude* so.'
> This horrified me. It seemed so infernally petty, and more than that . . . it was the saying of a vulgar little mind.'[27]

When Murry published this passage in Katherine's *Journal* of 1927, Elizabeth immediately recognized her words and was wounded by Katherine's unanswerable sentence. Both in her own journal and in a letter to Murry the following day, she attributed her 'vulgarity' to her (rather exaggerated) fear and awkwardness in Katherine's presence, and described the generous feelings that her reserve and pride prevented her from expressing when Katherine was alive. Neither Elizabeth nor Katherine wanted to appear soft and sentimental and they were unwilling to reveal their deepest feelings:

> Read K.M.'s *Journal* . . . finished it. Found disconcerting things about me in it—one of them more than disconcerting—'She has a vulgar little mind.' . . . Can I help it? I was very shy always with her, afraid of her while intensely admiring. Perhaps embarrassment made me say vulgar things. . . .
> I used to be dreadfully *embarrassed*—afraid of displeasing her, of being stupid, slow. I admired her so—well, abjectly, and my very anxiety to give satisfaction made my spiritual fingers be all thumbs. I always came away feeling as if my skin were off, and miserable with the conviction that I must have bored and repelled her. Yet I adored her. . . . If only I hadn't been so much afraid of Katherine! . . . But at least I had enough intelligence to worship hers.[28]

The tranquillity of Montana, the comfort of the Châlet, the company of Murry, the quiescence of her disease and the artistic example of Elizabeth inspired Katherine's creative imagination and made these months the most fruitful of her entire life.

Katherine wanted to get the deepest truth out of her ideas, felt 'It's always a kind of race to get in as much as one can before it *disappears*',[29] and wrote her stories, which she called 'spasms', in a rush of inspiration. Murry reports that there were no notes or drafts for her completed stories and the original manuscripts were 'written at ever increasing speed so that the writing towards the end is hardly more than a hieroglyph.'[30] Katherine felt guilty when she was not writing, never made her illness an excuse and worked at an astonishing pace, especially after Clement Shorter, the editor of the *Sphere*, had commissioned six stories at six guineas each.[31]

The most significant of these stories is the satirical yet sensitive 'Garden Party' in which, as Katherine explained to William Gerhardi, she tried to convey 'the diversity of life and how we try to fit in everything, Death included. That is bewildering for a person of Laura's age.'[32] Mrs. Sheridan attempts to preserve her innocent Eden and has her elaborate garden party despite the accidental death of her working-class neighbour. Her daughter Laura, who feels intuitive and imaginative sympathy for the bereaved family, and does not want to disturb their mourning, is bribed and distracted by a new hat that symbolizes the trivial vanity and moral corruption of her mother's life and values. After the enjoyable garden party has ended, Laura takes a basket of left-over food to the poor family and sees the dead father; her childishly impossible attempt to synthesize the pleasures of life and the experience of death illuminates the contrast between snobbery and social responsibility. Mrs. Sheridan's inability to respond to Laura's finer feelings and moral awareness illustrates Pascal's *pensée*: 'Pity for the unfortunate does not clash with our appetites. On the contrary, we are glad to offer this evidence of friendship, and to acquire a reputation for kindness without giving anything.'[33]

Katherine's third collection of stories, *The Garden Party*, was published by Constable on February 23, 1922 and went into a third printing that spring. The reviews were similar, though more positive and extensive, than those she had received for *Bliss*. Rebecca West in the *New Statesman* emphasized Katherine's brilliant technique and poetic response to beauty: 'Her choice of the incident that will completely and economically prove her point is astonishing. . . . One of the results of Miss Mansfield's poetic temperament is that beauty is the general condition of her story.'[34] But she was surprised by Katherine's perverse response to her praise and wrote recently: 'Though I gave her a very good review she was nobly disinterested and always expressed the greatest dislike for me to her friends.'[35]

The *Saturday Review* lauded Katherine's genius and 'instinctive' art,[36] and Joseph Krutch in the *Nation* also admired the richness of detail that gave her stories the 'poignancy of actual life'.[37] The *English Review* called Katherine a 'feminine Maupassant' (most of the other reviewers mentioned her affinity—and inferiority—to Chekhov), and then criticized the book as cruel, passionless and cynical.[38] And though Robert Littell and Conrad Aiken noted her remarkably skilful diction and style, they also had serious reservations about her narrow and somewhat superficial themes. Littell insisted: 'her art seems a little conscious, a little watchful, a little thin'; and Aiken affirmed: 'the language of associations which she speaks is, if brilliant, extremely small.'[39] The *TLS* noticed a new element of pity and thought the book 'stronger in tissue, wider in the range of its vision' than *Bliss*. But Malcolm Cowley, in the longest and most serious review, deftly analyzed her themes and settings (which were fascinating projections of her relations with Murry and her father), and concluded that *The Garden Party* was less successful than her earlier volume: 'One situation recurs constantly in her work. There is a woman: neurotic, arty, hateful, and a good, stupid man whom she constantly torments. . . . Another situation, which she repeats rather less frequently, is that of the destruction of a woman's individuality by some stronger member of her family. . . . She has three backgrounds only: continental hotels, New Zealand upper-class society, and a certain artistic set in London. . . . It is almost as good as *Bliss*, but not much different; from Katherine Mansfield it is immensely disappointing.'[40]

Katherine's modest fame enabled her to help a fellow writer, for when the young William Gerhardi, who had lived in Russia and was writing a book on Chekhov, sent her his novel, *Futility*, in November 1921, she gave him the same encouragement and assistance she had given to Brett and to Richard Murry. Gerhardi gratefully wrote: 'I was unknown to her. But she replied by return, read my book within a week, and found it a publisher [Richard Cobden-Sanderson] by the end of a fortnight.'[41]

By January 1922, after seven productive months in Montana,

Katherine began to hate the snow, ice and blizzards, and to long for the south of France. When she first came to Montana in July she admitted she was a frail half-creature, 'practically a helpless invalid'; in September she told Violet Schiff she was no longer an invalid but still coughed a great deal and could not walk; and when her disease forced her to remain in bed for six weeks from early December to mid-January, she described herself as 'locked' in lumbago. Disheartened by the return of her cursed illness and by all the clinical paraphernalia, and depressed by her 'parasitic' dependence on others, she felt she had been living mainly on 'nervous energy', longed for ordinary everyday life and decided to make a bid for health—her *final bid*. She remembered her dead brother and told Anne Rice and Brett that she did not want to die at an early age before she had finished her work: 'I'm sick of people dying who promise well. One doesn't want to join that crowd at all. . . . Ah, Brett, I hope with all my heart you have not known anyone who died young—long before their time. It is bitterness.'[42] At the very end of January she expressed in her *Journal* an irrational idea that would dominate the last six months of her life: 'I have a suspicion like a certainty that the real cause of my illness is not lungs at all, but something else. And if this were found and cured, all the rest would heal.' She desperately wanted 'To escape from the prison of the flesh—of matter'.[43]

Murry, who was very happy in Montana, later realized: 'If Katherine could have reconciled herself to living in the Swiss mountains where we were, her life could have been considerably prolonged. I think now that I ought to have strained every nerve to persuade her' to stay.[44] Murry was not entirely honest about his reasons for remaining in Switzerland when the gravely ill Katherine left with Ida for Paris: 'I at first intended to remain at the Châlet des Sapins, chiefly because I shrank from giving it up. I wanted Katherine to return there; it was to me the symbol of salvation and sanity.'[45] But Ida bluntly asserted that his motives were less high-minded than he suggested: 'Murry would not go; he was working well and enjoying the winter sports';[46] and Lea confirms that Murry stayed in Montana to finish his novel, *The Things We Are* (1922).[47] Katherine recorded in her *Journal* that Murry preferred to remain in Montana in order to free himself from the strain of her illness; in a letter she criticized his refusal to help her during one of the crucial moments of her life:

'Your work is more urgent than this affair in Paris has been.
... And also that remark: "Moreover, the rent is paid here!" ...
I have seen the worst of it myself i.e. going alone to Manoukhin,
having no one to talk it over, and so on. I want now intensely to
be alone until May.'[48]

Katherine had unusually bad luck with doctors, for their
treatment was frequently harmful and they were (with few
exceptions) dangerous, fraudulent or inept. She consulted twenty
doctors between July 1914 and October 1922, when she finally
abandoned her frantic quest for a medical cure.[49] She was inevitably sceptical of physicians ('Saw two of the doctors—an ass,
and an ass'),[50] and in a letter to Virginia Woolf she contrasted
their pretentious behaviour with the helpless humiliation of the
patient: 'Why *are* doctors so preposterous? I see them in their
hundreds, moving among sham Jacobean furniture, warming
their large pink hands at little gas fires and asking the poor visitor
if this will come off or pull down?'[51]

Towards the end of 1921 Kot told Katherine about a Russian
doctor, Ivan Manoukhin, who had worked at the Pasteur Institute
in Paris in 1913 and had been head of the Red Cross hospital for
infectious diseases in Kiev during the War. He claimed—in an
article in the *Lancet*—to have personally treated eight thousand
cases of tuberculosis in Russia and to have successfully cured the
disease by the application of X-rays to the spleen.[52] On December
4 Katherine wrote a simple but moving letter in French to
Manoukhin, who had left Russia after the Revolution and was
practising in Paris. She described her condition, minimized the
seriousness of her illness, emphasized her powerful wish to be
cured, and mentioned that she was a writer who still had a great
deal to accomplish: 'Les deux poumons sont attaqués et le coeur
en est embarrassé. Tout de même je ne suis pas une grande
malade. Je sens qu'il y a toujours de la santé en moi et j'ai le désir
le plus vif d'avoir assez de forces pour accomplir le travail—
je suis écrivain—que j'ai encore à faire.'[53] Though Manoukhin
did not reply to her first letters and was out of Paris when Ida tele-
phoned on December 18, she finally managed to reach him in
January.

After Kot's death in 1955, Murry unfairly blamed him for his
'quite pernicious' influence on Katherine and for encouraging
her in 'the dangerous dream of being completely cured by the

Russian, Manoukhin'.[54] Like most doctors, Manoukhin had had some success, and Kot had the best intentions when he told Katherine about him. The fault, in fact, lies much more with Murry for not insisting that she should have proper treatment in 1918 and for allowing her to leave the healthy tranquillity of Switzerland for the Russian's clinic in Paris.

Katherine journeyed to Paris on January 30 and found rooms in the large and chic Victoria Palace Hôtel at 6 Rue Blaise Desgoffe in Montparnasse, which had been suggested by Anne Rice. The following day she went to Manoukhin's clinic at 3 Rue Lyautey, off Rue Raynouard in Passy, and recorded in her *Letters* and *Journal* the conflict between her desire to believe in a miraculous cure and her intuitive scepticism about the doctor's ability to treat her disease. On the morning of January 31 she told John Galsworthy: 'I have not seen him yet—so—though it's still a miracle—one believes.' In the evening she honestly noted: 'I have the feeling that M[anoukhin] is really a good man. I have also a sneaking feeling . . . that he is a kind of unscrupulous impostor.'[55] Despite her serious doubts, Katherine agreed to begin immediately the painful, dangerous and totally ineffectual treatment, which cost 4500 francs for fifteen *séances*.

Katherine found Manoukhin 'a tall formal rather dry man (not in the least an "enthusiast") who speaks scarcely any French and has a lame Russian girl for his interpreter'. He was assisted by Dr. Donat, a handsome, white-bearded man with a stiff leg, who 'shouted so, pushed his face into mine, asked me *indecent* questions. Ah, that's the horror of being ill. One must submit to having one's secrets held up to the light, and regarded with a cold stare. D. is a proper Frenchman. "Êtes-vous constipée?" '[56] After Donat's rather crude examination, Manoukhin rashly claimed: 'I can promise to cure you—to make you as though you had never had this disease. . . . It will take 15 *séances*—then a period of repose preferably in the mountains for 2-3-4 months just as you like. Then 10 more.'[57]

Like most revolutionary treatments of that time, Manoukhin's 'cure' did much more harm than good because the powerful X-rays could neither be precisely focused nor controlled. Katherine began the *séances* with high hopes in February, but by mid-March she had swung from confidence to despair, and was suffering from an agonizing reaction to the irradiation of the spleen which she bravely described to Brett as a humorous martyrdom: 'One burns with heat in one's hands and feet and bones. Then suddenly you are racked with neuritis, but such neuritis that you can't lift your arm. Then one's head begins to pound. It's the moment when if I were a proper martyr I should begin to have that awful smile that martyrs in the flames put on when they begin to sizzle!'[58] This pain was compounded by the deadly boredom of a corpse-like confinement to her hotel room for three months.

Murry, who was feeling lonely, guilty and worried about Katherine, changed his mind, let the Châlet and arrived in Paris on February 11. Katherine completed 'The Fly' on February 20 and *The Garden Party* appeared three days later. Early in March she described their hermetic hotel existence in a letter to Richard Murry and expressed her fear that the isolation from normal life would hurt her art: 'We have two good rooms [134 and 135] and a bathroom at the end of a corridor down a little passage of our own. And it's as private as if we were in a flat. We work, play chess, read, Jack goes out, we make our own tea and work again. . . . [But] it seems to me we can't write anything worth the name unless one lives—really lives.'[59] Katherine suffered the burning pain of radiation and was confined to her room, except for visits to the doctor, until May. She then temporarily felt much better and began to enjoy life in Paris and to see people. She went to the Louvre, drove in the Bois de Boulogne and told Richard: 'It's terrible how Jack and I seem to get engaged. We are pursued by dinners and lunches and telephone bells and dentists.'[60]

Manoukhin knew a number of Russian *émigré* writers who had moved to Paris after the Revolution and he promised to introduce Katherine to Dmitri Merezhkovsky, the symbolist poet, Alexander Kuprin, the creator of Captain Ribnikov, who inspired the name of Katherine's doll, and Ivan Bunin, the author of *The Gentleman from San Francisco*, which had been translated by Lawrence and Kot and published in the *Dial* in January 1922. Katherine met Bunin, who had a tired, ascetic face and drooping eyes, in Manoukhin's flat in late May and was terribly disappointed by his faint recollection and condescending dismissal of her revered master, Anton Chekhov. As she wrote to her fellow enthusiast, William Gerhardi: 'I met Bunin in Paris and because he had known Tchehov I wanted to talk of him. But alas! Bunin said "Tchehov? Ah—Ah—Oui, j'ai connu Tchehov. Mais il y a longtemps, longtemps." And then a pause. And then, graciously, "Il a écrit des belles choses." And that was the end of Tchehov.'[61]

Katherine also saw the Schiffs in Paris, and in May they introduced her to their friend James Joyce. Katherine had recognized the importance of *Ulysses* when she read parts of it at the Hogarth Press in 1918, and though she was shocked by Joyce's language and repelled by his realism, she perceived (as few people did at that time) the brilliance of his technique, the depth of his characters, the greatness of his achievement and the truth of his vision. Joyce is 'immensely important', she wrote to Sydney Schiff, 'Some time ago I found something so repellent in his work that it was difficult to read it—It shocks me to come upon words, expressions and so on that I'd shrink from in life. But now it seems to me the *new novel*, the seeking after Truth is so by far and away the most important thing that one must conquer all minor aversions.'[62] In a letter to Violet Katherine described her meeting with Joyce, her fascination with the complex Homeric parallels in *Ulysses* and her pride in Murry's comprehension of the novel:

> I was so distressed that Sydney stayed such a short time on Wednesday. But Joyce was rather . . . difficile. I had no idea until then of his view of *Ulysses*—no idea how closely it was modelled on the Greek story, how absolutely necessary it was to know the one through and through to be able to discuss the other. I've read the *Odyssey* and am more or less familiar with it but Murry and Joyce simply sailed away out of my depth. I felt almost stupid. It's absolutely impossible that other people should understand *Ulysses* as Joyce understands it. It's almost revolting to hear him discuss its difficulties. It contains *code words* that must be picked up in each paragraph and so on. The question and answer part can be read astronomically or from the geological standpoint or—Oh, I don't know! And in the midst of this he told us that his latest admirer was *Jack Dempsey*.[63]

In May, when Katherine's health seemed to have improved significantly, she began to believe Manoukhin's promises and dared to write to Ida: 'As far as I can tell this treatment has been

(I hesitate to use this big word) completely successful. I hardly ever cough. I have gained 8 pounds. I have no rheumatism whatever.'[64] But if her initial hopes were high in this matter of life and death, her eventual disappointment was even greater. On June 3, just before leaving for her 'period of repose', she experienced her second *forte réaction*, began to lose faith and felt she could no longer bear the torture of a melting martyr: 'It's rather hard to work just now', she wrote to her much older and healthier cousin, Elizabeth. 'I am at the moment when one feels the reaction. After five doses of X-rays [and Katherine had fifteen] one is hotted up inside like a furnace and one's very bones seem to be melting. I suppose this is the moment when real martyrs break into song.'[65]

Katherine had endured her suffering in vain, for Manoukhin's theory was incorrect and his 'cure' had absolutely no positive effect on her disease. Katherine tried to believe, as she told her father in a confused letter: 'the spleen is the spot where the blood changes—if the spleen is fed with X-rays the blood is likewise fed.'[66] But a modern authority states:

> The theory *was* that radiating the spleen in small doses would stimulate that organ to release substances ('humoural sub-stances' now known to be antibodies) which would get into the blood stream and help combat the systematic infection of tuberculosis. There is no evidence that I know of that radiating the spleen causes release of these substances or that such treatment was of any value. . . . The premise was false and the treatment never helped anyone. White cells don't work *primarily* by dissolving as Manoukhin said. Nor does stimulat-ing the spleen help dissolve white blood cells. Moreover, low dose irradiation probably doesn't stimulate the spleen to do anything.[67]

Katherine was fortunate to survive this dangerous treatment, for Francis Carco described her as looking seriously ill when he saw her for the last time in Paris in 1922: 'Her beautiful sombre eyes shone with the same ardour, with the same fever. She emanated a sort of magnetism; but she had a sickly appearance and her poor little hands, so thin and pale, filled me with a frightful pain.'[68] And in London, where her literary reputation was beginning to grow, the young Evelyn Waugh noted in his diary: 'There are rumours that . . . Katherine Mansfield is not going to die after all.'[69]

In February 1922, while Katherine was having this treatment, she wrote one of her finest stories, 'The Fly'. The theme and central symbol of this intensely concentrated work derive originally from Gloucester's bitter statement about the gods' cruelty to mortal men: 'As flies to wanton boys are we to the gods;/They kill us for their sport' (*King Lear*, IV.i) and from Blake's 'The Fly': 'For I dance,/And drink, and sing,/Till some blind hand/Shall brush my wing,' and more immediately to Katherine's use of the fly-in-the-milk-jug metaphor to describe her own exhausted and impotent condition. For both the fly and the tuberculosis victim suffocate—in ink and in blood. In this autobiographical story, the fly represents Katherine and her brother Leslie, as well as the fate of all helpless people.

Katherine chose the name of Woodifield, a tuberculosis patient and friend of Ida in Montana, because of its similarities to 'Fairfield' and Beauchamp. The turning-point of the story, which takes place in late autumn, occurs when old Woodifield reminds the prosperous and confident boss (who is based on Harold Beauchamp) of their dead sons in Belgium, and complains that the *hôteliers* near the cemetery are 'trading on our feelings'. When Woodifield leaves, after making this fatal pronouncement, the boss locks himself in his office; he experiences extreme anguish because he can no longer feel grief for his dead son nor shed cathartic tears as he did six years before when (like Woodifield) 'he had left the office a broken man, with his life in ruins'.[70]

The boss's torture of the fly, a classic example of displaced aggression, is really a sadistic attempt to reassert his own omnipotence. The fly's plucky struggle to avoid suffocation symbolizes the destiny of mortals who think they have escaped horrible danger and are 'ready for life', but have actually lost divine protection and come under the influence of a malign will. When the boss kills the fly with the third black ink-blot, he drives out the demon of guilt and once again forgets his dead son. The greatness of this very short story derives from Katherine's ability to control and then detonate the highly compressed emotion and to make the central symbol express a universal theme.

When Katherine had her second attack of radiation sickness, she temporarily discontinued her treatments with Manoukhin

and returned to Randogne on June 4. The disastrous trip back
to Switzerland with Murry, who isolated himself from her illness
and was characteristically self-absorbed, caused a relapse,
destroyed all the progress she had made and brought her close
to death. As she confessed to Ida on June 9, less than a month
after her hopeful letter: 'I am almost as ill as I ever was, in every
way. . . . That journey nearly killed me literally. [Murry] had
no *idea* I suffered at all.'[71]

Their laundry did not come back in time, they left the hotel late,
there were no porters, swarms of people were travelling on the
Whitsun holiday, Murry gave away a 500 franc note by mistake,
the carriages were crowded and had no proper lavatories, they
lost their luggage tickets, Murry's fountain pen and Katherine's
precious travelling clock, and arrived at Sierre two hours late—
exhausted, dirty and depressed. After a brief lunch at the hotel
they had to rush for the little train up to Randogne, and Katherine
got thoroughly soaked and chilled in the open cart that took
them through a rainstorm from the station to the Hôtel
d'Angleterre.

Though Ida had praised the hotel, they found the small rooms
spartan and dreary. 'All was empty, chill and strange', she told
Brett the following day. '[An old grey woman] took us into
two very plain bare rooms, smelling of pitch pine, with big
bunches of wild flowers on the tables, with no mirrors, little
wash-basins like tea basins, no armchairs, no nuffin. And she
explained she had no servant even.'[72] Katherine immediately
began to cough and got an attack of pleurisy, just as she had
after the disastrous ride from the station to Garsington in
November 1918. She confessed to Ida and to her *Journal*: 'I am still
suffering from a kind of nervous prostration caused by my life in
Paris. . . . [There is] the strain of keeping going, of brushing my
clothes, of making the constant, renewed effort.'[73] Only when she
was taking a walk and suddenly, normally and naturally had to
urinate behind some bushes did she feel like an ordinary person
rather than an invalid.

Utterly weary, Katherine felt that wild horses would not drag
her away from the hotel for months, but her heart, strained by
Manoukhin's treatment, could not stand the high mountains.
She was restless, found it difficult to work and was extremely
anxious about her health. 'J[ack] can *never* realize what I have

to do', she told Ida. 'He helps me all he can but he can't help me really and the result is I spend all my energy—every bit—in keeping going. I have none left for my work. . . . [Jack] could not understand why I looked "so awful" and why everybody seemed to think I was terribly ill. Jack can *never* understand.'[74] Katherine and Murry, who disagreed about whether she should try to 'cure her soul' or her body, irritated and depressed each other, and agreed to a temporary separation.

At the beginning of July Katherine and Ida went down to the Hôtel Château Belle Vue in Sierre, where they had lived in June 1921, and she told the Schiffs: 'It's a relief to have Jones again. I have almost made her swear never to leave me even if I drive her away.'[75] Murry, who remained at the Hôtel d'Angleterre in Randogne, sought daily consolation from her cousin Elizabeth at the Château Soleil, and spent the weekends in Sierre with Katherine, who told him: 'With you it's love or nothing, and you are in love with Elizabeth when she loves you.'[76]

Brett, whose betrayal had evidently been forgiven, visited Katherine at the big, empty, dim Château Belle Vue in early July and described Katherine's desire for solitude and her exhausting spurts of creativity: 'In the mornings she was incommunicado. She would walk into the garden, but she did not want to be spoken to. She was to be invisible, and so it was. One afternoon she took me all over the hotel trying to find a room around which she had written a story ['Father and the Girls']. She had so changed things around that she just could not recognize it. Ill as she was, she would start a story and write all day, all night, without stopping until she had finished it, then drop off her chair into bed.[77] Katherine, who was then at the height of her artistic powers, finished her last story, 'The Canary', on July 7.

On February 19, 1918, the day of her first hemorrhage, Katherine had recorded in her *Journal*: 'How unbearable it would be to die—leave "scraps", "bits" . . . nothing real finished'; on January 29, 1922, the day before she left Montana for Paris, she noted: 'Tore up and ruthlessly destroyed much. This is always a great satisfaction. Whenever I prepare for a journey I prepare as though for death';[78] and on August 14, two days before she left Sierre for London, she made out her will and stated: 'All manuscripts, note-books, papers, letters I leave to

John M. Murry. Likewise I should like him to publish as little as possible and tear up and burn as much as possible. He will understand that I desire to leave as few traces of my camping ground as possible.'[79] It is ironic, in view of her last wishes, that Katherine's reputation, like Kafka's, rests largely on her posthumous works.

In January 1922 Katherine thought of Chekhov and her closest friends, and recorded: 'I can truly say I think of de la Mare, Tchehov, Koteliansky, Tomlinson, Lawrence, Orage, every day. They are part of my life.'[80] In late June Katherine wrote a witty letter to Kot and asked him to adopt Wingley, the son of a 'male mother' called Charles Chaplin: 'Would you care for a cat? . . . He is a beautiful animal, except for a scratch on his nose, one ear badly bitten and a small hole in his head. . . . I must confess he will not catch mice. But mice do not know that and so the sight of him keeps them away. He has a fair knowledge of French.'[81] Two months later she remembered her friends and relations in her will,[82] and then, on August 15, after living abroad for two years and putting her affairs in order, Katherine travelled with Murry to London to be examined by Sorapure, comforted by Kot and instructed by Orage.

CHAPTER FIFTEEN

Gurdjieff, 1922–1923

DURING THE last few months of her life Katherine suddenly embraced the mystical doctrines of Gurdjieff; she entered his Institute in October 1922 and died there the following January. Though her attraction to Gurdjieff seems surprising, it represented a triumph of the romantic and Russian over the cynical and sceptical side of her character, and was directly related to her mystical yearning for her dead brother in the autumn of 1915 and her flirtation with Catholicism in the spring of 1920. Her submission to the powerful charisma of Gurdjieff was a culmination of almost all the ideas and events that had dominated her final year: her passion for all things Russian, her absorption in *Cosmic Anatomy*, her impatience with her illness, her disillusionment with doctors and desire to cure her soul, her inability to face reality and acquiescence in self-deception, her separation from Murry and search for a dominant male, her acceptance of the teachings of Orage and Ouspensky. After refusing to enter a sanatorium and living as an invalid for five years while experimenting with numerous doctors and treatments, all of which failed to help her, Katherine irrationally decided that if she discovered certain psychic or spiritual truths her tubercle bacilli would simply disappear.

In January 1922 A. R. Orage sent Murry a book called *Cosmic Anatomy* (1921) by 'M. B. Oxon' and asked him to review it for the *New Age*. The Scottish author, Dr. A. R. Wallace, who had made a fortune as a sheep-farmer in New Zealand, had also written *Scientific Aspects of the Supernatural* and *Miracles and Modern Spiritualism*, and had first encountered Orage at theosophical meetings in the 1890s. He contributed £100 a month to subsidize the *New Age* and wrote many abstruse articles, under his Oxonian pseudonym, to mystify its readers. Like Orage, he was enthusiastic about crankish projects.

Murry despised *Cosmic Anatomy*, but Katherine was fascinated by it and copied many excerpts into her *Scrapbook* of January–June 1922. Wallace emphasized emotion rather than intellect, expounded a pastiche of occult doctrines, and suggested that the mind could control, transcend and even survive the body: 'If we have, while in the body, made psychic and pneumic links which are in any degree functional, these persist after the body's death, and in such cases we *may* find that the loss of the body is an advantage, a mere throwing away of a cumbersome machine, which leaves us able to concentrate our attention on elaborating the mechanisms which we have outlined in psyche or pneuma.'[1] It is extremely unlikely that Katherine (or anyone else) understood the book's peculiar combination of theosophy, Hinduism, astrology, cryptic diagrams, pseudo-physics and false etymology. For its pretentious mixture of tortuous language and muddled thought, its dogmatism and contradictions, make Yeats's *A Vision* seem, by comparison, a model of clarity and logic. But her enthusiastic acceptance of its doctrines does suggest that she was very susceptible to the influence of Orage and that her mind had moved far into the realm of the mystical. Though Katherine's mysticism gave her a certain consolation, it also hastened her death.

Katherine had written in a *Rhythm* review of 1912, just after she first broke with Orage and the *New Age*: 'Mysticism is perverted sensuality; it is a "passionate" admiration for that which has no reality at all. It leads to the annihilation of any true artistic effort. It is a paraphernalia of clichés.'[2] But in March 1922, when she was suffering intensely from radiation sickness, she wrote a letter to her eldest sister, Vera, that suggested her pathetic but desperate efforts to find a mystical solution for her physical illness: 'If it's a failure I shall go to Nancy [France] and try the new psychotherapeutics which are rather on the lines of our stepmother's subconscious mind treatment. I'm a desperate man now; I can't be ill any longer.'[3] And when Manoukhin's treatment—her miraculous and final bid for health—failed in June 1922, she came to believe that her disease was more spiritual than physical. She then decided to live, as far as possible, as if her illness did not even exist and to save her body by saving her soul. As Murry observed, Katherine was 'demanding that her disease should be physically or mentally annihilated, as it were, presenting Life or God with an ultimatum'.[4]

On August 15, 1922, Katherine left Sierre for London, ostensibly to consult Dr. Sorapure but actually to see Orage. She took the first floor of Brett's house at 6 Pond Street in Hampstead, while Murry lived next door with the Russian mosaicist, Boris Anrep. Katherine was examined by Sorapure, who reassured her about the condition of her heart; and she continued the radiation treatments with Dr. Webster until the end of September, when she decided that he was merely a superficial experimenter. She also saw her family and friends for the last time: her father, who was visiting England, was given a copy of *The Garden Party*; Kot, with whom she translated Maxim Gorky's *Reminiscences of Leonid Andreyev*; Anne Rice, who watched her slowly climb the stairs, clinging to the banisters; Ottoline, the Schiffs and Richard Murry. Katherine spent the first weekend in September with Murry, who had moved to a modernized seventeenth-century mansion at Selsfield, near East Grinstead in Sussex, which was owned by his friend Vivian Locke-Ellis, who had published Katherine's 'A Fairy Story' in 1910.

Despite her activities, Katherine was suffering from a fatal combination of physical illness and mental anguish, and later told her cousin Elizabeth: 'When I came to London from Switzerland I did . . . go through what books and undergraduates call a spiritual crisis, I suppose. For the first time in my life, everybody bored me. Everything, and worse, everybody seemed a compromise and so flat, so dull, so mechanical.'⁵ In May 1921 Katherine told Murry: 'I think nearly all my falsity has come from *not* facing facts as I should have done';⁶ and he affirmed that this preoccupation with truth became the devouring passion of her last years. Yet doctors have noted that illness often leads to a greater dependence upon emotions and that a sick person often craves magical cures.⁷ Katherine, who courageously faced bitter reality throughout her life, recognized the serious danger of deceiving herself but could not finally accept the fact that she would soon die of tuberculosis. As Frieda Lawrence harshly but honestly remarked, soon after she heard of Katherine's death: 'It was so sad and again so inevitable that she had to die— She chose a death road and *dare* not face reality!'⁸

By September 1922 Katherine had lost her gaiety and vitality, her hope of recovery, her creative inspiration and her faith in Murry. Just before Murry came to Paris in February she told

him, with defiant distrust: 'I now know that I must grow a
shell away from you. I want, I "ask" for my independence. At
any moment in the future you may suddenly leave me in the
lurch if it pleases you. It is a part of your nature.'[9] Murry, the
future author of *God*, did not enter his own occult phase until
after Katherine's death. He could not follow the mystical movement of her mind and claimed he was 'rigidly hostile to
occultism'. As he drifted apart from Katherine, they agreed to
separate until they had 'found a faith', and they did not live
together for the last six months of her life.

Murry, whose hostility to occultism did not prevent him from
participating in tumbler-turning experiments and yoga exercises
after he had moved in with his friend Bill Dunning at Ditchling,
Sussex, in November 1922, confessed: 'I could scarcely bear to
discuss the doctrines of Ouspensky with Katherine. The gulf
between us was painful to us both; and living under the same
roof became a kind of torture. I could not bear it. . . . She told
me she had felt that her love for me had to die. "It was killing
us both", she said. And it had died. "I felt that I could not bear
it—tearing my heart away from yours. But I managed to do it".'[10]
Just before joining Gurdjieff in October, Katherine regretfully
admitted: 'I remember what we really felt—the blanks, the
silences, the anguish of continual misunderstanding. Were we
positive, eager, real, alive? No, we were not. We were a nothing-
ness shot with gleams of what might be.'[11]

When Katherine left Murry she returned to Orage, a tall man
with a strong personality who, like Harold Beauchamp and
Thomas Trowell, disappointed her when she desperately needed
help. In November 1921, just before he sent *Cosmic Anatomy*,
she called him her 'master' and gratefully admitted that he had
taught her to write and to think. Though T. S. Eliot called
Orage 'the finest critical intelligence of our day',[12] a large part
of his mind was neither critical nor intelligent. In the 1890s
Orage had been a theosophist; after the War he came under the
influence of Dmitri Mitrinović, an attaché of the Serbian Legation
in London, who expounded a cabbalistic doctrine of Pan-
humanity; in 1919 he adopted Major C. H. Douglas's disreputable programme of Social Credit; and in 1922 became
Gurdjieff's chief English disciple. Edmund Wilson, who met
Orage in New York in the mid-1920s, called him 'a funereal

and to me a distasteful person',[13] but Katherine worshipped him.

Katherine saw Orage in London on August 30 and soon joined the Gurdjieff circle which was led by P. D. Ouspensky, a Russian mathematician who had met Gurdjieff in Moscow in 1914. Ouspensky came to London in 1921 and prepared the way for his master's ideas in *Tertium Organum* (1920), which claimed to succeed the systems of Aristotle and Bacon. Katherine attended several lectures by Ouspensky, a sympathetic man and excellent teacher, in his flat at 28 Warwick Gardens in Earl's Court, and in September wrote to Murry: 'There seems to me little doubt that the wave of mysticism prophesied by Dunning is upon us. . . . Orage gave a short exposition of his ideas and we asked him questions and made objections.'[14] Orage sold the *New Age*, which was in financial trouble, in the autumn of 1922 and, according to Denis Saurat (a French professor who visited Gurdjieff's Institute in February 1923) 'persuaded Katherine Mansfield to come here, having received almost a promise of her recovery'.[15]

Katherine's attraction to Gurdjieff was the fatal culmination of her life-long passion for Russians. When Katherine described her love for Maata in the summer of 1907 she exclaimed: 'My mind is like a Russian novel';[16] and Lawrence wrote of Katherine–Gudrun in *Women in Love*: 'The emotional, rather rootless life of the Russians appealed to her.'[17] Anne Rice recalls: 'She enjoyed being Katoushka in a peasant's costume of brilliant colour—yards and yards of it—convincingly using a few Russian words to give a local colour';[18] and she studied Russian at the Institute. In November 1922, while searching for still another cure, Katherine wrote to her father: 'I got in touch with some other Russian (Russians seem to haunt me!) doctors, who claim to cure hearts of all kinds by means of a system of gentle exercises and movements.'[19] And one of the great attractions of the Institute, where most of the disciples were Russian and spoke no other language, was that the painter Alexander Salzmann, a friend of Chekhov's widow, Olga Knipper, said the great actress might soon join Gurdjieff.

Katherine left London with Ida for the last time on October 2, ostensibly to consult the Russian Manoukhin but actually to see Gurdjieff, and she was once again torn between a medical and a mystical cure. Since the Victoria Palace Hôtel was full, she took a room at the more modest Select Hôtel in the Place de la Sorbonne, which cost only ten francs a day. Katherine, who had stayed at the Select during the bombardment of Paris in 1918, immediately wrote to Murry and Kot: 'My room is on the *6ième*, rather small and low but very possible. Shabby, but it gets the sun. Outside the window there's the Sorbonne roofs. . . . My room has sloping roofs like an attic. It is very simple and clean. One can work here.'[20]

Though the *séances* of the spring had failed disastrously, Katherine still had a great belief in Manoukhin, saw him immediately and agreed to endure ten more treatments. Like Gurdjieff, Manoukhin made cruelly deceptive promises and (it seems almost incredible) guaranteed 'complete and absolute health by Christmas'.[21] Katherine, who once told Virginia Woolf she wished she were a crocodile, the only creature, according to Sir Thomas Browne, 'who does not *cough*',[22] complained on October 9 that she now personified a cough: 'My cough is so much worse that I *am* a cough—a living, walking or lying down cough.'[23] After ten days of treatment Katherine finally abandoned all hope of a medical cure, and wrote to Brett that she was horribly cold and feeling worse than ever: 'I get up at midi and have to go to bed at about half past five. But I feel more ill this time than last time. I don't know what is the matter. I am sick all the time—and cold. But as I've never imagined cold before—an entirely new kind. One feels like a wet stone.'[24] Each day her disease destroyed a tiny bit more of her lung, and as she grew weaker she found it increasingly difficult to walk and to breathe. She would return from the clinic and lie breathless on her bed, with her body emaciated, her eyes glittering and her heart beating furiously.

On October 14, her thirty-fourth birthday, Katherine recorded in her *Journal*: 'Ever since I came to Paris I have been as ill as ever. In fact, yesterday I thought I was dying. . . . I am an absolutely hopeless invalid.'[25] And on October 18 she was once again forced to face the horrible truth that she was doomed: 'No treatment on earth is any good to me, really', she admitted to Murry, 'The miracle never came near happening.'[26] Though Katherine continued to write as an escape from illness, and had spurts of creativity late in 1920 and the latter half of

1921, she wrote no stories during the last six months of her life.

Katherine never found a doctor who could dominate and discipline her will during the long years of illness. When Manoukhin failed to perform his 'miraculous' cure, her fantasy of an omnipotent and magical physician, who would protect her against the dreadful consequences of her disease, was shattered. 'I had made him my "miracle",' she told Brett. 'One must have a miracle. Now I'm without one and looking round for another.'[27] She therefore turned for her salvation to mysticism, to the psychic control of tuberculosis and to the persuasive Gurdjieff, whom she supposed possessed the same powers in the spiritual sphere that she had once attributed to doctors in the realm of the physical. Gurdjieff, she told Murry, 'is the only man who understands there is no division between body and spirit, who believes how they are related.'[28] Gurdjieff's disciples believed that 'With a single blow he had got rid of all those difficulties which result from the Cartesian division of the universe into matter and mind. . . . The mind-body problem had entirely disappeared. There was no longer any need to explain how two such entirely different entities as mind and body could meet and interact, for mind and body had become one.'[29]

Orage came to Paris on October 14 and arranged for Katherine to be examined by Dr. James Young, an English psychotherapist who had been a surgeon for twenty years and then worked under Jung in Zurich before joining Gurdjieff in August 1922. (When Freud heard of his presence at the Institute, he exclaimed: 'You see what happens to Jung's disciples!'[30]) Manoukhin 'wrote to Gurdjieff telling him that his patient was in no fit state to dispense with her doctor's help and begging him to dissuade her from living at the Priory for the time being.'[31] And Ouspensky, who saw Katherine at the Institute at the end of October, confirmed Manoukhin's judgment: 'She already seemed to me to be halfway to death.'[32] Despite her moribund condition, Dr. Young allowed Katherine to 'pass' his medical examination so that Gurdjieff could benefit from the publicity of a famous convert. Murry disapproved of Katherine's commitment to Gurdjieff but was, as usual, too weak and indecisive to resist her impulse and influence her in a positive way. On October 15 she told

Brett: 'To-morrow I am going to see Gurdjieff. I feel certain he will help me. . . . I have no belief whatever in any kind of medical treatment',[33] and two days later she entered the Prieuré in the hope of curing her soul through a kind of religious penance.

George Ivanovich Gurdjieff was born in 1872 near Mount Ararat, on the Persian–Turkish frontier of Armenian Russia. He had experienced a *mélange* of oriental mysticism and told Ouspensky that from 1890 to 1914 he had travelled widely in the mysterious monasteries of Mongolia and India; had studied with the dervishes of Turkestan, the Sufis of Persia and the anchorites of Mount Athos, had acquired a knowledge of their rituals and religious dances, and had endured terrible hardships in his search for arcane knowledge. He was even rumoured to have been a Grand Lama as well as the chief Russian secret agent in Tibet. He shaved his head, wore an astrakhan hat, looked like a cossack out of Gogol's *Taras Bulba* and loved to provide his followers with lavish oriental feasts. C. E. Bechhofer described him as 'altogether Eastern in appearance, short, swarthy, almost bald, but with long black moustaches, a high brow, and piercing eyes.'[34] Katherine, in one of her more lucid moments, thought he looked 'exactly like a carpet dealer from the Tottenham Court Road',[35] and Gurdjieff actually did sell rugs throughout his life.

In 1914 Gurdjieff founded his Institute for the Harmonious Development of Man in Moscow, but was ruined by the Revolution and forced to leave Russia. Gurdjieff eventually established himself in La Prieuré des Basses-Loges at Fontainebleau, forty miles southeast of Paris, in July 1922. The Prieuré, originally a Carmelite monastery, had once been owned by Madame de Maintenon, and was bought by Gurdjieff with money provided by the theosophical Lady Rothermere, the wife of the wealthy English newspaper owner. The Prieuré, which had high shuttered windows, a fountain in the courtyard, large formal gardens and 200 acres of wooded land, was fully furnished but had not been lived in since the beginning of the War. Ouspensky's wife cooked for the *avant-garde* disciples who occupied the Prieuré in the summer, and who reserved the best rooms, in the part of the building called 'The Ritz', for visiting dignitaries.

Gurdjieff taught that the harmonious integration of the

physical, emotional and mental centres of man could be achieved by a method of conscious effort and voluntary suffering, and that development, self-knowledge and a higher level of awareness could be attained by an efficient concentration of energy. The Institute provided an artificial milieu which forced the pupil to experience himself in radically new physical and psychological postures. In Gurdjieff's system: 'The teacher sets a pupil some task to perform, a task which necessarily entails the pupil's having to struggle with his own personality, that is to say, to work on himself. The task forces him to go against what is called his "chief feature", or chief weakness.'[36] Bechhofer summarized the specific methods and goals of Gurdjieff's teaching: 'The aim of the institute is the development of the innate faculties of its members by first breaking down the artificial barriers of their personality and then by developing and harmonizing their various mental and physical centers, the means of doing this being self-observation; a practical course of dancing; manual and physical exercise; psychical analysis of every kind; and a series of tests, mental and physical, applied by Gurdjieff to fit each individual case.'[37]

But Edmund Wilson noted the difference between the ideal and the reality, and asserted: 'The Russo–Greek charlatan Gurdjieff undertook to renovate the personalities of discontented well-to-do persons. He combined making his clients uncomfortable in various gratuitous ways . . . with reducing them to a condition of complete docility.'[38] Gurdjieff had between fifty and sixty Russian and a few English disciples, mostly women of the arty and theosophical type. Katherine admired the Russians but disliked most of the English who, in happier circumstances, would have become her satiric victims. Though Gurdjieff did not preach chastity and had several illegitimate children, the men and women lived separately, except for married couples, and both sexes did the same strenuous work. The disciples broke down the 'artificial barriers' by eating and sleeping at irregular hours, constructing buildings, digging trenches and doing other hard manual labour. They also practised the Master's special kind of music and dancing which, according to Llewelyn Powys, who saw forty pupils perform in New York in 1924, seemed 'like a hutchful of hypnotized rabbits under the gaze of a master conjuror'.[39] William Seabrook also testified to the 'automatonlike, inhuman, almost incredible docility and robot-like obedience of the disciples, in the parts of the demonstration which had to do with "movement". They were like a group of perfectly trained zombies.'[40]

Gurdjieff was a forceful, quick-witted, sensual and attractive man, who had an exuberant and dynamic personality, great will power and enormous energy. In his autobiographical *Meetings with Remarkable Men* he boasts of his clever business deals, cunning exploits and political intrigues. But he wore an expression of habitual ferocity, demanded and received absolute obedience from his disciples, and ruled as a despot over devoted slaves. Gurdjieff tried to elicit 'genuine' reactions from his pupils by publicly antagonizing, shocking and humiliating them; and the disciples were extraordinarily submissive and helpless, filled with a mixture of fear and hope. They were determined to discover hidden significance in the Master's slightest whim and word, and ignored his violent temper, greed for money, personal lust, Byzantine extravagance and spectacular megalomania, which scarcely reflected the Wisdom of the East. Though Gurdjieff admitted: 'There is something sinister in this house, and that is necessary',[41] the desperate Katherine was attracted to the magnetic dictator who assumed all responsibility and authority, became an omnipotent father-figure and seemed to direct the lives of his obedient children with intuitive omniscience. Katherine could not speak directly to Gurdjieff, whose native languages were Armenian and Greek, and who spoke only broken Russian, and it is significant that she records no conversations with her Teacher.

In November 1922 Katherine told Murry: '[Lawrence] and E. M. Forster are the two men who *could* understand this place if they would. But I think Lawrence's pride would keep him back.'[42] Forster's views of Gurdjieff, who would probably have been antipathetic to his rational cast of mind, are not known, but Lawrence expressed his extreme distaste to Mabel Luhan, who tried to convert him to Gurdjieff's ideas, on the first anniversary of Katherine's death: 'I have heard enough about that place at Fontainebleau where Katherine Mansfield died, to know it is a rotten, false, self-conscious place of people playing a sickly stunt. One doesn't wonder about it *at all*. One knows.'[43] In the early 1920s Mabel gave Lawrence a copy of

Ouspensky's *Tertium Organum*, which he annotated extensively and which has been preserved in the Taos Public Library. Lawrence strongly disagreed with nearly everything Ouspensky said, and the essence of his rejection of the book is: 'Bosh and casuistry', 'Nonsense', 'Rubbish', 'Don't believe this.'[44] Lawrence, who valued vitality, freedom and individual truth, called Gurdjieff a 'charlatan' and 'mountebank', and felt that self-control could not be achieved by self-surrender.

When the dying Katherine passed through the high iron gates and entered the chill and dilapidated Prieuré on October 17 her fellow disciples included Orage, James Young, C. E. Bechhofer, who had contributed to the *New Age* in 1912, and a few well-educated Russians: Ouspensky and his wife, the pianist Thomas de Hartmann and his wife, the painter Alexander Salzmann, whose wife was the Institute's principal dancer, Olgivanna, the future wife of Frank Lloyd Wright, and Adèle Kafian, a young Lithuanian, who became particularly attached to Katherine.[45] Katherine was given a spacious and beautiful room in 'The Ritz', which had French engravings, antique furniture and a view of the garden, and said farewell to Ida. She then began to explore the Institute, a rather theatrical imitation of a Russian peasant village, complete with embroidered blouses, wooden shoes and exotic drinks, like kumiss and kiftir. The Institute became Katherine's ideal community, her Rananim.

Though she could barely walk and was far too weak to take part in the exercises or the heavy work, she ruined her hands scraping carrots and peeling potatoes in the communal kitchen. And the writer who had been called a 'brilliant and infinitely inquisitive sensibility', told Kot: 'I mean to learn to work in every possible way with my hands, looking after animals and doing all kinds of manual labour.'[46] She began to study Russian, arranged the flowers and observed the different kinds of work, including the slaughter of the pigs. Three days after she arrived, Katherine described her own daily activities, which were much more leisurely and orderly than those of the other disciples, in a long letter to Murry: 'I get up 7.30—light the fire, with kindling drying overnight, wash in ice-cold water . . . and go down to breakfast. . . . After breakfast, make my bed, do my room, rest, and then go into the garden till dinner, which is 11 a.m. . . . After dinner, in the garden again till 3 o'clock, tea-time. After tea, any light job that is going until dark—when all knock off work, wash, dress and make ready for dinner again at 7. After dinner most of the people gather in the salon round an enormous fire, and there is music—tambourine, drums and piano—dancing and perhaps a display of all kinds of queer dance exercises. At ten we go to bed.'⁴⁷

The projects that occupied most of the pupils were the construction of a large Turkish bath, which required elaborate plumbing, and a new theatre for the performance of the ritualistic dances, which resembled the Dalcroze eurhythmics described in the 'Water-Party' chapter of *Women in Love*. Thomas de Hartmann suggested the haphazard and amateurish aspect of the community: 'Almost immediately after our arrival we started to prepare a place to build a big hall on the grounds. Mr. Gurdjieff succeeded in buying, for practically nothing, the skeleton of a French Air Force hangar, and two big trucks soon brought it in sections. Everything was unloaded in one big heap and we began to put it together—quite a puzzle for inexperienced people. . . . Although cold weather had set in, we continued building. We had no proper tools and worked practically with our bare hands.'⁴⁸ When the theatre was completed, Katherine's imagination was stimulated by the valuable carpets on the floors and walls, the incense, the coloured lights and the exotic dances, and she told Elizabeth: 'It is a fantastic experience, impossible to describe. One might be anywhere, in Bokhara or in Tiflis or Afghanistan (except, alas! for the climate!).'⁴⁹

Katherine managed to tolerate the discomfort of the poorly heated Prieuré as long as she had a suitable room. But at the beginning of November, she was suddenly, and without any explanation, moved from 'The Ritz' to the dreary and noisy accommodation of the workers' quarters—which were worse than the servants' rooms in The Elephant—and had bare boards and a scrubbed table for her jug and wash-basin. Katherine accepted this spartan cell, which represented her extreme reaction against the luxurious life of Connie's Villa Flora and Elizabeth's Château Soleil, but she soon found it impossible to bear the dampness, draughts and icy cold, which she found worse than the severe winters of Switzerland. On November 11 almost all her laundry was stolen and she wrote to Ida for urgent replacements. She tried to justify her meagre and miserable existence of hard work, poor diet, little sleep, cold rooms and bad air, and bravely told Ida: 'Nothing is done by accident. I understand [very] well why my room was changed.'[50] But she offered no explanation, and later confessed to Murry that when 'she had been put into a small, cold room as part of the discipline of the place [she] had been on the point of collapse'.[51]

In mid-December, when Katherine could no longer endure the harsh and inhuman conditions, she told Murry she was about to leave the Prieuré: 'Last week when it was intensely cold I felt that I had come to an end of all that room had to teach me. I was very depressed and longing beyond words for some real change and for beauty again. I almost decided to ask him to send me away until the weather got warmer.'[52] But Gurdjieff was told of her desperate state and allowed her to return to her old room. Though Katherine had suffered intensely, she was still unaware of the gravity of her illness and boasted to Ida: 'This life proves how terribly wrong and stupid all doctors are. I would have been dead 50 times in the opinion of all the medical men.'[53]

In December Katherine seemed to have completely surrendered her rational faculty and spoke quite seriously of 'the monkey [Gurdjieff] has bought which is to be trained to clean the cows'.[54] The Master, not to be outdone by the doctors, decided to give Katherine the benefit of the traditional Caucasian peasant cure for tuberculosis. He told the workers to build a special platform for Katherine above the cow-byre in the old stables, and ordered her to spend several hours each day inhaling the fetid exhalations of the beasts—Bridgit, Mitasha and Baldaofim. Katherine still had absolute faith in Gurdjieff and enthusiastically described the tiny wooden balcony in a letter to Murry: 'There is a small steep staircase to a little railed-off gallery above the cows. On the little gallery are divans covered with Persian carpets (only two divans). But the white-washed walls and ceiling have been decorated most exquisitely in what looks like a Persian pattern of yellow, red and blue by Mr. Salzmann. Flowers, little birds, butterflies and a spreading tree with animals on the branches, even a hippopotamus.'[55] Adèle Kafian explained that the gallery was constructed so that Katherine, who had found it difficult to breathe the pure air of the Alps, could be fortified by this sovereign remedy and could 'renew her strength through the radiation of animal magnetism, or perhaps simply from the *healthy* smell of fresh manure'.[56] Olgivanna insisted that 'Katherine simply adored that place. She never ceased to express her gratitude to Gurdjieff for all that he had done for her'.[57]

Olgivanna also echoed *Cosmic Anatomy* and told Katherine: 'There is no death for one like you who perceives the possibility of sweeping death aside when the time comes as an unnecessary phase to go through';[58] Katherine agreed: 'The only thing to do is to get the dying over—to court it, almost. . . . And then all hands to the business of being reborn again.'[59] Katherine, who understood death far better than rebirth, lasted less than six weeks in this pernicious regimen and soon achieved her wish. As she told Murry in 1920: 'Not being an intellectual, I always seem to have to learn things at the risk of my life.'[60]

Although Katherine had not planned to see Murry until May, she suddenly changed her mind and, with Gurdjieff's approval, invited him to come to Fontainebleau for the opening of the new theatre on the Russian New Year. On January 9, 1923, Murry arrived at the Prieuré and Katherine told him that she might soon be leaving the Institute. At ten in the evening Katherine began to climb the long staircase to her bedroom on the first floor, forgot her habitual caution and—perhaps to show Murry how well she really was—ran quickly up the stairs without holding the banister. She was then overcome by a fit of coughing, was helped to her room and, as the paroxysm became uncontrollable, whispered 'I believe . . . I am going . . . to die'. She gasped for breath and put her hand to her mouth as the bright flame of arterial blood gushed fiercely from her lungs and oozed through her fingers. Murry rushed away to call Dr. Young, who arrived at once and turned him out of the room. Though Katherine stared at the door, her eyes wide with terror, Young forgot to call Murry until after she died.

Katherine's funeral took place in Fontainebleau on January 12 and was attended by Murry, his brother Richard, Ida, Brett, Katherine's sisters Charlotte and Jeanne, and Gurdjieff. Kot was extremely distressed because he was unable to get permission to leave the country. Katherine's large hearse was pulled by black-plumed black horses, and the mourners followed in carriages that wound slowly through the narrow streets to the Protestant church. The plain white coffin was placed in front of the altar and the French burial service was read by an ancient white-haired

9*

clergyman. At dusk Katherine was lowered into her grave in the communal cemetery at Avon, outside Fontainebleau.

When the disciples finally dared to ask Gurdjieff why Katherine had died, 'he always replied, with apparent sincerity: "Me not know." For him, she had not attained to real *existence* in his meaning of the word, she had no true "me", no soul.'[61] It is ironic that Katherine's death at the Prieuré and her dismal burial in a cheap coffin first attracted public fame and attention to Gurdjieff's Institute, and that Young, Orage and Ouspensky, who had indoctrinated Katherine and persuaded her to enter the Prieuré, all became apostates, broke with Gurdjieff and publicly renounced his teaching.[62]

CHAPTER SIXTEEN

Murry's Cult of Katherine

MURRY'S CREATION of the cult of Katherine Mansfield is unique in modern literature. In a repetitive torrent of forty books, articles, introductions, poems, and letters to the press, published between 1923 and 1959, he expressed his anguished self-consciousness, deliberately constructed his myth of Katherine and established a posthumous reputation far greater than she had enjoyed in her lifetime. The motives for Murry's literary crusade were closely connected with his own character and his relationship to Katherine, and were determined more by emotional needs than by intellectual convictions.

Though Murry was excluded from Katherine's room during her fatal hemorrhage, he took possession of her after death and transformed her into the docile woman he had always wanted. Her gravestone at Fontainebleau reads:

Katherine Mansfield
wife of
John Middleton Murry

as if that were her great claim to fame. It also bears the singularly inappropriate epitaph from *I Henry IV* (2.iii): 'But I tell you, my lord fool, out of this nettle, danger, we pluck this flower, safety'; for Katherine's story, 'This Flower' (1924), portrays a heroine who recognizes that she will never pass through the danger of disease to 'safety' and hides this fact from her rather foolish husband.

In his book on Keats, Murry writes with appalling egoism that 'Nothing more powerfully prepares a man's instinctive and unconscious nature for passionate love than prolonged contact with hopeless illness in a loved one'.[1] A year after Katherine's death Murry married his second wife, Violet LeMaistre, who looked astonishingly like Katherine and self-consciously imitated her dress, hair style, handwriting and mannerisms in order to win

Murry's love. Murry was still in love with the *idea* of Katherine, and since Violet wanted nothing more than to replace Katherine, they seemed well suited to each other. Murry took three years to discover that Violet was not Katherine, and admitted: 'It never struck me for a moment that there was a great difference between Katherine when I first met her, and Violet now.'[2]

Murry encouraged Violet's pathological attachment to his dead wife, and the spirit of Katherine hovered over their marriage. He gave Violet Katherine's engagement ring, bought their house with the royalties on Katherine's books, lived on the £500 a year that Katherine's posthumously published works brought in, named their daughter Katherine, and published both Katherine's and Violet's stories in his magazine, the *Adelphi*. When Violet contracted tuberculosis, she exclaimed: 'O I'm so glad. I wanted this to happen. . . . I wanted you to love me as much as you loved Katherine—and how could you, without this?'[3] Just as Katherine had turned away from Murry to Gurdjieff at the end of her life, so Violet fell in love with his friend, Max Plowman. After Violet died of tuberculosis in 1931, Murry, who may have been a carrier of the disease, pitifully asked: 'Am I attracted only by two kinds of women—one that I kill, the other that kills me?'[4]

Murry's guilt about his selfish and irresponsible treatment of Katherine led directly to the egoistic enshrinement of his wife. As high priest of Katherine's cult, Murry wrote an *apologia pro sua vita* and glorified his own role, image and importance. He exploited her tragic death, created a sentimental and idealized portrait which obscured her literary qualities, and made a good deal of money by publishing her posthumous works. Only three of Katherine's books appeared during her lifetime; eleven others were edited by Murry after her death. When Constable sent Murry a royalty cheque of £1000 for *The Dove's Nest* and *Poems* (both 1923) he recorded: 'It was by far the biggest cheque I had ever received, and ten times as big as any Katherine had received for her own work.'[5]

Lea believes that 'The greatest [of Murry's virtues] and the least conventional, was his honesty'.[6] But Katherine, who understood that his frankness was a pose that enabled him to project a false image of himself, was far more perceptive when she wrote: 'His very frankness is a falsity. In fact it seems falser than his insincerity.'[7] Aldous Huxley, who was editorial assistant on the *Athenaeum* in 1919, exaggerated this aspect of Murry whom he characterized as Burlap in *Point Counter Point* (1928), but he is worth quoting for his wit as well as for the essence of truth in his satire:

> When Susan died Burlap exploited the grief he felt, or at any rate loudly said he felt, in a more than usually painful series of those always painfully personal articles which were the secret of his success as a journalist . . . pages of a rather hysterical lyricism about the dead child-woman. . . .
>
> At the end of some few days of incessant spiritual masturbation, he had been rewarded by a mystical realization of his own unique and incomparable piteousness. . . . Frail, squeamish, less than fully alive and therefore less than adult, permanently under-aged, [Susan] adored him as a superior and almost holy lover . . . [who would] roll at her feet in an ecstasy of incestuous adoration for the imaginary mother-baby of a wife with whom he had chosen to identify the corporeal Susan.[8]

Huxley perceives not only the falseness of the cult and Murry's exploitation of his grief, but also the emotional immaturity and childish role-playing of both Katherine and Murry, and he describes the destructive aspect of Murry's 'mystical' love in the metaphor of sexual perversion.

D. H. Lawrence's story, 'Smile' (1926), is also based on Murry's response to Katherine's death, and portrays the selfish reaction of a man who sees his wife's body in a convent and feels an ambiguous mixture of guilt, self-pity, indifference and lust for a young nun: 'He did not weep: he just gazed without meaning. Only, on his face deepened the look: I knew this martyrdom was in store for me! She was so pretty, so childlike, so clever, so obstinate, so worn—and so dead! He felt so blank about it all!'[9] Lawrence, who knew Murry well, emphasizes his passivity and confusion.

Murry's 'In Memory of Katherine Mansfield', an atrociously sentimental poem in archaic diction and (like Shelley's 'Adonais') in Spenserian stanza, was published on the first anniversary of her death. It is a fine example of the insincerity and idealization of Katherine portrayed by Huxley and Lawrence:

> For she was lonely; was she not a child
> By royalty and wisdom, captive made
> Among unlovely men, beating her wild
> Impetuous wings in anguish, and dismayed. . . .
> A child of other worlds, a perfect thing
> Vouchsafed to justify this world's imagining? . . .
> A princess manifest, a child withouten stain.[10]

Lea points out that these lines 'were eight-year-old verses, re-conditioned for the occasion'.[11] The third and fourth lines idealize Katherine by alluding to Arnold's (inaccurate) description of Shelley as 'A beautiful and ineffectual angel, beating in the void his luminous wings in vain'.[12] There are significant analogies between the legends of Shelley and Katherine, for as Richard Holmes writes, 'where events reveal Shelley in an unpleasant light, the original texts and commentaries have attracted suppressions, distortions and questions of doubtful authenticity, originating from Victorian apologists.'[13] Though Murry knew about Katherine's bitter and destructive sexual experiences, her lesbianism and abortion, he stressed her perfect purity, and called her 'a child withouten stain'.

Murry had opposed Katherine's submission to the mystical rigours of Gurdjieff and insisted in 1951 that his 'prejudice against occultism was great; and it is as deep-rooted now as it was then'.[14] But he emphasized Katherine's 'spiritual' qualities one month after her death when he described a mystical experience in that confessional mode which exasperated critics and embarrassed friends: 'Not many months ago I lost someone whom it was impossible for me to lose—the only person on this earth who understood me or whom I understood. . . . I became aware of myself as a little island against whose slender shores a cold, dark, boundless ocean lapped devouring. Somehow, in that moment, I knew I had reached a pinnacle of personal being. . . . The love I had lost was still mine, but now more durable, being knit into the very substance of the universe I had feared.'[15]

This essay characteristically reveals far more about Murry than about his ostensible subject and provides a preview of the visitation which he later described in God (1929). Since Katherine had been dangerously ill ever since her first hemorrhage in February 1918, her death was probable rather than 'impossible';

yet in October 1922, three months before she died, Murry admitted his total ignorance of her thoughts and emotions: 'I feel I don't *know* anything. You've passed clean out of my range and understanding: and so suddenly.'[16] Murry's self-conscious response to this experience is aesthetic rather than personal, for he converts it into literary terms. His description of himself as a little island devoured by the ocean recalls Arnold's 'To Marguerite' just as his feeling that Katherine is knit into the universe echoes Wordsworth's 'A Slumber Did My Spirit Seal'. But his egoistic point is that Katherine's death led *him* to a vague 'pinnacle of personal being'.

Only Murry could write a book called *God*, and only he could begin the book with a very long first chapter about himself—as if to place the Deity in proper perspective. In this chapter he once again describes the 'mystical' experience of February 1923: 'When I say that "the room was filled with a presence", the "presence" was definitely connected with the person of Katherine Mansfield. . . . The "presence" of Katherine Mansfield was of the same order as the "presence" which filled the room and me. In so far as the "presence" was connected with her it had a moral quality, or a moral effect: I was immediately and deeply convinced that "all was well with her".'[17] This awkward passage merely proves that Murry could easily convince himself of anything he wanted to believe. But his conclusion that 'all was well with her' echoes her· *Journal* entry of October 10, 1922, which he used as the optimistic but misleading conclusion of the book: 'With those words Katherine Mansfield's *Journal* comes to a fitting close. Thenceforward the conviction that "All was well" never left her.'[18] Though Katherine's death only three months later suggests that all was *not* well, his 'mystical' experience prompted him to re-affirm that statement against all contrary evidence.

Murry's final attempt to exorcise the guilt-ridden memory of Katherine occurred—rather oddly—in his Introduction to Mantz's bibliography of Katherine's works (1931), when he described his dream of her rising, like a Gothic heroine, from the flowers of her coffin: 'As I watched, Katherine Mansfield raised herself wearily out of the shallow turfy grave. With her finger-tips she took back the hair from her still-closed eyes. She opened them at last, and looked at the garden and the house, and smiled. Then, as though weary, she sank back to sleep again. It was peace; it was good; and what she had seen was also good.'[19] Once again, after his *second* wife had died of tuberculosis, Murry has the dead Katherine absolve his guilt in the language of the God of Genesis, who divided the light from the darkness and 'saw that it was good'.

But Murry's virtuous and high-minded statements about Katherine were constantly undermined by his own egoistic behaviour and falsification of their relationship. In his book on Keats, which is also about Katherine, Murry praises Fanny Brawne, who 'jealously cherishes, in a secrecy that is sacrilege to disturb, the memory of her love'.[20] Yet when Murry lectured on Katherine at the University of Michigan in 1936, Professor Clarence Thorpe was amazed by his violation of their intimacy and wondered: 'How could a literary man discuss his wife in such a way in a public lecture?'[21] Though Murry told Ottoline Morrell: 'the only thing that matters to me is that [Katherine] should have her rightful place as the most wonderful writer and the most beautiful spirit of our time',[22] he always confused the 'writer' with the 'spirit', emphasized her 'purity' at the expense of her genuine qualities, bathed the reality of her life in pathos and pain, distorted her actual achievement and inflated her reputation.

All this quite naturally angered the friends who knew and admired the real Katherine Mansfield. Kot maintained that when Murry published her letters and journals he ' "left out all the jokes", to make her an "English Tchekov" ';[23] and when Murry published the *Journal* in 1927 Kot sympathized with Ida, who was extremely angry, and wrote to say that it marked the end of his relationship with Murry. In 1928 Lawrence told Dorothy Brett, with characteristic exaggeration: 'I hear Katherine's letters sell largely, yet Murry whines about poverty and I hear he *inserts* the most poignant passages himself. Ottoline declares that in the letters to her, large pieces are inserted, most movingly.'[24] Lawrence criticized Murry for assuming the role of acolyte chosen to bear the chalice of her fame, and warned that hyperbolic statements about Katherine would provoke a critical reaction against her: 'You are wrong about Katherine. She was *not* a great genius. She had a charming gift, and a finely cultivated one. But *not more*. And to try, as you do, to make it more is to do her no true service.'[25]

Murry, who was called 'the best-hated man of letters in the country',[26] misrepresented his relationship to Katherine. He claimed: 'We fell in love and were married' in 1912 and Mantz repeated this statement in the biographical notes of her bibliography.[27] In fact, they lived together for six years, and Murry, who felt that their liaison might sully the image of her 'spiritual purity', obscured the truth to 'protect' Katherine.

He also elevated the commonplace events of their life to the level of the mystical and the tragic. He writes of their unhappy stay in the cold, cramped and sordid Rose Tree cottage in Buckinghamshire in the autumn of 1914: '[I] told her that I had a sense of an infinite beatitude descending upon me. So, she said, had she.'[28] But their beatitude was interrupted by Katherine's affair with Francis Carco in February 1915. Murry writes of his departure from Katherine in Bandol in December 1915: 'The anguish of separation had begun, the terrible feeling that our love was totally at the mercy of an alien world',[29] but in December he voluntarily returned to London, jealous of her dead brother and ashamed of his jealousy.

Murry falsifies their attitude towards the War as well as the nature of his love for Katherine. In 1929 he emphasized their tragic involvement in the War and interpreted Katherine's disease in terms of his own feelings: 'Katherine Mansfield's illness [was] as much a circumstance of the war as any death at the front; but it has become *for me* the personal symbol of that universal suffering';[30] but in 1951 he records their casual disregard of the slaughter: 'It was not by any effort of the will that we ignored the war, which was then [April 1916] at one of its blackest periods—the carnage around Verdun. We did it spontaneously, and without a tremor of conscience.'[31]

Murry exaggerated Katherine's attachment to him and categorically states: 'The greatest obstacle she had to overcome in taking the plunge and making the final decision to enter the Institute had been her fear of losing me. . . . By risking losing me, she had found her love for me: it was entire and perfect.'[32] But on October 10, 1922, one week before she entered Gurdjieff's Institute, she analysed their relationship and saw with a penetrating clarity the fundamental falsity of their marriage: 'What have you of him now? What is your relationship? He talks to you—sometimes—and then goes off. He thinks of you tenderly.

He dreams of a life with you *some day* when the miracle has happened. You are important to him as a dream. Not as a living reality. For you are not one. What do you share? Almost nothing. . . . Life together, with me ill, is simply torture with happy moments. But it's not life.'[33] Though Murry always glorified his 'entire and perfect' love for Katherine, he asked Frieda Lawrence—with whom he had an affair after Katherine's death in 1923 and after Lawrence's in 1930—'Why, I ask myself, was it *you* who should have revealed to me the richness of physical love?';[34] and later told Frieda: 'I just didn't know what man-woman love could be until I met Mary', his fourth wife, in 1938.[35]

It is clear, then, that Murry used his very considerable authority as a critic and as Katherine's husband, literary executor, editor, biographer, and guardian of manuscripts to create a misleading picture of her character and their marriage. This distortion over-shadowed her literary reputation and established the sentimental cult which still survives in France.[36] Murry is an indispensable but thoroughly unreliable guide to Katherine, for he could not disentangle himself from her legend, could not distinguish between the woman and the artist, and could not form an objec-tive and consistent view of her work.

Murry's editing and criticism of Katherine's work was the decisive influence in establishing her posthumous reputation. Her stories, *Journal* and *Letters*—which were published in 1928 in an incomplete and heavily edited volume—have been trans-lated into twenty-two languages; all her fiction is still in print; the Penguin paperback edition of *The Garden Party* continues to sell more than 12,000 copies a year; and to commemorate the fiftieth anniversary of her death the BBC presented six programmes starring Vanessa Redgrave, which dramatized her life and work. As early as 1926 Gerald Bullett called her: 'The one short story writer of indubitable genius who has appeared during the present century';[37] and her technique and style have influenced (to various degrees) the feminine sensibilities of Elizabeth Bowen, Katherine Anne Porter, and Eudora Welty, all of whom have written about her. According to Carson McCullers's biographer, the librarian of Columbus, Georgia, 'had to buy a new Mansfield book of short stories for the library because Carson had literally "read the pages to pieces".'[38]

Christopher Isherwood, who has written one of the best

essays on Katherine's work and a novel—*The World in the
Evening* (1954)—whose heroine, Elizabeth Rydal, is modelled
on Katherine, has recorded: 'I myself felt a strong personal
love for her at one time in my life.'[39] Isherwood has recently
said that he was attracted to her evocation of New Zealand
and was moved by the poignant life of her *Journal*, by her
wanderings and her disease. But he became disenchanted by her
cuteness and smartness, and took her self-criticism, 'I look at
the mountains, I try to pray and I think of something *clever*',
as a personal admonition. But Katherine's statement about her
aesthetic point of view: 'I've been a camera. . . . I've been a
selective camera, and it has been my attitude that has determined
the selection',[40] probably influenced Isherwood's most famous
sentence, which appears on the first page of *Goodbye to Berlin*
(1939): 'I am a camera with its shutter open, quite passive,
recording, not thinking.' The books about Germany by Mansfield and Isherwood are both satires that portray sexual corruption and take place at the edge of doom—before the Great
War and before the Nazi regime.

In 1941 George Orwell harshly but honestly dissected her
weaknesses while recognizing her influence, and mentioned the
decline of her reputation, which Lawrence had predicted, in the
politically-conscious thirties: 'Nearly always the formula is the
same: a pointless little sketch about fundamentally uninteresting
people, written in short flat sentences and ending on a vague
query. . . . The spirit of Katherine Mansfield seems to brood
over most short stories of the past twenty years, though her
own work is almost forgotten.'[41] And Frank Swinnerton, who
knew Katherine in the days of *Rhythm*, has perceptively com-
mented on her reputation and originality: 'I think Murry had a
genuine admiration for her, and that only on her death did he
begin to cash in on her reputation. This reputation was increased
by reports of her illness, and the belief that any writer who
dies of consumption must be a genius. But the admission of
her talent was by no means universal; and the wider knowledge
of Tchehov's work which came when his tales were published
in more than odd volumes led to diminution of her claim to
originality.'[42]

Murry's desire was to protect Katherine's personal image
rather than tell the truth about her. Though he established

Katherine's reputation and created her cult by acting as her literary man-midwife, making a religion of her art, and substituting the delicate and sensitive for the cynical and amoral side of her character, his hagiography offended her friends and admirers, and perverted critical values and judgment. By writing far more about Katherine than any other literary critic and maintaining exclusive control of her manuscripts until his death in 1957, he created a false legend which eased his guilt and filled his pockets. Murry's voluminous writings about Katherine are subjective 'appreciations' rather than critical analyses and have little value today. It is both significant and appropriate that his reputation has declined at the same time that Katherine's has increased. When Murry's critical debris is cleared away, the Katherine that emerges from the ruins is a darker and more earthly, a crueller and more capable figure than in the legend.[43]

Notes

Chapter 1: Childhood

1. *The Diary of Samuel Pepys*, ed. Robert Latham and William Matthews, I (Berkeley, 1970), 292.
2. See C. R. Leslie, *Memoirs of the Life of John Constable* (1843) (London, 1951), p. 217 (January 20, 1833).
3. Samuel Butler, *A First Year in Canterbury Settlement* (London, 1923), pp. 100–101.
4. E. M. Forster, 'The Legacy of Samuel Butler', *Listener*, June 12, 1952, p. 956.
5. Hector Bolitho, *The New Zealanders* (London, 1928), p. 23.
6. W. H. Oliver, *The Story of New Zealand* (London, 1960), pp. 150, 157, 159.
7. Marion Ruddick, 'Memories of Katherine Mansfield's Childhood', MS Papers 1339, p. 5, Alexander Turnbull Library, Wellington.
8. Interview with William Craddock Barclay in Wellington, June 17, 1976.
9. Katherine Mansfield, *Letters to John Middleton Murry, 1913–1922* (London, 1951), p. 182 (February 24, 1918).
10. Katherine Mansfield, 'Juliet', *Turnbull Library Record*, 3 (March 1970), 8.
11. Unpublished letter from Katherine Mansfield to Ottoline Morrell, August 21, 1919, University of Texas.
12. Katherine Mansfield, 'Prelude', *Collected Stories* (London, 1973), p. 54.
13. 'The Little Girl', *Collected Stories*, p. 577.
14. *Letters to Murry*, p. 3 (Summer 1913).
15. Katherine Mansfield, *Letters*, I (London, 1928), 210–211 (August 14, 1918).
16. 'At the Bay', *Collected Stories*, p. 223.
17. Katherine Mansfield, *Journal* (London, 1954), p. 101 (February-March 1916).
18. 'Prelude', *Collected Stories*, pp. 31–32.
19. *Journal*, p. 42 (June 1909).
20. Letter from Jeanne Renshaw to Jeffrey Meyers, February 4, 1976.
21. *Journal*, p. 184 (December 15, 1919).
22. Katherine Mansfield, 'About Pat' (1905), *Scrapbook* (New York, 1940), p. 3.

23. Helen Hawke, 'Katherine Mansfield and Karori', *Stockade* (Wellington), 3 (September 1975), 4.
24. 'The Doll's House', *Collected Stories*, p. 395.
25. Quoted in Sylvia Berkman, *Katherine Mansfield: A Critical Study* (New Haven, 1951), p. 19.
26. 'The Voyage', *Collected Stories*, p. 329.
27. *Journal*, p. 106 (March 12, 1916).
28. 'The Little Girl', *Collected Stories*, p. 578.
29. 'New Dresses', *Collected Stories*, p. 549.
30. *Letters*, II, 142 (October 14, 1921).
31. Quoted in Ruth Mantz and John Middleton Murry, *The Life of Katherine Mansfield* (London, 1933), p. 152.
32. Quoted in Antony Alpers, *Katherine Mansfield* (London, 1954), p. 50.
33. Quoted in Mantz, p. 152.
34. 'Juliet', p. 8.
35. Quoted in Mantz, p. 153.
36. Katherine Mansfield, 'Maata', *Turnbull Library Record*, 7 (May 1974), 5.
37. Quoted in Philip Waldron, 'Katherine Mansfield's *Journal*', *Twentieth Century Literature*, 20 (1974), 13.
38. L.M. [Ida Baker], *Katherine Mansfield: The Memories of LM* (New York, 1971), p. 32.
39. 'Juliet', p. 9.
40. *Ibid.*, pp. 21–22.
41. *Ibid.*, p. 17.
42. *Ibid.*, p. 11.
43. Quoted in Mantz, p. 169.
44. Interviews with Oliver Trowell in East Brabourne, December 23, 1976 and with Dorothy Richards in Cambridge, December 31, 1976.
45. Quoted in Owen Leeming, 'Katherine Mansfield's Rebellion', *New Zealand Listener*, 48 (April 5, 1963), 6.
46. Quoted in Willa Cather, 'Katherine Mansfield', *Not Under Forty* (New York, 1953), p. 131.

Chapter 2: Queen's College

1. Sandra Darroch, *Ottoline: The Life of Lady Ottoline Morrell* (New York, 1975), pp. 49–50.
2. *Journal*, p. 104 (February–March 1916).
3. Interview with Ruth Herrick in Wellington, June 13, 1976.
4. Quoted in Alpers, p. 62 (January 24, 1904).
5. 'Juliet', p. 24.
6. Quoted in Mantz, p. 178.
7. Direct quotations are from Ruth Herrick, 'They Were at School Together', *New Zealand Listener*, 7 (September 25, 1942), 12. Other information is from my interview with Ruth Herrick.

8. *Journal*, p. 103.
9. 'Carnation', *Collected Stories*, pp. 665–666. Katherine used the name of Mlle. Séguin, who taught French at Queen's College from 1878 to 1911, in the title of her story about Geneva, 'Pension Séguin' (1913).
10. *Journal*, p. 105.
11. Copy of TS letter from Miss C. Oliver, Registrar of Queen's College, to Mrs. M. Amoore of the New Zealand Broadcasting Company, July 5, 1968, MS 119:66, Turnbull Library.
12. Quoted in Alpers, p. 60 (December 23, 1903).
13. Quoted in Mantz, p. 198.
14. Quoted in Rosalie Grylls, *Queen's College, 1848–1948* (London, 1948), p. 68.
15. Ida Baker, p. 26.
16. Interview with Ruth Herrick.
17. Quoted in Mantz, p. 184.
18. Beatrice Glenavy, *Today We Will Only Gossip* (London, 1964), p. 57.
19. Interview with Ruth Herrick.
20. Quoted in Mantz, p. 222.
21. News clipping of February 22, 1906 inserted in Katherine Mansfield Notebook qMS/ 1903–1922 (39:5), Turnbull Library.
22. Arnold played with artists like Mischa Elman and Nellie Melba from 1906 until the mid-1930s. In 1908 he met and fell in love with Eileen Woodhead, but her wealthy South African family opposed her wish to marry a musician, although she was studying the 'cello at the Royal Academy of Music. Arnold finally married Eileen in 1918 and had two children, Pamela and Oliver. He was Professor at the Guildhall School of Music (1924–54) and the Royal College of Music (1937–39), and died in 1966.
23. Quoted in Mantz, pp. 219–220.
24. Quoted in Alpers, p. 70 (April 24, 1906).
25. 'Juliet', p. 25.
26. Quoted in Mantz, p. 224.

Chapter 3: Return to New Zealand

1. Quoted in Vincent O'Sullivan, *Katherine Mansfield's New Zealand* (London, 1975), p. 48.
2. *Journal*, pp. 6–7.
3. Interview with Ruth Herrick.
4. "New Dresses', *Collected Stories*, p. 553; and Ida Baker, p. 33.
5. Interview with Edith Bendall in Wellington, June 12, 1976.
6. *Journal*, p. 21.
7. Rupert Brooke, *Letters*, ed. Geoffrey Keynes (London, 1968), p. 560.
8. 'Daphne', *Collected Stories*, pp. 471, 473.
9. E. H. McCormick, *The Expatriate: A Study of Frances Hodgkins* (Wellington 1954), p. 104 (letter of January 1918).

10. Letter to Vera Beauchamp quoted in Berkman, p. 24 (late 1906).
11. Quoted in Alpers, p. 76 (January 8, 1907).
12. Unpublished letter from Katherine Mansfield to Harold Beauchamp, June 26, 1922, MS 119:16, Turnbull Library.
13. Unpublished letter from Katherine Mansfield to Garnet Trowell, c. October 4, 1908, in the University of Windsor (Ontario) Library.
14. Unpublished letter from Katherine Mansfield to Vera Beauchamp, 1908, Turnbull Library.
15. *Journal*, pp. 22, 37 (October 1907, May 1908).
16. *Ibid.*, pp. 3, 4, 10 (1906).
17. Marie Bashkirtseff, *Journal of a Young Artist*, trans. Mary Serrano (New York, 1919), p. 452 (August 12, 1884).
18. *Journal*, p. 18 (August 27, 1907).
19. Quoted in Mantz, p. 281.
20. Millie Parker, 'Broken Strings: Miss Mansfield's Girlhood', Supplement to *New Zealand Herald*, February 3, 1923, p. 1.
21. Quoted in Ian Gordon, "Warmth and Hydrangeas', *New Zealand Listener*, 82 (May 8, 1976), 22–23.
22. *Ibid.*, p. 22.
23. *Journal*, p. 22 (October 1907).
24. *Ibid.*, p. 14; and Notebook qMS/1903–1922 (39:19), Turnbull Library.
25. Quoted in O'Sullivan, p. 55. The sentimental illustration is reproduced on the same page.
26. See Katherine Mansfield, 'Bendall', *Turnbull Library Record*, 5 (May 1972), 19–25.
27. *Journal*, p. 12.
28. Quoted in Gordon, p. 23.
29. Katherine Mansfield, 'Silhouette', *The Native Companion*, 2 (November 1907), 229.
30. Tom Mills, 'Katherine Mansfield', *New Zealand Railways Magazine*, 8 (September 1, 1933), 6.
31. Quoted in Alpers, p. 84.
32. Quoted in Mantz, pp. 275–276.
33. *Letters*, II, 199 (March 18, 1922).
34. *Journal*, p. 15.
35. *Ibid.*, p. 17.
36. *Ibid.*, pp. 17–18.
37. Notebook qMS/1903–1922 (39: 23a).
38. *Journal*, p. 19.
39. *Ibid.*
40. Unpublished letter from Katherine Mansfield to Vera Beauchamp, January 17, 1908, Turnbull Library.
41. *Journal*, p. 8.
42. *Ibid.*, pp. 12–13.
43. Notebook qMS/1903–1922 (39:17–18).
44. *Journal*, p. 14.
45. *Ibid.*, p. 17.

46. Notebook qMS/1903–1933 (39:23).
47. Quoted in Waldron, p. 13.
48. Oliver, p. 150.
49. Elsie Webber, TS description of the Urewera trip, 1956, MS 119:5, Turnbull Library.
50. Quoted in O'Sullivan, p. 68.
51. *Journal*, p. 29.
52. Quoted in O'Sullivan, pp. 64–65.
53. *Journal*, p. 31.
54. Notebook qMS/1903–1922 (2:34).
55. Quoted in Mantz, p. 305.
56. 'The Woman at the Store', *Collected Stories*, p. 565.
57. Quoted in Moira Taylor, 'A Child with the Children', *New Zealand Listener*, 75 (May 4, 1974), 14.
58. *Journal*, p. 20.
59. Harold Beauchamp, *Reminiscences and Recollections* (New Plymouth, New Zealand, 1937), p. 90.
60. Interview with Edith Bendall.

Chapter 4: Disorder and Early Sorrow

1. *Journal*, p. 5 (November 1906).
2. G. N. Morris, 'Katherine Mansfield: The Early London Days', *History and Bibliography* (Christchurch), 2 (August 1948), 102.
3. Unpublished letter from George Bowden to J. M. Murry, December 1933, Turnbull Library.
4. George Bowden, 'A Biographical Note on Katherine Mansfield', p. 12, MS/BOW/1947, Turnbull Library.
5. Interview with Dorothy Brett in Taos, New Mexico, March 21, 1976.
6. Quoted in Alpers, pp. 145, 361.
7. Ida Baker, p. 39.
8. Unpublished letter from Katherine Mansfield to Garnet Trowell, November 4, 1908, University of Windsor.
9. Letter from Rebecca West to Jeffrey Meyers, 4 February 1977.
10. Katherine Mansfield, 'Letters to Bertrand Russell', *Adam*, 370–375 (1972–73), 37, 40.
11. *Journal*, p. 157 (May 1919).
12. Katherine Mansfield, *Notes on Novelists* (London, 1930), p. 220.
13. *Letters*, II, 163 (December 13, 1921).
14. 'Juliet', p. 23.
14a. All the letters from Katherine Mansfield to Garnet Trowell are in the University of Windsor (Ontario) Library.
15. Interview with Dorothy Richards.
16. Letter from Douglas Trowell to Jeffrey Meyers, January 17 1977.
17. Unpublished letter from Richard Murry to Ruth Mantz, June 10, 1973.

18. Holograph notes in Margaret Scott's copy of Ida Baker's *Memories*, based on her conversations with Ida Baker in 1971.
19. Ida Baker, p. 157.
20. *Scrapbook*, p. 18 (March 1914).
21. Bowden, 'A Biographical Note', p. 1, Turnbull Library.
22. Mantz, p. 319.
23. Unpublished letter from George Bowden to J. M. Murry, December 1933, Turnbull Library.
24. Ida Baker, pp. 45–46.
25. Bowden, 'A Biographical Note', p. 1.
26. Unpublished letter from George Bowden to Anthony Alpers, February 3, 1950, Mansfield q920/1949–50, Turnbull Library.
27. 'Mr. Reginald Peacock's Day', *Collected Stories*, p. 145.
28. 'The Swing of the Pendulum', *Collected Stories*, p. 780.
29. *Scrapbook*, p. 39 (1915).
30. Lady Ottoline Morrell, *Ottoline at Garsington*, ed. Robert Gathorne-Hardy (London, 1974), p. 148.
31. Bowden, 'A Biographical Note', p. 6.
32. Unpublished letter from George Bowden to Anthony Alpers, November 16, 1949, Mansfield q920/1949–50, Turnbull Library.
33. Quoted in Alpers, p. 119.
34. Unpublished letter from George Bowden to Lucy O'Brien, March 10, 1948, University of Texas.
35. Mantz, p. 320.
36. *Journal*, p. 40.
37. 'A Truthful Adventure', *Collected Stories*, p. 547.
38. Garnet travelled with his orchestra to Durban, South Africa, where in 1923 he married Marian Smith, the daughter of a Canadian judge whom he had met in London when she was studying music. In 1929 they returned with their two sons to her home in Windsor, Ontario, where there were greater opportunities in music. Garnet taught the violin during the 1930s, worked in the Ford Motor plant in Windsor from 1939 to 1945, and died of cancer in 1947.
39. *Journal*, p. 41 (April 29, 1909).
40. Quoted in Mantz, p. 321.
41. *Letters*, II, 13 (to J. M. Murry, February 1920).
42. *Journal*, p. 289 (January 21, 1922).
43. I am grateful to Werner Alferink, who obtained this detailed information from Herr Josef Wolf, the Archivist of Bad Wörishofen.
44. *Journal*, p. 41 (June 1909).
45. *Ibid.*, p. 42.
46. 'At Lehmann's', *Collected Stories*, p. 743.
47. Floryan was born in southeastern Poland, then under Russian domination, belonged to the impoverished landed gentry, was educated at Cracow University, and studied aesthetics and art history in Munich and Paris from 1909 to 1911. He had a wonderful voice, a fine repertoire of Slavic songs, and a profound interest in

the dramatic poet and painter, Stanislaw Wyspianski, who had recently died of syphilis in Poland. Katherine, who had published poems in the *Lone Hand* (Sydney) and the *Daily News* (London) in October and November 1909, wrote an idealistic but rather poor poem 'To Stanislaw Wyspianski' in January 1910, which was translated by Floryan and published in a Warsaw weekly that year; she also translated part of Wyspianski's play, *The Judges*.

Floryan, who was a drama critic in Cracow during 1911–12, met Bernard Shaw late in 1912, obtained the Polish rights to *Pygmalion* and eventually translated forty-two of Shaw's plays. He was always in financial difficulty and frequently pressed Shaw for money, but these demands merely irritated the playwright, who constantly chided him for his lack of responsibility. Floryan ignored these admonitions and characteristically sold the letters from Shaw that portrayed him unfavourably. He lived in London from 1913 to 1929, and died in Cracow in 1964. This information about Floryan, which comes from the Polish Encylopedia, from Floryan's translation of his interview in *Zycie Literackie* (September 30, 1956) and from Alexander Janta's unpublished draft of an Introduction to the Floryan-Shaw correspondence, was kindly sent to me by Dan Laurence.

48. *Letters to Murry*, p. 579 (October 31, 1920).
49. *Journal*, pp. 193, 165 (January 12, 1920, June 1919).
50. Glenavy, p. 70.

Chapter 5: Orage and the *New Age*

1. Unpublished letter from George Bowden to Anthony Alpers, November 16, 1949, Mansfield q920/1949–50, Turnbull Library.
2. Bowden, 'A Biographical Note', p. 14.
3. Ida Baker, p. 54.
4. John Middleton Murry, *Between Two Worlds* (London, 1935), p. 215; and Ida Baker, p. 75.
5. Unpublished letters from George Bowden to Anthony Alpers, November 16, 1949, January 1, 1950 and February 3, 1950.
6. Bowden married in 1919, had one son, taught singing in various American universities, published a book called *F. Matthias Alexander and the Creative Advance of the Individual* in 1965, and died in Palma de Majorca in September 1975 at the age of 98.
7. Unpublished letter from George Bowden to J. M. Murry, December 1933, Turnbull Library.
8. Unpublished letter from Ida Baker to Garnet Trowell, July 20, 1910, University of Windsor.
9. Orage was born in 1873, became an elementary school teacher at the age of twenty, entered theosophical circles, joined the Independent Labour Party, married in 1895 and was divorced in 1904. Two years later he moved to London and met Beatrice Hastings, wrote two books on Nietzsche, and edited the *New Age*

(which he bought with money from Bernard Shaw and a wealthy theosophist) from 1907 until 1922. He introduced Katherine to the ideas of the Caucasian mystic George Gurdjieff; joined Gurdjieff's Institute at Fontainebleau at the same time as she did, in October 1922; remained there for a year; and then spent seven years in New York as Gurdjieff's principal disciple and propagandist. He returned to England to found the *New English Weekly* in 1932, and died two years later.

Beatrice Hastings, a married woman who lived with Orage and was a frequent contributor to his magazine until they separated in 1914, was born in South Africa in 1879. An attractive woman who looked a bit like Katherine, she had dark skin and brown eyes, was vivacious, intelligent, caustic and intensely emotional, and sometimes combined her sarcastic and malicious wit with Katherine's in the correspondence columns of the *New Age*. Beatrice, who was nasty to Katherine in Paris in March 1915, condemned the *New Age* circle in her hysterical pamphlet of 1936, and, after many unhappy alcoholic years, committed suicide in 1943.

10. Philip Mairet, *A. R. Orage: A Memoir* (London, 1936), p. 121.
11. Quoted in *ibid.*, p. 59.
12. Ida Baker, p. 54.
13. F. A. Lea, *The Life of John Middleton Murry* (London, 1959), p. 30.
14. Ida Baker, p. 55.
15. William Orton, *The Last Romantic* (London, 1937), p. 270.
16. Ida Baker, p. 62.
17. Alpers, p. 137.
18. Ida Baker, p. 68; and Murry, p. 208.
19. Holograph note in Margaret Scott's copy of Ida Baker's *Memories*.
20. 'Juliet', p. 15.
21. Quoted in Orton, p. 281.
22. *Letters*, II, 160 (December 5, 1921).
23. 'Juliet', p. 20.
24. *Letters to Murry*, p. 567 (October 18, 1920).

Chapter 6: Murry, *Rhythm* and Bohemia

1. Richard Murry, 'Katherine Mansfield', *Radio Times*, July 4, 1973, p. 54.
2. Dorothy Brett, *Lawrence and Brett: A Friendship* (Philadelphia, 1933), pp. 17–18.
3. Letter from David Garnett to Jeffrey Meyers, November 24, 1975.
4. Frank Swinnerton, *A London Bookman* (London, 1928), p. 74.
5. Frank Swinnerton, *Swinnerton: An Autobiography* (New York, 1936), pp. 110–111.
6. D. H. Lawrence, *Women in Love* (New York, 1961), p. 4.
7. Aldous Huxley, *Those Barren Leaves* (London, 1955), p. 11.
8. *Letters*, I, 208 (to Ottoline Morrell, June 27, 1919).

9. Aldous Huxley, *Letters*, ed. Grover Smith (New York, 1969), p. 948 (January 27, 1963).

10. Aldous Huxley, *Those Barren Leaves*, pp. 11, 18.

11. Quoted in Michael Holroyd, *Lytton Strachey: A Biography* (London, 1971), p. 660.

12. Victor Pritchett, 'Katherine Mansfield', *New Statesman and Nation*, 31 (February 2, 1946), 87.

13. Notebook qMS/1903–1922 (11:36), no date, Turnbull Library.

14. Murry, *Between Two Worlds*, p. 209.

15. Dorothy Brett and John Manchester, 'Reminiscences of Katherine Mansfield', *Adam*, 370–375 (1972–73), 85–87.

16. Quoted in Dan Davin, *Closing Times* (London, 1975), p. 94.

17. Unpublished letter from Frances Cornford to Irene Wilson, September 1, 1929, Cornford MS Papers 269, Turnbull Library.

18. Lea, p. 7.

19. Quoted in Colin Murry, *I At the Keyhole* (New York, 1975), p. 86.

20. D. H. Lawrence, *Collected Letters*, ed. Harry Moore (London, 1962), p. 821 (November 17, 1924).

21. Brett, *Lawrence and Brett*, p. 18.

22. Murry, *Between Two Worlds*, p. 80.

23. Frank Swinnerton, *Background With Chorus* (London, 1956), p. 151.

24. Murry, *Between Two Worlds*, p. 186.

25. *Ibid.*, pp. 202, 208.

26. *Ibid.*, p. 183.

27. *Ibid.*, p. 214.

28. Hugh Kingsmill, *The Life of D. H. Lawrence* (New York, 1938), pp. 83–84.

29. *Letters to Murry*, pp. 247, 259, 522 (May 17 and 23, 1918, April 14, 1920).
    Anne Rice was born in Philadelphia in 1879, one of eleven children of an Irish-American family. She moved to Paris in 1906, did many illustrations for *Rhythm* during 1911–13, lived in Cornwall in the summer of 1918, when she did the fine portrait of Katherine (now in Wellington), and designed the cover and decorations for Lawrence's poems, *Bay* (1919). In Paris Anne met the art and theatre critic, Raymond Drey (1885–1976), and married him in 1913; had one son, David, in 1919; and lived in London from the time of her marriage until her death at the age of eighty in 1959.

30. Notebook qMS/1903–1922 (12:22), 1918, Turnbull Library.

31. Murry, *Between Two Worlds*, p. 232.

32. Quoted in Lea, p. 31.

33. 'A Married Man's Story', *Collected Stories*, p. 434.

34. *Letters to Murry*, p. 106 (December 24, 1917).

35. Unpublished letter from Katherine Mansfield to Virginia Woolf, April 1919, in the University of Sussex Library; *Letters to Murry*, p. 407 (November 23, 1919); and *Scrapbook*, p. 149 (December 1919).

36. *Journal*, p. 285 (January 1922).
37. J. M. Murry, 'The Hill of Vision', *Rhythm*, 2 (June 1912), 34.
38. J. M. Murry and Katherine Mansfield, 'The Meaning of Rhythm', *Rhythm*, 2 (June 1912), 20.
39. 'Present-Day Criticism', *New Age*, 10 (April 18, 1912), 589.
40. Katherine Mansfield, 'Green Goggles', *New Age*, 11 (July 4, 1912), 237.
41. Hugh Kingsmill, *Frank Harris* (New York, 1932), p. 12.
42. J. M. Murry, 'Who is the Man?' *Rhythm*, 2 (July 1912), 39.
43. Quoted in H. S. Ede, *Savage Messiah* (1931), (New York, 1971), p. 89.
44. *Ibid.*, p. 90.
45. Floryan Sobieniowski, 'Stanislaw Wyspianski', *Rhythm*, 2 (December 1912), 311, 316.
46. Murry, *Between Two Worlds*, p. 237.
47. Mervyn Horder, 'Conversations with Martin Secker', *TLS*, December 10, 1976, p. 1565.
48. Edward Marsh, *A Number of People* (London, 1939), p. 227.
49. Murry, *Between Two Worlds*, p. 267; and unpublished letter from J. M. Murry to Katherine Mansfield, December 2, 1919, Turnbull Library.
50. *Letters to Murry*, p. 532 (June 1920).
51. Christopher Hassall, *A Biography of Edward Marsh* (New York, 1959), p. 226.
52. *Ottoline at Garsington*, p. 180.
53. Quoted in Gerald Brenan, *Personal Record, 1920–1972* (London, 1974), p. 57.
54. Letter from Enid Bagnold to Jeffrey Meyers, July 2, 1976.
55. *Ottoline at Garsington*, p. 188.
56. *Ibid.*, p. 150.
57. Frank Swinnerton, *The Georgian Literary Scene* (London, 1951), p. 185; and letter from Frank Swinnerton to Jeffrey Meyers, April 4, 1976.
58. Campbell, who was born in 1885 and educated at Charterhouse and Woolwich, had served in the Royal Engineers and was then a barrister at the Inns of Court. During World War I he had an important post in the Ministry of Munitions and later became Director of the Bank of Ireland. He succeeded his father as Lord Glenavy.
59. *Letters to Murry*, p. 60 (December 16, 1915).
60. Horder, p. 1565.
61. Cannan was born in 1884 and educated at Manchester and Cambridge. He had come to London to study for the Bar, but became instead the drama critic for the *Star* in 1909 and a contributor to *Rhythm* in 1912, and wrote *Peter Homunculus* in 1909 and *Mendel*, a novel about the painter, Mark Gertler, in 1916. The Cannans's marriage was dissolved after his megalomania became madness. He published nothing during the last thirty years of his life, and lived in a mental home until his death in 1955.

Chapter 7: Friendship with D. H. Lawrence

1. Frieda Lawrence, *Not I But the Wind* (New York, 1934), p. 70.
2. Violet Hunt, *I Have This to Say* (London, 1926), p. 259.
3. Brigit Patmore, 'Conversations with Lawrence', *London Magazine*, 4 (June 1957), 34.
4. Huxley, *Letters*, p. 813 (November 20, 1956).
5. Lawrence, *Letters*, p. 189 (to Ernest Collings, February 24, 1913).
6. Frieda Lawrence, *Not I But the Wind*, pp. 67–68.
7. Lawrence, *Letters*, p. 238 (Autumn 1913).
8. *Ibid.*, pp. 238–239.
9. *Letters*, II, 138 (September 24, 1921).
10. Quoted in Lea, p. 42; and *Letters to Murry*, p. 431 (December 5, 1919).
11. Murry, *Between Two Worlds*, p. 344; and quoted in Alpers, p. 194.
12. *Scrapbook*, p. 148.
13. Lawrence, *Letters*, p. 268.
14. Catherine Carswell, *The Savage Pilgrimage* (New York, 1932), pp. 22–23.
15. J. M. Murry, *Reminiscences of D. H. Lawrence* (1933), (Freeport, New York, 1971), pp. 88–89.
16. *Journal*, pp. 67–70.
17. Quoted in Leonard Woolf, *Beginning Again, 1911–1918* (London, 1964), p. 252.
18. D. H. Lawrence, *The Quest for Rananim: D. H. Lawrence's Letters to S. S. Koteliansky, 1914–1930*, ed. George Zytaruk (Montreal, 1970), p. 42.
19. D. H. Lawrence, *Reflections on the Death of a Porcupine* (1925), (Bloomington, Indiana, 1963), p. i.
20. Lawrence, *Letters*, p. 396.
21. *Ibid.*, pp. 401–402.
22. Murry, *Between Two Worlds*, p. 376.
23. Lawrence, *Letters*, p. 435.
24. *Ibid.*, p. 440.
25. *Ibid.*, p. 442.
26. Murry, *Reminiscences*, p. 70.
27. *Letters to Murry*, p. 85.
28. Unpublished letter from Katherine Mansfield to Ottoline Morrell, *c.* March 1916, University of Texas.
29. Frieda Lawrence, *Not I But the Wind*, p. 84.
30. Lawrence, *Letters*, p. 444.
31. *Ibid.*, p. 565 (November 1918).
32. Unpublished letter from Katherine Mansfield to Beatrice Campbell, May 1916, copy in Turnbull Library.
33. Murry, *Between Two Worlds*, p. 413.
34. *Letters*, I, 67–68.
35. Quoted in Harry Moore, *The Priest of Love* (London, 1973), p. 260.
36. John Dickinson, ed., 'Katherine Mansfield and S. S. Koteliansky:

Some Unpublished Letters', *Revue de littérature comparée*, 45 (1971), 84.

37. Quoted in Alpers, p. 225.
38. Unpublished letter from Katherine Mansfield to Ottoline Morrell, January 1917, University of Texas.
39. *Ibid.*, 1917.
40. *Ibid.*, May 1916.
41. *Journal*, p. 146 (September 20, 1918).
42. Quoted in Murry, *Reminiscences*, p. 73.
43. Lawrence, *Letters*, p. 452.
44. *Letters*, I, 72.
45. Lawrence, *Rananim*, p. 86.
46. Murry, *Between Two Worlds*, p. 288.
47. D. H. Lawrence, 'Smile', *Complete Short Stories* (New York, 1964), II, 584.
48. Murry, *Between Two Worlds*, p. 411.
49. Quoted in Frank Swinnerton, *Figures in the Foreground* (London, 1963), p. 102.
50. Unpublished letter from Katherine Mansfield to Ottoline Morrell, July 21, 1921, University of Texas.
51. Lawrence, *Letters*, p. 483.
52. *Ibid.*, pp. 500, 640. The anonymous review, 'Real Life and Dream Life', *Nation*, 28 (February 5, 1921), 639–640, was by Katherine's friend, H. M. Tomlinson.
53. Carswell, p. 198.
54. Lawrence, *Women in Love*, p. 256.
55. *Letters*, I, 315–316.
56. *Ibid.*, I, 79.
57. *Ibid.*, I, 215–216 (to Dorothy Brett, October 27, 1918).
58. Lawrence, *Letters*, p. 565.
59. *Ibid.*, p. 894.
60. *Letters*, I, 226.
61. Lawrence, *Letters*, p. 583.
62. Lawrence, *Rananim*, p. 164.
63. *Journal*, p. 198.
64. Lawrence, *Letters*, p. 620.
65. *Letters to Murry*, p. 470.
66. Quoted in Lea, p. 83.
67. *Letters to Murry*, p. 473.
68. Unpublished letter from J. M. Murry to Katherine Mansfield, February, 6 1920, Turnbull Library.
69. *Letters to Murry*, p. 505.
70. E. M. Forster, 'D. H. Lawrence', *Listener*, 3 (April 30, 1930), 753.
71. F. R. Leavis, ' "Lawrence Scholarship" and Lawrence', *Sewanee Review*, 71 (1963), 30–31.
72. Quoted in Edward Nehls, *D. H. Lawrence: A Composite Biography*, (Madison, 1959), III, 424.

73. *Journal*, p. 207.
74. Lawrence, *Letters*, p. 643.
75. *Ibid.*, p. 673. Lawrence is probably referring to three stories by Katherine published in the *Sphere* in August 1921.
76. *Scrapbook*, p. 135 (November 1918).
77. *Letters to Murry*, pp. 620–621.
78. *Letters*, II, 131.
79. Unpublished letter from Katherine Mansfield to Violet Schiff, October 1921, British Museum. Lawrence published a chapter from *Sea and Sardinia* in *Dial*, 71 (October 1921), 441–451.
80. Dickinson, ed., p. 90.
81. Unpublished letter from Katherine Mansfield to Ottoline Morrell, August 26, 1922, University of Texas.
82. *Letters*, II, 223.
83. *Ibid.*, II, 230.
84. *Journal*, p. 191.
85. *Letters*, II, 175.
86. *Ibid.*, II, 267.
87. Lawrence, *Letters*, p. 704.
88. *Letters*, II, 234.
89. *Letters to Murry*, p. 671.
90. *Ibid.*, p. 688.
91. D. H. Lawrence, *Letters to Thomas and Adele Seltzer*, ed. Gerald Lacy (Santa Barbara, 1976), p. 64 (February 3, 1923).
92. Lawrence, *Letters*, p. 736.
93. Quoted in Lea, pp. 117–118.
94. *Letters*, I, 177 (to Ottoline Morrell, May 24, 1918).
95. Lawrence, *Letters*, p. 1135.
96. Frieda Lawrence, *Not I But the Wind*, p. 195.

Chapter 8: Koteliansky and Carco

1. Lawrence, *Letters*, p. 239 (?Autumn 1913).
2. *Journal*, p. 55 (March 23, 1914).
3. Quoted in Murry, *Between Two Worlds*, pp. 277–278.
4. *Ibid.*, p. 284.
5. Unpublished letter from Katherine Mansfield to J. M. Murry, May 11, 1915, Turnbull Library.
6. Glenavy, p. 79.
7. Quoted in Lea, p. 44.
8. Brett, *Lawrence and Brett*, p. 17.
9. Leonard Woolf, *Beginning Again*, pp. 249, 251.
10. *Letters*, I, 21.
11. Quoted in Ruth Mantz, 'In Consequence: Katherine and Kot', *Adam*, 370–375 (1972–73), 107.
12. Mark Gertler, *Selected Letters*, ed. Noel Carrington (London, 1965), pp. 77, 79.

13. Quoted in Margaret Scott, 'Note to "Bendall"', *Turnbull Library Record*, 5 (May 1972), 19–20.
14. *Letters to Murry*, p. 14.
15. *Scrapbook*, p. 23.
16. Murry, *Between Two Worlds*, p. 346.
17. Notebook qMS/1903–1922 (34:12), 1916, Turnbull Library.
18. *Journal*, pp. 69, 71.
19. Quoted in Lea, p. 43.
20. 'Je ne parle pas français', *Collected Stories*, p. 68.
21. Interviews with Montague Weekley and Frank Lea in London, January 5, 1977 and December 20, 1976.
22. *Journal*, p. 62.
23. Frieda Lawrence, *Memoirs and Correspondence*, ed. E. W. Tedlock (New York, 1964), p. 358 (letter to J. M. Murry, August 2, 1953).
24. Glenavy, p. 81.
25. 'An Indiscreet Journey', *Collected Stories*, p. 634.
26. *Journal*, p. 76.
27. *Ibid.*, p. 78.
28. Francis Carco, 'Montmartre à vingt ans', *Mémoires d'une autre vie* (Genève, 1942), p. 351. My translation.
29. *Journal*, p. 75.
30. *Ibid.*
31. Francis Carco, *Les Innocents* (1916), (Paris, 1927), p. 131. My translation.
32. Carco, *Mémoires*, p. 352.
33. "Je ne parle pas français', *Collected Stories*, p. 87.
34. Katherine Mansfield, *Je ne parle pas français* (London: Heron Press, 1919), p. 25.
35. *Letters to Murry*, p. 149 (February 3, 1918).
36. Quoted in *Journal*, p. 240 (March 9, 1921).
37. *Ibid.*, pp. 58–59.
38. Quoted in Lea, p. 43.
39. Quoted in Murry, *Between Two Worlds*, p. 343.
40. *Letters to Murry*, p. 20.
41. *Ibid.*, pp. 24, 28 (March 22 and 27, 1915).
42. *Ibid.*, pp. 504–505 (March 25, 1920).
43. Beatrice Hastings, *The Old 'New Age'—Orage and Others* (London, 1936), p. 28.
44. *Letters*, I, 26 (May 15, 1915).
45. *Ibid.*, I, 33 (May 25, 1915).
46. Quoted in Murry, *Between Two Worlds*, p. 278.

Chapter 9: Leslie, Bandol and 'Prelude'

1. Interview with Edith Bendall.
2. Glenavy, p. 82.
3. *Journal*, p. 88.

4. Unpublished letter from Katherine Mansfield to ?Sylvia Payne, March 4, 1908, Turnbull Library.
5. Quoted in Moira Taylor, p. 14.
6. *Journal*, p. 84 (October 1915).
7. *Letters*, I, 34 (to S. S. Koteliansky, November 19, 1915).
8. *Journal*, pp. 86, 89.
9. *Ibid.*, pp. 86, 95–96.
10. Murry, *Between Two Worlds*, pp. 373–374.
11. Huxley, *Those Barren Leaves*, p. 46.
12. John Manchester, 'Prologue' to Dorothy Brett's *Lawrence and Brett: A Friendship* (Santa Fe, 1974), p. vii.
13. D. H. Lawrence and M. L. Skinner, *The Boy in the Bush* (London, 1963), p. 390.
14. Interview with Dorothy Brett.
15. Brett and Manchester, pp. 86–87.
16. John Dickinson, ed., 95–96. Brett, a lively, frank, kind and responsive woman, spoke generously of Katherine, Murry, Lawrence, Frieda, Gertler, Carrington, Ottoline Morrell and Virginia Woolf, and made it easy to understand why so many extraordinary people liked her and became her friend.
17. *Letters*, I, 35 (to Anne Estelle Rice, December 8, 1915).
18. *Letters to Murry*, p. 63 (December 22, 1915).
19. *Journal*, pp. 108–109 (c. March 1916).
20. *Letters to Murry*, p. 53 (December 14, 1915).
21. *Ibid.*, p. 66 (December 23, 1915).
22. Murry, *Between Two Worlds*, p. 378.
23. *Letters to Murry*, p. 63 (December 21, 1915).
24. *Ibid.*, p. 77.
25. *Ibid.*, p. 84 (March 1916).
26. *Journal*, pp. 93–94 (January 22, 1916).
27. Dickinson, ed., p. 87 (July 1919).
28. Quoted in Carolyn Heilbrun, *The Garnett Family* (London, 1961), p. 166.
29. Murry, *Between Two Worlds*, p. 417.
30. *Letters to Murry*, p. 88.

Chapter 10: Garsington and Bloomsbury

1. Quoted in Holroyd, p. 599 (letter to David Garnett, July 14, 1915).
2. Quoted in *ibid.*, p. 597.
3. Osbert Sitwell, *Laughter in the Next Room* (Boston, 1951), p. 18.
4. Lawrence, *Women in Love*, pp. 9–10.
5. Lawrence, *Letters*, pp. 379, 543.
6. *Ottoline at Garsington*, pp. 148, 150, 183.
7. Virginia Woolf, *The Question of Things Happening: Letters, 1912–1922*, ed. Nigel Nicolson and Joanne Trautmann (London, 1976), p. 174 (August 15, 1917).

8. Lady Ottoline Morrell, 'K.M.', *Katherine Mansfield: An Exhibition* (Austin: Humanities Research Center, 1975), p. 10.
9. Letter from Ottoline Morrell to Rosamund Lehmann, 1931, quoted in Miron Grindea, 'Only One K.M.?' *Adam*, 370–375 (1972–73), 11.
10. Letter from Julian Vinogradoff to Jeffrey Meyers, February 27, 1976.
11. Brett and Manchester, p. 85.
12. Huxley, *Letters*, p. 118 (December 29, 1916).
13. Katherine Mansfield, 'The Laurels', *Turnbull Library Record*, 6 (October 1973), 6.
14. Bertrand Russell, *Autobiography, 1914–1944* (New York, 1969), p. 58.
15. *Journal*, p. 105 (February 1916).
16. Quoted in Ronald Clark, *The Life of Bertrand Russell* (London, 1975), p. 314 (1916).
17. *Ottoline at Garsington*, p. 167.
18. 'Letters to Bertrand Russell', p. 38.
19. Quoted in Clark, p. 309; and *Autobiography*, p. 20.
20. Bertrand Russell, *Portraits from Memory* (New York, 1956), pp. 111–112.
21. *Ottoline at Garsington*, p. 167.
22. Virginia Woolf and Lytton Strachey, *Letters*, ed. Leonard Woolf and James Strachey (London, 1956), p. 61.
23. V. Woolf, *Question*, p. 107.
24. Christopher Isherwood, 'Virginia Woolf' (1941), *Exhumations* (London, 1969), p. 155.
25. Dora Carrington, *Carrington: Letters and Extracts from Her Diaries*, ed. David Garnett (London, 1970), p. 242 (to Gerald Brenan, April 27, 1923).
26. Gerald Brenan, *South From Granada* (London, 1957), p. 139.
27. *Letters*, I, 80 (August 1917).
28. Leonard Woolf, *Beginning Again*, p. 204.
29. *Letters*, I, 235.
30. *Ottoline at Garsington*, p. 150.
31. Interview with Dorothy Brett. Julian Vinogradoff and A. S. Frere agreed with Brett, during interviews on December 21, 1976 and January 6, 1977.
32. Quoted in Quentin Bell, *Virginia Woolf* (London, 1972), II, 37.
33. Quoted in *ibid.*, II, 45 (October 11, 1917).
34. Leonard Woolf, *Beginning Again*, pp. 204–205.
35. V. Woolf, *Question*, p. 551 (to Lytton Strachey, August 24, 1922).
36. Virginia Woolf, *A Writer's Diary*, ed. Leonard Woolf (New York, 1954), p. 349.
37. *Journal*, p. 121.
38. V. Woolf, *Question*, pp. 144, 159.
39. *Ibid.*, p. 248.

40. *Letters*, I, 80 (August 1917).
41. V. Woolf, *Writer's Diary*, p. 56.
42. Interview with Dorothy Brett.
43. Unpublished letter from Katherine Mansfield to Ottoline Morrell, July 1917, University of Texas.
44. V. Woolf, *Question*, p. 224.
45. *Ibid.*, p. 241 (to Duncan Grant, May 15, 1918).
46. *Letters*, I, 208 (August 1918).
47. V. Woolf, *Writer's Diary*, p. 12 (April 17, 1919).
48. Quoted in Bell, II, 70–71.
49. Unpublished letter from Katherine Mansfield to Virginia Woolf, ?August 1919, University of Sussex Library.
50. *Letters*, I, 83.
51. V. Woolf, *Question*, p. 258.
52. Virginia Woolf, *Diary, 1915–1919*, ed. Anne Bell (London, 1977), p. 167 (July 12, 1918).
53. V. Woolf, *Writer's Diary*, p. 2.
54. V. Woolf, *Question*, p. 293.
55. Virginia Woolf, 'A Terribly Sensitive Mind' (1927), *Granite and Rainbow*, ed. Leonard Woolf (New York, 1958), p. 74.
56. *Letters to Murry*, pp. 380–381.
57. *Novels and Novelists*, pp. 108, 111.
58. V. Woolf, *Diary*, p. 314 (November 28, 1919).
59. Quoted in Leonard Woolf, *The Journey Not the Arrival Matters* (London, 1969), p. 41 (1932).
60. Unpublished letter from Katherine Mansfield to Sylvia Lynd, September 24, 1921, Turnbull Library.
61. V. Woolf, *Question*, p. 243.
62. V. Woolf, *Writer's Diary*, p. 12.
63. *Letters to Murry*, p. 102.
64. V. Woolf, *Question*, pp. 515, 540, 546 (to Janet Case, March 20; to Ottoline Morrell, August 1; and to Roger Fry, August 13, 1922).
65. Letter from Gerald Brenan to Jeffrey Meyers, October 3, 1975; and Russell, *Autobiography*, p. 58.
66. Unpublished letter from Katherine Mansfield to Ottoline Morrell, December 2, 1918, University of Texas.
67. Unpublished letter from Katherine Mansfield to J. M. Murry, January 22, 1920, Turnbull Library.
68. *Letters to Murry*, pp. 419–420.
69. Quoted in Leonard Woolf, *Beginning Again*, p. 206.
70. *Ibid.*, pp. 205–207.
71. *Ibid.*, p. 207.
72. Bell, II, 117.
73. *Ibid.*, II, 118 (December 21, 1925).

Chapter 11 : Chelsea and Return to Bandol

1. *Letters to Murry*, p. 91.
2. Murry, *Between Two Worlds*, p. 433.
3. Huxley, *Letters*, p. 227 (to Leonard Huxley, January 25, 1924).
4. Quoted in Stephen Hudson [Sydney Schiff], 'First Meetings with Katherine Mansfield', *Cornhill*, 170 (1958), 209.
5. Ida Baker, p. 101.
6. *Letters to Murry*, p. 92.
7. Ida Baker, p. 102.
8. Huxley, *Letters*, p. 140 (to Juliette Baillot).
9. Quoted in Bell, II, 45–46 (diary of October 11, 1917).
10. These included 'Mr. Reginald Peacock's Day', a satire on George Bowden; 'The Common Round' (the first version of 'Pictures'), based on her experience in films; 'Feuille d'Album', about the ineffectual amours of a young painter in Paris; and 'The Dill Pickle', a description of Katherine's meeting with her former lover.
11. *Journal*, pp. 123–124.
12. Siegfried Sassoon, *Siegfried's Journey* (London, 1945), p. 52.
13. *Letters*, I, 75.
14. *Ottoline at Garsington*, p. 192.
15. Quoted in Lea, p. 58.
16. *Letters to Murry*, p. 109.
17. *Letters*, I, 87.
18. *Letters to Murry*, pp. 106–107.
19. Gertler, *Selected Letters*, p. 151 (to Dora Carrington).
20. Murry, *Between Two Worlds*, pp. 454–455.
21. *Ibid.*, p. 450.
22. *Letters to Murry*, p. 112.
23. *Scrapbook*, pp. 72–73.
24. *Letters to Murry*, p. 114.
25. *Ibid.*, p. 116. See also p. 210.
26. *Ibid.*, p. 118.
27. *Ibid.*, pp. 150, 152.
28. Notebook qMS/1903–1922 (14:1), Turnbull Library.
29. *Letters to Murry*, pp. 154–155.
30. *Journal*, p. 130 (February 19, 1918).
31. *Letters to Murry*, p. 124.
32. *Ibid.*, p. 127.
33. *Ibid.*, p. 150.
34. *Ibid.*, p. 149.
35. Ida Baker, p. 107.
36. Interview with Dorothy Brett.
37. *Journal*, p. 53 (1914).
38. 'Psychology', *Collected Stories*, p. 117.
39. *Letters to Murry*, p. 96.
40. Ida Baker, p. 120.

41. *Letters to Murry*, p. 181.
42. *Ibid.*, pp. 163–164, 177, 185.
43. *Ibid.*, p. 181.
44. *Ibid.*, pp. 169, 179; and *Journal*, p. 220 (October 1920).
45. Katherine Mansfield, *The Aloe* (London, 1930), pp. 155–156.
46. Quoted in Ida Baker, p. 186 (March 15, 1922). For a similar use of the word 'share' see E. M. Forster, *Maurice* (New York, 1971), 192.
47. Quoted in Ida Baker, p. 203 (June 14, 1922).
48. Ida Baker, pp. 127, 189.
49. *Journal*, p. 129. See J. M. Murry, *Keats*, 4th ed. (New York, 1955), p. 22, quoting Keats: 'I know the colour of that blood—it is arterial blood—I cannot be deceived in that colour; that drop is my death warrant. I must die."
50. *Letters to Murry*, pp. 173–174.
51. *Ibid.*, p. 218.
52. *Ibid.*, p. 221.
53. *Ibid.*, p. 224.
54. *Ibid.*, p. 227.
55. *Ibid.*, p. 238.
56. *Ibid.*, p. 241.

Chapter 12: Cornwall and Hampstead

1. *Letters to Murry*, p. 653 (February 8, 1922). The reference is to *Antony and Cleopatra*, I.iv.47.
2. *Ibid.*, p. 624 (January 19, 1921).
3. Walter Pagel, *Pulmonary Tuberculosis*, 4th ed. (London, 1964), p. 428.
4. Letter from Ida Baker to Jeffrey Meyers, February 14, 1976.
5. Lewis Moorman, 'Katherine Mansfield', *Tuberculosis and Genius* (Chicago, 1940), p. 115.
6. Letter from Dr. Sheldon Cooperman to Jeffrey Meyers, May 31, 1975.
7. Quoted in Ida Baker, pp. 113–114 (April 18, 1918).
8. *Letters to Murry*, pp. 257–258 (May 23, 1918).
9. Mary Middleton Murry ['Katherine Mansfield and John Middleton Murry'], *London Magazine*, 6 (April 1959), 71.
10. Unpublished letter from J. M. Murry to Katherine Mansfield, early April 1918, Turnbull Library.
11. Quoted in Mary Middleton Murry, *To Keep Faith* (London, 1958), p. 167 (diary of March 10, 1954).
12. *Letters to Murry*, p. 266 (May 27, 1918).
13. *Ibid.*
14. *Ibid.*, p. 288 (June 7, 1918).
15. Murry, *Between Two Worlds*, p. 485.
16. *Letters to Murry*, pp. 252, 265 (May 20 and 27, 1918).
17. *Letters*, I, 204.

18. Quoted in Ida Baker, pp. 119, 122 (June 22 and July 1, 1918).
19. *Letters*, I, 204–205 (June 1918).
20. *Ibid.*, I, 208–210 (August 21 and 25, 1918).
21. *Ibid.*, I, 223, 235 (January 13 and June 28, 1919).
22. *Letters to Murry*, p. 262; and *Journal*, p. 153.
23. Quoted in Ida Baker, p. 118 (June 14, 1918).
24. Quoted in Alpers, p. 259 (June 1918).
25. Leonard Woolf, *Beginning Again*, p. 204.
26. Murry, *Between Two Worlds*, p. 490.
27. *Scrapbook*, pp. 133–135 (November 1918).
28. Quoted in Nehls, ed., III, 425.
29. Ida Baker, p. 128.
30. Quoted in Alpers, p. 308. Whether or not, as Anne Rice claims, Sorapure 'was a foundling left on the doorstep of a Paris convent', he was born in 1874, was a Catholic and was educated at St. George's Jesuit College, Kingston, Jamaica. He earned an M.B. after five years at Edinburgh University, did postgraduate work at St. Andrews University where he was house physician at the Royal Hospital, returned to Kingston for five years as Chief Surgeon at Government Hospital, and was then Chief Surgeon at women's hospitals in Liverpool and London. He married and had three children; and held the Chair of Histology and Pathology at Fordham University Medical School from 1906–10. Like Katherine, Sorapure was a colonial outsider who moved about a great deal, and though he had extensive experience before he treated her, he specialized in gynaecology and pathology rather than in tuberculosis, which caused his death at the age of fifty-eight in 1933. (Anne Estelle Rice, 'Memories of Katherine Mansfield', *Adam*, 300 (1965), 84; and 'Medical School Notes', *Fordham Monthly*, 25 (1906–07), 273. See also Sorapure's obituaries in the *Lancet*, February 11, 1933, p. 337 and the *British Medical Journal*, February 25, 1933, p. 348).
31. *Journal*, p. 168 (June 21, 1919).
32. Sylvia Lynd, 'Katherine Mansfield', *Weekly Westminster Gazette*, 1 (January 20, 1923), 12.
33. Friedrich Nietzsche, *The Case of Wagner*, trans. Walter Kaufmann (New York, 1967), p. 165.
34. *Journal*, pp. 70, 272 (January 21, 1915, November 24, 1921); and *Letters*, II, 229 (to Arnold Gibbons, July 13, 1922).
35. Quoted in Ida Baker, p. 199 (June 5, 1922).
36. Bashkirtseff, pp. 405, 416, 456 (March-August 1884).
37. *Letters to Murry*, p. 365 (November 1, 1919).
38. *Journal*, p. 238 (January 1921).
39. John Keats, *Complete Poetical Works and Letters*, ed. Horace Scudder (Cambridge, Mass., 1899), pp. 426, 432, 438, 442 (February-July 1820).
40. *Letters to Murry*, p. 109 (December 24, 1917); p. 395 (November 17, 1919); p. 266 (May 27, 1918); p. 427 (December 4, 1919).

41. Katherine Mansfield and S. S. Koteliansky, trans., 'Letters of Anton Tchehov', *Athenaeum*, 1 (June 6, 1919), 441.

42. *Journal*, p. 333 (October 14, 1922).

43. *Letters to Murry*, p. 674 (October 15, 1922).

44. Katherine Mansfield, 'Letters to Richard Murry', *Adam*, 370–375 (1972–73), 34.

45. Quoted in Ida Baker, pp. 162–163 (Spring 1921).

46. *Ibid.*, p. 128.

47. *Journal*, p. 207 (August 12, 1920).

48. *Ibid.*, p. 166 (June 1919).

49. Katherine Mansfield, MS Papers 119:10, Turnbull Library.

50. Quoted in Leslie de Charms, *Elizabeth of the German Garden* (London, 1958), p. 238.

51. *Journal*, pp. 183–184.

52. *Letters*, I, 221 (December 18, 1918).

53. V. Woolf, *Diary*, p. 216 (November 9, 1918).

54. *Journal*, pp. 147–148 (October 1918).

55. *Ibid.*, p. 166 (June 1919); and quoted in Lea, p. 176.

56. Interview with Frank Swinnerton in Cranleigh, Surrey, December 29, 1976.

57. Lawrence, *Letters*, p. 643 (March 2, 1921).

58. *Letters to Murry*, p. 482 (February 22, 1920).

59. *Letters*, I, 227.

60. Letter from Enid Hilton to Jeffrey Meyers, January 23, 1976.

61. *Letters*, I, 240 (August 13, 1919).

Chapter 13: Ospedaletti and Menton

1. *Letters*, I, 243 (October 1, 1919).

2. *Letters to Murry*, p. 318 (October 6, 1919).

3. *Ibid.*, p. 437 (December 8, 1919); p. 366 (November 2, 1919); and p. 422 (December 1, 1919).

4. *Ibid.*, p. 437.

5. *Journal*, p. 184 (December 15, 1919).

6. *Ibid.*, p. 187.

7. *Letters to Murry*, p. 406 (November 23, 1919); and p. 343 (October 19, 1919).

8. *Ibid.*, pp. 449–450 (early January 1920).

9. *Ibid.*, pp. 399–400 (November 20, 1919).

10. *Journal*, p. 216 (September 1920).

11. *Letters to Murry*, p. 360 (October 30, 1919).

12. Letter from Katherine Mansfield to J. M. Murry, November 20, 1919. Turnbull Library. The powerful image of 'blind breasts' was probably influenced by the 'blind mouths' of the bishops in Milton's 'Lycidas', a poem in Katherine's *Oxford Book of English Verse*.

13. 'Prelude', *Collected Stories*, p. 53.

14. *Letters to Murry*, p. 359 (October 29, 1919).
15. *Ibid.*, p. 50 (December 19, 1915).
16. *Ibid.*, pp. 386–387 (November 12, 1919).
17. Quoted in *Journal*, p. 251 (May 19, 1921); and *Letters to Murry*, p. 401 (November 21, 1919).
18. *Ibid.*, p. 352 (October 24, 1919); and p. 376 (November 6, 1919).
19. Murry, *Keats*, p. 22.
20. Quoted in Mary Middleton Murry, *To Keep Faith*, p. 27 (diary of August 1939).
21. Mary Middleton Murry, *London Magazine*, p. 70.
22. Frieda Lawrence, *Memoirs and Correspondence*, p. 387 (January 1955).
23. *Letters to Murry*, pp. 424, 426–428 (December 4, 1919).
24. *Ibid.*, pp. 441–443 (?December 9, 1919). Murry's salary went up to £1,000 p.a. in early 1920. To be fair to Katherine—and to Murry—most of her letters to him, like the one of October 6, 1920 (p. 552), were kind and loving: 'Your letter—surely the most wonderful letter a man ever wrote to a woman—or a Boge ever wrote a Wig —almost made me cry out: "Forgive me, forgive me." '
25. Quoted in Lea, p. 75 (December 8, 1919).
26. *Journal*, p. 192.
27. Unpublished letter from Katherine Mansfield to Ottoline Morrell, January 20, 1920, University of Texas.
28. *Journal*, p. 192 (January 11, 1920); and *Letters to Murry*, p. 469 (?February 7, 1920).
29. Quoted in Lea, p. 116 (March 23, 1923).
30. Unpublished letter from J. M. Murry to Katherine Mansfield, December 5, 1919, Turnbull Library.
31. Unpublished letter from J. M. Murry to Katherine Mansfield, February 20, 1920, Turnbull Library.
32. *Letters to Murry*, pp. 464, 466–468 (January 31, February 4 and 5, 1920).
33. Quoted in Ida Baker, p. 159 (*c.* March 1921).
34. Quoted in de Charms, p. 243 (?August 1922).
35. Unpublished letter from Katherine Mansfield to Harold Beauchamp, November 1, 1921, Turnbull Library.
36. *Letters to Murry*, p. 455 (January 13, 1920).
37. *Ibid.*, p. 459 (January 22, 1920).
38. *Letters*, II, 24 (March 1920); and *Letters to Murry*, pp. 388–389 (November 13, 1919).
39. *Letters to Murry*, p. 457 (January 21, 1920).
40. *Ibid.*
41. *Ibid.*, p. 460 (January 23, 1920).
42. *Letters*, II, 16 (February 1920).
43. *Letters to Murry*, pp. 471–472 (February 8, 1920).
44. *Ibid.*, p. 484 (February 23, 1920).
45. *Ibid.*, p. 511 (April 1, 1920).
46. *Ibid.*, p. 471 (February 8, 1920); and p. 398 (November 19, 1919).

47. Quoted in Ida Baker, p. 149 (*c.* March 1920).
48. *Letters to Murry*, p. 568 (October 21, 1920).
49. *Novels and Novelists*, p. 103.
50. Wyndham Lewis, 'Introduction' to *The Apes of God* (1930), (London, 1955), p. [2].
51. George Painter, *Proust: The Later Years* (Boston, 1965), p. 339.
52. *Letters to Murry*, pp. 529, 521, 522, 520, 530.
53. Katherine Mansfield, 'Fifteen Letters to Virginia Woolf', *Adam*, 370–375 (1972–73), 19.
54. V. Woolf, *Question*, pp. 438, 441 (August 1 and 24, 1920).
55. *Letters to Murry*, pp. 536, 541 (September 16 and 23, 1920).
56. *Ibid.*, p. 556.
57. *Ibid.*, p. 502 (*c.* March 24, 1920).
58. *Ibid.*, p. 549 (October 1, 1920). A. E. Ellis's *The Rack* (1958) is a much greater and even more terrible book.
59. *Novels and Novelists*, p. 282.
60. Benjamin Goldberg, ed., *Clinical Tuberculosis*, 5th rev. ed. (Philadelphia, 1946), pp. C–83.
61. *Letters*, II, 115.
62. *Ibid.*, II, 84.
63. *Letters to Murry*, p. 568 (October 21, 1920).
64. *Ibid.*, pp. 595–596 (November 14 and 17, 1920).
65. Lea, p. 80. This explanation was confirmed in an interview with Colin Murry in Dittisham, Devon, January 3, 1977.
66. Katherine Mansfield, 'Letters to Sydney and Violet Schiff', *Adam*, 300 (1965), 105 (January 19, 1921).
67. Quoted in Hudson, 'First Meetings with Katherine Mansfield', p. 210.
68. *Letters*, II, 96 (March 14, 1921).
69. *Letters to Murry*, pp. 69–70.
70. *Ottoline at Garsington*, p. 192.
71. Lea, p. 81. See also Mary Middleton Murry in the *London Magazine*, p. 71: Murry's love for Katherine 'made him faithful through all their long separations. . . . He once said to me: "It never entered my head *not* to be faithful." Just that, quite simply.'
72. Letter from F. A. Lea to Jeffrey Meyers, July 27, 1976.
73. Interviews with Ruth Mantz in San Francisco, December 24, 1975; with Enid Hilton in Ukiah, California, June 25, 1976; and with John Manchester in Taos, New Mexico, March 21, 1976.
74. Unpublished letter from Katherine Mansfield to J. M. Murry, March 2, 1920, Turnbull Library.
75. Unpublished letter from Katherine Mansfield to Ida Baker, March 13, 1921, Turnbull Library.
76. Katherine Mansfield, Notebook qMS/1903–1922 (25:2–3), Turnbull Library.
77. *Journal*, p. 208 (August 19, 1920).
78. Brett and Manchester, p. 88.

79. Manchester, 'Prologue', pp. xi–xii.
80. Letter from John Manchester to Jeffrey Meyers, July 12, 1976.
81. Interview with Dorothy Brett.
82. Letter from Enid Bagnold to Jeffrey Meyers, July 2, 1976.
83. *Letters to Murry*, p. 70 (December 25, 1915); and quoted in Lea, p. 81.
84. Wyndham Lewis, *Blasting and Bombardiering* (1937), (London, 1967), p. 53.
85. Interviews with Julian Vinogradoff in Banbury, December 21, 1976; and with Juliette Huxley in London, December 22, 1976.
86. *Ottoline at Garsington*, p. 226.
87. *Journal*, p. 233 (December 27, 1920).
88. *Letters to Murry*, pp. 621 (December 12, 1920).
89. *Ibid.*, pp. 610, 621 (December 3 and 12, 1920).
90. Katherine Mansfield, MS Papers 119:10, Diary of December 9, 1920, Turnbull Library.
91. Quoted in Ida Baker, pp. 154, 162.
92. *Journal*, p. 228 (December 19, 1920).
93. Quoted in Ida Baker, p. 162 (March 1921).
94. Unpublished letter from Katherine Mansfield to Elizabeth Bibesco, March 24, 1921, University of Texas.
95. *Letters to Murry*, p. 587 (November 6, 1920).
96. Edward Shanks, 'Fiction', *London Mercury*, 3 (January 1921), 337; and Desmond MacCarthy, 'A New Writer' (1921), *Humanities* (London, 1953), p. 182.
97. Anon., 'Unpleasant Stories', *Saturday Review* (London), February 19, 1921, p. 157; and Malcolm Cowley, 'Page Mr. Blum', *Dial*, 71 (September 1921), 365.
98. J. W. N. S[ullivan], 'The Story-Writing Genius', *Athenaeum*, April 2, 1920, p. 447; and [Walter De La Mare], 'Prelude', *Athenaeum*, January 21, 1921, p. 67.
99. Anon., 'Miss Mansfield's Stories', *TLS*, December 16, 1920, p. 855; and R. H., 'Bliss', *New Republic*, 26 (March 23, 1921), 114.
100. Conrad Aiken, 'Katherine Mansfield' (1921), *Collected Criticism* (New York, 1968), p. 291.
101. *Letters*, II, 138 (to Sylvia Lynd, September 24, 1921).
102. 'The Stranger', *Collected Stories*, p. 358.
103. Unpublished letter from Katherine Mansfield to John Squire, December 1, 1920, Stanford University Library.
104. Lawrence, *Letters*, p. 239 (?Autumn 1913).
105. *Journal*, p. 158 (May 1919).
106. Quoted in Ida Baker, p. 116 (May 21, 1918).
107. *Letters to Murry*, p. 425 (December 4, 1919).
108. *Ibid.*, p. 601 (November 27, 1920).
109. Morrell, 'K.M.', p. 11.
110. *Letters*, I, 221 (December 18, 1918).

Chapter 14: Switzerland and Paris

1. F. Scott Fitzgerald, 'One Trip Abroad', *Afternoon of an Author*, ed. Arthur Mizener (New York, 1958), p. 161.
2. *Letters*, II, 98, 103 (to J. M. Murry and Anne Rice, May 1921).
3. *Ibid.*, II, 116–118 (May-June 1921).
4. See *British Medical Journal*, September 22, 1923, p. 519; and Lynden Macassey and C. W. Saleeby, ed., *Spahlinger contra TB, 1906–1934* (London 1934).
5. Quoted in John Sherwood, *No Golden Journey* (London, 1973), p. 189.
6. *Journal*, p. 289 (January 22, 1922).
7. 'Letters to Schiffs', p. 111 (December 3, 1921).
8. *Letters*, II, 161 (December 5, 1921).
9. *Journal*, p. 252. Katherine's Notebook in the Turnbull Library makes it clear that this passage refers to Murry and belongs after the entry of November 21.
10. Quoted in Ida Baker, pp. 170, 185 (September 7, 1921 and March 15, 1922).
11. Quoted in Swinnerton, *Figures in the Foreground*, p. 57.
12. Interview with A. S. Frere in Aldington, Kent, January 6, 1977.
13. Interview with Ruth Herrick.
14. Interview with William Craddock Barclay.
15. 'Letters to Schiffs', p. 102.
16. *Letters to Murry*, p. 586 (November 5, 1920).
17. *Novels and Novelists*, p. 7.
18. *Letters*, II, 140 (October 1, 1921).
19. *Journal*, pp. 284–285 (January 11, 1922).
20. Quoted in de Charms, p. 233.
21. E. M. Forster, 'Recollections of Nassenheide', *Listener*, January 1, 1959, p. 13.
22. Swinnerton, *Background with Chorus*, p. 149.
23. Interviews with A. S. Frere and Frank Swinnerton.
24. Elizabeth, *Elizabeth and Her German Garden* (New York, 1900), p. 61.
25. *Journal*, p. 286 (January 14, 1922).
26. *Letters*, II, 174 (January 15, 1922).
27. *Journal*, pp. 259, 291 (August 1921 and January 27, 1922). The critical entry was originally published in the *Journal* (London, 1927), p. 190.
28. Quoted in de Charms, pp. 253–254, 311 (September 7 and 8, 1927).
29. *Journal*, p. 287 (January 17, 1922).
30. *Scrapbook*, p. 224.
31. She finished 'Mr. and Mrs. Dove' in mid-July 1921; 'An Ideal Family' on July 23; 'At the Bay', a continuation of 'Prelude', and 'The Voyage' in August; 'The Garden Party' on October 14, her thirty-third birthday; 'The Doll's House' on November 2; 'Her First Ball' and 'Marriage à la Mode' in late autumn; 'A Cup of

Tea' on January 11; and 'Taking the Veil' in three hours on January 24.

32. *Letters*, II, 196 (March 13, 1922).

33. Blaise Pascal, *Pensées*, trans. J. M. Cohen (London, 1961), p. 70.

34. Rebecca West, 'Notes on Novels', *New Statesman*, 18 (March 18, 1922), 678.

35. Letter from Rebecca West to Jeffrey Meyers, February 4, 1977.

36. Anon., 'The Garden Party', *Saturday Review* (London), 133 (March 11, 1922), 266.

37. Joseph Krutch, 'The Unfortunate Mendoza', *Nation* (New York), 115 (July 26, 1922), 100.

38. Anon., 'The Garden Party', *English Review*, 34 (June 1922), 602.

39. Robert Littell, 'Katherine Mansfield', *New Republic*, 31 (July 5, 1922), 166; and Conrad Aiken, 'Katherine Mansfield' (1922), *Collected Criticism*, p. 294.

40. Anon., 'Miss Mansfield's New Stories', *TLS*, March 2, 1922, p. 137; and Malcolm Cowley, 'The Author of *Bliss*', *Dial*, 73 (August 1922), 231–232.

41. William Gerhardi, *Memoirs of a Polyglot* (London, 1931), p. 155.

42. *Letters*, II, 111, 165–166 (May 19 and December 19, 1921).

43. *Journal*, pp. 288–289, 291 (January 20 and 28, 1922).

44. *Letters to Murry*, p. 643.

45. *Ibid.*, p. 644.

46. Ida Baker, p. 174.

47. Interview with F. A. Lea in London, December 20, 1976.

48. *Letters to Murry*, pp. 654–655 (February 9, 1922).

49. Apart from the doctors involved in her miscarriage and abortion, she consulted Croft-Hill in July 1914, the New Zealander Ainger in December 1917, the English drunkard in Bandol in March 1918, the Irishman Pagello in Cornwall in May 1918, Victor Sorapure from September 1918 to October 1922, her cousin Sidney Beauchamp in November 1918, the Italian Ansaldi and German Bobone in November 1919, Foster in December 1919, Rendell in February 1920, Mee and the Frenchman Bouchage in October 1920, the Swiss Figli, Mercanton and Stephani in May 1921, Hudson in June 1921, the Russian Ivan Manoukhin and the Frenchman Donat in February 1922, Webster in September 1922 and James Young in October 1922.

50. *Journal*, p. 195 (January 23, 1920).

51. Mansfield, 'Fifteen Letters to Virginia Woolf', p. 20 (*c.* 1918–19).

52. Ivan Manoukhin, 'The Treatment of Infectious Diseases by Leucocytolysis Produced by Rontgenisation of the Spleen', *Lancet*, April 2, 1921, pp. 685–687.

53. Unpublished letter from Katherine Mansfield to Ivan Manoukhin, December 4, 1921, Turnbull Library.

54. Quoted in Glenavy, p. 192.

55. *Letters*, II 180; and *Journal*, p. 293.

56. *Journal*, p. 294 (February 3, 1922).

57. *Letters to Murry*, p. 645 (February 1, 1922).
58. *Letters*, p. 199 (March 19, 1922).
59. 'Letters to Richard Murry', p. 33 (March 3, 1922).
60. *Letters*, II, 212 (May 23, 1922).
61. *Ibid.*, II, 218 (June 14, 1922).
62. 'Letters to Schiffs', p. 114 (December 28, 1921). For Katherine's views on Joyce see also *Letters*, II, 171, 173, 208, 240.
63. Unpublished letter from Katherine Mansfield to Violet Schiff, May 1922, Cornell University Library.
64. Quoted in Ida Baker, p. 193 (May 11, 1922).
65. Quoted in de Charms, p. 233.
66. Unpublished letter from Katherine Mansfield to Harold Beauchamp, March 18, 1922, MS Papers 119:16, Turnbull Library.
67. Letters from Sheldon Cooperman to Jeffrey Meyers, September 8, 1975 and July 24, 1976.
68. Carco, *Mémoires*, p. 355. My translation.
69. Quoted in Christopher Sykes, *Evelyn Waugh* (Boston, 1975), p. 37.
70. 'The Fly', *Collected Stories*, p. 426.
71. Quoted in Ida Baker, pp. 200–201.
72. *Letters*, II, 213.
73. Quoted in Ida Baker, p. 200; and *Journal*, p. 322 (June 1922).
74. Quoted in Ida Baker, p. 201 (June 9, 1921).
75. 'Letters to Schiffs ', p. 117 (August 9, 1922).
76. *Letters to Murry*, p. 671 (October 13, 1922).
77. Brett and Manchester, pp. 88–89.
78. *Journal*, pp. 129, 292 (February 19, 1918 and January 29, 1922).
79. Partially quoted in University of Texas: Humanities Research Center, *Katherine Mansfield: An Exhibition* (Austin, 1975), p. 52, and in Lea, p. 113n.
80. *Journal* (1927), p. 223 (January 20, 1922). Lawrence's name was omitted from the 1954 edition, p. 288.
81. Dickinson, ed., p. 95 (June 17, 1922).
82. She left her carved walking stick to Kot, other personal possessions to Ida, Anne Rice, her father, her three sisters, Murry's brother and mother, and favourite books to De La Mare, Tomlinson, Lawrence (whose letter she had forgiven), Orage, Fergusson, Campbell, Sorapure, the Schiffs and Elizabeth.

Chapter 15: Gurdjieff

1. 'M. A. Oxon' [A. R. Wallace], *Cosmic Anatomy, or the Structure of the Ego* (London, 1921), p. 184.
2. K[atherine] M[ansfield], 'Review of Victor Neuberg's *The Triumph of Pan*', *Rhythm*, 2 (July 1912), 70.
3. Unpublished letter from Katherine Mansfield to Vera Bell, March 20, 1922, Turnbull Library.
4. *Letters to Murry*, p. 642.
5. *Letters*, II, 267–268 (December 31, 1922).
6. *Letters to Murry*, p. 634 (May 19, 1921).

7. S. Vere Pearson, 'The Psychology of the Consumptive', *Journal of State Medicine*, 40 (1932), 478.
8. Lawrence, *Letters to Thomas and Adele Seltzer*, p. 69 (February 10, 1923).
9. *Letters to Murry*, p. 654 (February 9, 1922).
10. Quoted in Lea, pp. 90–91, 94.
11. *Letters to Murry*, p. 669 (October 11, 1922).
12. Quoted in Mairet, *Orage*, p. 121.
13. Edmund Wilson, 'The Literary Consequences of the Crash', *The Shores of Light* (New York, 1961), p. 494.
14. *Letters to Murry*, p. 662 (September 20, 1922).
15. Denis Saurat, 'A Visit to Gourdyev', *Living Age*, 345 (January 1934), 429.
16. Waldron, p. 13.
17. Lawrence, *Women in Love*, p. 203.
18. Rice, p. 77.
19. Quoted in Harold Beauchamp, p. 209.
20. *Letters to Murry*, p. 664 (October 3, 1922); and Dickinson, ed., p. 99 (October 5, 1922).
21. *Letters to Murry*, p. 666.
22. *Letters*, I, 241 (August 1919).
23. *Ibid.*, II, 252 (to Dorothy Brett).
24. *Ibid.*, II, 257 (October 15, 1922).
25. *Journal*, pp. 331–332.
26. *Letters to Murry*, p. 676.
27. *Ibid.*, p. 643 (December 19, 1921).
28. *Ibid.*, p. 671 (October 13, 1922).
29. Kenneth Walker, *Venture with Ideas* (London, 1951), p. 71.
30. Quoted in Louis Pauwels, *Gurdjieff* (New York, 1972), p. 192.
31. *Ibid.*, p. 253.
32. P. D. Ouspensky, *In Search of the Miraculous* (New York, 1949), p. 385.
33. *Letters*, II, 258.
34. C. E. Bechhofer, 'The Forest Philosophers,' *Century Magazine*, 86 (May 1924), p. 67.
35. Quoted in Alpers, p. 347.
36. Walker, pp. 99–100.
37. Bechhofer, pp. 71–72.
38. Wilson, p. 494.
39. Llewelyn Powys, *The Verdict of Bridlegoose* (London, 1926), p. 163.
40. William Seabrook, *Witchcraft* (New York, 1940), p. 207.
41. Saurat, p. 431.
42. *Letters to Murry*, p. 688 (November 19, 1922).
43. Lawrence, *Letters*, p. 770 (January 9, 1924).
44. E. W. Tedlock, 'D. H. Lawrence's Annotations of Ouspensky's *Tertium Organum*', *Texas Studies in Literature and Language*, 2 (1960), 209, 212, 213.
45. Gurdjieff later attracted other notable disciples: Frank Lloyd

Wright; Olga Knipper; Margaret Anderson, the editor of the *Little Review*; Georgette Leblanc, the actress and mistress of Maeterlinck; and Dorothy Caruso, the wife of the operatic tenor.

46. *Letters*, II, 260 (October 19, 1922).
47. *Letters to Murry*, pp. 677–678 (October 20, 1922).
48. Thomas de Hartmann, *Our Life with Mr. Gurdjieff* (London, 1972), p. 107.
49. *Letters*, II, 268 (December 31, 1922).
50. Quoted in Ida Baker, p. 224 (December 22, 1922).
51. Quoted in J. M. Murry, *God* (London, 1929), p. 22.
52. *Letters to Murry*, p. 695 (December 17, 1922).
53. Quoted in Ida Baker, pp. 222–223 (December 12, 1922).
54. *Letters to Murry*, p. 695.
55. *Ibid.*, p. 692 (December 6, 1922).
56. Adèle Kafian, 'The Last Days of Katherine Mansfield', *Adelphi*, 23 (October-December 1946), 36.
57. Olgivanna, 'The Last Days of Katherine Mansfield', *Bookman* (New York), 73 (March 1931), 8.
58. *Ibid.*
59. *Letters to Murry*, p. 669 (October 11, 1922).
60. *Ibid.*, p. 476 (February 11, 1920).
61. Pauwels, p. 314.
62. Gurdjieff gave up his pupils and sold the Prieuré in 1933, died in Paris in 1949 and was buried, according to the Greek Orthodox ritual, near Katherine in the cemetery at Avon. Harold Beauchamp lived until 1938. Ida typed Katherine's manuscripts for Murry for £10 a month, and then worked as a housekeeper for Elizabeth Russell in London and in the New Forest village of Woodgreen, where she had lived from 1942 until her death in 1978. Brett followed Lawrence to New Mexico in 1924 and died in Taos in August 1977. Richard became a painter and lives in London. Edith Bendall and Ruth Herrick are in Wellington, Katherine's sister Jeanne in the Cotswolds, Frank Swinnerton in Surrey and Dolly Trowell in Cambridge.

Chapter 16 Murry's Cult of Katherine

1. Murry, *Keats*, p. 28.
2. Quoted in Lea, p. 140.
3. *Ibid.*, p. 144.
4. *Ibid.*, p. 187.
5. *Ibid.*, p. 124.
6. *Ibid.*, p. x.
7. *Journal*, p. 296 (February 8, 1922).
8. Aldous Huxley, *Point Counter Point* (London, 1965), pp. 170–172.
9. D. H. Lawrence, 'Smile', *Complete Short Stories*, II, 584.
10. J. M. Murry, 'In Memory of Katherine Mansfield', *Adelphi*, I (January 1924), 664–665.

11. Lea, p. 113.
12. Matthew Arnold, 'Shelley', *Essays in Criticism: Second Series* (London, 1906), p. 252.
13. Richard Holmes, *Shelley: The Pursuit* (New York, 1975), p. 353n.
14. *Letters to Murry*, p. 642.
15. J. M. Murry, 'A Month After', *Adelphi*, I (July 1923), 94–96.
16. Unpublished letter from J. M. Murry to Katherine Mansfield, October 1922, Turnbull Library.
17. Murry, *God*, pp. 30–31.
18. *Journal*, p. 255.
19. J. M. Murry, 'Introductory Note', to Ruth Mantz's *A Critical Bibliography of Katherine Mansfield* (London, 1931), p. xv.
20. Murry, *Keats*, p. 76.
21. Quoted in Lea, p. 227.
22. Quoted in Darroch, p. 258.
23. Quoted in Glenavy, p. 69.
24. Lawrence, *Letters*, p. 1105 (December 10, 1928).
25. Quoted in Carswell, p. 198.
26. Quoted in Richard Rees, 'John Middleton Murry', *Dictionary of National Biography, 1951–1960* (Oxford, 1971), p. 761.
27. J. M. Murry, 'Katherine Mansfield', *New York Evening Post Literary Review*, February 17, 1923, p. 461; and Mantz, *Bibliography*, p. 17.
28. Murry, *Between Two Worlds*, p. 311.
29. *Ibid.*, p. 375.
30. Murry, *God*, p. 14.
31. *Letters to Murry*, p. 85.
32. *Ibid.*, p. 699.
33. *Journal*, pp. 332–333 (October 14, 1922).
34. Quoted in Frieda Lawrence, *Memoirs and Correspondence*, p. 362 (September 24, 1953).
35. *Ibid.*, p. 302 (May 27, 1946).
36. See Christiane Mortelier, 'The Genesis and Development of the Katherine Mansfield Legend in France', *AUMLA*, 34 (1970), 252–263.
37. Gerald Bullett, *Modern English Fiction* (London, 1926), p. 114.
38. Virginia Carr, *The Lonely Hunter: A Biography of Carson McCullers* (New York, 1975), pp. 51–52.
39. Christopher Isherwood, 'Introduction' to *Great English Short Stories* (New York, 1957), p. 233. See also 'Katherine Mansfield', *Exhumations* (London, 1969), pp. 80–89.
40. Conversation with Christopher Isherwood, July 31, 1976. The quotations are from *Journal*, p. 269 (October 1921), and A. R. Orage, 'Talks with Katherine Mansfield', *Century Magazine*, 87 (November 1924), 38.
41. George Orwell, 'New Novels', *New Statesman*, 21 (January 25, 1941), 89–90. See also Orwell's more sympathetic review 'Sensitive Plant', *Observer*, January 13, 1946, p. 3.

42. Letter from Frank Swinnerton to Jeffrey Meyers, April 4, 1976.

43. The cult of Katherine still thrives in Helen McNeish's soppy edition, complete with soft-focus photographs, of the Mansfield-Murry correspondence, *Passionate Pilgrimage: A Love Affair in Letters* (London, 1976).

Select Bibliography

I.
Katherine Mansfield:
  Collected Stories. London, 1973.
  Journal. London, 1954.
  Letters. 2 vols. London, 1928.
  Letters to John Middleton Murry, 1913–1922. London, 1951.
  Novels and Novelists. London, 1930.
  Scrapbook. New York, 1940.

II.
Adam International Review, 300 (1965), 1–14, 76–118 (special issue on
  Mansfield).
Adam International Review, 370–375 (1972–73), 1–128 (special issue on
  Mansfield).
Alpers, Antony. *Katherine Mansfield*. London, 1954.
Berkman, Sylvia. *Katherine Mansfield: A Critical Study*. New Haven,
  1951.
Carco, Francis. *Les Innocents*. Paris, 1916.
Carco, Francis. *Mémoires d'une autre vie*. Genève, 1942. Pp. 346–355,
  463–468.
Charms, Leslie de. *Elizabeth of the German Garden*. London, 1958.
Glenavy, Beatrice. *Today We Will Only Gossip*. London, 1964.
Hudson, Stephen [Sydney Schiff]. 'First Meetings with Katherine
  Mansfield.' *Cornhill*, 170 (1958), 202–212.
Lawrence, D. H. *Letters*. ed. Aldous Huxley. London, 1932.
Lawrence, D. H. *Collected Letters*. ed. Harry Moore. 2 vols. London,
  1962.
Lawrence, D. H. *The Quest for Rananim: D. H. Lawrence's Letters to S. S.
  Koteliansky*. ed. George Zytaruk. Montreal, 1970.
Lea, F. A. *The Life of John Middleton Murry*. London, 1959.
Mantz, Ruth and John Middleton Murry. *The Life of Katherine Mansfield*.
  London, 1931.
Meyers, Jeffrey. 'Katherine Mansfield, Gurdjieff and Lawrence's
  "Mother and Daughter." ' *Twentieth Century Literature*, 22 (December
  1976), 444–453.
Meyers, Jeffrey. 'Katherine Mansfield: A Bibliography of International
  Criticism, 1921–1977.' *Bulletin of Bibliography*, 34 (April-June 1977),
  53–67.

Meyers, Jeffrey. 'Katherine Mansfield and John Middleton Murry.' *Married to Genius*. London Magazine Editions and New York: Barnes & Noble, 1977. Pp. 113–144.

Meyers, Jeffrey. 'D. H. Lawrence, Katherine Mansfield and *Women in Love*.' *London Magazine*, 18 (May 1978), 32–54.

Meyers, Jeffrey. 'Murry's Cult of Mansfield.' *Journal of Modern Literature*, 7 (February 1979), 15–38.

Meyers, Jeffrey. 'Katherine Mansfield's "To Stanislaw Wyspianski".' *Modern Fiction Studies* (1978)

Meyers, Jeffrey. 'The Quest for Katherine Mansfield.' *Biography*, 1 (Summer 1978), 51–64.

L. M. [Ida Baker]. *Katherine Mansfield: The Memories of LM*. New York, 1971.

Morrell, Lady Ottoline. *Ottoline at Garsington*. ed. Robert Gathorne-Hardy. London, 1974.

Murry, John Middleton. *Between Two Worlds*. London, 1935.

Orage, A. R. 'Talks with Katherine Mansfield.' *Century Magazine*, 87 (November 1924), 36–40.

Orton, William. *The Last Romantic*. New York, 1937.

Woolf, Leonard. *Beginning Again, 1911–1918*. London, 1964.

Woolf, Virginia. *A Writer's Diary*. ed. Leonard Woolf. New York, 1954.

Woolf, Virginia. *The Question of Things Happening: Letters, 1912–1922*. ed. Nigel Nicolson and Joanne Trautmann. London, 1976.

Woolf, Virginia. *Diary, 1915–1919*. ed. Anne Bell. London, 1977.

Index